DIE WISE

DIE WISE

A Manifesto for Sanity and Soul

Stephen Jenkinson

North Atlantic Books
Berkeley, California

Published by
North Atlantic Books
Berkeley, California

Cover photo by Ian MacKenzie
Cover and book design by Jasmine Hromjak
Design assistance by Natasha Kong
Author photo: Mark Tucker
Printed in the United States of America

Die Wise: A Manifesto for Sanity and Soul is sponsored and published by the Society for the Study of Native Arts and Sciences (dba North Atlantic Books), an educational nonprofit based in Berkeley, California, that collaborates with partners to develop cross-cultural perspectives, nurture holistic views of art, science, the humanities, and healing, and seed personal and global transformation by publishing work on the relationship of body, spirit, and nature.

North Atlantic Books' publications are available through most bookstores. For further information, visit our website at www.northatlanticbooks.com or call 800-733-3000.

Library of Congress Cataloging-in-Publication Data
Jenkinson, Stephen.
    Die wise : a manifesto for sanity and soul / Stephen Jenkinson.
        pages cm
    ISBN 978-1-58394-973-3 (paperback) — ISBN 978-1-58394-974-0 (ebook)
    1. Death. 2. Grief. 3. Bereavement. I. Title.
    BF789.D4J457 2015
    155.9'37—dc23   2014036180

6 7 8 9 10 KPC 21 20 19 18
Printed on recycled paper

North Atlantic Books is committed to the protection of our environment.
We partner with FSC-certified printers using soy-based inks
and print on recycled paper whenever possible.

HONOR AND FLOWERS

The death trade is awash in contention when it is not subdued by conviction. You find that out when you start wondering why it is the desolate endeavor it has become, and whether it could be otherwise. In times when you're intemperate enough to wonder this aloud, some people put up with you and some people don't. Some stand with you before they know why, and some after. Each of them has a hand in you managing to get anything worthy out into the world. For what there is in this book that might yet earn its keep I owe garlands and gratitude to many.

To those at work in the death trade then and now, and to those allies and adversaries who got me there and for a time kept me there, particularly Michele Chaban: all praises for your labor. May the ragged caravan of sorrows and mystery carry you in hard times.

To those many dying people, all now dead, and their loved ones who burdened and blessed me by including me in their dying time: I remember it all. May you hear your song sung in these pages.

To those who will fail to live forever: May something here find its use in your coming days.

To those robust and jangling scholars of the Orphan Wisdom School past and present, whose willingness to learn dangerous things in a troubled time grants me wild nights in which I plant my dreams for some coming generation's chance of a better day: May your hearths and roads be blessed, as you have blessed mine.

To those faithful keepers of our fields, seeds, varmints, and fences and roof, especially and always the staunch ally of our days Daniel Stermac-Stein: May your people know you and claim you.

To those many young people who have sought me out, anger in one hand and sorrow in the other, figuring somehow that perhaps the lateness of our hour alone might be reason enough to try: May the years after our time together prove your judgment good and your purpose right.

To the firm midwives and allies of our noblest endeavors and givers of grandchildren, Natasha Kong and Christopher Roy: May the mists and the wildflowers of your hearts find each other and the swaying green of the fields be a sign of it.

To those staunch allies from the Wedding Days years ago, most of whom have rightly scattered to their lives, and to those who came to us after with those rumors of ceremony stirring: Nothing is forgotten. May the swirl of blessings you learned now gather at your door.

To the wizards of sound and light who've lent their learning and skill to setting my little boat of dreams and principled sorrow into the current of the marketplace, including Ian MacKenzie, Dave Vollrath, Scott Pond, Mike Strait, and Charles Sue Wah Sing; to Tim McKee at North Atlantic, who kept me in mind; to all those who have conjured the many teaching events for this work of mine to appear in their towns in Canada, nobly among them Anne Pitman, Dana Bass Solomon, David Henderson, Kaz Amaranth, and Rachelle Lamb; in the U.S., faithfully among them Reed Larsen, Bodhi Be, Lucia Camara, Douglas Varga, and Karen Paule; in Poland, stoutly among them Dorota Kožusnik-Solarska and Dorota Ostoja Zawadzka; in the U.K., keenly among them Neda Nenadic and Duncan Passmore; in Mexico, so generously Susana Dultzin; to the National Film Board of Canada and especially to Tim Wilson for his film Griefwalker and for his indefensible, insoluble insistence that something of all this be heard in the world years ago, before most others wanted it: May your days be hung as garlands 'round the necks of your families and friends, and may they brag of having had you among them, as I do. There are others remembered but unnamed: You are there still, with us.

To the teachers and storytellers, the blazing stars in the night of our times, the burden carriers and great rememberers in whose steps I found reasons and ways of continuing, chief among them Leonard Cohen, landsman, Jewish patron saint of my school unawares, and defender and master practitioner of elegant longing; Martín Prechtel, giver of immense, detailed, and field-tested choice; and especially the ancient tower and father of my younger days Dr. Hugh Morgan Hill, Brother Blue, and his wife, Ruth Hill, to whom I owe the best of my voice: May your labors be flowers on the altar of life and your names be spoken in the time to come.

To my children, Jesse and Gabriel, and to all their ways of living life sometimes in the ebb and flow of this work of mine: May your days become your own true days, proof of how it all could be, and may this sanity I am bargaining for be planted in your world, soon.

To all the Gods of the holy places and their peoples, including all Gods who remain sure that they are the only ones and all peoples who remain sure that they are too: May humans and Gods find each other again, as it was, and may their time together out on the edge of town commence and continue.

And always to my swarthy, earth-loving, raucous, and life-filled wife, Nathalie Roy, mother, midwife, physician, and priestess to every worthy thing I have done these years together, honey and hearth of our home, dreamer for us both when I stayed too long awake, pilot of our little boat of life, unwavering witness to what is needed, keeper of our altars and our holy things: Would that you take this book as a little love letter in place of those unwritten while I made it.

February 1, 2014

Tepoztlán, Mexico

FOREWORD

The Hawk and the Otherworld

Where I come from we have a word: *Yarak*. It can be described as the supreme readiness of a hawk as it prepares to hunt. This book has Yarak.

Die Wise is the book on initiation that you have almost certainly not been waiting for. There's no jungle feathers, no vision pit, no tundra vigil. Yet every word is wrought firm with such erudition, wit, and occasional old time bullishness that you realize, suddenly, that you are standing by the edge of the fire, and staring out at a vast dark forest. The battery on your cell phone is dead and never recovering. Please don't mistake this for a promise of comfort. From here on in we are trading comfort for shelter. Deep news tends to arrive with dismay. The price of breaking a trance is high.

Initiation? Isn't this a book about modern North America? About strip-lit hospices, and doctors fiddling with pens delivering bad news as swiftly as possible, soporific infusions to lead gently to a dreamless death? Well, the next time someone tries to peddle you the notion of initiation without a daily maintained recalibration of death and dying, you can be sure they're a mimic.

This is the one initiation that we will all face, regardless of gobbling ayahuasca in the amazon, regardless of whether we grow green-tongued and sweat-browed from wheat grass smoothies and palates. It's coming.

Stephen Jenkinson enables us the courtesy of not answering big questions with big answers. There is no one-size-fits all here, no three-point plan, no sound bites. Disarmingly, he doesn't appear to be selling anything whatsoever. What we are witness to is a man that took the long way home, that did the work; this book is road tested in ways many of us hope never to experience. His handling of language is particularly fine: inventive, exacting, straight-up, refreshing.

Die Wise is filled with generosity, but of a very specific timbre. Generosity, in its archaic, regal form, was to gift the very soul of a community, not pander to its temporary polemics. Generosity at root is not always about a warm, cozy glow. This book is another kind of animal entirely, this book is a soul gift. And I don't think the soul is convinced by much. But sorrow, handled with skill and suffused with literate beauty, is still high currency. So I ask you not to turn your head away from the deftly curated grief. Please don't betray the moment. Our developing fidelity to grief is what may, just possibly, mark us out by our children's children. That we may be a fertile bough of something real over their gorgeous little heads.

We could call this capacity *Hireath*. It's a Welsh word that has no direct English counterpart. But the nearest we can get is still something rather beautiful: *The Old Hurt*. A noble thing, highly prized, the root of all functioning ritual. And that hurt is something no Celt would dream of being without, it's the very weft and weave of true culture. It's nothing to do with clinging to grievance, rather wearing certain hard-earned melancholies like a cloak. To those with eyes to behold it, it's the essential markings of an elder. And we are drowning in its deficit. After twenty years of initiatory work in the wilds of Snowdonia, I recognize its cadence immediately. Its gorgeous and unusual scent.

It's one thing to present a book of victory stories—and we're all sick of them—quite another to read of a man that bent his head and, in his way, kissed the dying. That was always what brought the tribe together; peering through the blue smoke and speaking inventively of elegant sorrow. That kind of grief is a curious catnip to the pre-history that lurks in your bones.

And suddenly you realize this book *is* a great victory. Jenkinson takes deep mythic inventiveness and applies it to the hemorrhaging, numbed out, individualized to the point of unutterable loneliness condition of our times. Oh, and there are old words for that too: The Wasteland.

The notion that we could live forever is a very old one in the myth-world. And was not without intelligence, but, by god, did we ever take that story and run with it, run with it until it was grievously free of all the binding ceremonies and elaborate mythologies that grounded it to something more useful, ran with it till it became grievously toxic. Scalped free of all earthy resonance, we now squat in the departure lounge of its aspiration—never quite achieving its promise but never quite getting our true, ancestral inheritance on the matter. A holding pattern of tacit depression prevails. We're trapped in a vast airport with very bad food, unmentionable music, and a queue to the restroom.

Maybe there *is* some part of us that lopes on after death in the form of a rowan tree or a blue crest of stars, but our part of the old debt—and its wondrous un-payable nature—was that our very bones and hair and rash opinions would feed the soil, worms, vultures, bears and minerals of our place. We got beautifully devoured. We gave up the landlords' portion. And that we didn't run backwards into the arrangement either. That we would now be trying to ascend that arrangement is a heartbreaking and recent and wretched degradation of events. But it's true; we touch so little these days. We let the diggers do it for us.

We are becoming a ghost cult. Ghosts because anything of weight tends to be consciously unwitnessed, or, if even suspected, resolutely shunned. We decide to un-witness. When we don't have thirty pairs of curious eyes on us it creates a suspicion we need thirty million. And that something is deeply wrong with us when we don't get it. And so a protracted annihilation of substance and character begins, a kind of long-winded, low-key suicide attempt.

Because we privately suspect we are ghosts we presume we can float through life, trusting only the erratic, far distant pulse of our "feelings," and gaze bemused when our children are ripped almost crazy with sorrow when we separate. Well, read this book for their sake if not your own. Life is way too short not to stake your staff in the ground.

It may be that we are so phobic of death, our dead don't even know they are dead anymore. May it not be so.

With long-tempered musings, Jenkinson also reaches back into European history: the departures to North America and quite what the People of the Boats were running from and to. I should tell you that the man is philosophically ambitious. In this rumination we glimpse a Europe constipated with tyranny, choked with lack of rolling wilderness, no longer ground for any decent dream.

Do we who stayed remember you who left? When the ships sailed from Plymouth it was not just to the *New World* they sailed, to us you were also sailing to the *Otherworld.* Not just as dreamers, adventurers, but those riven with terror. To us, when you left you became spirits. How does dying wise function when to we who stayed you are already dead?

So in some deep and barely mentionable way, this work is a message back from the land of the dead concerning our facility to steward that very journey; about the hundred thousand times we betrayed imagination for fantasy, about who we are and where we might still be headed. What follows is a Hawk across the Waters, carrying news of the Otherworld.

Please don't mistake this for yet another book colluding on a generalized, axe-swinging assassination on every conceivable dimension of modern life. That's an easy target—clichéd, flabby—and *Die Wise* is doing something more sophisticated. It holds a door to a hundred acres of thought long banished from the West. *Die Wise* is not an endorsement to change your name to Eric Buffalo-Rainbow or anything of the sort. The opposite. Change it back.

A true story-man, Jenkinson paints image after image on the cave wall of his parchment. The vastness of the ideas are often brought into the agility of story and so invited slowly into the body. And his teachers come too: we learn that to stand well in this world you also have to learn to bend your head, and he offers clear and coherent praise to his own brilliant tutors. They are present and honored and witnessed. There is much gracefulness present, and again, that word generosity.

It also contains such ribald humor that I blame it entirely for spitting out half a mug of tea in the hushed confines of my local library.

Die Wise is prophetic insight rather than pastoral affirmation. And that is fitting in times like these. I ask you to consider the subtitle of the book; *"a manifesto for sanity and soul."* Manifesto it is. Sheesh. Not a gentle suggestion, or generalized pondering or any of the lily-livered half-wishes we renege on the moment we whisper their name. This is a rebel keen, and absolutely proper.

So, we have a lone rider hurling his very character, intelligence, and being—a being that has been slowly and not-so-tenderly refined to a fierce skill maker—at vast forces that are always ravenous and always present. Address them directly, and without artistry, and they will turn your very heart to stone. But here is the shelter of a shield in which to behold Medusa. Get educated. Study will suit you. There is fresh hay everywhere here.

This is the inheritance that no one ever told you about—wild and curious, unblinking, sorrow-eyed and courageous chested, shuddering the rain from its feathers, ready to launch into the dusking light.

Stand up. You are needed. It's time. *Yarak Yarak Yarak*

Dr. Martin Shaw
Southern curve of Dartmoor, Devon
Winter, 2014

CONTENTS

OVERTURE: NIGHT

You and I clamber up the rough path,
drops gathered on lichen and granite.
The wind blows rain in our faces.
A dozen yards below our feet
the escarpment drops away ...
I think of those secret lives
forever hidden whose songs we will not hear.
From one end of this valley to the other are nothing
but reasons to live.

> Thomas R. Smith, "Escarpment Trail,"
> in Keeping the Star, page 40

STARS It's dark. You are standing in a field, far from the house. This is the midnight sky of your younger, wilder days. It is ablaze, aching with stars. It is the vault of heaven, indigo sea of time pierced by light from the other side. The horizons are gone and the Bridge of Sighs, the one they say the dead walk to leave this world, dazzles you. Dew settles on your shoulders and you're atremble, no longer full with comprehension and certainties. Every idea you have seems too small for the world. The blessings tumble. You lived long enough to see a night such as this, and you're stilled by it. There are unlikely companions in the field with you, everyone quiet. Someone looks up into the night sky and says, "You see that star right there? Could be it isn't there anymore." All conviction is sent reeling. Nothing is truer than this. The mysteries roll. You are welcome. If that didn't quite happen in your earlier days, it has now. If it did, then it's happened again.

I

You need witnesses for wonder. Some things in life are too hard to see by yourself because they take up the whole sky, or because they happen every day, unwinding above your busyness, or because you thought you knew them already. Wonder takes a willingness to be uncertain, to be thrown. We have a lot of information these days, and few are enamored of imprecision or subtlety. But *starlight traveling a bewildering distance for so long that there is every chance that it doesn't even exist anymore, and all of that having already happened, and you standing there, your face blazed in the dark by a starlight gone, seeing it all, what is and what isn't there enthroned by your witness:* That is a marvel, and surely that is how awe is born in us. With somebody there alongside you in the darkness, you can think unauthorized thoughts. You can see what's gone, or whether it's gone, or both. Fantastic.

A book about dying is a book awash in the great mystery of what is to become of us, and so it is a book about time. A book about dying should wonder again and over again whether the river of time and life flows toward the future and the not-yet and carries us there, as most of us are taught, or toward the past and the known, toward all who have been, as some of us suspect. The night of wonder must be a long one, and sometime before dawn it will come to this: When I die, am I past? Am I gone? Lost?

This is when the midnight sky, riven by all the light givers that have been, starts whispering. You *can* see something that isn't there anymore, and you have more proof than you need that the past is not quite passed. So I am counting on this possibility: That out of that encounter with confounding starlight could come marvel and gratitude for being here, alive, for now, and with them come the beginnings of an answer to that bewilderment, that human-scaled mystery: What will happen when I die? I'm counting on more: The times of dying, of real and proper sorrow, could be woven by a gratitude for being around long enough to be overwhelmed by something that happens every day, by ordinary awe. And each of us could be gathered in by the raveling covenant of sorrow and thanksgiving as our days end. Here's what happens every day: The past has tangible presence and isn't gone. People are born, and people die, and there are signs.

Gratitude needs practice, though. Gratitude for the things that don't seem to help, that aren't sought out or welcome—that's a demanding kind, and it is needed in hard times. A book about dying should have that kind of gratitude in it, bleeding through from the other side of sorrow. Drink enough of the sweet, strong mead of grief and love for being alive and it isn't long before you're sending a trembling, life-soaked greeting out to everything that came before you and to everything that will follow, a kind of love letter to the Big Story. You're even willing to include yourself and your days going by in the roiling mystery of it all, not as alone as you once were. And this willingness is a gift for those who see you trying to pull it off and for those who are coming after you who might hear of your one bewildered human example. It's all they'll need, a sign of how a human can live his or her days. All of this from looking into the night sky and seeing what's mysteriously there to see, what is there and what is gone, with witnesses.

Maybe this swirl of awe and marvel and good intent for the world and gratitude for ourselves in it is where all the religions came from. That is where our feel for the sacred in the world is conjured, surely, the ordinary, staggering mystery of where it all comes from before it is born here among us and where it all goes after it dies away from us, the starry midnight courtship of the heart that whispers, "What is gone is still with you, still here. As you will be."

RIVERS My farm is a sixty-acre strip of stony land washed to where it is by a glacial run, huddled under those kinds of midnight skies. Lately it is some beaver swamp, some pasture, a roofless cedar log barn, and a secret little stream trickling down off the mountain that makes the spring forest around it hold green light all day long. We call it a farm mainly to keep our hopes up. We do farm the place, and that is a detailed chorus of pleading, cajoling, and bargaining with everything done to the land before we got here. We have vague but promising signs that the land may have forgiven a bit the old trespasses of clear-cut, pesticides, and overplanting. Only two families have lived on it since the place was taken from the surrounding forests and the Algonquin people in the

3

mid-nineteenth century, but those farmers left their signs: a rusting harrow in a tumbled-down log outbuilding, an evening star cut out of the barn's western eves that let dusty light in at day's end when the roof was still on, crumbling split-rail cedar fences and played-out soil. This place, as anybody who works land around here knows, should never have been cleared and farmed. It can feed the remaining trees and bush and the animals who live here, but it can't feed much else, not without help. It's sand, mostly. Our way of helping is to dig into the ground the spirit and the body of everything that withers and dies here. So far, the deals we've struck with the place are holding.

Partly because of my traveling and teaching schedule, which supports our farm habit, and partly because we don't plough with a tractor, this is still mostly a dirt farm. That is what I used to tell the customs people when they wanted to know my occupation: dirt farmer. Once I was asked if I was bringing into the U.S. any monetary instruments totaling $10,000 or more. I reminded the customs officer that she knew I was a farmer. "Oh, right," she said. "Sorry." Ours is a fair way of life, more than fair. But it isn't much of a living. A dirt farm it is likely to remain, and we turn out a bumper crop year after year without the heavy, crippling labor that used to be done here in years past. For now we plant clover, bury cardboard to encourage the worms, and hope that small green patches of people food will bear the early frost or show up in time to feed the scholars at our school. Patience and a manageable mortgage are mandatory for this kind of thing.

The name of the river I live beside when translated into English comes out something like "the place of full life," which does it some justice. We've come to call it the River of Abundance and Time, which is a better rendering. Across the road from our skinny farm is a granite and oak ridge a day's walk long that neighbors call The Mountain. The Mountain is not a mountain by almost any standard but a prairie one, but it rises sudden and unannounced from the land around it, steep and still bearing the marks of the upward tectonic forces that made it, and so locally it is highly regarded as a proper mountain. My friend and I climbed The Mountain one morning. Not being much of a mountain it wasn't much of a climb, so we had energy enough to sit for a while and take in the great arc of the River of Abundance and Time as it rolled in its true course out of the purple western hills, through two grand lakes and on to the Mattawa in the east. We could see for forty kilometers, anyway, in every direction.

It was a beautiful sight. I admired aloud the valley before us that the great melt of water had carved ten thousand years before, the old torrent of which the current River of Abundance and Time is for now a subdued memory. After a minute my friend said, "Valley? What valley is that? Where's the other side?" He was right, of course. It isn't a valley at all and has probably never been. I'd just assumed there was another mountain explaining the river running between them. But it isn't so. The river is where it is without any obstacle, without another side. Or you could say, the other side of the river—what makes it a river and not a lake—seems to be gone. But a long time ago some other, subtler thing made a home for the River of Abundance and Time, and still keeps it right where it is. This book about the wisdom of dying is, partly, about that subtler presence on the other side that binds all things to their course.

The river was dammed farther up about a half century ago to control the melting runoff, so now it flows slow and steady most of the year like most old-timers do, no longer too rambunctious, hardly able to act as in days gone by on the mad flush of spring. A half-hour's paddle downstream from our place the river pours into to a large lake which is a favored cavorting spot for people from the city. Judging by the summer traffic, they are untroubled by the price of gasoline—or the end of gasoline—and all that goes with it. Holiday weekends are raucous times on the river, and you can be tested by the mayhem. On one of them I stayed home, making me the local exception, and lived through a prolonged reminder of why being here on those weekends isn't wise. The buzz and the roar of two-stroke power plowing the river in front of the house to a muddy froth was constant, and it sent endless waves of erosion up and down the shoreline. This is how one of the local people accounted for it all: It's a free country.

Somewhere in the helpless, molar-grinding consternation of that weekend, a couple of thoughts struggled up toward me through my anger like lake trout through dark water:

*What if those people could stand on the shore watching
their wake wash a bit of the shore away?
And what if each of us could stay put long enough to
see the rippling trail of everything we did rolling out
behind us?
What if we stopped long enough to see the long train of
unintended consequence fan out from every innocently
intended thing we did?*

A taste for the consequence, for what endures: Maybe then there'd be a chance for things to be different.

TIME Sit on the shore while everything else goes on by you, and get through the low-level anxiety and the boredom and the feeling that you've already seen it all. That's a good time to learn. Here's what's there to see. Everything we do and don't do makes a wake, a legion of waves and troughs that pound the shores at the edges of what we mean, grinding away on the periphery of what we know. They go on, after the years in which we lived our individual lives are long passed. If we don't learn that simple, devastating, and redeeming detail of being alive—that what we do, all the jangle of our declarations and defeats, lasts longer than we ourselves do, that the past isn't over—then the parade of our days stands to indict much more than it bequeaths. This is something that we have to learn now. Many of us count on our best intent winning the day or getting us off the hook of personal or ecological consequence. It hasn't, and it won't.

This is not true just of people with boats on small rivers with nowhere to go but back and forth. Everything that is alive and moves in the world, all the winds and worms and wrens and willows leave in their passing some kind of similar wake too. All lives are lived in the swirls and eddies of what has gone along before them. Then, with a little time passing, we ourselves, our lives and all we hold dear, become what has gone before, a swirl or an eddy or both. Things might be different, we could really learn something, if we could see our lives from the shore of Life: "Ah look, there's my life going by, trailing everything I meant and didn't mean, the end of it clearly in view."

Sometimes it's so clear: Time carries everything toward what has been, toward the past. That's where we're headed, to join all who have come before. That's the understanding of time that the word "obit" (as in "obituary") comes from. It means "to go to meet." The weather of time is blustery, reversing and scattering, but the past is the *current* of time. Ah, modern life is a hard one to live though. We bank on a future. We keep our options open. We trade on potential. In our busyness and in our spare time we are crafting antidotes to this current of time, little weirs to contain the past and what it means for us now. Sometimes we are on the boat, roaring down the river of our days, certain that they are *our* days. Sometimes we are on the shore, standing beside an old white pine that leans away from the roar and the churning roil of what we've done, its roots a little barer and washed clean of the earth that has given it life all these years. When was the last time you stood anywhere for a moment and saw that what you meant and felt and how you loved and lost and what you said and held off saying might already have become waves lapping somewhere else, washing upon a shore you've already passed by, where someone else is standing, where an old white pine used to be … proof that you've been, sign of how you've been? It could turn into your prized possession, having learned the endurance of what you did, the willingness to know how it is, and the skills of living accordingly. The whole thing needs witnesses, though, people who will testify. That's how it lasts.

What does it take to get us to stand quietly, like somebody under a clear midnight sky, taking all of it in, stilled by the staggering pitch and pull of life? Things going well doesn't seem to help with this. Good fortune isn't persuasive on this matter, and it rarely gives people pause. It's when the news isn't good news; that's usually the time you find the limits of what you can bear to know. Then, maybe only then, you might be able to see that the waves of what you believed and did and held off from doing will still have their ripples, long after you're done. They outlast you. And this is tremendous news. When you are still enough for long enough, sometimes the river, the boat, and the waves and eddies—all of it—can turn into what you mean when you say, "My Life." If you can do that, you can change things. Your life becomes a little friendlier to the world, to what the world needs from you. It becomes a little friendlier to the endings of things too. This is a book about dying, yes, but it's more about that kind of change.

LIFE WORK If you live long enough in a certain kind of way, with help, you can awaken to the idea that *you were born to a certain task or purpose.* This is an antique idea in most of the places I've lived. If you can manage that some day, let the feeling of being lucky soothe that other feeling of being haunted or mournful for not having awoken to it until now. Time goes by, and if you manage to find out what that purpose is, well, many of your days will be their own reward, and you will be in rare company. If against all odds and propriety somebody pays you for doing what you were born to do, you will find out what the old desert saints meant when they said, "Blessed." That is a great trifecta of human life.

Most of the things I did in the early going—divinity school when I'd never gone to church, shipwrecked in the Mediterranean when I was supposed to be in school, married and divorced and married again, very nearly dying a few times from misadventure or medical malfunction and then, for reasons no one knew, not—gave me a hint that there could be something called "my life's work." I came to the thing by default, having tried on a few other people's life's work or having tried living as if there's no such thing. Then I began to see the idea and the shape of what I was born to.

As a rule, nobody in our time asks you to do your life's work. More often, at least in the early going, you have to do your life's work as a self-appointed task. And in the early going you're not very good at it, which can be humbling. It is a learning thing, expensive, demanding, relentless. That's how it has gone for me at least, paring down the list of reasons I was born until only a few likely candidates were left standing.

People who know such things say that there are older ways of life, still here in the world, against the odds, where people are asked to do their life's work, and are helped to find it. These places have village bards, or village drummers, who are the great rememberers. I knew one of these people when I was a young man, and he crafted my days for me. I've met a few along the road since. They recount and play the polyrhythms of human life, all the contrapuntal extravaganza they can learn, but they don't play or tell the Rhythm inside those rhythms. They know it—everybody in a sane culture knows it—but they don't play it, and they don't tell it. That is the work of the Gods, they say, to play that simpler, steadier Rhythm, to tell that one Story. That Holy Rhythm is the time signature of life itself, sometimes a loping cadence that drives whole villages down to the river to pray and sometimes a thrum that carries someone out to walk in a snowy field at day's end while the light is dying and the shadows go violet, with witnesses, staring out, remembering. And so your life might go, as you quicken to your purpose: You get far enough into the sway of it to learn that you've been playing everything around the Rhythm, everything but the Rhythm itself, trying all the possibilities you found until all that's left is to be told and played by the simple, ragged syncopation of your days. That's when the Rhythm finally is able to have its way with you. That's how finding what you were born to do seems to be, like answering at last someone who's been calling your name faithfully for years. You play the rhythms and you learn the Rhythm, and you move accordingly: The ancestors of us all would have known that as *the way of human being*.

DEATH I have worked and taught for two decades in the death trade. During most of that time I was lucky enough to know a blessing when I saw it. I have sat with hundreds of dying people and their families and had the burdensome privilege of trying to help them die. I managed the counseling services of a very large urban palliative care program. I designed, launched, and directed a center for children's grief and palliative care from scratch, and was assistant professor in a prominent medical school. I have taught in more conferences, workshops, and retreats than I wanted to. A major documentary film was made about my work in the death trade, and many tell me that it is a useful thing in a troubled time.

Early on in the business I saw that what passed for a fitting and deserved dying was very often sedated dying or managed dying or defeated dying or collapse. I saw far too many people with well-controlled pain and symptoms die in an unarticulated, low-grade, grinding, and unspectacular terror anyway. I saw that antidepressants and sedation were the rule and not the exception. I saw the full panoply of medical technology unfurled for the benefit of dying people, and I saw that there wasn't much practice wisdom nearly as vast or as well tested that was guiding that technology's use. I saw the death phobia that permeates our time brought to bear upon dying people in the name of caring for them. And I saw that as a culture we have a withered psychology of coping and accepting where we might once have had a mythology and a poetry of purposed, meaningful dying. This poverty was the constant companion and chimera of almost every dying person I worked with. I discovered that few wanted to die well, fewer still, wisely. Most didn't want to die at all, and they spent their dying time refusing to do so.

So I started to do what no one was asking me to do. I worked a long time on the idea of a good death. I wondered how it is that things have come to what they are now, for dying people and their families and their caregivers. I started teaching that dying people deserved dying-centered care, a complete novelty then and probably now. I started asking all the old ideas that permeate the palliative care field in North America to earn their keep, and I found that many of them couldn't do so. And then I started asking dying people to die well. Not encouraging them or inviting them or offering them the option or waiting until they were ready, but imploring them to do it, often obliging them to do it. I began to teach the idea that dying well is a right of all dying people and an obligation that must rest upon the culture in which they are dying.

This book tells you something of what I learned and what happened when I began dreaming aloud that it could be different. I have taught many of the ideas in this book to thousands of people working in the palliative care field in North America and Europe, and to thousands more who will one day be on the receiving end of that care. The reactions have been mixed, to be honest. Many people working on the front line in medicine, continuing care, and counseling institutions have some genuine relief when they hear these things, because they corroborate the uneasiness and hollow feeling these workers frequently have about how people die in their care, and because it gives them a sense that things could—must—be different. Their gratitude is often confused and unclear, but it is palpable. Further up the food chain in palliative care organizations, where people in managerial positions tend more to identify themselves with the current treatment options and where they have the responsibility of delivering on the status quo, there's been considerably more reluctance even to consider some of these ideas, and there's a good amount of hostility and derision about them too. This continues to be so.

The care of dying people is as grim as it often is not because the caregivers want it that way, nor because they don't care or are burned out or too rigid to change or not smart enough. Dying people and their families don't want it that way either. Things are the way they are mainly by default. A real alternative, one that has a clinical, cultural, spiritual, and political depth and corroboration in which we can plant the noble motivations and sentiments and the training that so many of us bring to this work, is rare. It is rare too for the families that are trying to care for their dying loved ones. It is painfully rare for those people among us who now, without much fanfare or warning or teaching about it under their belts, are dying. As it stands, some version of what you will read in these pages is coming to us all, our imaginations being stilled or addled by what passes for compassion and sanity and the way it goes, looking landward for some sign of shelter, some home for our great love of life and our last days, often sedated, vaguely, chronically distraught.

Dying wise: That's that antidote. Dying wise is the rumor around which all the attempts to control and manage and detoxify and assuage and domesticate and diminish dying swirl in our corner of the world. Dying wise is a thought unthought—a rumor—in a culture that does not believe in dying, and it will take about as much courage and wisdom as you can manage to do it. Dying wise is a life's work. Dying wise *is* the Rhythm, the Story, around which human life must swirl.

This book is an unblinking gaze into the maw of what we have done to dying and to dying people in the name of caring for them, and it is a rankling plea for how it all could be. I began years ago in the palliative care business, but I ended up in the redemption business. I am demanding wisdom. I am making a plea for redeeming our way of dying. This book offers a way of doing so.

I've included in *Die Wise* quite a few stories about dying people and their families. None of these stories report fact, but all of them are true. There were real people, and I have been faithful to them in the stories. People indeed said many or probably all of the things I have ascribed to them, but they and their stories are not facts. Facts happen once and typically fade and so have nominal use, I would say. But true things are true because they happen and happen again, sometimes in heavily altered form, and so are a trustworthy signature of the Makers of Life, as clear as the whorls of their thumbs. So the stories here are given to you as a kind of polestar by which you can make your way. Dying is tough sledding, to be sure, and the stories of others who came before you can help. Blessed with a good or well-exercised memory, you can recognize these true things through the length of your days and moderate the general demand made upon you for facts. The stories I tell here can help with that too. They are true stories.

This is a book that could be useful to you if you read it sometime before Your Time comes. That I can promise. It is a book for those of you working in the death trade with all kinds of good intent about helping people. Most especially it is for those of you who have the news of your dying in hand or who are waiting for the news that seems certain to come in, and for those who love you. It is a book for all who will fail to live forever.

Against the usual instincts though, I am asking all who read this to forego their normal hope for a plan, a grand scheme to fix what's wrong to kick in after thirty pages. It won't happen here. That is a big part of why it is the way it is at the end of our lives, this problem-solving reflex. It is that way with most relationships in trouble: We instinctively try harder to do more of what we've been doing that got us into trouble, trying to fix what we are hardly willing to learn.

Instead, we have to earn our way toward a better day. We will earn that by staying a long time with the way it is, by wondering: How is it that what seems so inevitable and so natural *to us* about our lives ending is so foreign to most of the world's peoples? What is it like, really, to die in our time and place? Instead of a new plan to replace the old plan, a few lines scratched into the shoreline sand with a twig from an old white pine—that's how we'll begin. That is how we'll begin to remember how it has come to be as it is, and to remember that dying hasn't always been as crazed as it is now. To get the crankshaft cranking and for all our sakes, here are the articles of faith, an overture to what I ask you to consider in this book. These are the bones of an Orphan Wisdom that I am certain, without much proof, we remain capable of remembering and treasuring and acting upon.

DYING WISE IS A RIGHT OF EVERYONE. Most would agree, but the agreement means little until we are willing to proceed as if dying well is also a shared responsibility, *binding upon us all.* Opting out of that agreement because of personal belief or professional prejudice will rob others of a chance to see and learn the possibility and the labor involved in dying well. We have to widen the circle of responsibility far beyond doctors and nurses until it includes extended family and neighbors and legislators and funeral directors and school curricula designers and nursing home managers and dying people themselves. All of us are bound to each other now by the shared obligation of securing good dying from the mayhem of managed, muted expiration that has become the norm.

DYING WISE IS A MORAL OBLIGATION. Dying well is not a matter of enlightened self-interest or personal preference. If you can begin to see how dying badly poisons the social, political, professional, and personal discourse about the purpose and meaning of health care and social welfare and being born and dying, if you get a glimpse of how the concentric circles of mayhem and spell casting attending a bad death do not end with that death but actually accelerate and deepen and turn into best practice manuals and family mythologies that have generations of unintended consequence, then you can know each death properly as another chance to die well and to learn the adult mystery of deep living in the face of what often seems to rob life of its depth. Dying well must become an obligation that living people and dying people owe to each other and to those to come.

DYING WISE IS A POLITICAL ACT. As soon as you begin to see how dying well challenges the old madness that passes for compassionate care and the orderly, meaning-free shuffle of a managed death, then you begin to know dying well as a great service and gift to those who are not yet dying. Dying well is the same kind of act as Gandhi's cotton spinning or salt harvesting: a nonviolent insurrection that dares the status quo to oppose it or prevent it. Dying well gathers adversaries. Of this you can be sure. Dying well means dying knowing that there is much at stake for the greater good. Whose death is it, anyway? It is all of our deaths, one death at a time, until our time comes. It is one enduring place where we can declare what and who we are willing to be to each other. We can reclaim our way of dying and decide upon it, and we must do so now. We can take it from the hands of professionalization and privacy and legislated monopoly only by assuming the greater responsibility of learning about death during the course of our lives, and teaching it if we are able, and by being an exemplar, an incarnation of what we advocate when our time comes.

DYING WISE IS AN ACT OF LOVE. It carries an abiding faith in life, it carries love for the world, and it asks that same faith and love of those who attend to it when it comes. Dying well is not the end of parenting, but the fullness of parenting, not the end of a marriage, but the last great act of a married life. Dying well is a bequest that you leave to those you love, probably the only thing that in the end will not be eaten by moths, apportioned by lawyers, or bought for quarters in a yard sale. Dying well is the way you could be known by those you won't live long enough to meet, the way by which they might feel loved by you after you die.

DYING WISE IS SPIRITUAL ACTIVISM. It doesn't require you to change your religion or get a religion or free yourself from one. Dying well is a portion of what your religion owes the world, as part of earning its keep, and what you owe your religion, as a part of you earning yours. It whispers to those terrified and depressed by a terminal diagnosis—those with and without a religion—that there is such a thing as dying wisely and well, that it can be done. Dying is not the collapse or the eclipse of wisdom. It is the sum of a soulful life. It dares and pleads with all professionals and volunteers and family members and neighbors to be partners in learning and championing the great, worthy spiritual project of dying wisely and well. Seeing the end of your life is the birth of your ability to love being alive. It is the cradle of your love of life.

DYING WISE IS IMMENSELY HARD LABOR. In a time and place that is death-phobic and grief-illiterate, dying well is mostly a sedated rumor. We suffer in our dying time from our addled language, from our assumptions about trauma, and because we think dying is what happens to our bodies. We suffer because we have little wonder about what passes for common sense about dying. We suffer from a withered mythic understanding of living and dying that will not stand the test of time. We deserve better than we get when it comes to dying, and until we change all of this, dying will ask more of dying people than should be asked of them. Dying is not what happens to you. Dying is what you do.

DYING WISE IS A SUBVERSIVE, TROJAN HORSE KIND OF DEED. Dying well nails you to the wheel of the world. It binds you to your people, to your ancestry and to those who will come after you. Dying well loves life. How we die, and how we care for dying people, and how we carry the dead: Taken all together, this work makes our village life or breaks it. That much and more is at stake in every terminal diagnosis, at every deathbed, at every memorial service. Dying well subverts the confounded compassion of a death-phobic culture. The ending of our lives is the shore that the current of our lives laps up against. How we live and die, the whole gaggle of decisions, torments, convictions, loves, and losses, all of this rolling on is the river of our days. Dying, and helping someone die, is a time for watching that river roll on and getting to know its eddies and its ways. It is a time for standing still beside the old pine, or beside where it used to be, learning life. Dying is not a time for not dying.

My farm, as I found out, *is* the valley between the river and the mountain. Since the River of Abundance and Time and The Mountain are still there, our long and narrow farm gets to be there between them, and we get to live on it, and make of the life granted us our lives. And so it seems to me that those things that become our life get to be where they are and how they are because the things that are not our particular lives are still there, enduring. Like rivers do, our lives find themselves by running alongside what will never be our lives, what will never happen, or what will always be. *How* we die is ripples in the river of life, little signs for others to come; *that* we die is the shore that the river of life obeys.

In our darker and lonelier days we can feel constrained or rebuked or turned away from by those more enduring things—things like dying—that our way of living won't change, that have no regard for what we mean, that will be there, God willing, long after the roil of our life goes on by. That is one of the things that can make dying so hard: looking around and realizing that everything you see, including the poorly built buildings and the questionable souvenirs, will outlast you.

But live your days, friends, and if you can get up a little higher along the edge of your life to see maybe a hundred acres of what you've lived from the east to the west, stand there long enough to say some unobservant thing. Guaranteed that you will. If you are lucky you'll have some companion make that climb with you and say without rancor, with just enough humor, "What valley is that?" Somewhere in there you will learn how to be a companion on someone else's climb up the little mountain of their days.

And then it will be your turn. Would that a companion or two show themselves. This is a book for that kind of companionship.

1

THE ORDEAL OF A MANAGED DEATH

What Happens When We Don't Let Dying Change Everything

No matter how old you are the first few times you come across the sleek monolith that is modern medicine in an urban center, you will probably feel as though you come from somewhere very early in the century before last. You might feel like a bumpkin just fallen from the back of the turnip truck, a hapless immigrant from the old country washed up onto the shore of a stainless steel land, carrying your uncertain health in a satchel dangled from a stick. Surely you will feel small and insubstantial in your blue gown and your paper slippers, and you will wonder where you were while all this became your "health care system." It has become more elaborate, more specialized, and more foreign to your usual life than anything you could imagine. At some point, your usual life will probably depend upon it. The way we die has been drawn up into that system so thoroughly that it is likely your grandparents wouldn't recognize anything that will be routine care when it is your turn. High-tech health care has become an undeclared war on dying itself, nothing less. Caveat emptor.

Cobalt and Courtesy: A Few Things to Know about Palliative Medicine

At the end of the Second World War, Western countries led by the U.S. had their armament-based economies rolling in very high gear. The war effort gave them considerable sway for domestic technological innovation. Winning the war didn't hurt, either. Coming out on the winning side lent to the ideology and its technology a heady feeling of the inevitable and the just. Whatever helped win the war was good, God was with the good guys, Europe was a tribal disaster, and the New World was bound to steer the rest of the world toward freedom and sanity, toward the brave, new, secured leisure-time future that everyone deserved.

Like many other wars in human history, this one was won and lost far from most of the battlefields. Touch and go as it was for several years, the Allies won it finally in the research and development departments, in the boardrooms and the laboratories of what came to be called the military-industrial complex. The manipulation of physics and chemistry turned the tide and won the war for freedom and democracy, where our shock and awe finally trumped the other guys' blitzkrieg. There is nothing like winning to neutralize second guessers, doubters, and competing interests, and there is nothing novel or shattering in saying that America, along with its allies, forged a new religion during the war and in the years just after it. That religion had an incorruptible faith in the goodness of the brave-new-world technology. There were scant caveats or qualifiers. The advocates of nuclear science were poised to make an entire industry where none existed before, and while the fifties turned into what nostalgia mongers sell as the Fifties—great music, great subdivisions, great security—they did so. The aggressive, confident empire we know as medical technology was conjured during that time. Nuclear medicine was and still is the prodigal child of medical technology, trailing clouds of glory, taken to the bosom of the health sciences to become the science of health, master and servant both of the health-seeking sector in Anglo North America and beyond. Medical technology is one of the things that happened to the nuclear industry when peacetime was forced upon it for a while.

If there is one postmodern article of faith that has survived any demonstration to the contrary, it is that there is an inherent progressive benefit to technological innovation. Some are willing to concede that the occasional application has been ill-conceived or haphazard, but overall the dominant culture of North America still believes in technology. One such example is the idea that "Guns don't kill people." Machine guns and nuclear warheads and GMOs, even less so. The lion's share of technological innovation still aims to provide an increasing degree of comfort to those who have the good sense to benefit from it, and the means by which that is pursued is the fine-tuning of efficiency.

Cost-effectiveness is the screw that turns the wheel of efficiency. But there is a considerable cost to pursuing cost-effectiveness. Here is the logarithm of progress: The more you pursue being saved from the drudgery of going through your days, the ordinariness of being around, the venality of physical limitation or vulnerability, the more is taken from the physical world to provide you that salvation and the more remote you will be from what grants you your security. *That is an ecological and spiritual fact.*

You might say that it has always been that way, and we're doing pretty well, or you might say that this is what the world is there for, so that we can wring some comfort from it. There are two problems, at least, with that. The first is that this objection, without hesitation, proffers comfort as a need—a dangerous and irrational proposal. The only needs that postindustrial people easily acknowledge are felt needs: If I miss it, or long for it, or had it once and lost it, or can't make do without it, I need it. Comfort has become this kind of need. Cell phones might be a good example: Twenty years ago they were a clumsy, tumor-generating innovation that hardly worked when you wanted them to and made you look foolish in your car. Now you are obliged to be on call eternally. "Come *on*. I left you a *message!*" Walk down the street of any major North American city and watch how there are more people talking to the phone than there are people talking to anyone you can see.

The second is that it *hasn't* always been that way. Smaller-scaled cultures with minimal technology tend to be willing to consider *what human comfort costs the world*. This older calculation of need weighs the accumulation of a kind of obligation to the world accrued by those who pursue it, the kind of obligation bequeathed to coming generations. When the hole left by trying to meet that need is deeper and wider than people's ability to begin to fill it through their way of living, worshipping, and loving, then the balances tip, and the obligation is not something people can deliver on. When that unlived debt—perhaps unlivable debt—is about to be passed on to their children's children, then *what is being pursued is no longer deemed a need*. It is too expensive, and anything that expensive is not in the realm of human need. By that old calculation, the world is a living thing and a spirited thing, the time-deepened repository of all the living and the dead, the always-accumulating source of life, conjured and rendered by death. These cultures have a willingness to enter into obligation to the world in the course of being alive. Certainly they do, and in this fashion they resemble a bit the dominant culture of the West. But there is a serious reluctance to steal from the world and from the generations to come in order to live. Stealing from the world, by this way of seeing things, isn't living. It is anti-living, perhaps, or *death living*. It is a deep trespass.

The dominant culture of North America sees its needs differently. We are concerned with the cost to the individual and the economy for *not* pursuing and meeting our needs. Our way of doing business individualizes almost everything. Here the cost accrues only to the one pursuing need: If *he* can afford having his need met, he gets his need met. It is driven by the feeling of needing and intolerance for the frustration of that need. The real cost to the world by proceeding that way, by our way of doing business, is not hidden from us. Not at all. It is unwelcome, and until recently it seemed negotiable.

In our way of life the plan has always been that the accruing benefit be passed on to future generations. We have been less forthcoming about the inevitable debt, or trespass, that is passed on with it. The "benefit" depends now on innovation being continually pursued, and here's why: Because need in the current reckoning is an escalating proposition.

"More" and "better" are enduring offspring of innovation, and need has a remarkable ability to adjust outward and upward toward improvement and acquisition. This is the mantra of growth. The world is there to be made to respond to our need, *but the world has no need of its own,* and certainly no need of us. The spiritual debt people have in our way of living— if any—is toward themselves and, if generosity, surplus, and cost-benefit analysis permit, toward each other. Exploitation of the world as a resource is the means by which this spiritual debt is "worked out." There is progress. There is inefficiency. There is no theft;. Efficiency is our faith, our obedience.

A young father once called on me for some advice. His faith in the old recipes was shaky. He'd been doing work he scarcely believed in any longer, taking jobs with questionable consequence for the world, but he was bound to them by the moral order of having to care for his family. Pushed a little more, he did admit that he was bound to the idea that his children deserved more than he'd had as a child. The truth is that we are in the straights we are in now in part because of our pursuit of this mandate. I encouraged him to consider that, with all the evidence mounting, it is clear and relentless now that our children, in the deepest way this can be meant, deserve less, considerably less, than their parents had.

Older ways of life know the world as animate, as alive. That means the world is treated with the same regard and esteem as is every living thing in it. People living these older ways of life know themselves as *of* the world, made of the same things in the same ways. In modern, sophisticated ways of life the world is inert and inanimate, a staging ground for life, but not itself alive. People living in that way tend to feel a bit like visitors or strangers to the world, uniquely wrought. But this faith in the unprecedented, singular self turns out legions of solitary, stand-alone people. This faith is hard on companionship. These people fan out over the countryside, compelled by need, bent on getting those needs met.

There are cultures that know that the ways of the world include them and that the ways of the world need them to be able to continue. These cultures know that the essence of being human is the learned capacity to maintain the world, or to care for the world as they are cared for. They understand themselves as needed by the world in order for the world to continue, not as fodder or raw material but as caregivers. Their technology is grown in accordance with their ability to maintain the world.

Needy cultures count on the world being self-sustaining, autonomous, and ordered. The world exists as a kind of need-gratification machine. For them the essence of being human is to triumph in turning the world into raw material whose end product satisfies them. Their technology spirals from success to success, from one logistical problem solved to the next. Progress, in other words. Caveat emptor, again.

Many times I've asked health care audiences what they think of when I say, "cobalt." For a few of them it is a place in northwestern Ontario, close to nowhere, which is half true. For the rest, you can see the generational split open up in the room. The younger people, anyone under forty-five or so, think of it as a color. Many of the older ones get a grave look in their eye. "Do you remember," I ask them, "hearing stories of your grandma or uncle coming home from the hospital with burns that wouldn't heal?" That's what "cobalt" means to people over age sixty: old people going to the hospital sick and coming out much older and ravaged and treated and scarred and scared beyond describing by what the doctors can do to you in there, with machines, you draped in lead and the technicians behind protective screens, looking at you through safety glass, hundreds of healthy miles away. Grandma was of the first generation of people exposed to cobalt treatments—radiation therapy. For cancer patients in those days, going for treatment was a lot like going away to war. They were mostly on the receiving end of what happened. It changed their ideas of what was possible in this world for the rest of their lives. They weren't sure that everything was going to be okay no matter what they were told. They couldn't tell a soul about any of it and have anyone see what they had seen. It was a lot like going to war. Cancer patients were—and mostly still are—armies of one, separated from the people around them by what they've seen and by what's been done to them in the War on Cancer in the name of getting better, for however long they live thereafter, Lazaruses all.

Medical technology has a religion, and it *is* a religion. It has a foundational creed that grew out of its own success. The creed is a dead simple one, known by any and all who have availed themselves of its many gifts, its brevity and power of persuasion the envy of anyone who works in advertising. The creed is memorable, easy to translate into almost any walk of life that needs it—and almost every walk of life does. It is part commandment, part aphorism, part the plea of common sense, and taken altogether it is a kind of life you owe to your loved ones: *If you can, you should.* It is the unchallenged mantra of most large health care institutions, emphatically so in big city hospitals that have pride and fundraising staked on their status as the best, the brightest, the newest, and it is the plea on the lips of most scared, diagnosed patients and their loved ones: *If you can, you should.*

We are in a state now, and have been for at least fifty years, where burgeoning medical technology imagines itself to serve best by leading. It no longer just provides an enviable range of treatment options when we need them most. It treats by compulsion. Gone, if it was ever there, is the option of doing little, of under functioning, of opting for nothing when wrestling with illness and death in the presence of a remarkable range of options that doesn't include doing nothing. Gone is any real questioning of treatment at all. The treatment options are debatable, but treatment is not. The treatment options of medical technology en masse have redefined "reckless and irresponsible": None of the options is in itself reckless and irresponsible, depending on the context, but failing or refusing to invoke the range of options might be.

To be honest, this happens much more subtly than in the naked and aggressive characterization I have made. I don't know if I have met anyone inside the med-tech system that wants it to be this way, but it is this way anyhow. For the 50 percent or so of people being diagnosed with cancer this year who will survive the coming of their disease, there aren't many qualms with being bullied somewhat by the "no option" option. They have bought their restored health with their narrowed ability to choose, and it isn't likely that many of them will stand on the principle of demanding their right to the real choice of doing nothing while enjoying the improved health the lack of choice availed them. For these people it would seem as sane as pining for impotence.

But for that other 50 percent, for those who come what may will die by the disease found in them this year, they are in the same slipstream, missionized in their illness by the same med-tech monotheism that will tolerate no other God, the same optionless option that relentlessly follows them more or less to the day of their death: *If you can, you should.* Those people learned early on in the diagnostic and treatment process that they owe their families and their close friends the unspoken, unwritten, and unsuspected debt of trying everything there is at least once, until health and wealth and sanity and give-a-shit are exhausted. And it is often only this exhaustion that produces for the first time the real choice of *enough already,* of *stop.* In other words, most of them will probably collapse into the waiting arms of *enough,* instead of seeking that embrace. All of this is unfolding daily in cities all over North America, where patients and families have no idea at all what can be done to them in the name of *If you can, you should.* What can be done is considerable.

To say it again: I do not mean that this is a conspiracy foisted on an unsuspecting public by Big Pharma with the easy compliance of boards of directors of hospitals, surgeons, lab technicians, and general practitioners. I don't mean that it isn't, either. I mean that people on all sides of the exchange are proceeding daily in the centripetal sway of this religion, and very few of them would be able or be willing to recognize how pervasive, persuasive, and necessary it has become. We use the term "consumer" to describe a patient's relationship to the swell of medical sites and services, but the thorough practice of *If you can, you should* raises a real question about who is consuming and who is consumed by this technology. This has considerable consequence for people who are slowly dying—and slow dying is increasingly the norm—in the active care of the med-tech system.

Within the health care regime the language often changes when a patient is tacitly acknowledged to be a dying person. Professionals will start talking with patients and families about "quality, not quantity." They will talk of "palliative radiation," of "comfort-giving measures." It sounds like the approach has changed, and in some ways it has. The ostensible goal has changed, from cure to … Well, that's the dilemma. What comparison can you make between "cure" and "keeping you comfortable"? None, really. One is a goal, the other is a collapse. Strangely enough, what animates the treatment program is almost unchanged. It sounds different on paper—healing versus palliating—but the energy is strangely similar. The religion is often still there, still persuasive and compelling and making its claim equally upon the patient, the family, the paid help, barely moderated by the fact that the person in question is now discernibly, measurably, and soon visibly dying. When the practitioners are in a team meeting they can afford to be honest with each other about whether it is justified to do another round of blood work or to offer more chemotherapy, and oftentimes they are. But it is usually a different story when the patient and family are present, when no one wants to be accused of giving up, when doing what can be done often still comes first.

Here is a story that illustrates how our med-tech arsenal appears from the outside looking in; I saw this kind of situation unfold more than once working in a large, multicultural urban setting: There is a child whose parents were born black- or brown- or yellow-skinned in a developing country, whose parents came to the West for a better life, and that child is dying. After various treatments are tried and exhausted, the parents are taken to a private meeting room and told with sensitivity that there is nothing more the hospital can do to cure their child. At some point in the meeting the anger boils over, and one of the parents says, "Of course there is more you can do. You have the machines and the medicine. You can do anything. You're saving the medicines for the white children."

This doesn't come from racially determined decision making nearly as much as it comes from the parents' certainty that white man–technology can do almost anything. Where did the parents get the idea that the hospital can do anything? It isn't because they are naïve or not acculturated. It is because they were taught that there is *always* something new to try, some new technique or drug or machine. They are easy converts. They have seen the fundraising slogans on the billboards outside the hospital too. They know that miracles are more engineered than they are prayed for. They know that there is always something to be done, and they, like most parents, want it all.

Look to the table of contents of any palliative care textbook, and you'll see that certain phrases show up in the titles of the articles over and over. Most of the physical, emotional, social, spiritual, even political challenges and limitations inherent in the experience of dying are met with an approach that is usually called "Management of …" or "Control of …" Medical technology provides to sick and dying people and the people charged with their care a diagnosis-to-death approach that is generally called "pain and symptom management." It is pervasive and rarely challenged as the gold standard in the care of dying people. Its practitioners will argue the self-evidence of its merits this way: You can't do or think about much else if your pain isn't well managed, and you can't help people with anything if you can't control their pain and symptoms. This is true to some degree, but it has an influence on how dying is understood and treated and practiced *which is far in excess of its ability to help.* It is a coded way of saying that the body comes first, or the disease comes first, or what we can do about the disease comes first. It says that dying is best understood and responded to as *a metabolic, physical fact* with emotional and psychological side effects. Pain and symptom management, practiced as it often is as the first order of business with the greatest efficacy, regularly collapses everyone's attention to the body and the disease, and it perpetuates this working definition of dying without questioning—or even owning up to—the assumption.

Ask most dying people how they are doing, and listen with this in mind. Their first, usually most enduring and often only response is to talk about what their body is doing. This isn't inevitable. It is a learned response, learned often during the diagnostic and treatment phase of an illness. Offer a dying person a home visit from a physician, and it will be usually welcomed. This is true also of a visit from a nurse. But offer a home visit from a nonmedical practitioner, a counselor, and the welcome vaporizes and the compliance plummets. The patient and family are saying: The body comes first. I am what my body needs, and my body needs this medical expertise. Whatever *I* might need I can likely conjure myself. Or at least it can wait. This considerable focus on the body, the treatment of dying as primarily a physical reality, and the preoccupation with pain and symptom, all of it is carried on in broad daylight with the general willingness and compliance of everyone in the treatment stream, usually with the full support and encouragement of everyone who loves the one who is dying.

At this point in my teaching events there will be people who will ask whether I am opposed to pain relief in any medical, chemical form, and whether I am advocating a cold-turkey, white-knuckle endurance test for dying people. That is not what I have in mind for anyone. I'll say plainly that when it is my turn I'm sure I'll want whatever pain and disease symptoms I might have treated and managed. That is what I would ask of anyone qualified to deliver it, absolutely. But there is almost no limit—certainly no limit tolerated—to the expectation we bring to medical technology. I wonder if we can make this overarching focus on the body and on pain and symptom management earn its keep and pay the rent for all the practical, emotional, and political real estate it takes up in the real process of dying that happens every day in urban North America. This is not too much to ask.

Pain and symptom management invokes the ideal of what has to be called a managed death, and behind that ideal, as behind most ideals, there is curled in the dark corners a much feared thing. More and more as the twentieth century wore on and became our lifetimes, the great fear and the great indignity became the possibility of an unexpected death. I don't mean a sudden death as much as the kind of death that should have been anticipated and wasn't, that should have been tracked and measured and fought and treated and wasn't. An untreated death is a nightmare death in a culture that has so much expertise, so much technology, so much mastery and money and machinery. Once we have bought lock, stock, and barrel the fantasy that we can do almost anything if we get it in time, unexpected death and its uncontrolled pain and rampaging symptoms, and our impotence in the face of those things, mock the diagnostic arsenal and the treatment panorama. They mock the ability, utility, and sheer mass of what we know how to do. For an information-flooded, competence-addicted, novelty-enamored culture, any chaos and randomness that carries us off is insulting, unbecoming, and a terror. We all know the stock response: *We can't just stand there and do nothing.* Refusing to use all the med-tech options at hand has become tantamount to doing nothing.

The receding religiosity of the urban North American dominant culture is a lament to a chosen few, liberty to a few more, and an apparent nonevent to the majority. But when that receded religious sense meets dying after dying has been reduced to a largely physical, metabolic event—and that is what I saw most working days—the going is very rough for all concerned. The word "religion" is related etymologically in spirit and meaning to the ideas of measurement, regulation, and control. In this older sense of its meaning, religions of all stripes provide to their advocates what is these days called a narrative, a story or bundle of stories of the way things are and will be and must be, and these stories serve an explanatory, sense-making purpose. By structuring an understanding of "how," they conjure a "why." In this sense-making function at least, palliative care in North America has sponsored the replacement of religion by technology.

Of all the teaching requests I have received from palliative care organizations over the years, one concern dominates. I have been asked over and over again to teach how to help dying people "find meaning at the end of life." I am sure this is because people in those organizations are routinely sitting beside dying people and staring with them into the void of what is to be, and they sense the shudder running through all those for whom dying is the end of meaning, the annihilation of meaning, the anti-story. Many of these professionals are working without such a narrative, without the ordering, meaning-making story that a religion can provide. The second most common teaching request I get? "Teach us how to survive doing the work." This tells me that storylessness is contagious.

Whether the meanings that the various religions carve out of life for death are working and delivering on their promises is something we will come to later in this book. But here is a little story that illustrates pretty well how it can be when we come to the time of dying without stories about it.

I was asked once to see the parents of a young boy who had been given a spate of treatment regimes that had failed and bifurcated to a handful more options, and ultimately to one experimental option. The results of the experiment were always more likely to have benefitted research projects, med-tech innovation, and maybe some other child in a time to come, but it too failed. Now the boy was dying. The parents had readied themselves for this for some time, and this was not the crisis they were grappling with. Their home town was in a Bible Belt area, and before they had come to the city for the experimental treatment they routinely found people on their front lawn, even their front steps, praying for their child's full recovery and recommending strongly that the parents join them then and there.

The parents had by their own estimation no religious understanding of life, and by the time I met them were feeling more and more hostile to any offers of prayer, spiritual reflection, and the like extended by the hospital staff. They were leery of meeting with me because they suspected I had some kind of religious agenda for them and their son's death. They'd had it with this life and with the afterlife too, but this was not their crisis, either. Their crisis was that, out of thin air, on the day when he had been removed from the trial drug regime because his body could no longer take the side effects and apropos they thought of nothing, without any prior religious upbringing their son had asked them whether there was such a thing as angels and whether he would still be their son after he died and whether he would see them again, someway, somehow. Their crisis was how to answer their son while, as they put it, staying true to their beliefs.

Well, what beliefs? Some believe that when you die, that's it. Some believe in keeping faith with the treatment-regime religion that their child's unfolding death is mainly or most importantly a physical, medical event. Some believe that their child's questions about angels and heaven and whether the child will ever see them again are not really the child's questions, but confusion brought on by a lot of drugs and symptoms and pain and the reckless and useless ideas of well-intentioned people trying to confuse and ease the child in a hard time. If you believe all of that—and many people do—what story will you tell your child about his or her coming death? What will you say to your child when he or she asks you if they'll still be your child after they die? Not "Will you think of me as your child?" not "Will you remember me as your child?" but "Will I still be your child?"

You would think, hoping never to find out for yourself, that any parent in a painful moment like that would know what to say and would give blanket assurance to their child that they will be his parents forever, just as divorcing parents tell their children. These parents had been through so much treatment with their son for so long, and had been thoroughly gathered into the religion of the body that is at the heart of palliative medicine, that they just could not make that seemingly inevitable leap from finding a fix, from pain and symptom management, to knowing what I call the whole-person sadness of their son finally, after everything, dying.

Their knowledge of him as a young person, as their son, had been seconded to the project of pain and symptom management, and the news of the exhaustion of treatment options seemed to change nothing in their way of caring for him or even in their way of talking to him. They responded to him not so much as parents but as care providers, and they responded from the poverty and the exhaustion of their willingness to go with *If you can, you should.*

They were in that wretched time trying to be the parents they knew they should be, no doubt. No doubt too their beliefs about what happens to you when you die, and after, and what dying is like, and what it does to you now and later, and what you should believe when you are dying, none of them came from anything they knew or learned about dying and death during the course of his long illness. During the time when they could have and should have been learning about dying and death, he was not dying. He was in treatment. None of what they knew or believed came from any hard and fast experience with dying, even though he had been dying for some time. Most of it came from stumbling across dying in the fitful, haunted, death-phobic early years of a new century in a place that knows dying mostly as what happens to your body, not from what dying is and means and asks of you when you are an eight-year-old boy or the parents of one.

This thinned or narrowed understanding of death is what animates most of the palliative care that is defended as "best practice" in most health care centers in most urban settings in Anglo North America, in my experience. There are all kinds of written material on "whole-person care" and "patient-centered care," but commonly the med-tech religion both underwrites and undermines the intent of such a broad vision. There remains considerable, primary focus on the body. The preoccupation with pain and symptoms is not a conspiracy of medicine foisted on an unwilling, unsuspecting public. It speaks to a poverty of options in its philosophy, not its tool kit. It is carried on with the general willingness and compliance of everyone in the treatment stream, with the full support and encouragement of pretty much everyone up and down the line. It is not a deliberate thing, not a decided thing, nor is it something more practitioners would necessarily defend if asked to do so. Practitioners want to believe that the kind of care they provide derives from the convictions and the motivations they bring to the job. But the dicta of the workplace are entrenched, and we have the technology, and technology is more and more dictating to us all how dying should properly be understood and managed. More and more, medical technology has become—maybe by default, because so many of us have no other—*the* story of our dying. The religion of medical technology goes like this: Dying is what we can *do* about dying. Palliative medicine is a creation of rapid med-tech innovation unaccompanied by any similarly rapid innovative practice wisdom guiding its use, governed by the unimpeachable human-centered conviction that dying is a manageable metabolic event that should be managed, animated by the root conviction that *If you can, you should.*

The Iatrogenic Nightmare of Palliative Care

The chances are very good that everyone receiving palliative care in this culture at this moment has had their life extended by palliative medicine. That means that most people who are dying of a known disease are living the benefits—or at least the consequences—of our med-tech expertise. Their lives are the outcome of our best practices in this field. Another way of saying this is that their lives have become what we have done to them.

People who are offered palliative chemotherapy and radiation are being offered "more time," the second-best scenario, a distant second to the preferred "enough time" or "all time." They are asked to submit themselves to a regime of calibrated toxicity with foreseeable side effects and somewhat foreseeable intended consequences. Rolling the knucklebones of their fate, they gamble for more time. For the lion's share of patients, they get some version of what they gambled for. "More time," you should know, is no longer much of a dream for palliative patients or for those in the business of palliative care. It is largely a fact of palliative life. Certainly in my time working in medically driven palliative care, almost every patient referred to me for "difficulty in adjusting to diagnosis" had gone through a treatment phase that had extended their days beyond what number they would have had without the treatment. So far, you'd think, so good.

It's the same story, for the most part, with dying-related pain and symptoms. The old nightmare of raging pain and rampaging, uncontrolled symptoms is, depending on where dying people are dying, on how informed and competent their physicians are, and how compliant with treatment protocol they are willing to be, just that: an old nightmare that in the new dawn of palliative medicine has faded largely to memory.

Listen carefully to any dying person, and you will find in the early days of their dying that most fear pain above all else. This is their nightmare scenario: a resolute, intractable pain, swelling to a crescendo mainly at night when everyone who could do something about it is asleep, the solitary hell of a pain-filled solitude. So they welcome any promise, any attempt to control that pain and make it livable while they die.

Here is what I have seen, over and over: dying people in the early and middle stages of their dying, still fairly healthy considering everything, their dying no longer unknown, no longer questioned, their symptoms fairly well managed, their pain fairly well controlled, utterly terrified, unspeakably riven by dread, numb when they are not panting with the horror of it, up many hours of the night with a raw, unspeakable, pain-free or pain-managed terror. This makes them prime candidates for sedation or antidepressants. Here's why: Their terror should have been quelled by having their worst fear managed. Yes. Of course. It should have done.

How can this be? How has it come to pass that, as technology and medical expertise crest in ever-achieving high water marks and physicians become ever-more skilled in soothing our ailments, as our worst nightmares are managed down to annoyances, our end-of-life terror peaks and more of us die sedated now, I am sure, than did our aunts and uncles and parents and old friends even twenty years ago?

The answer I think is simple, as in "uncomplicated," and very diffi-cult, as in "immensely hard to bear." As I said, almost every dying person has had their life extended. Almost every dying person who submitted to treatment got some version of what they wanted. Almost no dying person has done this, though: They have not walked into the oncologist's office, negotiated the terms of their treatment fingering the rosary of their inter-net medical savvy in their pocket, signed up for the deal and then asked anyone who would listen, "If we gamble for more time and win, and if as I come out the far end of your palliative chemotherapy, maybe hairless or vomiting or spent, I suddenly find myself in the grace period that I want and everyone wants, what should I do with it? What should I do with the More Time that I get?"

They haven't done so not because they aren't curious or intelligent peo-ple, not because they are addled by fear or pain and can't think obvious thoughts, not because they are intimidated by imperious health care types who won't give them the time. It isn't likely that anyone around them has thought this thought either. No, the reason is that for almost anyone with an opinion on the subject, More Time is its own reward. When you get your heart's desire, when the prayer is answered, surely you won't have to ask, "What now?" Isn't that in the nature of a prayer answered, that you'll know what to do with it when it happens? How could that ever be a problem?

The radiologist or the oncologist might answer the question this way: "Well, that isn't my field, really, but Social Work is down the hall, Chap-laincy is around the corner, and, if all else fails, Psychiatry is next door." Friends and family will probably answer the question this way: "Well, just go out there and live," or, "Just carry on as you have," or, "Get your affairs in order," or, "Enjoy as normal a life as possible, under the circumstances." "And what," the patient should then ask, "are 'the circumstances'?"

Almost everyone gambles for it and wins, and almost no one knows what to say to this question. It turns out that More Time is almost never its own reward. When something happens that routinely, it stands to rea-son that by sheer force of exposure most people working in palliative care or in the medical community or in the helping professions could be relied upon to answer well when a dying person asks, "What should I do with my More Time?" But that's not what happens. The question is rarely asked and very rarely answered to anyone's satisfaction. This is not because the professional caregivers are calloused drug peddlers or closet bureaucrats, nor is it because the family members and friends are burned-out misanthropes or unlearned bit players in this medical drama. It is because the More Time almost never looks or feels or goes the way people imagine it will when they are bargaining for it.

More Time bears no resemblance to anything most people have lived. More Time is a fantasy of the resumption of a life interrupted. But More Time, when it finally kicks in, is the rest of a dying person's life, and the rest of that life will be lived in the never-before-known shadow of the inevitability of their dying. For the first time in their lives they will live knowing that they will die from what afflicts them. Most referrals that came to me were for palliative patients who were "having difficulty adjusting to diagnosis," but this was rarely an accurate understanding of what was going on. Their real difficulty was in adjusting to the consequences of having had their days extended. *Their real affliction was almost always More Time.* More Time means more time to live their dying. It means more symptoms, more drugs for the symptoms, more drugs for the side effects of the first drugs, more weakness and diminishment and dependence to go along with more time with the kids or the grandkids, or walks in the park with the dog. That's not all it means, not necessarily, but More Time almost always means more dying. No one is born, no one walks in the park or sits looking out the window knowing how to die like that, slowly and visibly and knowingly. Very few here on these shores, where death phobia rules, learn how, or want to.

Palliative medicine in the last thirty years has taken people living with a life-threatening disease, or people in treatment with no intent of cure, and created from them an entirely new social, ideological, political presence among us. Most people now call them The Dying. Maybe it is better to say that The Dying were created by More Time. The Dying have been obliged to narrow their understanding of themselves down so radically during the course of their treatment that they become to themselves mainly a bundle of symptoms ridden by an attitude. They can talk doctor with the doctor, pharmacy with the pharmacist, they know a lot more than most people do about chemistry, histology, anatomy, respiration rates. When you ask them what is happening to them, they can read back to you their medical chart. They know probabilities, survival rates, side effects. They know about the possibilities of More Time, about *If you can, you should.*

The Dying have discovered without wanting to that pain does not equal suffering. They have lived long enough to realize that they were utterly wrong about what they once feared most, without any sense of how to live with the error, without any skill in how to wrestle their deeper, enduring terror. It isn't pain, after all, that is unendurable. It isn't living that is undoable. It is dying in a death-phobic time and place. The Dying are obliged to live in a way they have never done before, and no life skill or old competence can be brought to bear. They are asked to live dying, when nothing about how they've lived looks as it once did. They are delivered to a place no longer among the living, only one foot uncertainly planted in a vestige of a life they once knew, the other angling off like a broken limb in an unknown, unbidden direction. They have only qualified, temporary citizenship in the Land of the Living. Their prognosis is their one-way ticket out of that country. By being given More Time, they have been given more death. Imagine that there is such a thing, because there is. There is more death than there has ever been, and for certain more death than there has to be. More days were given to them by others, but more dying they will have to do on their own.

When you wrestle More Time from the jaws of cancer, and your More Time is lived with the coming of your death ever present; when the ever presence of your death comes to you in a time and place that doesn't believe in limitation or frailty or limited productivity or aging or non-competence or not being in control—or death—you will not get what you bargain for when you take palliative treatment. Instead it conjures a vague curse that makes most of your days and all of your nights a gray-knuckled endurance test where you must fashion for yourself, seeing your death from a long way off, a way of dying. When all around you do their mad cheerleading and think good thoughts and refuse to let all this be a big part of their lives, they will ask you to do the same for the sake of getting along and getting by. You are now of The Dying. It isn't what you imagined. It isn't what you rolled the knucklebones of your fate to win. But these are your winnings.

So, in our time, somewhere over the last twenty years or so, the old nightmare of a chaotic, untreatable, unexpected death was mostly tamed, and it is now a thing that lives mostly in the bad old days. In the hole left by the taming of that old nightmare a new one has grown. It is a natural child of the old nightmare, but born of the ways and means by which we gained our freedom from it. One day no one will be surprised that things have come how they have come. One day it will seem obvious, inevitable, that this new nightmare should have grown in place of the old.

Dying people get the best of our pain and symptom technology and they tend to lose their old fear of pain. They get the best of our palliative chemotherapy and radiation and they have More Time to die in. Their families plead for the palliative medicine system to *do something* and it does, and those families live months and years in the inarticulate, insubstantial purgatory of not knowing any longer how to have a dying person in their midst, with little good guidance on how to do so. Dying people answer research questionnaires to determine their quality of life, but neither they nor most people around them are willing to ask for quality of death, or advocate for one, or make one, or imagine quality of death as the last privilege of a dying person. Almost no one imagines that pleading for quality of death becomes the job description of someone who has wrestled More Time from the med-tech ether, but it does.

> When I pulled up to the house I knew something more than the referral had told me. I'd been asked to see a fifty-something husband and father who was probably midway through his dying, who had made his living as a mental health professional with medical training

in his background, who was as they say "showing difficulty in adjusting to the news of his prognosis" now
that the treatment phase of the disease had quietly and
without fanfare or much notice given way to the palliative phase.

The house was new and large, on a street of older,
smaller homes. It was set apart and had a kind of aloneness about it on a street in a subdivision in a city that
already had a good amount of aloneness built into it.
Anyone toward the end of his working life who buys a
home in a substantial subdivision in one of the fiercest
real estate markets in North America and then tears it
down and builds a bigger place than he wrecked, that
man has *plans,* and the means to plan, and those plans
include being around to admire the tangible fruits of a
life's work. They don't include dying in the house before
the paint is dry and the dust has settled. They don't include dying without a choice. They sure don't include
"having difficulty adjusting to diagnosis."

I made my way up the winding approach to the
house, climbed the prodigious stone steps and stood in
front of the oversized door, looking in vain for a bell.
No button, no knob, nothing to twist or push or pull.
A house like this with no bell? Home security these days
being what it is, I figured that there must be some kind
of motion-detecting camera device pinholed in the ma-
sonry somewhere around the door. A house like this
must be well protected. They must know I'm here. They
must have seen me coming up the steps. I don't look
typically professional or businesslike, and it is usually
important to strike a note of competence early on, but I
stood in front of that dark, massive door and I couldn't
figure out what the competent thing to do might be. I
waited some more. Now I imagined them watching me

through the camera, standing at the door, just standing there, not doing anything, looking obviously out of my league. "Why isn't he knocking?" I argued with myself about the merits of knocking. Maybe this is the wrong door. Maybe there is a service entrance somewhere, and that's the one I should be standing at. But that would mean going back down the stairs and skulking around the ground floor of the house looking for it. Nothing about that would look good. I gave up. I couldn't figure the thing out. I knocked.

Eventually his wife came to the door and let me in. She hollered back into the house to her husband that "the Steve guy" was here.

"Who?" I heard him yell back. "That Steve guy. I told you. The hospital guy. We have an appointment."

He yelled again, "For what?"

"I don't know," she said, and pointed me to a room to wait for him to appear. Now, this appointment was at her request, and it wasn't a promising start, never mind the doorbell situation, for her to disavow any knowledge of why I was there. Maybe you can hear the code being spoken and the spell being cast: They all know in a general sense why I'm there, but thou shalt not know, and it's business as usual, given the circumstances.

Eventually he came downstairs, moving slowly, easing himself into the wraparound lounge chair. He looked at me briefly when we said hello, looked away again. His wife sat down, looked at me, looked away too, waited. I made an introduction for myself, described how the palliative services worked, what they could expect from us. They had no questions about that. So I asked the question I always ask at about that stage in the proceedings. I ask it because I want to hear what they say, and what they don't say, about what has been and what is to come.

I asked him, "With everything you've been feeling, all the changes, and with everything you've been told so far, what is your understanding of what is happening?"

His answer was swift.

"Oh look. I know I'm dying, okay. There are a couple of things you should know about me. One is I've had a history of illness, thirty years of it. I know this stuff. I know how to be sick, okay. This is nothing new for me. The other thing is that I'm not afraid of dying. That's not my problem."

It's very rare in my line of work that people will tell me within minutes of meeting that they know they are dying, and that they're not afraid to die. Most are waiting to find out if they're going to die, most think of it in the future tense, most hate the whole enterprise, most secretly believe that if you say it aloud you'll make it happen or make it happen sooner or make it worse. Most people toward the end of their lives believe in Word Voodoo, and they won't say much that they think could swing things out of their diminishing favor. This man was an exception, in some ways.

"My problem is this. I know what's going to happen. I know how it's going to go. Sooner or later the pain will be too great. I can handle pain. I've got experience with that. That's not the problem. My problem is that eventually the pain will just get too bad. And then there's the breathing. Eventually I won't be able to breathe. I don't want to go through all that. All I want from you guys, when the time comes, I want you to sedate me. That's it. Not to take the edge off. I want you to sedate me so I won't wake up again, when the time comes."

That kind of request is rare too. It took me a minute to hear what he was asking for.

"You're asking us for terminal sedation? So I can be sure, you want us to sedate you so that you'll die from the sedation. That's what you're asking for, when the time comes. Have I got it right?"

"Terminal sedation. Exactly. I don't want to go through shortness of breath, any more of this. When the time comes, I want to know that you'll sedate me and end this. We wouldn't make dogs go through what I've gone through already. It's immoral. It's barbaric, and you can't defend it. I have a right to not suffer. You guys are in the business. I've talked to people. I've been on the internet. I know how it's done. But I can't physically do it, when the time comes. I can't ask my family to do it. I know it's against the law. The law's wrong. The law's an ass. So if I'm going to have you guys around, I want to know you'll do that for me, when I ask for it. I don't need anything else from you. I don't need any counseling or anything. I'm fine. I just need you to take me out when the time comes."

The law, as this man knew, is fairly clear on this point in my jurisdiction. Any medical treatment that will foreseeably cause someone's death, or any treatment intended to cause death, is some kind of murder. The application of the law usually centers on intent.

The truth is that in most urban centers across North America, some version of terminal sedation in the context of palliative care happens fairly frequently. It isn't discussed openly except in philosophical terms, but it is done, and most people working in the business know it is done. The people who are supplying terminal sedation are sedating people who will die in any event. That is pretty much a given. The fine point goes like this: Sedation is intended to ease irreversible suffering at the end stage of a terminal disease. That is the goal. The unintended but typical side effect of doing so with enough medication is that the dying person's death probably happens sooner than it would otherwise have done.

The dying person's intent is that they die sooner than the disease process would dictate. That is suicide, in the usual judgment. The attending caregiver's intent is that the dying person's "terminal agitation"—death anxiety, to call it properly what it is—be ended. That is terminal sedation. The legal issue, the ethical thorn, is when does terminal sedation become assisted suicide, suicide by physician? Or is that what it is?

Either you obey the law about assisted suicide and let your obedience soothe whatever qualms you have about being able to end someone's suffering but choosing not to, or you know the limitations of the law in this matter and decide with all the considered honesty you can afford what your obligation might be as one human being to another human being who is—there is no other way of saying it well—obliged to suffer. He or she is obliged not by the disease but by the medical innovation that has given him or her More Time and, by the inability of the law to keep pace with that innovation, to suffer.

Though all of this swirled in the room—all family members were professionally trained people, they all knew there were implications to what he was asking—none of this was what we would all have to wrestle then and in the coming weeks. Our man's problem was not that he feared pain or shortness of breath, not that he had a history of physical disease that might predispose him to hyperbole or imagined mayhem where there wasn't any, not even that he eventually would become weakened to the point where he could not act on his own wish and end his life, or that he might have to rely on others to do it for him.

Our man's problem was that he was still alive. Because of the treatment he'd received his life had been extended far beyond what the disease dictated, but he gained that additional life knowing that he would die in the foreseeable future of the disease he was being treated for anyway. His suffering was not in the time to come. He was suffering *now,* not from what was going to happen but from what had already happened and was still happening, and *from what had not happened.* He said he wanted to be sedated when the time came. But when would that be, and what would that time look like? What would be the sign that it had come? What more had to happen to propel him into the time of the unendurable, the indefensible, the dog's life?

Our man's idea of dying, his ideal, was the comedian's throwaway line: He didn't mind dying, but he didn't want to be there when it happened. His idea of a proper death, the least of his rightful entitlements, was to die not knowing he was dying, to wake up dead, as they say. But his great and personal hell was that it was already too late to have that kind of death. He already knew that in some fashion he was dying, and still *it wasn't happening.* That was the nightmare he'd been delivered to by his medical treatment: It would take longer to die, so long that it never seemed to be happening. His every waking minute—and, judging by his dreams and insomnia, every half-sleeping minute too—was lived knowing he was dying. He had bargained for months of illness and an hour of death, but instead got an eternity of wakeful agitated, motionless, unremarkable, endless, symptom-riddled, ordinary dying.

As things unfolded, without much increase in the symptoms he feared most, his demand for sedation escalated to where he began to ask for it when there was pain and when there wasn't, when he thought he couldn't breathe and when he could. Doctors sometimes develop a jaundiced eye when regaled with "unsubstantiated" pain reports. Despite repeated assurances that we would not let him suffer the intractable pain and terrifying shortness of breath he feared, he drew no consolation or comfort from it. From his point of view, with no real changes in either, he was already in the "when the time comes" time because he had decided so. Fearing it was the same as it being true. It no longer mattered when we came to his house, when we titrated the pain medication, when we sedated him. It would always be too late. When he did die in the middle of the night, one of his wife's first acts was to leave us a voice message saying that we had failed him and balked at the moment of truth—a moment that had come and gone months before.

So this is the new iatrogenic nightmare, the malady caused by the cure, that has become palliative care for many. With little worsening of dying peoples' physical pain and symptoms, more and more of them want to die sooner, and they can't, at least not of the disease that is killing them. This is what is fueling the accelerating debate about and request for assisted suicide or terminal sedation. More physicians are in the impossible position of defending, or at least acquiescing to, the longer death that their patients are living. More families caring for a dying loved one are at a loss about what they should wish for, and untold thousands have guilt years later that when it came to it they just wanted their loved one to die already, because no one could do it anymore. Instead of the old nightmare of uncontrolled pain and unexpected death, we have a new nightmare of controlled pain and an unexpected wish to die, a wish that can't be accounted for by worsening symptoms and can't be soothed by reassurances that no one will be allowed to suffer. They *are* suffering. Dying people are suffering a torment we once thought would only come to those in the hour of their death. Now the hour of death is months long, sometimes longer. Now, in the middle of the More Time that they prayed for, dying people more often than not cannot bear the answered prayer.

The Right of Life

In my experience people are great fans of stories. As much teaching as I have done in as many cities and settings, for as many crowds and countries, I see that most people want a story. Whatever good ideas you might have, however elegant your theories, whatever prestige you can conjure with your overheads and your Power Points, none of these can touch a story worth telling and worth hearing. None of them will have the arc of necessity about them, none will carry that mystery of recognition that jumps up at the telling of a story worth hearing, none of them will be remembered months, years, or lives later and told in trying times. Stories have all this power, and more.

Stories need a certain regard, though. There are cultures in the world where stories are heirlooms, as precious as the shinbones of the ancients—they *are* the shinbones of the ancients, played like flutes on the lips of the griots—and belonging only to a few. There are stories that can be heard only by a few, or by a few at a time, in ceremonial chambers made in hours of ritual, offering, speechifying. The Anishinaabeg people in my part of the world have stories that can only be told when the land sleeps under snow, when the saplings snap, when the night sky is so blue-black that the stars are like ragged holes dug through from the other side to let the light of the Other World into this one for a time. The reason these stories can only be told then? That's part of the story that can't be told but by those to whom it belongs, in winter. And if you are somehow honored by being present when these stories are told, don't think that this confers on you the right to tell them. It isn't so. Those stories have been paid for many times over by their tellers, and telling them is their job. It is a privilege to be told a story that is not yours to tell. Our culture, where stories are often told for amusement or distraction from pain or boredom and belong to no one, still has the hardest time distinguishing privilege from right, and not just in storytelling.

I have told this story many times, and I'll tell it again here. I remember the man in the story with great respect, and he is among us. He is Martín Prechtel, now an author and teacher in the U.S. but once an apprentice to a Mayan shaman, a man with a mighty capacity for storytelling. He is the kind of raconteur you'd like to grapple with, but because you couldn't contend with what he can do with his words, your wisdom might win out and you'd listen instead. This is proper. In a culture so addicted to psychology, to the hallowed, endless habit of killing your father or mother every chance you get by trying to cut the legs out from under people of wisdom and learning when you meet them, really listening to someone because they carry something you've never known is rare. On this day—and I take no credit for it—I mostly listened.

> The storyteller is a man who has the indigenous capacity for dense brevity of speech. It is thrilling to be present when someone able in this skill begins stirring the cooking pot of Remember When. This brevity isn't parsimony. It wasn't that he spoke in a clipped, ungenerous way. His epic harangues trust the words they ride on, and his memories don't hobble thousands of words when making a friend of a good phrase can get the work done of including you, the listener, in an understanding of something you weren't there to see when it happened. So this was how the talk was going, murmurs and eruptions, epic declarations and amens. We had quieted for a moment, giving the last story the proper room after its telling. Then, apropos of nothing I can recall, he looked out over the piece of the world we had been admiring and said, "Hey unh. It's very strange, where you come from."
>
> Well, amen. I've been where I come from for a while now, this dominant culture of North America, and I

can say with confidence that there's nothing in what he said that I can dispute, not then and not now. If anything, his observation is truer now than when he spoke it. What passes for natural around here would not be recognizable in the natural parts of the world, truly. I waited for the rest of what I was sure was coming, an elaborate rendering of our particular madnesses, of the consequences of our way of life for ourselves and for the world, but there was nothing else. I looked over at him and saw that he was entirely satisfied at the catholic scope of his observation, its self-evidence and decent accuracy being plain to all with an eye for the way things are. He felt he had done good justice to the subject at hand, and he rested on the achievement.

In cultures where food is not plentiful it is precious. Even food prepared poorly or without spice, for example, could be good food. A small meal in a bowl carries the immense story of its growing or hunting, the whole sweeping saga of how the seed or animal came to the people, all the times that the same food has been eaten in the same way as now, joining those at the frugal feast with all those who did so before. Cultures rich in stories know storytelling in a similar way. What we might call a short story is for them a feast, and recognizing the years taken in learning and living a story that takes only a minute to tell, they take a good long time to hear it. This is the story hearer's skill, his or her half of the project.

We enjoyed a few quiet minutes. The storyteller had grace to go with his discernment, and he knew that while we sat quietly some had some hope that he would say a little more from his own experience of the strangeness of where we come from. He had been dealing with tourists from El Norte for years. "Well," he said, "it seems to me that where you come from, every-body wakes up every day expecting to live." He shook his head slowly back and forth a few times. This for him was not just an example of how strange it is here, where I come from. It was the fullest expression and the essence of our strangeness, perched on the trembling branch of our morning habit. That was his unnecessary but gracious gloss on what was already a full and true thing. He was done with the subject.

This was said without any rancor, without malice or the surgical assassination or irony passing for repartee that many of us learn at school or from sitcoms. He wasn't pleased to know this about where I come from, nor was he pleased that this was so. He said this with a real sorrow for us, and a feeling of bewilderment that we could against all evidence to the contrary and against what would be best for our lives continue to get up in this way, every day, expecting to live. I tell you this story, having years in the death trade, with the same bewilderment.

Consider this: Is it inevitable that we awake with the expectation to live so firm and unquestioned? Is it possible to awake in some other way? Should we? Most hearing this story for the first time imagine that people waking up with no particular expectation to live have been robbed of it by the fatalism of their religion or the squalor of their daily life or the resignation to a basic misery of their high infant mortality rate, or the like. Many of us feel that if they could they'd wake up like us, raring to go and fueled with the just and sanctified certainty that their life is a right to be exercised. Without that choice among them, there must be a current of depressive, diminished expectation. If we could, some of us would marshal our considerable clout and connections and do something for these people. The most enterprising of us would bypass the World Health Organization and the NGOs altogether and take matters into our own hands, to rid these people of their depression, to give them the fair chance they deserve to have some version of what we have, and to give them the chance to expect to live as we do, a basic human right, as we would say.

Places like this have physical and emotional hardship that most of us here have never contended with or imagined. With all the infant mortality, haphazard death from treatable disease, and privation of the "basic needs" which tourists who go there take as a given, with all of that and more in place, still depression may not be the result. Sorrow and lament no doubt, much of it. But depression isn't the inevitable consequence of that kind of hardship. I have been to the place I am from, many times, and I've made my living there. I have seen "waking up expecting to live" every day on the job, and I've seen what it does for us. I have seen that there is a diminished ability to suffer. There is little instinct or capacity for grieving. There is a headlong flight away from discomfort, hardship, dying. There is a degree and kind of depression here that would be declared some kind of emergency if it were known for the widespread thing it is. Waking up as we do is job security for all the mental health professionals in your yellow pages.

This culture believes in expecting to live. It is our right, a positive, life-affirming way of life, unassailable, proper, natural. But the coincidence of expecting to live and depression as two enduring parts of our life here is something to be noticed. There is every possibility that waking up each day expecting to live and the widespread depression we know is here are connected, that one has some role in causing or contributing to the other. And it could just as likely be that expecting to live is not the life-affirming proposition I have repeatedly been told that it is. Expecting to live is life affirming only if your belief about life is that it is generally self-initiated and self-directed, that we all have a more or less equal opportunity to make something of our lives, that limitation and boundary are the unnecessary but lamentable consequences of our unwillingness to go big or go home, and that dying is just one of many lifestyle options available. Waking up every day expecting to live is how people who hold life at arm's length do so. It is our ten-foot pole. It affirms, no matter any evidence otherwise, what we believe our lives should be if life is good, if there is a God worthy of the name superintending the story.

But if your idea of life includes wearing out early or late and dying and death, if it includes your own personal, inevitable, and omnipresent dying, no matter how many good thoughts you think or how much broccoli

49

you eat or how good a person you are, as it should, then waking up every day expecting to live is something you would do *in spite of* what life is like, *in spite of* what you know of it, not because of it.

Expecting to live is training wheels on the spaceship of our entitlement: That is how life is mostly lived in our part of the world. Expecting to live is soon enough eclipsed by a conviction of greater swagger and consequence. Sooner or later we begin demanding to live as a basic right of our presence on the scene. Where I worked for several years there is a collection of large, formidable buildings running down both sides of a six-lane street for a block. Most people there know them to be hospitals, but I know them to be temples. Their religion is Quality of Life, but their God is the demand to live. Demanding to live is the God they serve. If this sounds a little overstated to you, tour one of them. Notice where the different services of the temple are found. The boardrooms and executive suites are usually high up, with good views and very good furniture. The brave new technology wings, the ones named after their benefactors with slogans about cure, are usually very sleek and seem well funded. The rehab services take what the med-tech wards no longer need and generally make do. The chronic care wards are the poor cousins of medicine, bedraggled and on floors that have seen better days, but still in the building, still above ground. Now try and find palliative care, if there *is* such a service in your hospital. I know of institutions where palliative care is in the basement, beside Custodial Services. No accident, no coincidence. Care of the dying is the place where demanding to live did not prevail, despite everyone's best practice. There is a running gag in medicine that there is no such thing as dying; there is only a failure to thrive. In a culture that wakes up every day demanding to live, dying is a failure, at least temporarily, of the way that culture lives. But the treatment of every new sick or disabled or broken or depressed or dying person is where the culture reaffirms its belief that a long, full life is the inalienable right of all.

There is a general pride that our part of the world enjoys the best quality of life in the world. We point to three indicators of this achievement: lowest infant mortality rate, comfort-giving material/technological innovation, longest average life span. Everything costs though, friends. Our creaturely comforts have cost the world considerably, as we are finally, unwillingly learning. Our lowest infant mortality rate is bought in part by obliging infants with considerable birth abnormalities who would otherwise have died from them to live with them instead, often well into their childhoods and beyond, and by asking their families to learn how to do that. Our superb life span is purchased in part by extending old people's lives far beyond what their illness or their disease would have allowed, while still not entirely ridding them of that illness or disease. We should add a fourth record to the string of our achievements: I suspect that we also die the longest. We are not allowed to die on schedule. Often we do, but it isn't encouraged. Our idea of what dying on schedule is like has been so skewed by the med-tech competence in distorting that schedule, funhouse mirror–style, that "natural death" is mostly a matter of opinion and personal style instead of a matter of dying.

Every natural thing in this world has the innate skill of obedience. With the North American history of slavery in plain view, and with every weekend Buddhist looking to kill every Buddha they meet on the road, obedience generally goes against the North American grain. As adults, we are not big on obeying. The quality of being obedient is not much sought or taught, except to small children while they are small. Etymologically, obedience has nothing to do with being some kind of slave. It means instead a willingness and an ability to listen to what is, to attend to it. Obedience is following the grain of things. With that skill of obedience, every natural thing knows above all how to be itself, come what may. Dying is a natural thing, and left to its natural self each living thing knows how to die. The body has the genius of a natural thing, and it knows how to obey the accumulation of time, wear and tear, disease and symptoms. It knows how to stop. But med-tech, not in any sense a natural thing, knows how to subvert the way disease and symptoms have of keeping and marking time, and in doing so it subverts the body's knowledge of how to stop.

"April is the cruelest month," T. S. Eliot wrote, and it isn't a botanical or calendric fact. April ends rest, torpor, slumber. It ends the ending of things, by prodding every seed, sap-filled vein, leaf bud, and body capable of going on into stirring again and pressing forward. The winter of a person's life is the time of slowing down, sagacity, and dying, or it should be. But the April of our lives, when we are sickened and dying in the harrowing early years of this century in a death-phobic, death-intolerant place like this one, ends our death and prolongs our dying. The cruelty of it is unimaginable were it to be recognized as cruelty, but it is not. Medical technology and the temples downtown and the distraught, cheerleading families aren't serving cruelty. They are serving the demand to live. This is the strange God who claims their attention, their fidelity, their obedience. I am sure this is why, year after year, more people seem to die in late winter, before April obliges them to rise up one more time.

I had the great good fortune years ago when I needed it most to be found by a teacher whose capacity for obeying life was massive and whose willingness to show it to me over and over was somehow not exhausted by the hard time I had learning it. His given name was Hugh Hill, and his street name was Brother Blue. He, his wife, and I toured some corners of Canada and the U.S., he the storyteller, me the band, his wife the guiding light showing us what was needed. One night we were backstage, preparing for the show. The house was humming with the quiet electricity of an expectant audience, and we were properly alert to the occasion. I was, given that we never rehearsed, that every performance was truly a one-off event that hinged on my iffy ability to improvise from the slightest shift Blue made in the bottomless repertoire of stories he carried and remembered, scared. In the final moment before we took the stage, he took one of each of our hands in his and prayed hard for our ability to do something useful that night. Midprayer, eyes open and riveting, he told me to find one person in the third row and play to them all night. He said, "If you can see what that one person has walked through, from their earliest time, from all their growing up time, through everything they wanted to believe in that didn't believe in them, through everything that couldn't last, through every heartbreak that got them to tonight, you'd fall down on your knees in awe, and there'd never be another stranger." With Blue's prayer in mind, I tell this story.

The man I was sitting beside had been diagnosed ten months before with a progressive disease that would in the fullness of time end his life. He had taken the treatment offered him, whose purpose was to slow the disease, and the treatment was successful. The man couldn't open his eyes. There was something about the combination of disease and surgery and drugs being used to treat him that made his eyes so sensitive to light that he found it unbearable to see. He was day blind. He had bargained for more time, he was now in the more time he had bargained for, and his towering anger was an obstacle for the care team and a terror for his wife. He raged, for the most part, wordlessly. It was in his sighing, in the grinding of his teeth, in his sleepless nights. His wife cultivated the practice of divining what he might want or need from the tone and object of his rage, day and night.

We had never met. I was another stranger in his living room. His wife gently encouraged him to speak with me, and I couldn't tell if he was drug addled, sleep deprived, hostile, all or none of the above. I only had my words, my tone of voice, and my timing, and it was a huge challenge to be conversational and faithful to the bottomless but terminal diagnosis that had brought us together.

I introduced myself, and then he snapped, "What have you got for me?"

"What do you mean?" I asked him. "Do you have any new drugs with you? Do you have a new operation? If you didn't bring something like that with you, you don't have anything for me. You're useless."

His wife was embarrassed and mouthed the words, "I'm sorry."

I nodded to her and then said, "You know, I don't have either one."

"Well?" he said.

There is no room to argue in a moment like that. Being sympathetic might keep you in the room a little longer. But I don't think the question is, Where does his hostility come from? The question, rightly so, is, Do I have anything he could use? That is what is up for grabs.

I said to him, "Everyone in this house is suffering, and no one knows what to do. That's what I know about. I can teach you something about how to suffer."

"Who in their right mind wants to learn how to suffer?" he yelled.

I said, "Nobody I've met yet wants to learn. But the drugs and the treatments and the way you've been doing this so far seem just to add to the suffering instead of giving you some way to do it well. That's why I'm here, because you're close to the end of what they can do for you, and because you're at the end of what you know."

"Go on then," he said with a defeated wave of his hand. "Talk."

So that is how some of the harder meetings start. As we began talking back and forth you could tell how towering was his incandescent rage over what was happening and how stout was his refusal to be anything but betrayed by the ending of his days and by the manner of their ending. He said over and over that he just wanted all of it to end, to be drugged so he wouldn't know what was happening and didn't have to talk. I asked maybe two more questions whose answers were dead-end antagonism. Then he said something that has stayed with me ever since, probably because it was so livid, so naked and filled with rancor and hatred for what it had all come to. After a long silence where I didn't know if he had fallen asleep, he suddenly pulled his eyes open, reared up on his elbows, and said this to his wife and me, to the ceiling, to the world, to whoever had given him this end: "I hate my heart. I hate my kidneys. I hate my spleen. I hate my lungs. I hate my brain." With that, he collapsed back into the pillow with an exhaustion and debilitation that had advanced much deeper than had the disease.

You might think that he was making a list of all his afflicted organs, all the places the disease had withered or stupefied or blurred or half killed. I realized after a moment that, unlike so many other dying people who focused their animosity on the affected part of themselves, this man was making a list of all those organs in his body that were free of disease and still in some kind of working order. He hated their efficiency, their health, because they obliged him to continue living. He hated all in his body that was well. While he hated the doctors for treating him "unsuccessfully," he hated more the enduring parts of his body which had begun dying ten or more months ago and then stopped dying while the disease ground away in the places it was found. He was living the more dying that the God of demanding to live asked of him and gave to him. The closer his death came, the more sedated he was. He died in the distracted, reluctant twilight awareness of his dying that for much of the indigenous world might be the very definition of hell: argumentative, terrorized, and addled.

So now, go back for a minute if you would to that observation about how we go through our days expecting to live and ask, How might people in some other village or town rise up each morning? What does being alive mean to them? It isn't likely that they wake up every day expecting to die. They likely want to live at least as much as we do, and they want this for each other too. Experience has taught them not that life is cruel, random, arbitrary, unjust. Experience has taught them that life is *unlikely*, everything considered. Waking up each day, and having your children do so, is not written in the stars, not an entitlement, far from inevitable. It is not even the fair trade meritocratic consequence of being careful and living right. For all that, waking up each day is a gift. It is a gift that is not reward for playing by the rules. It is a gift from the Gods, giving each living person the capacity not just to go on, but to go on as if he or she has been gifted, to go on in gratitude and wonder that all the things of the world that keep them alive have continued while they slept. Wonder, awe, and a feeling of being on the receiving end for now of something mysteriously good: These are antidotes to depression. Please consider that our way of caring for dying people, and our ways of dying, would not be what they are if we would awaken somehow that way.

2

STEALING MEANING FROM DYING

What It All Has Come To

Long Life, Quick Death

Generally in our culture if you want to find out how it is out there, what people are thinking these days about a particular something, you pay some PR firm too much money to do market research, focus groups, and surveys, or you spend far too much time watching the media, certain that somehow what people are thinking survives the translation to news and current affairs programming. You could get a clipboard and an ordinary suit and try to stop people on their way to work to give you their opinions. Or you could get into the business of helping people die—not the most obvious way of finding out, but by far the most faithful, the most trustworthy.

I had the privilege most days of my working life to sit in small rooms with people who were afraid they might be dying, who thought they were dying, who didn't want to die, who were refusing to die, who were dying and didn't really know it. I learned about what they had in mind for themselves and for their lives, about how and why they planned as they did, if and what they thought about the Big Questions, about what life did to them while they were living, about whether they found out if the universe was a friendly place.

Most everyone has in mind for themselves their version of a longish life, it seems. Before there are any wishes for health or happiness, before people have a chance to ante up on the nobler, better-to-want things of life, I found that dying people tend to have wanted a longish life. I should say now that dying people don't seem to be wishing for a long life because they are dying people. Many of them, if you ask, aren't dying, at least not any time soon, at least not in any important or urgent sense of the word. Dying is very rarely a part of how they now see themselves. They mostly hold fast to that "self" and refuse to let it be touched much by the news of their prognosis. And dying people are not a special interest group like Breast or Testicular or Differently Abled or Deaf. Dying is gregarious and indiscriminate that way, promiscuous even, and it sets no one aside as unworthy and chooses no one out as more deserving, culpable, or defenseless.

So they planned for or counted on a longish life, whatever winter count that entails, and the news of their prognosis did little to change their belief that they had a right to that longish life. The second almost universal wish, typically unspoken but firmly at the wheel, is strange to most people's ear. When I am teaching on this point and ask, "What do people want for their lives beyond a fairly long time to live it in?" the audiences will almost always guess noble pursuits, honorable goals: health for themselves and their loved ones, a fair opportunity to do good in their communities, some kind of world peace. But I have never heard that these are the wishes of dying people. What I have heard is at first hard for the rest of us to recognize as a real wish. It is not an easy thing to want, and intuitively it doesn't make any sense to want it.

When the time comes, what is the other pillar holding up the pantheon of yearning that is North American life? Someone says, "Good death. Everyone wants a good death for themselves." It makes sense, but that isn't it. I don't believe I have heard that anyone has wished for a good death during the course of their lives, healthy or not, nor does it seem to be something they valued, like world peace. This might sound strange to you, given what I have done for a living over the last decades, but I've never heard anyone wish a good death on anyone they love, at least not in the early or middle stages of what is unfolding. Nor have I heard of anyone wanting a quiet death, save for many people working in the death trade and some well-read Buddhists who when push came to karmic shove opted for a quiet death.

But let's go further. Even if your experience in these matters is not mine, and you know people who have exercised their right to vote on this counterintuitive thing, and have made it known to you that, yes, it's true, they want some kind of good death, the hard and fast supplementary question is still there, looming, waiting: *How can you get the good death that you want for yourself?*

Some will barter for "painless" death, which on the whole does not exist, depending on what they mean by "pain." "Easy death" is another grail; a third is "gentle." Medical expertise, enough or more money, urban proximity to the newest and best technology, cope, hope, and dope—none of these things will without fail wrestle a good death to the ground for you, nor can they. No, the guarantee, the über option, the only surety of success that will deliver when all the other rickety schemes collapse under their own weight, is this: Good death is *quick* death. "Quick" is the midwife of "good" when it comes to dying in the staggering first years of our twenty-first century in dominant culture North America. The best death is not the one that hurts the least, but the one that has the least time to torment, to pain, to hurt, to last.

Now in the trenches it turns out that "quick" can't be measured by a clock or calendar. When people receive a terminal diagnosis they will usually ask for the prognosis too, and they mean to find out—though what they do with the answer will soon become the monarch of their torments—when? How much longer have I got? The span, the most likely time frame, the least likely. Not everyone asks, but almost everyone wants to know. Loath as they often are to tie the patient, family, and themselves to a prediction based always on a ragged mix of statistical probability and hunch, most physicians as part of "breaking the bad news" will knuckle under and give an answer: Based on your age, general state of health, location, and stage of the disease, most people with your diagnosis tend to live from _____ to _____. But that only answers the patient's question of, What has happened to people like me? To everyone before me? To everyone like me but me?

In the trenches, a quick death isn't quick because it ends soon. Quick death isn't quick even when it is brought up short by an unexpected piece of medical mayhem that hastens the inevitable, or by terminal sedation, physician-assisted suicide, or euthanasia. These are all opinions from the outside, and they are all lunges toward the elusive quarry of quick death. They are also responses to the fact that dying has already made an appearance. A quick death in a death-phobic culture is really only possible when you don't see it coming. That is the prerequisite for dying quickly, that *you don't know what is happening.*

If you have the chance as your life goes on to pass some time with old people, you should. Not with people who are getting old, but with those who got there. I've spent many superb hours out in the bush with a trapper friend of mine who tells the story that when he was young and starting out, an old trapper took him in and began showing him the ropes. When it would happen that they'd be out checking the beaver traps at -25°C with their hands in the cold water and their butts in the wind, and they'd be three-quarters through the day with no fur on their sled and little prospect of any, the old fellow would look out over the frozen world and say to my friend, "Yes sir. We're passing a nice, quiet time." And that's what you should do with old people, if you get a chance: pass some nice, quiet time.

If you do, try to get a good look in their eyes from every now and then. Now this has to be a respectful thing. I don't mean to stare them down, or to bore a hole down inside them to see how they got the way they are. Just try to catch a glimpse if you can of what's there; not *why* it's there, but only what it is that is there. I think Rumi said somewhere that the eye is a miracle: small enough to fit easily in your smallish head, big enough that the whole world will fit into it. You really can see something of the whole world in the eyes of an old person.

One of the things you'll see, with respect, is that those eyes have seen the collapse, the withering, the end of a lot of things. They've seen the end of their old idea of a good time, the end of their spunk and their give-a-shit, and the end of their plans for what they would do with it if they had it, and the end of their vitality and of most of what they thought was vital. They've seen a lot of death of all kinds. They've seen the entire generation of their grandparents long ago go to ground, all of their parents, aunts, and uncles, all the people they were born to who welcomed them into the world and didn't, who would show them the ropes and would not, die and end. They've seen the first source and proof of anything human they knew put in the dirt. They've seen most or all of the generation of their friends and enemies and peers and competitors buried and gone, and probably a good number of the generation younger than them, dead and no more. In all, a stunning pageant of the departed, all of it in there. Looking in their eyes, you'll see what seeing death does.

And somewhere in there, first once and then often and then probably each time they look up, their own death has taken a seat at the groaning board in the banquet hall of their life and become finally their most faithful, most constant companion. Their own death no longer one possibility among many, no longer a threat or an injustice or a mockery, no longer the world turning on them or God leaving them to their own devices. Only another true thing, or maybe the truest, only the one born when they were born, their twin making room for himself or herself in their knowledge of how it is. That's what you'll see, if you are patient and fortunate and willing.

Those old people have seen their deaths coming from a long way off. Because of that, they won't be dying quickly. They'll be dying slowly. Because of that, because their death is not any longer dread or rumor, they have been slowly dying. They've been dying for some time by the time you are looking respectfully and indirectly into their eyes. Regardless of the state of their health—and here let's wish them good health and a long life for it—they've been dying for some time. That is not the idea of their death that you are seeing: That is their death, truly. And your death is in there somewhere, if you can bear it.

So the algebra of the thing comes to this: Long life and quick death, they don't happen together. They aren't peaceful cohabitants in the banquet hall of your life. You cannot have both and you will not. What most people are bargaining for will not come to pass, and though it was never possible and so will never be one of their many losses, still it will seem like the end of their dignity, the final unkindness, the least of their entitlements or pleas come to naught.

The irony of the thing is this: Most all of us, instinctively, know this to be true. It is strange, it is unfamiliar, it has never had a place in our plots and plans for ourselves, but we know it, somewhere in our knowing parts. We know without wanting to know it that *knowing we could be dying somehow begins our dying.*

And that is where the most lunatic of all the lunatic ideas this culture harbors about death is born: that you have a right not to know that you are dying, or that you will die. Some years ago a place I worked for subjected itself to that exquisitely irksome minuet called "A Strategic Planning Exercise for the Future of the Organization in Five-Year Installments." This involved being led by a stranger unfamiliar with the daily grind of caring for dying people through the exercise of articulating just what each of us imagined the tasks and goals of the organization, self-appointed and otherwise, to be. Some of them were inevitable, if hard to measure: to be good at what we do, to be a mentoring organization to others, to advocate for change. But when we got down to the "what we do," things got interesting for us. I thought that an early and useful thing would be for us to make some statement about what we actually did, day in and day out, before we talked about what we wanted to do, some declaration about the business that we conducted. I suggested that we could begin by acknowledging that we were in, as I have called it before and since, the death trade. This was met with grim silence, as if I was rubbing someone's face in it by using the word "death." I went further and pushed hard for the inclusion of the principle that a good death was everyone's right, which met with unanimous if moderate assent. And then I pushed for what to me was the obvious, other half of the statement: A good death was everyone's obligation to pursue and provide and act upon, including patients and families.

This is gravel in the machinery of bioethics at the end of life. Some began to qualify, "Well, if that's what the patient wants." Others said, "We can't push good dying on people," or, "Well, it depends what you mean by good death," or "Our job is to provide, not persuade." Or, "Who are you to say what a good death is?"

I saw what seemed and still seems to be the ludicrous, impossible-to-defend sum of these objections coming, and I said, "It seems that what you will do, pushed to it, is defend everyone's right to die badly." After a moment's pause, someone said, "Yes, I will. I will defend someone's right to die as they choose, even if that choice is to die badly. Whatever that means."

To my mind this amounts to arguing that everyone has a right not to die, if that is their choice. Most of what happens under the cloak of palliative care, unless someone calls an end to it, proceeds as if people have the right not to die and tries to deliver on that right. I understand the principle that was being defended here, the inalienable right of choice and self-determination, the principle of humility and service before the suffering of another. But there was no acknowledgement of the enduring, intergenerational, and culture-wide consequences of dying badly, and there was no willingness to ask more of the dying person—including asking them to pursue a good death for themselves—than the dying was already demanding of them. There certainly was no willingness to question this right not to die and not to know that you are dying.

I have been persuaded by everything I've seen on the job that the beginning of dying, to the extent that it is thought about at all, is not much understood. I have a small question that I ask from time to time to see if the answer ever changes. It never does. From conference to workshop, from village to city, from professional crowd to general public, the answer is fairly constant. I ask, "When do you begin to die?" This is easily one of the hardest things to figure and maybe the most mysterious of our life's companions. The reflex answer that comes fastest and first—and this frequently from an audience of people who work with dying people every day—is: "You begin to die the moment you are born." There is almost universal consent to this proposal wherever I go, and the audiences are usually well satisfied that in a bewildering slurry of moral, ethical, and existential dilemmas, none of which allows much certainty or quorum of acceptance, this is a true and obvious thing, that you begin to die the moment you are born. Birth causes it. People in the womb are exempt, and the eerie implication is that they aren't alive, not yet.

If this is true, that you begin to die by being born, then the next time you, in a state of fair or perfect health, in the prime of your days, should find yourself at the deathbed of a dying person in the full grip of the immanence of his or her death, you are well within your rights as a purveyor of the obvious and the compassionate to coax onto your face your best collegial and sympathetic expression and take the weakened, cooling hand of the dying person in your warm, living hand and in a voice both soothing and full of a shared understanding of a shared moment look into the dying eyes of that person and say, "I know. Me too."

Don't guffaw or dismiss this, but tell me instead that it doesn't follow like left follows right that if you begin dying the moment you are born then all that separates you from someone in the last days of their life is the clock and the calendar, and that because of that we are all in the same terminal boat, and that we should somehow draw consolation in our last days from knowing that all of the healthy, alive people around us are dying too. As if they were.

This is an insult to a dying person of the most sublime and profound kind, of course, and you would likely never say such a thing. If you believe this business about beginning to die once you're born, then every birth you hear about will suddenly look different, and it will no longer be the unmitigated good news that it once was. If you believe this, then one day you'll look down on every swaddled newborn and think, "Not bad for a dying kid." But you wouldn't say that. You wouldn't think that. You wouldn't see that in the crib, because it's not there to see.

Most healthy or even moderately ill people will not likely respond well to your revelation that they like you long ago began to die. But if you're going to not say it to a dying person, then withhold it for the right reason: It isn't true. In the turmoil of what all this could mean for how you work and how you live the days you are granted, you might find some willingness to think the hard thought that *you begin to die when you see your own death.* Your own death: It isn't something that is prompted by bad health, not necessarily. It is something you can see in another person's death, or in the death of a star, or the last stubborn falling leaves of November, or in the grayed exoskeleton of a crayfish on the beach of your spring break vacation, or in the proper final withering of every idea you hatched at age fourteen and defended ever since against any evidence to the contrary about what love should mean or do or feel like, or how long it should last, or why.

I've long been a believer in etymology. I find over and over that there is much to be learned in being surprised by the secret lives of ordinary words, by their long history and often great changes of meaning over time. The verb "to palliate" is a good example. Most people who have heard or used the word understand it to mean something about the kind of care dying people receive, some kind of comfort-giving measures. "Palliate" comes from "pall," whose Old English root means "cloak," or "shroud," borrowed in turn from the Latin for "robe," which is ultimately from the Latin for "skin." So when we palliate someone we are in one sense clothing them for protection from the slings and arrows of how it is, and we are in another sense covering and concealing things. This is what pall bearers are carrying, the death hidden in the box, shrouded by the flag. In a death-phobic culture, palliative care has come to be the kind of care motivated by compassion and concern that masks or conceals dying. This older meaning of the word is there whenever we have a discussion of whether and how a dying person should be told that he or she is dying. Usually this becomes an issue because there is a strong belief that knowing that you are dying increases the suffering that dying brings to the point of being intolerable. It isn't dying that really kills you, in other words; it is knowing that you are dying. Knowing, for a culture like ours, is where the real pain and suffering are generated. This is one of our great, mobilized fears, and it prompts the cone of silence that descends whenever dying needs talking through. Somewhere in this fear is a shard of unwelcome certainty: We are fairly certain that dying is prompted not by knowing that we're going to die, but by knowing we could be dying.

I think that in a strange and secret way we know that we begin dying when we see our death, when we suspect that that is what is going on, no matter. I think this in part because of the extraordinary energy and vitality given in this culture to the project of not knowing that we are dying, and because of the unhesitating willingness of caregivers of all stripes to collude with this refusal to know through the usually clumsily crafted projects of positive outlook, hopefulness, and live-instead-of-die advocacy, and because the etymology of the verb "to palliate" comes closer to "to conceal, to cloak" than it does to "to help." I cannot think of anything else that would explain the strange idea of our right not to know a true thing about our lives. I was teaching a palliative care course once, and I asked the group to defend the proposition that you deserve to know that you are dying. A woman who had been in the work for years answered, "I don't believe it is a right. I don't believe that anything good comes from knowing that you are dying. All it does is hurt and make things worse." This pall is the sign: We believe that knowing is the beginning of our dying, hence our investment in distraction, in not knowing, in the compassion of the shroud.

> My first phone call to the patient's home had gone pretty well. The man had advanced brain cancer and was no longer able to communicate well, and so I spoke at length with his wife, who had a number of good questions about the services the center I worked for provided, what they could expect from us. Toward the end of our talk she began to soften a little, and she allowed that her small family—they had one child, a son of nineteen years—needed an opportunity to begin talking about what was happening to them and about what was going to happen. They hadn't done much talking so far, and she could recognize that each of them was afraid of hurting the other two by speaking too directly.

This is one of the great constants of working with the families of dying people. The rest of us imagine that the years they've had together will automatically transform such a family into a compassionate, informed care team that with a little guidance from a health care professional will just know what to do and be willing to do it. The fact that they've never done anything remotely like what they face having to do doesn't change the assumption much. When they don't know what to do, when they are often wrong about how the rest of the family is doing, when they are dismayed to see that the best part of everyone doesn't materialize or is inconstant, they are doubly despondent and confused.

One of the central fantasies around which families with a dying loved one gather is the Myth of Everlasting Hope. Everyone seems to know that everyone's job is to keep the faith that there is nothing inevitable about the person they love's terminal diagnosis prevailing. Everyone knows someone who knows someone who didn't die on schedule. These stories move in palliative family circles the way contraband copies of Solzhenitsyn's novels circulated in Brezhnev's Russia. Countless times I've been challenged to answer the question that tolerates but one answer: The doctors could be wrong, couldn't they? If they've ever been wrong, of course, they could always be wrong. In any case, with all this parsing of the possible going on, families seem to know that their first obligation, the ultimate expression of their love for the dying person, is to challenge anyone who proceeds as if that person is dying. Likelihoods are idle speculation. Changes can unchange. Being willing to consider that the gathering evidence of diagnostic precision, that timetables of tested probability and mounting symptoms might, when taken together, require the family to change its thinking is heresy. It is betrayal. It is giving up. And Thou Shalt Not Give Up.

One result: No one in the family lets themselves know what they know, and they especially don't let anyone else in the family know what they suspect and fear. When they are together—whether the dying person is present or not—they are one party, united under the banner of We Believe. Of course, there is secret knowledge all around the house that what has been predicted is coming to pass right in front of them, but this is not a loving thing to know, and very much not a loving thing to acknowledge or say out loud. Most families believe deeply in "Word Voodoo": If you say the wrong thing, you can make it happen.

On my way to the house I called to make sure they were home and expecting me. She assured me that everyone, including the teenage son, was looking forward to meeting me: polite and considerate, but generally a huge overstatement of the case. After giving me a good sense of what had happened since we had last spoke, the patient's wife said, as an afterthought: "Don't use the D word, though."

Though I'd heard the fear and the belief in Word Voodoo many times, I'd never been told not to use the D word. "Don't use the D word," I said.

"Yes, thank you," she said, thinking that I understood the etiquette and would refrain. So I asked her:

"Didn't you tell me that your son spends time every morning with his dad before he goes to school?"

"Yes," she said. "And he helps his father to bathroom when he's at home?"

"He does, yes."

"He sees that his father can no longer eat by himself and can't get out of bed?"

"That's right."

"And when he comes home from school he lays beside his dad and tells him about his day and can tell that his father can't really follow what he is saying or make himself understood when he tries to talk."

"That's right."

"Well, if I don't use the D word when I'm there, what secret am I helping you keep?"

How else to understand people in the last month of their life together in this world trying to be pleasant and trying in vain to live a normal life?

Maybe the secret helps the days go by. If a thing is never spoken between people who know each other well, and each knows the thing well, maybe it's not a secret. Maybe, in the name of loving someone when you no longer know how, in the name of caring for someone when you are at the end of any caring you've ever done before, surrounded by well-intended people who don't know what to say or do and by a culture that makes no room for the change in everything that dying rightly brings, being silent together about what is now "living" in your house looks a lot like love. It's a powerful thing, that ability to tell the truth when the truth is upon you, but it has another power entirely when you don't tell it.

To Die, Not Dying

As care of dying people has been professionalized over the last fifty years, so also has it largely passed into the hands of medical practitioners. Medical practitioners are as much servants as purveyors of the creed *If you can, you should.* Their expertise by virtue of their training is in the care and management of physical symptoms and pain when a cure is not possible. To someone with a hammer, they say, everything looks like a nail, and the medicalization of the care of dying people has had considerable consequence for how we now understand what dying is. In a tertiary care setting, in an outpatient chemotherapy clinic, in a home-based palliative care program, dying is essentially something that happens to your body. It is a measurable, metabolic, biomedical event with an imperceptible beginning and an emphatic end. The free use of the medical arsenal available depends on seeing dying in this narrow, somatic way.

Medical practitioners without specific training in what is called psychosocial and spiritual care of dying people are inclined to keep dying simple and physical. Their bedside discussions are still largely about pain and symptoms and their management, about what could be done. Typically the medical practitioners and the patients and the families all enter into a covert conspiracy to keep conversations to the empirical, the physical, the medical. When the patient is asked, "How do you feel today?" most everyone knows that this refers mainly to the impact of their disease on their body. Patients learn this well and early. They know what the patient record says about them, and this is the language they begin describing themselves with. Without anyone wishing for this to be so, patients become symptom bundles, their pain and symptoms problems to solve, their anxiety, fear, and despair things to manage. This isn't to say that medical practitioners don't feel the sorrows and impotence of not being able to change the course of things, or that they are not as a profession good at responding to the nonphysical aspects of dying. It is only to say that their training predisposes them to see dying in terms of what they can do about it, not in terms of what dying might ask of them.

I was read to probably in the womb, I'm sure of it. By the time I was born I'd already heard—felt—many stories, and I was born into the epic coming and going that every story worth a damn tells us we are born into. Much as I loved stories from an early age, and as much as I beat the odds and continued loving stories through the formal education of my childhood years, when the time came I suffered grammar. I suffered it badly. I could not see or hear language that way, as a codified rulebook, though I tried. I could not even see the merit of the thing, try as I did. Years later and without much employment, I ended up teaching English as a second language to Latin American kids sent north for finishing by well-off parents who feared that the civil wars that haunted El Salvador, Guatemala, and Chiapas at the time would find their children too. Then I discovered how little of the English grammar had stuck to me. Being the mongrel it is, and claiming for itself a regal pedigree of structure that given its speckled partrilineage cannot be, I found myself having to make up reasons to explain why the language does what it does. The story of why English prepositions aren't based in Greek or Latin when so much English is, for example, was one of their favorites, and utterly my invention.

But, I bow to it: Grammar, like the mosquito, has its use, and we'll try to employ it in wondering about dying. You will remember that the English language verbs have tenses (three main ones, a miserly number considering that many indigenous languages have rafts of tenses, and this paltry choice forces us to see life in a strange, progressive, and linear fashion), and they have voices. In another miserable victory for our binary, oppositional way of seeing things, there are only two voices for our English verbs: They are either passive or they are active.

I have a hard-earned twenty dollar bill in my pocket on this snowbound early spring morning. I take it out and put it on the kitchen table with all the seed trays planted last night, far out of my reach. That twenty dollar bill is yours for the taking. Please give me—in proper English—an example of the verb "to die," in the passive voice, in a sentence.

Many times I have taught this idea, and I have learned a lot from it. All the different audiences have tried to solve this riddle in the same way. At first their answers change "to die" into an adverb and use it to describe some kind of dying, or an adjective to describe all kinds of death, none of them alert to the fact that they are not using "to die" as the verb of their sentences. When that doesn't work, they move on to use other verbs that approximate what they think "to die" means. Finally, the grammatically adroit people start using "to die" correctly as the verb of their sentences, but they are using it actively in the past tense.

This has taught me a great deal, this unexpected use of a past tense to solve the riddle of a passive voice. This isn't grammar, mainly. This is teleology, epistemology, theology. We think of time as a line irreversible and unbendable. We see everything as hurtling headlong from the present toward the future, from the known to the unknown. We are rational and progressive. At least one foundational religious tradition of this culture takes our dead from us and calls them gone and consigns them to God and to what is lost and no longer and will never be again. Once a thing, a dream, a person is gone, and there is nothing to be done. No wonder the past tense conjures a quiet, relentless passivity—and so it is with us. In trying to answer a grammar riddle we are stalemated by our theology, and the only solution seems to be to get the feel of passivity by *losing*. Goneness: What might have been or what was, both now lost to us, claimed by the past. "I lost my mother last month," people say.

Who among you has come to the Rubicon of this riddle? The answer, as best as I can figure with my limited English grammar, is that it can't be done. You cannot use the verb "to die" in the passive voice in a sentence and obey the rules of grammar and the style manuals. You'd think you should be able to do it, that every verb will allow for an active way of doing and a passive way of being done, but I can't find it. And so I bow to the language on this epic grammatical detail as a great teacher. The language we use every day wants us to know that dying is not passive, can't be passive. Dying is active. Dying is not what happens to you. Dying is what you do.

Dying is what you do. It is not what is done to you. While the disease process is doing what it is doing, you are doing what you are doing, so the language teaches. This is good grammar, but can you recognize the phenomenology of dying in it? Dying in the English speaking world is usually an affliction, a malfeasance, an arbitration, certainly something coming from somewhere beyond your plans and abilities to steal your plans and abilities from you. It is an intrusion, a violation, a visitation of Nothingness, a grim reaping. It is almost never spoken of as something you do, or could do, or ought to do, and this is where our confusion spirals into the great fear and loathing of the contemporary death experience. The "disease trajectory," as it is called in the trade, is somewhat predictable, fairly trustworthy in its unfortunate way, with a ring of the inevitable about it. But what you *do* in the face of that inevitability—there is nothing inevitable about that. What you do while the disease goes as it goes is entirely up for grabs, just as our grammar says it is. And almost nobody knows this.

This grammatical stalemate is a great teacher also. It whispers that perhaps the only way you can fight the angel of active dying to the ground of passivity and victimization is to change the verb altogether. The answers I get to this riddle all point to one word, very passive, to change things. *Either you die,* you find out from this riddle, *or you are killed.* There are your choices: die or be killed. Either the cancer kills you or you battle cancer and win and carry the stain of your vulnerability the rest of your shadowed days as a survivor, or the cancerous broken heart kills you and the obituary they make for you begins this way: "After a long and courageous battle ..." Or you die. Those are the choices. We should be able to tell the difference between dying and being killed.

There is an island north and west of where I live that is called by God's own name. The English name of the island is a parsimonious translation of a word that in the Anishnaabeg language means something like "mystery," which may well be God's own name. The original people in that part of the world, like original peoples all over this continent, once thought there was room enough for everyone. They kept moving over to make room for the European, moving over, moving over, and found out after a few generations that they were the only ones who thought there was room enough for everyone. So some of them dug in their heels on this island a couple of hundred years ago, and they are there now. Most of their ancestors signed no treaty, and in the government's headlong crusade to solve "the Indian Question" by treaty or land theft or boarding school, God's own island was overlooked. The mystery might be that in spite of it all they are still there.

There are a few small towns on the island, none of which have much in the way of sustained government support for real health care. They have to band together, an uneasy partnership of native and white groups, to advocate for anything and be heard. Under the fierce leadership of a gravel-voiced nurse who'd heard me teach at a conference the year before, one of these partnerships approached me to come and talk about caring for dying people. Together we wrangled some possible venues and audiences, and a few months later I was there. For my gravel-voiced partner, who had mad, brave, and hearty hopes that the communities she worked and lived in might from these talks begin to wonder about doing their work together differently, the organizing of this event was her way of loving the place she was working for. She's no longer there, I hear, but I salute her bravery and willingness to work with the enduring legacy of colonization and discrimination, and I tell this story with fondness and gratitude for her invitation to make me a part of her work.

The centerpiece for this tour was to be an event for nurses, social workers, and doctors in the biggest bar

73

in town, a nineteenth-century, main street, brick-faced building that had meeting rooms upstairs where the old hotel rooms used to be. By my nurse friend's estimation, she had to feed them to get them all there. We sat down to eat. As village people can do when suddenly seated with a stranger from the Big Smoke, they spoke to each other about who and what they knew and gave me the occasional sidelong glance, wondering what they'd let themselves in for now. After a formidable dinner we trooped up to a room where all the chairs were laid out in a semicircle, save one, which faced them all. I took the seat that must be mine. I faced forty or so people who descended soon into postprandial torpor. Behind me was the bar, and a long table with easily ten kinds of desserts people rarely have at home. It was clear to all that this affable but languorous group had to get through me to get to the dessert table and the beer. Another unpromising beginning.

Well, I'd come a long way and not for nothing, so I put the bit between my teeth and started plowing the field of their remoteness. As always, I asked that people give their certainty about these things a rest for the duration and allow their wondering muscles a little exercise. I fixed my sights on the great work and sordid mystery of dying here in our part of the world, and began to make my usual case for the general death phobia and grief illiteracy of the times. I was starting to catch my stride when I saw in the back row the challenge start to gather. It turned out he was one of the town's few doctors, a younger man that the folk were likely glad to have among them. I didn't know him, but I knew this: Like many rural places this place had a hard time attracting doctors to their area, and so there were government incentives to draw them away from the urban centers. This doctor was probably sitting on his isolation pay, with nowhere to spend it, and working through his term in the sticks. Anyone from the city was fair game for his mixed feelings about his current gig. His general demeanor made it clear that he was supremely under persuaded and more accurately informed than I was. So here, for sure, would be one of tonight's adversaries.

A few minutes more and he'd heard about enough. He raised the index finger from one of his folded hands to ask a question.

"Yes, sir," I said.

Well-mannered and extending the grace I have learned from years of meeting with contention, ill humor, attack, and worse when I wonder aloud with people about what dying asks of us, I gave him the floor that was for the moment mine to give. He managed the pause to good effect, and then came to the line: "Really," he said, "you are making this much more complicated than it is or needs to be." "All right," I said. "Good. I've come a long way, and now the chance to have this simplified. Please simplify it for us."

"Well, we all know it. Everyone knows they are going to die. There isn't a lot to discuss here."

I waited for a little more, but there was none to come. He was done, satisfied. He'd dismounted and hobbled his horse, certain that he'd defended the townsfolk and civilization against me and my big city ideas. He may have been eying the éclairs.

I have unrestrained regard for anyone who loves words, the spoken word in particular. I saw a piece of film once that showed Tibetan monks in a sunny monastery courtyard going at it hammer and tongs, debating their Buddhism in a standing position with wild hand jive and reckless eye bulging, and what looked an awful lot like good-natured chest thumping. They were like Mongolian wrestlers, or Mongolian wrestlers were like them. After my time of gray-tweeded, monotoned, anemic, academic nonconversations at the Ivy League divinity school that made the unlikely move in the late 1970s of taking me in, attendance at which put me off the spoken word for a few years, that movie, just the look of loving to speak, was one of the things that got me going again. I loved those guys instantly and was ready to sign up with and defend any religion that loved the spoken word the way they seemed to. On the other hand, I am testy and worse when this love of mine is slandered as "just words," or "semantics," or "only your opinion," and I can do a pretty good impression of a Mongolian wrestler myself when the right and obligation and the ability to speak and speak well (the right and obligation of all who *can* breathe) is trivialized or humiliated. If you have struggled for life and struggled for breath—I have done both, times over—then you don't struggle with words. You struggle on their behalf. Words come to you as gifts, the way life has done, un-expected and against the odds. You struggle in their name. When the *pneuma,* the wind of the soul, blows through the feast hall of your chest and you can say so, that is one time when life is *already* good enough. The job then is to be good enough for life.

I have all this and more with me when I am asked to teach. Our man the doctor didn't know that, but he did prompt it. So with a flourish and a bit of a bow to him I said, "Would you object, sir, if we put this idea of yours, that everyone knows they're going to die, to a vote?" He wasn't sure at all what I was up to. He shrugged the shrug of one with only a mild inkling of the coming weather and no concern for it. His hand gesture said, "Go ahead. Knock yourself out."

"All right, then," I said to the people, who with the promise of conflict had begun to stir a little from their digestion, "the proposition is this: 'Everyone knows they are going to die.' All in favor, please raise your hand."

The poor people hadn't a clue what I was asking of them. So I encouraged them and repeated the proposition. This was a real vote, I assured them, and I'd be glad of their wading in on the thing. Their gaze slid slowly back and forth, from me to their man the doctor. I knew they were in a bind, and they knew it too. I was leaving in a day or two, but they had to work with the doctor for the foreseeable, and they'd no idea where I was going with this. They'd already sensed that, as they used to say in my mother's home town, I might be a bit of a live wire and so perhaps a little interesting, but not someone you would trust with your only cow, or your holy cow, or your livelihood.

After a moment, they all slowly raised their hands and sent their flags up the pole, showing good sense. It was unanimous, then: That night, everyone knew they were going to die. I'd anticipated as much and so had a supplementary request to make. To the doctor I said, "You've won the vote, sir. Well done. Now, if you would, make the case."

"What do you mean?" he asked.

"Proof, if you would. We both know you are an evidence-based practitioner, as they say, and that you've good training in it. This can't be difficult. So, some proof. Proof that everyone knows what you say they know. Proof of the thing so obvious to us all, proof that what you say is true. After all, you said it like it was a fact, the most obvious thing in the world, and not your opinion at all. It shouldn't be hard." He'd lost his patience and his stirrups.

He said, "Well, that's ridiculous. There's no case to make. Everyone's going to die," he snarled. "That is true, very true, in a sense," I said to him. "So far as we know, everyone will die. I could not agree with you more. But that is not what you said, my friend. That's not what this roomful of your townsfolk voted yes to. You said, 'Everyone *knows* they are going to die.' I'd like you to show me that. I'd like you to make the case for *that*."

The young doctor remained in his seat but withdrew from the discussion, and who could blame him? It was a strange challenge: Prove somehow that what everyone knows is true is true. The actual, observable truth of it, if you go by people's behavior when the time comes, is that everyone knows that *everyone else* is going to die. Generally, in my experience of the thing, the dismay of learning that your best friend or your beloved partner will die is dwarfed severely by the bolt from the blue shock of learning that you too will die. There is nothing in what I have seen working in the death trade for years that persuades me for five minutes that everyone knows they are going to die. You simply cannot tell that we know we're going to die from how we live. What is it called in training modules designed for physicians, the first discussion of diagnosis and prognosis with terminally ill patients? It is called "Breaking Bad News." Why is it news? It is not news because it is so sudden: Most people receiving that diagnosis have had symptoms and suspicions for a period of time before the consult. It is news because prior to its broadcast, it wasn't a known thing.

For most of us, our death is not a known thing. It is a rumored, suspected, and feared thing. That is why it is news. Fear is not knowledge, not even remotely. It has tremendous consequence and power, but it is not knowledge. The machinery of fear is diabolical in its perfect symmetry. It works like this: Imagine that fear has a voice that sounds very much like your own. Imagine that it is not really "fear," anyway. It is "*your* fear." In this way fear is a lot like a mortgage: You use the phrase "my mortgage," but it is up for grabs who owns whom. Your fear's voice finds your ear every time it speaks, and an unexpectedly willing ear it is. Your fear's voice doesn't fulminate, generally, or vilify too much, and it isn't too bellicose most of the time. Those are anger's voices, and anger is the poor, unsophisticated, adolescent sibling of fear. Fear's voice is measured, concerned even. Fear's voice has something of the barrister in it, and the capacity for reasoned argument and persuasion.

Eventually it will say, "Well, look. You don't want such and such a thing to happen, right?" And of course you don't want that thing to happen, so there is quick agreement on that. Your fear feels informed, intelligent, alert to the possibilities. But the ante is upped when the feared thing comes around again, as it always will. Fear's voice will say, "We can't let that happen. You know what it'll be like if that happens."

The truth is that you don't know what it will be like if that happens. The feared thing, almost always, is the thing that hasn't happened yet. That is where fear lives, in the not yet, the not now, the not me. Fear is full of uninformed anticipation masquerading as heightened awareness. Fear knows enough to mobilize, stir, run, and fight, but it knows next to nothing about the feared thing. *Fear is not knowledge.*

For the last few months now I've had a half dozen whitetail deer nosing around my farmhouse. The winter has gone on a long time, the snow is still two feet in the bush and frozen, and the deer are beginning to starve, so I have feed out for them most nights. The wolves and coyotes will get a few of the weaker ones, and maybe the rest will get by until they begin scratching up the ground again in six weeks. They are animals of perfect grace. Their capacity for stillness could teach something to stones. But they are heart attacks on four feet, waiting to happen. They have a bottomless ability to be instantly terrified by something changing around them, or by nothing changing around them, and they explode through the bush with unimagined power starving or not with almost no provocation. They gallop madly for thirty yards, stop on a dime, and raise their heads with a look that says, "What?" Nothing has killed them yet, they probably have not seen much in the way of killing, but they proceed to my eyes as if their death lurks in every leaf, grass blade, squirrel chirp. *They seem to know they can die*—you can tell—and they head the other way.

Most people's reaction to the news of their death shows clearly that they did not know that this would come to them one day. You can see in many that they feared that this is what was happening to them, but there is nothing in their reaction or in their premorbid way of living that bears the mark of *having known this all along.* With respect, I disagree with the young doctor. Everyone knows that everyone else is going to die. Each person does not know that he or she are going to die. They do not know they are dying when they are, which is why they need to be told. There are many working in the death trade today who will vehemently defend this not knowing as a fundamental right of all people. This is compassion to them.

But I take the young doctor's objection for the greater teaching that it is. His comment raises up the least expected other truth, the fact that is so counterintuitive, so nonsensical at first blush: Because people do not know that they are going to die, because dying is what you do and not what happens to you—and only because of that—*it is possible for people not to die.* And many, many do not die.

This sounds I know like lunacy, or like a Ouija board session, or like a first-year philosophy class discussion. What could this mean, that it is possible not to die? It means that if dying is what you do, it is more than possible that you will not do it. You may be afraid to do it. You may refuse to do it. You may not know how to do it. You may not know that it is something you do instead of something that happens to you. Any or all of these together could well end up in you not dying. Your metabolism will cease of course, and so will mine. Our hearts will slow and ebb and flutter and go quiet altogether. Our kidneys, spleens, and livers will no longer clear our systems, and our bodies will go septic and shut down. Our lungs will heave shallowly and then barely and then not at all. Even our brains, because of all this, will slowly stop knowing that this is what is happening. But this is our body doing what it knows how to do when it cannot continue as it once did. This is our body being itself at the end of its days, but *we* are doing none of it.

Most of this will happen regardless of what we do or refuse to do. All of this taken together is not what dying is. It is what our bodies do at the end of our bodies' lives. It is not what we are doing. It is at most a negligible part of what dying is. The rest—what this book is about—might be done, and it might not be done. It is more than possible not to do it. Most of the people I have worked with in the death trade have, at least at the outset, refused to do it. They do not spend their dying time dying. They spend it—I mean *spend* it, here, as in *exhaust* it—not dying.

This kind of statement deserves a story, and certainly needs one.

Sometime during the 1990s a single woman from a North African country decided or was otherwise compelled to come to the city I lived in. She came alone—a curiosity and a tragedy in her culture, to be alone. She soon found a small group of her country folk in that city, joined their church, and that small congregation became her family. Her life went along. She developed some health problems in her early forties. As her appointed and protective kinsman, the pastor of the church accompanied her to all meetings with the physician. Tests revealed that she had metastatic disease that was slow, progressive, and untreatable. The woman was referred to an outpatient palliative care service without being told what it meant to be in palliative care. At the pastor's insistence, she was not told that she would die in the fullness of time from that disease.

I got a call from a nurse working with this woman. The pastor had become a serious obstacle to the provision of good care to her, and the nurse was hopeful that I could be useful in that conflict. I asked the nurse to arrange a meeting with the woman, the pastor, and whoever else was involved in caring for her. At the appointed hour the pastor appeared with several deacons from the church, Bibles in hand, a typed agenda for the meeting prepared, without the woman. It was their decision that this meeting could only distress her. The pastor began by describing everything about his culture that I, as an urban North American, could not understand or appreciate. His was a tribal people, he said, where I only understood isolation and solitary life. His was an African people, he said, where I had a kind of mongrel history that went back a few generations at most. His was a Christian people, he said, where I had no congregational faith discernible to him. His was an immigrant congregation, he said, and I had no serious tolerance for anything that diverged from the cultural norm I was born into. With his turf claimed, he came to the subject at hand. He was speaking for the woman at her request, he said. They all knew that she was seriously ill. They knew that it was our intent that she should know that she would die from this disease, and that this was foreseeable. They would not let her know this.

As the pastor saw it, this woman's job as a person with a terminal diagnosis was to pray for cure, for health, for healing and a full recovery, for a miracle if it came to that. This was her moral, religious, ethical, and cultural duty. Learning the truth about her prognosis would seduce her away from her prayer and probably bring her to despair and hopelessness, and this he would not allow. We on the professional side did not know what God could do or would do now or at the eleventh hour, he said, and he would not let any of us suggest otherwise. There was nothing assured about her death.

Her ability to pray for health, he'd decided, depended on her being healthy and knowing herself as such. Her capacity for prayer of any kind would be compromised by the medical truth that gave rise to her prayers in the first place, he decided. The pastor, well intentioned, had the woman praying for something that with our medicine and experience we knew would almost certainly not come to pass. I asked him to consider the real likelihood of what kind of last days he was designing for this woman. She would likely get worse without being told why. Her accumulating symptoms would have no reason, no story to them, no purpose or cause. As we tried to ease her end-stage shortness of breath, he would have her using that breath to pray for health. In the hours that were likely her last, while she still had some awareness and lucidity, she would not be able to be sheltered from the inescapable truth that the thing she had prayed for was not coming to pass, and would not. Her last conscious awareness of her earthly life would be lived knowing that she was surrounded by good people who had proceeded as if none of this would or should happen, obliged by them to pray for something that did not appear, knowing that she spent the last months of her life in unrequited longing, dying a secreted death that should not have happened, her prayers unanswered, dying not dying.

We were fired, of course, from anything except strict medical management of her pain and symptoms, and we were not permitted to be with her unattended. It was to me a sad prospect. The pastor was certain that God's hand would be in her miraculous delivery from cancer, but he couldn't find that hand in the cancer, not anywhere in the illness or the dying. The African woman was excused from that young doctor's universal declaration that everyone knows they'll die. She wasn't allowed to know when the future tense had become the present, because her pastor and most people I have met in the death trade are certain that little or no good comes from knowing that you are dying while you die. Her job was to not die, as she died, as it is most dying people's self-appointed task in the dominant culture of North America.

❧

Death is always a prospect with us. It is almost always talked about in the future tense when it is talked about in personal terms, as a thing that could happen, if enough things go wrong for long enough. Death is something that happens to us if we live the wrong kind of life in the wrong place for the wrong reasons with the wrong people, long enough. No one in their right mind, in our way of thinking, would die. Anyone in their right mind would refuse it.

When people refuse to tell their dying spouses and dying children and dying friends and dying grandparents and elderly, dying parents that they are dying, they believe they are saving them from dying by saving them from knowing they are dying. This is somehow easier, better, the best of the beggared options. And when people hope for themselves a long life extinguished by a quick death, a death which they neither see nor expect, what are they hoping for? When people bargain with the extremes of their lifestyles and their longings to die before the denouement of age, or before infirmity unsteadies their hand or their nerve, what are they bargaining for? They are bargaining to be killed, not by the entropy of a body in time but by something silent and sudden and incapable of error or hesitation. That's what the singer was bargaining for when he sang, "I hope I die before I get old." For a culture that doesn't believe in death, that believes that everyone will die but shouldn't have to, being killed is the solution to the problem of dying. Seeing death as a pacifying victimization, as an affliction from the great beyond, as just desserts from an unjust life or, as it is often talked about these days in some religious circles, a nonevent, an illusion, an automatic transition: None of this comes from what dying is like or from knowing death well. All of it comes from *our* kind of death. It comes from our refusal to die, from enthroning sudden death as the savior of our last days.

What have you bought from me now with your willingness to think a few of these unauthorized thoughts? You come, however uncertainly, to the counterintuitive fact that for us it *is* possible not to die. Being killed is one way not to die. Not knowing you are dying—or will die—is another. Hating death or refusing to die are others.

So this is our grail, the noblest of the ignoble outcomes, the only just way that our life's end can be vindicated: that we expire without the preamble of slowing down, that we stop without coming to a stop, that we end without any ending, that we are gone without any leaving. A death-phobic culture despises dying for the competence-reducing, control-dismissing, meaning-annihilating random chaos it makes of the end of someone's life. A death-phobic culture relieves its citizens of any obligation to die well, of any obligation to death, by offering up this newer, nobler option: We can die not dying. And we call this a life-loving thing.

> The address was in the suburbs, and the drive gave me a little time to ponder what I would do when I got there. I was looking forward to this meeting. For once I had a feeling that I might have something like a curious reception, or a willing one, even a learned one. The patient was a Protestant minister in his late fifties. He'd probably had much of the same kind of schooling that I did, and I looked forward to being able to cut to the matters at hand quickly and confidently with someone whose life's work had probably brought him into contact with many of the challenges we might talk about. As an ordained man, he'd had many occasions during the course of his illness to ponder and wrestle the great questions, and I'd be able to trade on that when we met.
>
> The lung cancer had progressed quite a bit further than I'd guessed from the information I had. When his wife answered the door I could hear the hum of the portable ventilator and saw the clear breathing tube snaking down the hall toward the room where he waited for me. He was gaunt and had the ashen look that many people with breathing problems have. He sat bolt upright in his chair, straining always up, toward the air, the way they do. When you struggle to breathe, every organ in your body is enlisted. His eyes even, they

glared a little, unblinking, as if they could bring in a little air if they were open far enough.

In the first few minutes, as always, I tried to give him a feel for who I was, what I was there to do, what I was going to ask of him. When I asked, as always, what he thought was happening, husband and wife offered up, delicately, their understanding that he was quite ill, but that things were going pretty well, better than expected, considering. His wife mentioned in passing that he was still working, as an example of how well he was faring.

The reverend was speaking in one-breath sentences, which means that he had enough breath for maybe ten words at a time. They seemed to be reasonable people. She must have meant—I hoped this is what she meant—that he was attending the odd committee meeting at the church or taking phone calls from concerned parishioners. When I asked about it, he said, "Oh, no. Preach every Sunday." There was a long pause. "Haven't missed one yet." And a longer pause. "Gotta keep going."

I was thinking about the parishioners in the pews on all those Sundays that he hadn't missed, how they'd been watching him get weaker and more winded in the last month or two while he had to keep going. I thought of the great opportunity that lay before him and them to keep the truth of dying in front of them, right there in their church services. I thought of how their Communion and their fellowship could be unforgotten for the rest of their lives at least, how they would tell the story of the minister's dying before their eyes, and how those who didn't see it happen but heard about it would be able to imagine that this was a human thing, not a heroic thing, a possible thing. Even the people who were put out by it or found it altogether too much, even they would be able to see something they'd never seen before. Maybe a few of them would be able to live a little differently on the other side of the minister's death. Maybe a few of them would be able to die differently.

So I asked, "Are you talking about your illness in your sermons?"

"Oh no," he said again, "Too depressing. All week, hard lives. On Sunday, need a break. Too hard."

I asked him, "The people need a break when they come to church on Sunday?" He nodded yes. "And I guess the scene at the door at noon, shaking their hands and saying good-bye, would be pretty awkward if they thought they might not see you next week."

He brightened a little at what he thought was my agreement with his decision, and he wheezed, "Exactly."

The Reverend knew the code of conduct for dying people in this culture just as well as I did. He knew the moral obligation that dying people have to live as normal a life as possible, under the circumstances. He knew that he was winning as long as he didn't let the disease change things much, as long as he kept going. And he knew that people don't know what to do when someone is dying, what to say. So he was, as far as he could tell, being compassionate. He was right, wasn't he, about the awkwardness at the church doors, about what the noontime good-byes might be and might not be? Wasn't he right, too, about how hard it can be to have a dying person in the midst of the living?

On that November day, taking some of the energy and lucidity and breath and time that he had left and mixing it all up with my own energy and lucidity and breath and time, and making a meeting of two human beings with them, I wondered hard on how I could respond. In those moments I know I owe dying people something that they never ask from me. It is a strange kind of self-appointed debt, I guess, almost never recognized by the debtor, but I do my best to make some payment on it. I owed a debt to him, and also to his parishioners, and the deacons of the church, and to all their families and all the people who might in time hear of the dying and death of this minister, to give them some chance to experience this dying as a living thing, as something that believes in life and imagines another way for us of dying well. So in the crazy accounting that these kinds of debts tolerate, I asked something more of him, something that it seemed no one and nothing else had asked of him or had a right to ask of him.

I said, "Reverend, tell me this. This man you've been preaching about for thirty or forty years: They say he knew when he was dying, as the story goes. Just like you. He had people looking to him for all kinds of guidance and good example, just as you do. He could see his death coming from a good ways off, they say, as you can. As his life was coming down the road toward him, when it was his turn to die, did he tell anybody, do you remember?"

The minister looked blank. He had no answer.

"It's been a while since I read about it, but it seems to me he told everyone around him that he was going to die. That's what they call the Last Supper, isn't it? Which is strange, isn't it? It couldn't have been easy, everybody gathered there to a feast and him putting a real damper on the proceedings by talking about dying. But he said that he was feeding people something by telling them about his death. He fed everyone by telling how it was with him. How could telling something which makes so much heartache and awkwardness feed the heartbroken and awkward people? Well, the news was the food. And he said it: 'Here, eat this. Eat the end of my days. Drink in my dying.'"

I don't know that hearing that old familiar story in that kind of way did much in the way of helping the minister. But I don't know that it didn't, either. I wasn't asked back, I remember that. Maybe that's why I wasn't asked back. What I am fairly sure of is that him dying in front of his parishioners without him saying a word about it had probably gone a long way toward making him look heroic, stoic, admirable. It would easily be recalled in the years to come as "a long and courageous battle." That's what dying, not dying looks like, though: enviable, singular, sane. I still feel badly for him when I remember that meeting, how narrow his choices really were. All those people gathered every Sunday for the great transubstantiation, trying to make do on the dry wafer and watery wine of a long and courageous battle.

What Is It about Living That Dying Proves?

I know that there are many nurses, physicians, social workers, and therapists of all stripes who were taught and now believe that in the harrowing business of caring for dying people and their families, with all the raw emotion, the unsorrowed sorrow, the not-yet-wept-for caravan of withering things crowding the death room, it is neither wise nor compassionate to move quickly or obviously to the tasks of helping those people die. More typically, most people in the trade are content in the early going to talk symptoms, trade experiences, focus on the physical, or visit, and they believe in those things. One of the deep lessons that you can learn in the death trade, one of my personal, burdensome favorites, is that each meeting with another person is the last of its kind. My figuring, rightly or not, is this: I am there not because someone is sick or bewildered or lonely or devastated or having difficulty adjusting to the news of their prognosis, though they are usually all of this and more. They all have only one sure thing in common. I am there only because someone is dying—if they are not I wouldn't be—and because someone is dying in a time and place that has banished any opportunity long ago they might have had to learn how to die and now asks of them that they do so hopefully, positively, and not very obviously.

So they are dying without map or guide, without any widely shared sense of what will be after, with nary a soul close by who knows how it is. These people in my experience don't need another relationship. They don't need a partner on their journey. It's not a journey like any other they've known, and even if it was the helpers around them aren't going too far down the road with them, the truth be told, nowhere close to where they are going. And they sure as hell don't need permission to die from someone who's never done so, who has no plans to do so, who is no more inclined to do so than they are. They don't need someone showing up who, mostly unawares, will take some of what is left of their energy, their lucidity, their capacity to give a shit or to sit up. They don't need someone who will steal their time by colluding with the general refusal to know that dying is in the room, and *should* be, in the name of helping them. I don't say dying people don't want any or all of these things—they usually do—but only that it is a poor thing to do to them.

So what do dying people need from the rest of us? They need the rest of us to know something enduring and true and useful about what dying is and what it asks of us all, and they need us to be able to act on this wisdom when the time comes. And the time is always coming, meaning that people are constantly dying among us, meaning that we have all the reasons and all the opportunities we need to learn and to practice this wisdom. It will take the rest of this book to get us there, by coming back to three essential questions:

> *Why is it so hard to die?*
> *Why do we have to learn how to do it?*
> *Why, if dying is so common, is it so much a mysterious, troubling thing among us?*

You may be surprised at the courage and the discernment you will need to keep coming back to these questions. The part of you that wants to be helpful and supportive will regularly be demanding, "Just tell me what to do. Just tell me how to fix it." And the question that I hope will keep shimmering up out of the pool of your frustrated desire to help people who are suffering is, "Fix what?" It takes a lot of courage to spend time with the dilemmas, the nightmares, the things we do to dying people in the name of compassion that just don't help, but that is what we will try to come back to: What mayhem are we trying to fix?

People working in the death trade can make appointments and care plans galore with dying people, but they do so in the undertow of knowing that, with little notice or none, those appointments and care plans will end. Being with dying people can teach you with certainty that there won't be another time like this: You ought not to plan as if you'll have a chance to do something, anything, again. It won't make you desperate, likely, to learn this lesson, and if you and they are lucky it won't make you cling all the more tightly to your job or your own loved ones, blessed as you'd be to have them for a while longer. Instead, learning it will drop you solidly into the only time you know with some certainty, *now*, together with the only people you know are there with you. And then you can look upon your time with dying people, and then with everyone, as something never before seen and never to be seen again, as something to be honored and cherished as the singular sort of miraculous thing that it is.

Everything swings on the hinge of "and then." You are willing to see your dying, and as soon as you do it can change how you understand your life. Your dying changes your eye, it changes what you see, and in that way your dying begins first in your seeing. *Your dying changes what your life means.*

For anything like this kind of alchemy to happen, your willingness and your sweat equity is required. It is enormously expensive to have your dying change what your life means, and you start paying from the cache of ideas you've nursed along for years about what living and dying are for. Dying changes what life means if you are *willing* for it to be so, as a rule, and only if you are willing to pay, to lose your old ideas, often by handfuls at a time. I've taught for years that dying must be allowed to change everything. You might think it inevitable that dying has that power, but a couple of decades in the death trade persuaded me without doubt that there is nothing inevitable about it. It is enormously hard work, to get your dying to tell your life's story. We have elaborate ways of eluding and betraying our dying in how we live, and almost all of them are provided—though not free of charge—by the culture we are born to. In the next section I am going to wonder about how dying has come to mean what it means and what that has done to how we die. This wondering is not hunting, and it is not seduction. It is courtship, which means it is a matter of the heart—the root word of "courage"—and the intellect, which also means it is a slow, elegant, old time approach that is needed.

There is a law in physics known as Heisenberg's Uncertainty Principle, and it goes something like this: In the realm of small particle science, the small particles themselves are altered by the technology you have to use to find and observe them. It can't be otherwise. If you expand that by a few orders you get this: However it is that you approach the thing you seek, that thing responds to your approach and your way of seeking, so much so that what you end up finding is the sum of the reactions of the sought-after thing to your way of trying to find it. *You find your looking,* in other words, *and you will see your eyes.* What you will find is a faithful rendering of your own consequences.

The Western mind, so informed by the Enlightenment, has an "essentialist" way of going through the world. We still believe that "the thing itself" is always available and attainable, and mystery is always vanquishable, if we improve the technology and fine-tune the theoretical model. Each advancement in technology advances us toward these consequences, though, toward what the technology does to the world and to our ways of seeing things, and we cannot fix our way out of it. The Uncertainty Principle shows us that "the thing itself" isn't out there waiting to be found.

It is changed by our search for it. It is changed by our desire to find it. It is changed by us *being there* at all. This is a "relational" understanding of physics, where nothing hangs in isolation, remote and austere, where everything has to do with everything else, where the nature of a thing is a consequence of the presence of all other things. It only seems like an ontological dead end if you wish it were otherwise, if you don't want to be part of the story.

Objectivity is the Enlightenment's way of trying to contend with this uncertainty principle. The idea is that the true nature of a thing is very available to you, provided that you obviate yourself to the point when you are purely receptive, when you are a nonevent in the process of observing: You get out of the way, and now you are capable of objectivity. In the helping professions this is called Therapeutic Neutrality, where you as the counselor manage and minimize your own feelings to the point where they are no longer a part of the process, or at best a parallel process. What you get for your trouble, though, is your own life turning into an unworthy or troublesome opponent of your work as a helping person, and that's what you see when you go looking objectively. In less-than-elaborately-skilled hands this continually turns into a therapeutic mandate or mantra or commandment: Thou shalt not be afflicted by that which thou proposes to treat in others. Objectivity usually invalidates experience by characterizing it as prejudice, but objectivity itself *is* a prejudice. Whether or not objectivity is possible, it has never struck me as a worthy, laudable achievement. It is to me better understood not as the quieting of the self, but as the View from Nowhere—probably not helpful in working with people and not a lot to write home about.

Another example: If you were born after the Victorian science/religion schism that bedeviled Western thought, worship, and jurisprudence well into the twentieth century, and your way of seeing the natural world has a "survival of the fittest" hue to it, then it will probably happen that every time you are in the bush you will feel a little bit at risk, as if the bush is somehow hankering after your blood, as if the only way you will survive that kind of exposure is to exert your muscle power and your connivance over the rocks, trees, insects, and animals you might come across. You'll feel unfit, in other words, separate and remote from the very place you stand. Of course, none of this is true *about the bush.* The life of the bush doesn't depend on us showing up and being mauled and turned into food. None of that is required for the life of the bush to continue. In fact, the bush might fare better if we don't show up at all, especially when we continue to show up feeling alien and unfit, as we are wont to do. The story about the wild being red in tooth and claw is a story we bring to the bush, not one we find there. "Survival of the fittest" characterizes *us,* not the bush. It is a story that lives unvanquished in our eye, so much so that we have no capacity to see anything that we haven't brought with us. That is all that we will see. And it goes further. If we go into the bush that way and behave as if all of this is true, anything that can move will make as much distance from us as it can, and anything that is fixed in place will hide its face from us and be as invisible as possible. In other words, the wild hides from people who bring their fear to it. There is the Uncertainty Principle at work. We see mostly what we have done to the bush, because we have changed it by going there in the way that we do. We have changed it by seeing it in the way that we do.

This *does* have something to do with dying well, and with taking care of dying people, and especially with trying to figure out how dying has come to mean what it means for us. Here is a hard thing for us to know and remember, as obvious as it might sound: Not everyone in the world knows what we know, fears what we fear, sees what we see, loves what we love. Not even most people in the world. Nor would they want to, given the choice. I am not talking about people only in Mali or Mongolia. I am talking about people in our midst, with a different history, an entirely different inclination and capacity for seeing things. An indigenous understanding of life and the world, to use a broad generalization, bears almost no resemblance to our own. This is very hard for us to imagine, since we are probably fairly sure that underneath it all (here's the essentialist model at work again) we are seeing and talking about the same life and the same world that indigenous people are talking about and seeing. The truth is, though, that an indigenous understanding has the capacity to see every important thing in the world, and the world itself, much differently than we do.

One of those important things is the place that humankind is given in the natural order of things. The foundational religions of contemporary North America, biblically rooted, teach that humans are (or were) the "crown of creation," the center of the divine architecture and purpose. The made world was given to humans to take what is needed and wanted. Humans in that sense are owners of the world. With the fall from grace humans ushered the dark side of that proprietary relationship into the world and ever since have been chained to the world as caretakers (tillers of the soil, herders of the animals) and subjected to the world's rhythm by having a limited life span. Our creation legends say it plainly: Life means what it does because human beings are its proper heirs and managers, a standard agriculturalist's vision. Life means what it means because of how human beings live. We impose meaning upon an otherwise meaningless tangle of life.

Generally speaking, an indigenous understanding of life, one not mauled by conversion, bears no resemblance to this story. In indigenous ways of seeing, creation is a web of connectedness and mutual reliance. The earth itself is the fundament, the giver of "livingness," you could say. The plant world, being in a way the skin of the earth, or being the way the earth has of being itself, is the life upon which every living thing depends. The animal world lives as the plant world lives, faithfully obedient to its ways, which is a radical re-understanding of what to most of us seems "dependent." And then there are human beings, upon whom from our first appearance in the world up to the present moment nothing in the world depends for its life. The dependency flows entirely in the other direction. We have always been the most *dependent* beings in the world. (In these modern times, given the enormous impact that we continue to have on the natural order of things, it may already have come to pass that what the world does need of us to continue at all is our willingness to live as *true human beings,* by which I mean deeply obedient to the natural world, inextricably bound to the health of the world for our health, permanently indebted to the world for whatever gives us the capacity to be human.) Nothing naturally occurring in this world depends upon human beings for its life. Humans are not a mandatory part of the natural order's health or ways. On the other hand, *our* capacity to live at all requires the interdependence of all those other things, and so *our obligation to what gives us life is greater than that borne by any other living thing.* Human life means what it means because of how life is, of which humans are a small and deeply obligated, dependent part. *We are heirs to the meaning of life and not its creators,* from an indigenous point of view.

If nothing of the natural world needs our lives, then nothing needs our deaths either. If you think in terms of interment—leaving aside for now our utterly foreign and essentially unsustainable burial practices, which make our bodies toxic and make it impossible, no matter what we intone over the grave, for us to return to the earth—the mass of plant and animal death that returns base elements to the earth dwarfs any contribution we could make to soil health by our deaths. We are eaten by nothing, and we see to it that this is so. If nothing in our part of the world benefits from our dying, we are challenged by two riddles:

> *All the deaths of all living things feed life;*
> *what does our death feed?*
> *All of life's deaths mean that life continues;*
> *what does our death mean?*

If your creation legends put you at the center of life—drink in a deep draught of this irony—then the meaning of your death is fugitive, uncertain. So we who are heirs to this "crown of creation" story have a problem if we are to let the news of our dying change what our living means, a serious, intractable problem that has loomed up at the deathbed of almost every dying person I have worked with. There is something in our basic understanding of life that makes us strangers to the natural world and its ways, and it makes our death—the meaning of our death—unnatural.

Let's go deeper. There is a saying I mentioned earlier: To a man with a hammer, everything looks like a nail. I've learned in the last two decades that this is many times more brilliant a thing than I had thought it was, and it is worth some wonder. It's a saying about anticipation and prejudice, about poverty of options, and it has a lot to tell us about what dying in our time and place means to us. "To a man with a hammer": This means that, though you may know your one tool well, you likely will ask it to do what it wasn't designed to do and perhaps cannot do. This isn't really a recommendation to go out and get a lot of things. It means that it is a good idea to have a variety of ways and means available to you, to do justice to the vast diversity that the world is. "Everything looks like a nail": a much more volatile proposition. It means that your meager tool kit, your poverty of options, changes two things fundamentally. It changes your eyes, and it changes the thing your eyes are looking at. The poverty is contagious, in other words, and the world itself is susceptible to it.

So what happens to dying, what do we make it mean, when we bring to it the inarticulate fears, the anemic rationalism, the lack of familiarity and the poverty of any mythic or poetic answer we might have to the question "Why?" The answer for several hundred years has been that we hammer away at it until it is the first, last, and often only nail needed for the coffins where our imaginations are interred.

A few years ago I was asked to speak at a national palliative care conference that was taking place in the cavernous, epic loneliness of a big-chain hotel ballroom. To think on it now, a ball is inconceivable in a place like that. It is a good spot for one of those mass Moonie weddings that were happening some years ago, or a new car convention. Ballrooms like that are built not for the courtship of one heart willing to see another, but for the seduction of one heart selling another to the highest, most remote bidder.

I dreaded the ballroom setting. The room was actually endless, in every direction but up and down, and had something like a thousand people in it. After the welcoming speeches and the processions of flags and delegates, and after the stage was cleared of the choir singing hopeful, inspirational songs, and after the short introduction by someone who seemed to think well of me but didn't know me, I stood on an endless stage in an endless room, so far from the seated people that I couldn't see beyond the fifth row, flanked on either side by massive, rock concert–scale screens showing nothing—since I don't use slides, overheads, or Power Points—but me. And I knew, because we wouldn't be together again like this, that I could not do the talk the organizers had asked me for, just as I had never done it and never will. I wasn't after all going to do the conference keynote address for them about "Finding Meaning at the End of Life."

Consider the last part of the phrase: "the End of Life." When someone is dying it is the end of many things. Don't listen to those placid detachment specialists who tell anyone who'll listen, "It isn't death, it isn't an end, it's a transition." No friends, it is endings of all kinds, incontrovertible, non-negotiable, no matter what you believe. It ends marriages and families as they once were, workplace dynamics, headlines, plans for retirement, plans for childbearing, all manner of hopefulness, and on and on. But for all that, the dying of anyone, no matter how you might or might not feel about them, is not the End of Life. Most everything we can know about our life is ending as we die, that is a true thing, but life isn't ending *because* we die. I don't know how many people in how many cultures beyond the one I'm born to, and beyond the cultures that made this culture, who deliberately and desperately mistake the human life span for life, but I know truly that this North America does. The end of life hasn't happened, and all the evidence you need to see this clearly is there. So this is a very poor, misleading, and misinformed, sorrow-mongering thing to say, the End of Life, and it is a phrase that shouldn't have a place in the care of dying people or in our way of dying. The End of Life is a hammer, in other words, and it turns dying into annihilation, demonstrably and falsely so. "The End of Life" is the end of the meaning of life, and when that is your hammer then that is what your dying becomes: the end of the meaning of life.

But this is not the reason that most people in the West have a hard time finding meaning at the End of Life. *There isn't an end of life for meaning to hide in,* but that isn't the hard part. I've been asked to teach on this "Finding Meaning" idea at least fifty times, and I've never done it. People who ask me to do it seem to believe that finding meaning at the end of your life is bound to be good for you and worth the effort. Where is it written? But that isn't why I don't teach on that theme either. This is why: What if your life, anyone's life, isn't a maze or a puzzle? What if it is not a test or a smudged mirror, or a guide book with a dozen pages torn out by the last user, or a Rubik's Cube for you to twitch over until everything lines up and you win? Meaning isn't hidden away from us, or withdrawn because we haven't been good or didn't study hard enough or long enough, or because it was lost in the Fall. Meaning is not a fugitive or a tease or a prize going only to the best and brightest and to those who live up to their potential.

Here's a malignant story: The Gods, bored one day, decided to make humans, and imbued us with an appetite for meaning. They gave us to understand that the meanings were hidden. But they weren't. There weren't any meanings. The Gods watch us making holes in life looking for the hidden meanings of life, wringing our hands in futility and pushing each other out of the way. That is how the meaning of life came into being. This is their entertainment.

It isn't godly behavior, I'd say. The meaning of our lives isn't sitting under a rock somewhere waiting for us to find it. That is theology speaking, and it is a crippling story whose time is done. It comes from the idea of heaven as a remote meritocracy that you have to earn your way into and from the idea that the impermanence of your life means you have to trade it in for a better, more enduring deal. It means that your dying time is ground zero where you *find out* if your life was a worthy thing. You won't *find* meaning in your life, or in the end of your life, especially if you haven't been on the prowl for it or had a hankering for it before then. When Finding Meaning is your hammer, it turns dying into a desperate kind of scavenger hunt, a last-gasp lunge at holding back the tide of Meaninglessness that our cultural poverty on this issue prescribes to us in our dying time.

Earlier in this book I talked about the med-tech arsenal that we use in responding to "life-threatening illnesses." If med-tech is your hammer, what does it turn dying into? It turns dying into "what we can do about dying." It turns dying into something that shouldn't be happening now, something we can interfere with or control or contain or almost always prolong, or at least have some kind of vote on. Here is what that looks like in a normal day in the palliative care business. In the health care system I worked in for many years, the provincial government paid most physicians according to the number of billable units—multiples of seven-and-a-half minutes, if I remember correctly—they racked up, and the remuneration varied according to the kind of work done in those units. In the case of the very difficult office visit where the physician has to "break the bad news" to the patient, this was a typical scenario. An appointment of, say, forty-five minutes was allotted, which is a long meeting by today's medical practice standards in my part of the world. You might imagine that the lion's share of the meeting was devoted to the bad news and the patient's emotional response to it, but that is not typically what happened. Usually the news was given in the first three minutes or so, with more or less skillful empathy. The patient's reactions almost all surfaced within those same three minutes. What are the remaining forty-two minutes for? They're for working through the various treatment options available in palliative care. Three minutes to describe what we can't do anything about; forty-two minutes to describe what we can do about what we can't do anything about. As soon as that kicks in, it has turned the epic life drama of dying into the treatment of symptoms, the treatment of side effects of the treatment, the treatment of side effects of the drugs, the treatment of secondary, escalating symptoms, the treatment of secondary side effects, and so on. In other words, med-tech turns dying into what is happening to your body, with you on the receiving end. With a med-tech hammer in hand, dying turns you into a victim and med-tech activates your defenses. It places some measure of control over what is to become of you into your dying hands. Dying means physical diminishment and how it can be forestalled, which, given how immense the experience actually is and what it asks of all of us, isn't much meaning at all.

These are the stories of dying that religion and medical technology have given us. What of psychology, then? Surely, you might hope, counseling and therapy give us a way out of this poverty of the imagination when it comes to dying. In my experience, however, that is not usually the case. Without having read a single book on the subject of dying, you would still be able to tell me fairly quickly what was going on with someone who had received a terminal diagnosis but steadfastly refused to talk about it or to behave as if anything much had happened to change their lives. You would probably say, "They are in denial." And if the person with a terminal diagnosis sat looking out the window for hours at a time at nothing in particular, didn't eat much, and couldn't sleep through the night, you might figure that he or she is depressed. In both cases some kind of counseling would be recommended so that this person could "work through their anger and bargaining, and begin accepting the news." Acceptance is the grail, the prime indicator of mental health, the gold standard of dying well in our part of the world.

> The twenty-nine-year-old woman I was meeting for the first time had stage-three lung cancer; she already required nasal prongs when sitting to avoid shortness of breath. After introducing myself and the palliative care service I represented, I asked what her understanding of what was happening might be. She proudly declared that she had been informed that she was seriously ill, but that she didn't let it be a big part of her life. She looked over to her mother, who gave her the thumbs up, and then looked back at me and said, "My yoga teacher says I'm on the right track."

Most people who are mental health practitioners might agree with the yoga instructor, and back in their office might check "yes" on that place in the assessment form where it asks, "Patient adjusting well to diagnosis?" And what is the sign that she is adjusting well? Her life is carrying on in as normal a manner as possible, under the circumstances. Normal life, so far, has survived the diagnosis. Is this acceptance? Is it denial? Are either of these questions even remotely helpful in understanding what is going on with this woman? They are not, I would say. Neither of them has anything to do with what dying is, or what it asks of anyone. They are psychological ideas that are not tutored by the realities of dying. Both of them hint strongly that there should be a steady self in there somewhere that is supposed to prevail *in spite of dying.*

The counseling that is given to dying people generally isn't learned from the experience of dying. In our helping professions, dying is almost never understood as a reliable teacher. It is an adversary, and what it does to people is the counselor's job security. So the counseling models are imported into "the care of the dying" from the field of mental health. Most grief counseling is usually trauma counseling by another name. The working definitions of "denial," "bargaining," and the rest are psychological concepts rooted in the assumption that grief is loss, that dying is traumatizing, that getting the news requires Critical Incident Intervention, that counseling is about coping and hoping. None of this knows dying as a legitimate or necessary or purposeful outcome of a terminal diagnosis, only an inevitable, calamitous one. All of it is used to manage the debilitating trauma of the "news" that the patient will not last.

What if dying is not a "mental health issue"? What if "coping with loss" is not the same as dying? What if it is this insistence on *dying being a trauma* that is the traumatizing thing about dying in our time and place? If psychology is your hammer, then dying is an intrapsychic event, a threat to whatever remains of your mental health. The gold standard of mental health in our culture—well adjusted, verbal, accepting—is supposed to endure dying and withstand the utter loss of the meaning of life that it threatens. If psychology is your hammer, then your prevailing state of mind as a dying person is supposed to be pretty much unchanged by a terminal diagnosis, and dying is the opposite of mental health, just as it is in medical circles the opposite—not the proper end result—of physical health.

Just think that thought for a moment: If you are healthy enough long enough, you will die. If you have a positive-enough outlook on life long enough, your life will end. It won't end because of what you do, nor because of what you don't do. Those things say something about when and how, but nothing about *why* you die. Does this sound "depressed"? Does it beggar all the self-help books, the be-all-you-can-be seminars, to be willing to know that this is the truest thing about your life, that it will properly and justly and surely end? In my years working in the death trade, I saw dying people constantly trying to find a way to live *in spite of the fact that they were dying—not because of it.* They felt they had to choose between living and dying, and they almost always did choose. Almost all of them chose against dying in the early stages, and when the symptoms and the drugs got to be too much they gave up, to use the lethal phrase that is current among us. For those patients and their families, a terminal diagnosis meant that one part of their life, the dying part, the symptoms, the effected organs, the side effects, was the enemy. Their willingness, as it is usually called, to "fight this thing," and the willingness of doctors, lab techs, and family and friends to do the same, was their only friend. Dying people, and all those arrayed to help them, labor along dragging a burden bag that they willingly hoist over their weakening shoulders every day. Inside the bag, fortune cookie–style, is a note that says, "You cannot live, dying." You have to choose. If making the most of your mental and physical health and maximizing your potential is the hammer of your life, then dying is turned into something that insults and endangers your health. Dying is the opposite, not the result, of your health, just as dying is the opposite, not the result, of your life.

> I am speaking to a man who is in every medical and biological sense of the word a dying man, but who refuses to know or discuss his death. I ask him what he thinks is happening, given everything he has felt and heard and read. He allows that he is seriously ill, but then begins telling the story of the neighbor of a cousin who six years ago was diagnosed with something like the same cancer he has and though she was younger the woman was given the same hope-lacerating prognosis as he has been given—two years, plus or minus—and she is still alive these six years later, and he intends that outcome for himself, because if it *does* happen it *can* happen, and if that cousin's neighbor can live, so can he.

All of this sounds like a death-phobic culture means it to sound: hopeful, positive, life affirming, enabling one kind of good outcome. The dying man is fighting his death here, and he has given it meaning: It is one option, the most ignoble and arbitrary, among many. For a dying man who hates his dying life, the story of the lone, heroic victor should be his story too.

When that cousin's neighbor got her medical news six years ago, maybe ninety-nine other people in the same metropolis on the same day at the same stage of life and disease got the same prognosis. Things went along as things do, and each of those ninety-nine people died on schedule, as foretold by the doctor. But our man is not concerned with or interested in their stories, not one of them. He doesn't even want to know their stories and has no problem with them not being told. Their story is that they got sick, died, and disappeared. For him, for everyone who loves him, those are not stories to be told at a time like this. And generally, whenever there is no one around who believes what I believe, they *aren't* told. Why? Because those ninety-nine aren't here anymore to tell the story? Because those ninety-nine didn't eat enough broccoli or think enough good thoughts when they had the chance? Because they didn't love being alive enough to beat the cancer?

Ah no, we tell the story of the One, over and over, and let the ninety-nine tell their own stories if they can, their mouths full of dirt, the dead left to bury the dead. And what meaning do we give their deaths? There is no merit in knowing or telling the story of their death. There is only merit for the dying man in the story of the one who didn't die. Not dying: *That* is the story to be told.

One morning in early winter I was on the highway en route to my farm from the big city. Normally that is a four-hour enterprise, lots of time to think big thoughts or worry big worries. This was one of those mornings that come to you once in a while full to bursting with the real promise that many a thing can be and will be. On mornings like those, even in winter, you feel ripe somehow, able. I had cold, clear air, two empty lanes, and my mind was on the ramble. I wasn't listening to the radio droning away, and then I was.

The host had patched in three trauma ward nurses to a four-way conversation about the slings and arrows of their kind of work. It happened that each of them had experience in neonatal intensive care, which is among the most taxing ways to make a living there is, I'm fairly sure. The host was genuinely in awe of these women's workday, what it asked of them, and what it did to them, and he praised them often, as I would have done. Along the way, in describing how hard the work must be, he added this summary statement as the final word on working with dying children: "And, of course, the hardest thing of it, children aren't supposed to die." There was a pause after he said this, and then each of the nurses in turn murmured their agreement. They all said their amens to this article of faith and moved on.

Children are not supposed to die? No one objected. Three people who had between them probably seen hundreds of children die, and all of them went along with this. Children *aren't* supposed to die: That was the bedrock of their job description and of their motivation for being in that difficult work. If children do die—and they do the world over—then what are we saying about life when we say that they are not *supposed* to die? Are we saying that we don't approve, or are we saying that it isn't right, isn't just, isn't proper, isn't natural that children die? If children aren't supposed to die, then what does their dying mean? What is it about life that dying children prove? What does death mean when the ones who are dying are children?

If they're in Uganda or Chad or Haiti, then dying children mean lack of hygiene, malnutrition, no clean water, wretched public health infrastructure, the miserable limit of Western humanitarian relief schemes and our benevolence, the continuing toll of European colonialism, or age-old tribal enmities erupting again. If dying children are in any big city in Anglo North America, they mean that we haven't raised or spent enough research and development dollars, and we need to raise and spend more. They mean that our med-tech religion is good, but not yet good enough. One dying child is one too many! And we won't rest until … Until what? Until there are none? Until every child reaches adolescence? And then? Until every adolescent reaches their twenties? And then? If the world is good, and life is to be believed in, does everyone deserve to live into their sixties or seventies, or what? And do we then come to everyone in their eighties, now that everyone makes it that far, and say, "Well, you've now received the fullness of your entitlement. You are our victory over the arbitrariness of life. You are already in your grace, your bonus years, the end of what you deserve. How does that feel?" Are *they* supposed to die? If children are not supposed to die, who *is* supposed to die? Where does this "supposed to" come from?

You can get a lot of strong feeling going on this question of children's death. That is because children dying seems to focus our deepest convictions about whether life is fair or just or purposeful. Dying children are ground zero for our beliefs about most of the Big Things. They activate our convictions about Supposed To. Having children, and having them meet and exceed their peers, those are high on our list of natural inevitable-if-the-world-is-halfway-just entitlements. When it happens otherwise, the first casualty is the willingness of parents, siblings, aunts and uncles, grandparents and godparents, and beyond to continue believing if they ever did that there is a natural order of things, that it is good that there is, and that the natural order of things now includes the dying of the young person they love and counted on to outlive them. People will say as if they are reading from Leviticus or Luke or some other book: It isn't right. In a place that doesn't believe in dying and uses the death of children to fight it, just as every children's hospital uses the idea of—and the fear of—dying children to raise money, dying children mean the end of justice. The dying of children is the place where the domesticated life fair to humans gives way to the bloodied, aloof, Godless life of chance and chaos, where what is just is beggared by what is so.

I don't want children to die, here or anywhere, and there are places in me that are wrecked by the thought and the work experience of children dying on my watch. I had spinal meningitis as a child in the 1950s. I am a grown, dying child who didn't die, amen. My own children, those born, have lived to see their twenties, praise everything holy, and when they were younger I would have done—and did do—what I could to steer them from their deaths. I wanted them to live, and to live beyond me, and so far they have. And I want the same for you, and for you who did not have it go that way I want that you can rise up somehow and try again to love life. But what I want for my children and for you, natural though it might be, is of little consequence in the nature of things. Or you could say, it is a small, understandable part of the nature of things. The nature of things just isn't the same as human nature.

An Angel or an Executioner

Well, this is a pretty grim story so far, and it seems to get worse with every paragraph. What can we *do* about all this? you're probably wanting to know. Can we do anything about it? My short answer is: yes. We can, and we must. It is very much up for grabs if we will, though, especially if the last fifty years are any indication of our priorities where dying is concerned. In order for anything to turn itself toward sanity, we will need a stout combination of willingness and capacity. The first we can only seem to conjure when we are forced to. It seems to take a monstrous turn of the Wheel, an unhinging of our plans, a big hole blown in our belief about how things should be for us to begin thinking about these things at all, let alone deciding to live otherwise. As to capacity, that takes heavy, expensive, and prolonged learning, not much a valued commodity when information and self-determination rule the day. But here is one possibility, as a way of getting the thing into some kind of motion: Don't wait. Imagine that everything *is* up for grabs, whether you've got the news or not. Imagine that everything that your life and your death mean is decided by how you live and die, while you live and die. Here's a hint about how to get started: If the meaning of life isn't *necessarily* anything at all, then try to imagine that you have to *make* meaning instead. Imagine that *the meaning of things,* especially of human things, *is itself a made thing,* and imagine that you can make meaning every day.

If you haven't been deliberately making meaning in your life by the ways you've lived it, then your time of dying is going to be a hard, hard proving ground, a tough, under-the-gun place to do so. You don't make meaning from the ether, or hocus-pocus it into view by the force of your will or by getting to all the weekend workshops in your area that you can afford. Meaning is made while you live, in all the small true moments that become your life, and it is all but inevitable that your way of living will become a part of the meaning of life that others—your grandchildren, say, or someone else's grandchildren—will with some cobbled-together version of willingness and capacity live or not. The crucible for meaning in your life is how you wrestle with the way things are.

> I heard a brief bit of an interview done with George Harrison's widow a year or two after his death. She was asked whether George had died well, and she responded that after having tried whatever he tried to be cured, he had known for a couple of years that he was slowly dying, and that as a practitioner of meditation he had some readiness—some combination of willingness and capacity—that held him in good stead. Then she said that George had one day a few months before he died said something that was uncharacteristically harsh of him. He said that if people waited until the end of their lives to get to know God, they were waiting an awfully long time, and that there was such a thing as "too late." George Harrison was speaking from the trenches of how it is these days to die, so we might rely on what he saw there. And I remember long ago the poet Robert Bly passing this on to a few of us sitting down together: "They say that if you love God you might find Him in twenty years, but if you hate God you can find Him in two."

Trying to get to know something of the holy during your life, and along the way hating the holy and the way things are from time to time for

having to learn the way things are, that is how the meaning of your life—
and the meaning of the ending of your life—gets made. In my experience,
most of those dying people who think about any kind of God come to the
firestorm of hating God, as do many of those who haven't thought about
God much at all.

The American poet William Stafford pleaded with his readers to treasure candor, clarity of speech. At stake, he claimed, was any capacity we
might have for a "mutual life" in dominant culture North America, and
the darkness that would entomb it is palpable. Our mutual life, where dying is concerned, is very much lost in the dark, friends. I myself am a faithful witness to that. Our culture is a death-phobic thing to die in, probably
irrevocably so, and many of the unbidden, unexamined thoughts and feelings we have about dying come from there. The darkness around is deep
indeed, and it is only by enormous labor and courage and well-crafted
speech that we are going to make our dying mean something more than
what it has meant. That is the least of what we owe to those we will not
live long enough to meet.

Maybe you've heard this one: There are no atheists in a foxhole. When
the going gets tough, some kind of God is going to emerge where your
agnosticism used to be. This is true for many self-avowed atheists too: As
their death approaches, should they want to have been right their whole
lives about the God thing? Should they want now to have been wrong
their whole lives? The going gets very tough when dying is in the house
and you end up, maybe in spite of yourself and your old vows, planting
the flag of your last months in some kind of conviction about what it all
means, what it is all for. Dying abhors a vacuum too. By this I mean that
eventually most dying people decide that their death is either an angel or
an executioner, and that's the story they die by.

The hard truth is that most people in my experience choose the executioner. No one says that out loud, of course, but you can read it in the
stance they take, in the language they use and don't use when they talk

about how they're doing and why. Most people seem to back into their dying time. Their disease is the battleground, but their dying is the executioner. When the possibility of dying becomes the certainty of "I'm sorry, there's nothing more we can do," then most of the "got-tos" of life just leech out the souls of people's feet and down into the ground. The *reasons* for things wither, and dying means the end of anything meaning much of anything. That's when your dying has become your executioner, and when that happens you have two choices before you: fight or quit. Either choice crafts an executioner out of your death. Either way, your executioner has it in for you. Either way this thing is coming for you with bad intent. The grim reaper, and all that. Obituaries are one place where the secret religion of our last days shows itself: "After a long a courageous *battle* ..." they say. So the families of dying people assemble on the sidelines of this lethal, final contest under the unfurled banner that in Gothic script reads, "Thou shalt not quit," and they cheerlead their loved one into the perpetual-motion machine of palliative care, where you can almost make out in the rumbling drone the mantra, "Do something. Do something."

"Fighting," though it sounds like a life-affirming response to something that is life threatening, backs you into a corner. It gives you a palette with three shades of gray and says, "Go paint the masterpiece of your last months." The problem with fighting your death when you are a dying person is that this battle will almost always become an intolerant, uninformed mania masquerading as a rational life choice. Fighting death gets you the T-shirt that says "Choose Life," as if you had a choice to make between them. St. Paul and Dylan Thomas are both cheerleaders in fighting death, the one leading with a sneering dismissal, the other with filial rage.

Though sometimes they lose, fighters fight to win. That is their purpose. They fight to end the fight. Even if you get very good at fighting, the purpose remains the same. If you fight your terminal diagnosis with the chemo and positive thinking and the rest, and you end up realizing that you've been dying all along—if you end up realizing that a dying person is what you have *become*—it means one thing: that you lost. That is the gray secret of your end-times: Fight your executioner to your heart's content if you will, but he will no less be your executioner. You might change how you feel about him, but if you fight him you will not change his job description. In other words, *you won't change what dying means by fighting it.* It will always mean "loss." That's the riddle's answer. When you are dying, fighting means that you will lose. It is like the proverbial Beckett play: You fight, you lose. It's like Vegas: You fight long enough, you lose. What the obituary means but never says is that after a long a courageous battle, *you lost.* Fight your death and your life is stalemated, a worse outcome by far than losing. For us it seems mainly to be either that we are victimized by our dying or we are in charge of our dying. Having only two choices—especially when they are really two sides of the same coin—is the same scam as having two choices of cola in Walmart.

Life. We talk about it enough. We *use* the word. It is *there,* after all, carrying everything we think of it and more. What life *means,* though, is roused up into the light by the way we wrestle it in the course of putting one foot before the other. "Wrestle" doesn't mean "fight." It seems adversarial—we've all felt it, probably—when life doesn't look like what we have in mind. The sea, for instance, is malevolent and seems to have a taste for humans the moment there is a question of whether we'll make the shore. But that idea shows up mostly in disaster novels written by people without much fondness for water, and it isn't what the sea *means.* The sea doesn't become any more itself when we go down in it, and its continuing ability to be the sea doesn't need humans awash, adrift, or at its bottom. We make that meaning when we fight the sea. A good seaman loves the sea at times, heeds its signs and portents other times, might even hate it when he loses his senses, and comes to them later and realizes it is something of himself that he was hating. He will always have a fine regard for its many ways of being itself, no matter whether he approves of the current, the swell or the squall of the moment. But a good seaman fighting the sea? He doesn't. He wrestles the sea by sailing upon it and by making his way.

You can fight your boss or your employee, but win or lose, the proceeds at the end will be small. If you fight your spouse on matters of principle, something good might come from it, though the aftertaste of winning and losing will probably cast a spell on your house that can last for years. This, for whatever good comes from it, will all be gathered up and become your life together or what your life together means. Fighting your zeitgeist or the nature of your times could have nobility in it, and you might have some transient bragging rights if you are a faithful witnesses to the fray. For many philosophers and politicians this is the meaning of their lives. The death notices of politicians have always struck me as particularly thin and sad because so often their politics are taken for their lives. "He was a fighter," they say.

I was asked to write a short chapter for a book an American publisher wanted to do on palliative care. Theirs was an ambitious project. Judging by the prospectus they sent me it was destined to be a huge wad of a thing, a kind of North American response to the English *Oxford Handbook of Palliative Care.* The mysterious part of their invitation was the subject they were asking me to write about: suffering. There were no qualifiers, no context, nothing to fit into, just this wide-open invitation to write about something I'd been teaching for years. I decided to risk it all, take them at their word, and refuse to write about how to cope with suffering, how to minimize suffering, how to palliate or medicate or manage or avoid or fight suffering. All these approaches do no one any good, to my mind, and have already been done over and over in almost any book you can find on nonmedical palliative care. I decided to write this short chapter on how to suffer.

I was pretty sure that I wouldn't make it past the first editorial go-round. They wanted evidence-based practice and they wanted research, and you can't do much research on how to suffer. There is almost no one out there who wants to learn how to do it. Suffering is never identified as anyone's goal of care. Dying in almost any palliative care textbook, and for most of those who write them and who read them, is a complex tangle of problems, and dying people are on the receiving end of problem-solving strategies. So I wrote about suffering as a skill, as something to be learned and taught and defended. I was certain that my chapter, if it made its way into the book, would be in the section with bowel management and pain management and terminal anxiety management and depression management. As it happened, the editors put the chapter in the first section, where the foundation principles of palliative care are discussed, a fitting place for consideration of the suffering of dying as a life skill, but a surprising one. (Later they seem to have had second thoughts. I've been told that the second edition of the book omits my contribution completely. If so, I wasn't notified.) Suffering, learning how to suffer, is how you make meaning from what seems random, chaotic, or pointless. This is what I mean by wrestling. Meaning comes from this kind of wrestling.

"How can any of this fighting mania change?" That way of asking guarantees that things will not change. "How can I change any of this?" That is the beginning of changing it, to choose differently without waiting to feel any differently about it all first. Try it this way: What if your dying is an angel? And what if your dying job, should you choose to accept it, is to wrestle this angel of your dying instead of fighting it? What if you wrestle the angel of your dying life instead of fighting the executioner of your disease?

Let the difference between the two unfold a little. Wrestling is a different thing entirely. Wrestling has choreography. The purpose of dancing, or any choreographed thing, isn't to get to the end, to have it be over, to resolve it, to let go, to accept. The purpose is to move, to dance. Wrestling has an intimacy to it that fighting will never attain. With our kind of military and medical arsenals we can fight our enemies from hundreds of miles away. That is what chemo is like. But wrestling brings you very close to your partner. Wrestling isn't what happens to you. It is what you do. And you will not be alone in it. Wrestling is dance. Not the tai chi kind of dance, where the partner is missing, but the ballet or the jive that only appears when two or more come to it together. Wrestling is articulation, the elegant courage of singing and dancing when song and dance tend as they do toward silence, knowing it will end. *Living your way of life wrestles the way life has of being itself: That is how meaning is made.*

Now, life has a few enduring constituent parts. Life has birth, the coming of life in it, surely one of the old sources of the human instinct for awe and worship. Life has maturing, the growing of life in it, the mystery and the manifesto we are calling DNA these days, surely an enduring biochemical and a spiritual fact, and as much proof as we'll ever enjoy of the presence of the holy in the world. And life has death in it, the resolute, rock-solid death of everything. Of the coming in of life, of the growing of life, of the death of the living, life is made. These three are whorls in the thumbprint of the Makers of the thing, and something like proof of the nature or the style or the purpose and intent of what has made it.

Now you have some feel for what I mean with this awkward question: What is it about living that dying proves? Change "fighting for your life" into "wrestling life for the meaning of your life," and you can feel the shift of possibility. You wrestle the constituent parts of life, and the meaning of your life is made. You wrestle life as you come into it, and you are known certainly by your mother as one who did not come quietly. Maybe you had other ideas for yourself, or maybe you glimpsed the heartache to come and hesitated. You wrestle childhood illnesses that come over and over to take your life and you don't die, and so you might be named accordingly, as the Malian national treasure Ali Touré was named Farka, denoting donkey, denoting someone tenacious and working hard to live. You wrestle the DNA of your skin color, what it is and what it isn't, in a bigoted time, and in time you can brag with hard-earned clarity as my teacher Brother Blue did: "I don't look like much, but I am *hard* to kill."

I know that asking you to imagine dying as an angel without losing sight of the finality and the sorrow and the grief that dying must bring amounts to a tough sell, but that is what I'm asking. It's much easier to see dying as an executioner, given our inheritance from the death-phobic culture that has given most of us whatever meaning we take from dying. If I were to ask, "Dying—angel or executioner? What do you say?" we know what the vote would be.

So let's start with the word itself. Etymologically, an "angel" isn't a fluttering, downy, rosy-cheeked purveyor of benevolence and good times. Its oldest meaning is "hireling, laborer, messenger." This means that an angel is, according to its truest nature, the one who labors by serving, by bringing the news or telling the story. How can you tell, then, when an angel is in the room or in your life? Will you inevitably feel comforted, secure, and affirmed in your understanding of how things should be? Not likely. Because it brings news, and because the news is probably strange to your ear and not part of your normal day—that's what news is, after all—an angel is likely to bring something more like doubt, dishevelment, disorder, maybe chaos, maybe anarchy. You know that an angel has come to call when you get home from work, come in through the front door as usual, and from that point on you can't be sure where you are or why. Nothing is where it once belonged, and you have an unbidden and distinctly unwelcome opportunity to decide anew what your life could look like, all of which has been well disguised as a disaster.

We live in a time when most of us have to get the news of our dying from someone else, usually a specialist, ironically, in health care. But how can our dying be "news" when everybody already knows they are going to die? We are not tutored in the ways of dying, nor in what it asks of us, nor in what it could mean. And so our dying is a stranger to us, brought to the doorstep of our ordered lives and introduced to us as our lifelong companion and faithful *accompagnateur* unto our last breath, and in that way more faithful than any friend or family member can be or will be, by … an angel. When an angel comes to call, very little of your life is untouched. From that moment on, if you work hard at it, your life will never be the same. That is the great labor of the thing, to let your life be changed utterly by the news of your death when all and everything around you is counseling steady as she goes, business as usual, as normal a life as possible under the circumstances. Whatever of your former life is left standing is probably the part that is most what you were born to learn about and be faithful to. Whatever of your life that is still standing is probably you. That is what the news of your death could mean: It could mean the beginning, unadorned, common, and singular, of your one true life and its work.

This doesn't make anything easier. This doesn't banish executioners, not at all. Terminal cancer is a true executioner, certainly, as are sudden accidents, heart attacks, political assassins, and famines. These are things we die of, things over which we have little or no say. They answer the question, "How do we die?" They tell us nothing about why. Cancer may be your executioner, but the news of your dying is your angel, or could be if you are willing. You fight your executioner by chemotherapy and radiation and good nutrition, and properly so, but you wrestle the angel of your dying by grief and wonder and sorrow and somehow in spite of any example or counsel around you by choosing the meaning for your dying time. By the manner of how you live your dying you will start answering the question, "Why do we die?" And that is how we will change what dying has come to mean to us.

If you wrestle death, your labor makes a proper place for it. If you fight death, there is no place for it. Death is defeat, the end of life. Demonize death and you turn life into a factory-farm canola field: flat, hollowless, no place for mysterious things of substance to gather. But come to your death as an angel to wrestle instead of an executioner to fight or flee from and you turn your dying into a question instead of an edict: What shall my life mean? What shall my time of dying be for? What is it going to be like, that cottage of darkness? If you work hard in your dying days, the answer could be, "Not like anything you've known." Dying turns into something you live. The trick here is that to be able to ask questions like that you have to know, somewhere in your bones, that you will die. When the time comes, you have to know that you are dying. That shift from the future tense to the present is a chasm that many people these days never cross, never even see.

3

THE TYRANT HOPE

The ability to wonder—if I put it like that it probably doesn't sound to you too much like an advanced skill. It probably sounds more like the ability to land on the ground when you fall: more inevitable than skillful. My wife says that the world would be a kinder place if every man had a tractor, and all I can add to that is that the kindness would be guaranteed if every man was full of wonder when riding it.

It is my experience that the capacity for wonder might be something we share with everything that is holy, and something that is easily and early forsaken by people and times where technique and information are boss. *Wonder is part fascination, part ability to believe in things as they are, part willingness to be confused, even devastated at times, by the epic myste-riousness of ordinary things.* The work of dying that each dying man or woman or child must do demands of each of them some ability to be drawn in, overwhelmed, sometimes devastated and always awestruck by the ordinary death that underwrites their lives. The same is true of their caregivers. Wonder is the sum of life's way of being itself, washing up on the shore of what you've known until now, leaving handfuls of treasure scattered among the small boulders of what you were sure of. You gather some of that treasure for no reason you can figure without telling anyone and stash it under the pillow of your dreams for a time not quite yet upon you. Wonder is a willingness, decked out as a skill, to be on the receiving end of how vast the world always is and of how unlike your ideas of how it should be it often is.

When I was very young I, probably like you, thought about a lot of things that, so far as I knew, no one else seemed to be concerned about. A few of them were of the "Why is the sky blue?" kind, or the "If the earth is rotating how come I don't get dizzy?" kind. These questions get your young wondering muscle tuned up for its possible future employment in the ragged enterprise of trying to be a real, useful human being in the world, if you are lucky enough to be born into a place and time and people that make room for wonder in their schemes and plans. The adults around you and I, though, had found little or no employment for their wondering muscle in the graying, flattening, rationalist, and literalist project of getting a job and fitting into this part of the world, just as it had been for their elders as well, and so on. So these questions of mine didn't find any similar, surviving wonder in most of the people I asked. When I asked those kinds of questions as if much depended on the answers, the answers I got solved the "problem of my young confusion" by slaying the wonder that lay at the heart of the question. The physics of the answers I got— what rotates around what, how the atmosphere distorts—bled mystery out of the world, turned the world into a machine, and sedated wonder with information. Information is where wonder often goes to die. There are tens of thousands of seven-year-old poets in any large town or small city staggering under the weight of the sheer mystery of ordinary things, but only a few handfuls of forty-year-old poets there shuffling their feet through the gravity of their times, fallen leaves in the gutter as the days grow shorter.

The greatness of a great question is that it can survive any and all answering, and still be left standing after the debates and harangues and rationalist assaults have bashed away at it. There are no great answers, you could say, but only great questions made greater when their answerers are nobly defeated by the awe and mystery of the way things are. Great questions are not problems to solve any more than great feasts are problems for stomachs to solve. They are not lacunae in the web of our intelligence, waiting to be filled with more intelligence. Great questions, given half a chance, *are* our intelligence. Intelligence should not be a siege machine in the efficiency army's assault on the tower of what we don't know yet, though in our time and place it is mostly that. Great questions are a proper throne for wonder, and there is much in our life that needs our wonder, and deserves it, just as we ourselves deserve the capacity for wonder that came to us early on but does not often survive our education.

> A great question happened to me as a child. I still love it, it is still great to me, and it is still a question: Can soap be dirty? I know it doesn't sound like much, but there's something there. You might remember that bar of soap in the bathroom in any public place and say emphatically, "Yes! Soap can be dirty. I saw it." But if you stay with the question a little longer, you might start to wonder whether the dirt on the soap makes the soap dirty, or whether the dirt has to be *in* the soap somehow to make it dirty. Then you might go further and wonder whether it isn't in the nature of soap to be cleanliness itself, so that soap will always be clean and dirt will always be on the outside of soap looking in. These are the kinds of things I wondered about as a kid, anyway.

Hope is the soap of palliative care, in a way. Hope is often the tower of sand where most dying people live out their days, staring through a small window down onto the fields of the longed-after things that will come no closer and the hated and feared things that will gather there instead. Hope is the siren song of anyone who loves a dying person, the conjuring chant taken up in the name of compassion. The preservation of hope is the base element in any plan made for dying people by the people paid to care for them. It is the root condition for proceeding. That is the conviction of most of us, dying or not. Hope is life loving, and it cannot be otherwise. Without hope, they say, what's the point? And it's always a rhetorical question. In my years at the bedside and at the podium in palliative care, I have never heard hope wondered much about, or challenged, or talked about as if it were anything other than goodness incarnate and the secret ingredient that makes Maslow's "hierarchy of needs" and living and dying make sense.

A few years ago some researchers proposed to test what variable had the most significant impact on physicians' ability to accurately predict the course of their palliative patients' disease trajectory. One of the things they discovered in their test group was that the prognostic accuracy decreased in an "overly optimistic direction" the longer the patient-physician relationship went on. As the physicians spent more time with their terminally ill patients and with the patient's test results and lab work and family and history and hopes and fears and care plan, the physician's estimation of how much more time the patients were likely to have changed apace, and this shift in the estimated time a patient had left was almost always, as the researchers call it, overly optimistic. The doctors consistently tended to grant More Time to the patient, and the patients consistently tended not to live the More Time granted to them.

The physicians' prognostic accuracy seems actually to have been compromised by prolonged exposure to the patient. On the surface at least, that feels odd. If you are a patient, you want the physician to spend a lot of time with you and your chart, believing as you would that more familiarity can only help matters. The physician likely believes the same thing in principle, and time and workload permitting will try to gain that familiarity by putting that time in.

How could prognostic accuracy be compromised by prolonged exposure to the patient? And why does the compromise tend toward granting *more* time to a patient's life? Maybe it is because increased exposure to the patient tends to have the effect of binding the physician more strongly to the patient's views and wishes for his or her care plan, and maybe this tends to compromise the physician's judgment as to prognosis, to make it more consistent with the patient's wishes. As time goes on the physician's experience, judgment, and training all seem to get hitched to the bandwagon of encouragement, support, and cheer-leading the patient in pursuit of what the patient wants. And if the patient is "negative" and has a grim or overly realistic view of what is to come? The physician will again tend toward advocating a more hopeful outlook in the patient, the belief being that only good can come from being realistically hopeful.

The article seemed to strongly suspect that what the patient wishes for is contagious, but I think the dilemma it describes goes a little deeper. Medical training is thorough in most things. I don't think it is very likely that most physicians would confuse their training and experience with their patients' wishes. There is a subtler something going on with this. It is not the *content* of what is wished for—the grail of More Time—that is contagious. The fact that the patient steadfastly wants what is already gone for good, often long after it has gone, perhaps this is the contagious thing. The patient's insatiable desire for what will never be makes the doctor's simple objectivity and prognosis look and feel ineffectual, impotent, even disloyal. Many a physician has been accused of giving up on patients when they attempt to refer those patients to palliative care.

It looks as though sympathy and discernment are hard bedfellows where dying is going on. The consequence of this conflict—I have seen this many times—tends to be that the physician will delay referring a terminally ill patient to a palliative care service. For any patient who is paying attention, this referral is the end of the physician's willingness to go along with the program for More Time. Patients' desire for a close, more personal relationship with their physicians seems often to compromise the physicians' judgment. It challenges the very firmly entrenched belief in palliative care circles that the physician must establish a relationship of trust with a patient prior to being able to "break bad news." Usually that trust depends on physicians clearly aligning themselves with the patients' views and wishes regarding their prognosis, and not prematurely challenging those views and wishes. This "relationship of trust," if it requires time to be established, is built on the assumption that there *is* more time, and will be. It is also built on the conviction that what the physician knows of what is to come must at least for a while take a backseat to the principle of maintaining that trust. This is an uncommon understanding of what a relationship of trust should look like, is it not? It also should make us wonder: When *is* a good time for prognostic candor? When will the old relationship of trust be challenged by a new willingness to be honest with the patient about what the physician has known all along? Will the patient's hope ever legitimately be undone by the physician's training, experience, judgment, and counsel? Is maintaining hope what the helping professions owe people who are dying?

Years later some research was done on the subject of what patients want to be told by their physicians about their diagnosis and prognosis. It found that patients wanted clarity, precision, lots of information, an accurate prognosis, measured but full disclosure of the nature, consequences, and outcomes of their disease … and they wanted their overall hopefulness about their outcome left intact and supported and sustained throughout the process of their dying. Now on the face of it, this can't be done. There are two solutions that I've seen used over and over. In the first, the physician isn't entirely candid about the prognosis. This is generally defended as being done in the best interests of the patient by proceeding with information sharing according to the patient's willingness and ability and readiness to hear it. In the second, the patient is more or less gently prodded into shifting the content of the hope to something more realistic, given the likely outcome.

Doctors and social workers usually invoke a patient or family-centered model of care that places the patient at the center of the care plan as its coauthor and quality-control person. This solution looks concerned and compassionate, and gives candor its proper junior position in the scheme of what the patient deserves. A second solution is to periodically recalibrate the content of hope—the hoped for thing—to compensate for the ongoing failure of the care plan to achieve or sustain patient health. This solution looks discerning, and it recalibrates the patient's wishes by invoking the principle of "realistic hope."

Each of these solutions, and all others that I have seen in my years in the death trade, accepts in principle and without qualification the presence and the necessity of hope in the work of helping someone die. There is everywhere I look an uncritical willingness to support the hope project, because there is everywhere a belief that hope is inherently good, inherently helpful, and inherently necessary, especially in the face of this most trying of life's travails. Wherever hope is discussed, it is discussed in terms of its content, but rarely in terms of its function. There is strong belief in the palliative care community that a great leap forward has been made when a patient is encouraged to change what he or she hopes for as their dying comes on. Nowhere that I know of is there much discussion of what hope *does* to someone who is dying hopefully. Everywhere hope's function is tied to its content: If your hope is for something that is foreseeable, or possible, however exaggerated your sense of the foreseeable might be, you ought to be hopeful, and that'll be good for you. But what does it *do* to you to be hopeful that way?

> The backyard lot of this housing complex had one of those inner-city commuter highways running through it. The drone of tons of metal hurtling through a former river valley was the background sound to everything. When people fought, read, thought, fled, made love, and made dinner there, they did it to the roar of strangers' cars passing through. When I finally found the right door into the place, I thought about what I knew of the people on the other side of it: The patient was about thirty-five, never married and no children, living with her mother only, a married sister in the city, all emigrated in the last five years from the Philippines. Stage-three lung cancer. I guessed a little more: She'd had no time to get well established in a job before she got sick. Maybe she had some kind of custodial, maintenance job somewhere, and maybe she qualified for the government health plan. There likely wasn't much

money between them, or they'd probably be living somewhere else. Likely she was a pre–Vatican II Catholic, and likely this was coming in for some hard service lately. Likely she had a nagging suspicion that coming to North America had something to do with getting cancer, and likely she was awfully bewildered at being in the hands of a high-tech oncology team.

Her mother was very reluctant to let me into the apartment. She said nothing before or after I introduced myself, but when it was clear to her that I wasn't going to get discouraged and leave, she just walked away and left the door ajar. After a little awkward deliberation with myself, I went in. Two wrong turns later I found the lady in question cross-legged on the couch in the living room, in a head to toe purple housecoat, staring intently out the window and away from me. Almost hairless from the latest radiation, quiet, and wearing what she was, she looked for all the world to me like a Buddhist nun. I sat on the opposite end of the couch and told her a little bit about who I was and why I was there. She didn't respond, but continued looking out the window. Somewhere in a bedroom upstairs, a young child cried loudly about not wanting to go back to school after lunch—the only sound in the place besides the highway din. Plainly no one in that home thought I was a good idea.

At times like that I remember a bizarre little event from my student days, and it gives me some leverage with which to negotiate the total collapse of social grace or the utter absence of a shared understanding of anything, not an uncommon experience in palliative care. As part of my schooling back then, I interned in the psychiatry ward of a local general hospital. The place was run by a psychiatrist who had a closet commitment to Gurdjieff, though he never let on how this influenced his work. He took me aside in my first week and told me what a rookie in psychiatry needed to know, concluding with this: "Of all the people that are admitted while you are here, a third of them will get worse no matter what we do, a third will improve no matter what we do, and a third will leave the way they came in, no matter what we do. Your job will be to figure out which third your patients belong to." So things went along, me trying to understand how anyone could come to work seeing it that way. Later I wondered how they could come to work otherwise, such is life in the psychiatry ward in a general hospital. Eventually I was teamed up with a cunning, generous, earthy mentor whose idea of teaching was to drag me around the ward with him and then retire to his office to discuss anything but work to give me a chance to express myself. One day he said, "There's a new admission I have to see, a young woman who had to be restrained overnight. She was pretty aggressive, and she's probably been sedated. She may not be in good shape, but we'll see. Come on."

The woman still had her straightjacket on and stared at the ceiling. It seems that those things are designed to drive their wearers to their wits' end and beyond in the name of calming them down, a Kafka solution to aggressive behavior. We filed into her room, and my boss started to introduce himself. He got three or four words out when this woman, doing a very close *Exorcist* impression, reared up on her elbows and snarled, "Fuck off," with the spittle flying. Without breaking stride my boss saluted her, said "Fucking off," turned and left the room and me standing there.

I caught up with him thirty feet down the hall, awfully concerned about how things went, and asked him how he could say that to someone in her state. He stopped in the hallway, looked at me and said, "What better response do you suggest? I just took her at her word. I did what she asked. Nothing else was going to happen then. We'll try again tomorrow."

So I wasn't too thrown when the lady from the Philippines wouldn't look at or speak to me. But I wasn't going to put her through too much awkwardness in her own home, and I wasn't going to take much of her time and energy when she clearly had other ideas of how she should spend it, so I went to the heart of the matter promptly. I asked her, "When there's no one here to ask you about your blood pressure and your bowel movements, what do you find yourself thinking about?"

Her answer came quick and assured: "I am very positive and hopeful about my situation."

Most people in my line of work would be reassured by her answer. They would hear a woman who is positively oriented to her circumstance, who shows no outward sign of depression or anxiety, who is acting in her own best interests, appropriately guarded. They would look around for other things to talk about, now that her mental status has been found to be hopeful and forward looking. They might wonder whether there is much more to be accomplished, at least until the woman hit the unfortunate but foreseeable wall of her hopefulness collapsing under the pressure of mounting symptoms and drugs. But to me, an answer to so uncommon a question that comes so fast and so assured doesn't bode well, for now and in the longer term.

I said, "Well, that's all right. But I'm not asking how you are doing, really. I'm asking you something more specific, about what you think about. What do you find yourself coming back to and back to in your mind when you're on your own?"

I admit that this isn't an easy question to answer. Neither you nor I would be able to answer this one on the run with any certainty or satisfaction. It takes some serious hesitation and pondering to catch up to what claims you in the times in between life's "got tos" and "going tos." Someone you don't know asks what you're thinking about most of the time, and you may have to think long and hard to figure out what it is. Someone with a terminal diagnosis, though, she knows the code, the propriety. She knows something of what is expected of her. Her next reply was slower in coming, and a bit rambling. It took a minute to take some shape and gather some of her meaning. In summing it up for her best as I could I said, "It sounds as though you are spending many of your days praying. Is that what you mean?

This too wasn't much of a daring summary. Her old-style Catholicism and her newly acquired and terrifying patient status made the guess about prayer an obvious one. She agreed that she was praying a lot of the time. Here most people in my line of work might translate this as clearly a good thing, and they'd leave well enough alone, being able to check the box on the intake form that says "Religious Affiliation: Yes or No." Prayer in the context of terminal diagnoses is natural enough, among those who still pray anyway, and it would probably be left at that. Instead, I asked her, "If you don't mind me asking, what is it you are praying for?"

Praying is its own reward for praying people, usually, and the news that someone is praying in the midst of a terminal disease process is generally tolerated in the helping trades and thought of as a good thing. But the content of someone's prayer, especially given how intense and private it can be, isn't typically asked about. Prayer is one of those dirty soap subjects: It has inherent merit, it is at the very least its own reward, even among those who don't pray, and it mostly signals to people in my line of work that the dying person has a predisposition to inwardness and a willingness to be reassured. But I am not always persuaded that prayer is the balm it often appears to be, and I'd like it to earn its keep the same way I have to earn mine. So I asked her what she was praying for, and her answer this time was halting, uncertain, a little lost. With a lot more experience on my side than she had on hers, I summed up her answer this way:

"It sounds to me like you are praying for more time."

She nodded slowly. How could she not be praying for that? You could plot your course across the Sahara, you could do any number of divinations with this unshakeable, enduring, and eternal instinct that people with a terminal diagnosis have for praying for More Time. That is how enduring, widespread, and predictable it is. Again, most people who receive palliative care have received More Time. More Time is almost never the balm that people bargain for. It never appears as it did in their hopes and dreams and prayers.

We were coming to a kind of crossroads in our short meeting. I'm with a dying person who is praying not to die, at least not now or soon, who will almost certainly die more or less on schedule and who is dying as we sit there together. This brings up the question, What else *is* there to say about it? I could veer away from where this was surely going and say nothing more about it, or I could keep going and meet her at the place where prayer and prognosis was taking us.

I said, "Okay. Last question, and then I'll leave if you'd like. It's not an easy question, but I'm going to ask it anyway, and I hope you can forgive me for asking. How would you know if your prayers had been answered? How could you tell?"

As I said, I went to the heart of the matter, and the heart of the matter for a religious woman with cancer is, Where do her beliefs meet her dying? Do they meet at all? Prayer *in extremis,* pared down, is usually part supplication and part demand. At such a time, though, no one I've met prays to stop praying or to get to the end of their prayer. A rosary is a circle of beads after all, without end. Praying people pray to keep praying, if for no other reason. This specific prayer for More Time when you're dying, though, is a very tricky thing. If it happens at all, when does it begin? Does it look like all the other time before it, or does it have a different way altogether? What is the sign that it's happened? How *would* you know if your prayers had been answered? What would change?

This was the first time she looked at me since I had sat down. There was none of the equanimity from her first answer, none of the praying person's contentment or the religiously affiliated person's sense that they know what is going to become of them. There was a raw, un-alloyed terror in her eyes; that was all. I knew her rick-ety certainty about praying was swaying, and I knew too that it was a terrible thing.

I said, "I know this is a hard question. It's almost im-possible to answer. I've thought about this a lot though, and if it is okay with you I'll tell you two answers that I've come up with." She gave me something like a nod, the kind of acquiescence that people with no real choice give, and so I continued.

"Let's say that against all your upbringing and against your own inclinations you pushed the oncologists until they finally gave you a number. Let's say they told you, though they didn't believe it would do you much good to know, 'Well, probably three to nine months.' So you stumbled out of that office and into the light of day with this news, with this sentence in your ears—'Three to nine months'—and nothing any longer looked like it did. Not the sidewalk or the road, not the trees or the people or the light itself, none of it looked as solid, and none of it looked like it included you anymore. Somehow you made it home. Once you were inside, maybe you went right to the kitchen, because in the kitchen is the fridge and on the fridge are the magnets and under the magnets is the calendar. And maybe you didn't know which date to flip to: Should you want the shorter estimate, the one that gives you the least likely time, so that the More Time can start sooner? Should you want the longer estimate, to give you more time to pray for the change you're praying for? You probably are a positive person and so you flipped to nine months, not three, and you circled the day with the yellow highlighter. And that's your goal, to get there. And if you get there, if you are still breathing by means normal or mechanical, *that* will be the sign. More Time will start that day. From that day on your prayers will have been answered.

"What will it be like, to see that day? You'll be able to move and speak and feel like a person who was worth the trouble, who made the cut, when you know there are lots of others who did not and will not. You will be one who was heard and deemed deserving, whose prayers have been answered. It'll be a hallelujah time, then. But until then, what? Keep praying, that's what. Keep praying for more time, like you and your friends and your congregation have been doing. Keep praying to see that day on the calendar.

"The other possibility, strange as it might sound, is that your prayers have already been answered, and you missed it entirely. Pretty hard to imagine. Not impossible, though, not at all. What if the fact that you and I are here talking about it is all the proof you're likely to get or need that you are in the middle of your More Time? What if this is what More Time is, nothing more and nothing less special than this? If that's true, then you could already *be* the person whose prayers had been answered, instead of being the person waiting to find out, and you could walk and talk and feel like someone who has been heard and found worthy. And you could feel like someone who made it, a prayer-answered person, today.

"And if your prayers for More Time have been answered already, would you go through your days any differently?"

This was an awful lot to take in, and our visit didn't last a whole lot longer. I know that she thought about this question about praying for More Time, about not knowing when it starts, just as I have many times thought about it since. It isn't a comforting thing to wonder about, but often at 3 a.m. it is the only thing to wonder about. No one who is dying is likely to ask you to help them wonder about their prayers, and I don't think waiting for them to ask you to do so is a fair thing to ask of them. Sometimes you have to wonder aloud whether hope is all it is cracked up to be and wait for the pieces to fall. Maybe you'll get to be there when they fall.

You know how it is when you have a mortgage. Many things that once were possible are no longer possible. Once you did things that now, for good reason, you no longer will do. You will put things on hold. You will wait. You will do without. You will do less with less, and all of this you'll do because the mortgage gives you some guarantee that the sacrifices you are making will come out well in the end. You live *in* your mortgage, and because of that one day, all going well and you don't sell, it will become your house.

Hopeful people generally have their one good eye on a future they imagine, the more jaundiced eye on a present they mostly tolerate, and both eyes on a past they have a hard time remembering well and letting go of. Hopeful people do not as a rule hope for what they have. They hope for what they do not have. They hope for what they once had to come again. Hopeful people do not in their hopefulness often vote "yes" to the present. They vote for the future. Even those with a greater agility of hope, who hope for more of what they have, they are still voting for a future in which to have it.

Here is the connection: Hope is a mortgage. It is not *like* a mortgage: It *is* a mortgage. Hope is a mortgaging of the present, for the sake of some possible future that might come to pass and just as likely might not. Being a hopeful person with a terminal diagnosis means that, like those doctors in the study, you are in some mysterious and compelling way not allowed to know what you know when you are dying. In a death-phobic culture like our own, *knowing you are dying is not as healthy as hoping you aren't dying while you are.* When hopeful people are dying, and when dying people are hopeful, they buy a house on a street called Not Now, in a town called Not Yet, according to a Freedom 55 investment plan called Anywhere but Here. They become fighters, and the obligation they hold their families, friends, and caregivers to is that there be nothing but positive, upbeat, hopeful talk around them, no matter the diagnosis, prognosis, symptom buildup or failing strength, phantom capacity or fugitive alertness, until they themselves give the unequivocal signal that they have given up hope.

As long as you are hopeful, you are never in the land you hope for. If you bargain for More Time, you never live in the land of More Time. Your more time is spent bargaining or praying or hoping for More Time. No one seems to hope for what they have, and hopeful dying people rarely get the More Time they hope for, no matter how much More Time they get. This understanding was inside the questions I was asking the Filipino lady. What you want rarely looks like what you get, but it almost *never* looks that way to hopeful dying people. The questions I asked her weren't taunts, not some unbeliever trying to take a dying woman's faith down. I myself am a praying man, but on my good days, when I know what I know, I am not a hopeful man. No, these questions were one way I had of asking her to consider that her unquestioned faith needed to earn its keep, that her hope for More Time owed her something other than More Hope.

The bargain for More Time is a gamble for More Life, in oncology, in palliative care, in any foxhole. More Life is the reward of More Time, so the hope goes. But More Life at the end of your life is lived in the distinct, ample, palpable presence of your death, and the chances are very good that if you are a dominant-culture North American you have not lived your life in the presence of your own death much before your diagnosis, if at all. So your More Life is asking something of you that no one warned you about, that no one around you probably understands or has thought much about. It is asking something of you that you have not much experience with, something that will probably show you to be the inelegant amateur that you are in this the epic waning of your days. Your More Life, it turns out, includes More Death, a lot More Death than you ever imagined could be in one life. As you try to live this thing that was to be its own fine reward, you find that More Life is mostly More Death. They were quick to offer you chemotherapy or radiation for your More Life, but there aren't many offers teaching you how to have More Death.

The doctors and the psychiatrists and the counselors are not unkind in this, certainly not knowingly or purposefully. They are not people living in a place called More Life withholding something from a dying person living in a land called More Death. They don't have some secret strategy of support. No, paid therapists and physicians and volunteers and families and dying people are mostly *hopeful* people in the time of More Death, and hope has often numbed many of them to the understanding of what More Death means. Hope is contagious, and it is to me a kind of obscenity at a time like that. Hope is an anesthetic of the spirit. Many people are fearful that if they speak of dying in a clear way "at the wrong time" they will disarm dying people at the very time they are supposed to be fighting. I've seen many times that family members and health care workers secretly believe that to speak of dying is to approve of dying, that grotesque Word Voodoo that mutes most of us when dying is in the room. And so the knowledge of the thing goes AWOL, and we wait for the riptide of symptoms and diminishing energy and lucidity to dare the dying person to learn how to do it with whatever is left of their capacity and their willingness to learn.

Hope almost always makes sure that it is too late to learn how to die for dying people in a death-phobic culture. That is what it does to them. Turning away from learning how to die well in the name of being hopeful, dying people consume probably as many antidepressants and as much antianxiety medication as do late-middle-aged people who have lost whatever they once had of a feel for why they are alive. Somewhere in the Mall of Hope—and research will someday show this to be so—this culture is incubating a considerable demand for physician-assisted suicide and for terminal sedation among dying people that cannot be explained by a concomitant increase in their symptoms or pain.

How could it be otherwise, then, that dying people and the people who love them and the people paid to care for them often understand dying as nothing more than a challenge to endure, as the low-grade curse of the passing of time when the prayers and the gambles for More Time have come to pass?

More extraordinary than Elisabeth Kübler-Ross's ideas in *On Death and Dying* by far was the unqualified, mass-market embrace these ideas enjoyed soon after they were published and continue to enjoy across the dominant culture of North America and beyond. Wherever I teach there are large numbers of people who can quote "The Stages" without ever having read the book, sounding as though they are reading from the book when they do so, many of them not knowing that there is a book that these ideas come from. The ideas in *On Death and Dying* were timely, but does that account for the massive influence they now have? I don't think so. In unpublished research, Dr. Michele Chaban has argued persuasively that Kübler-Ross's ideas were derived largely from her early work with people who had escaped a nightclub fire that had killed others and who were subsequently experiencing what we would now call post-traumatic stress disorder. Kübler-Ross seems to have identified the PTSD sufferers as people who had "nearly died." People who are close to dying people are not nearly dying themselves, though, and that is one dilemma in the scheme. The patients she worked with were never dying. They were exposed to what killed other people, and were traumatized by that, surely, but it is very possible that *they were not traumatized by dying*. Kübler-Ross appears to have applied these ideas about coping with trauma to the experience of "nearly dying," and she found what to her were compelling similarities. So it seems were born the famous five stages and the discussion around them. Kübler-Ross seems to me to have counted on the fact that dying was inherently a traumatic event, that it was in the nature of dying itself that the trauma was to be found. She then seems to have generated a strategy for purposeful coping—the five stages—to manage that trauma.

But ask yourself whether dying is universally traumatizing, across all cultures and times. It is not so. It is not so even here, where it is so rampant, and I cannot credit *On Death and Dying* for these exceptions. Dying is traumatizing when it is happening in a place and time that will not make room for dying in its way of living. It is not dying that is traumatic; it is dying in a death-phobic culture that is traumatic. The continuing extraordinary popularity of some of the ideas in *On Death and Dying* are partly a result of the fact that the author's assumption of the trauma of dying has found easy recognition and acceptance among people who have lived a death-phobic life and believed likewise. This death-phobic culture recognizes the trauma unto death sold in the book in its own experience. Look carefully in the tables of contents in palliative care textbooks, read the mission statements of palliative care agencies, study the Best Practice Manuals of palliative care associations. Explicitly or otherwise, you will find that most of them accept without pause that dying is trauma. What they prescribe is management strategies for that trauma, for the physical and metaphysical consequences of that trauma. Cope, Hope, Dope: the trivializing trinity, the barstool for dying people to teeter on in a place that will not tolerate death.

So, a culture that sells hope to dying people is selling them anesthesia and management. Hope, as much as anything else and more than most, traumatizes people at the end of their lives. Hope, like any good shuck and jive artist, sells itself and its absence as the only two options in town. In our good binary oppositional style of argument and contention, many of us imagine for dying people and the people who love them only hope or hopelessness: either the faint possibility that things can be otherwise or the withering misery of being pinned by the brute fact that they will not be. In a death-phobic culture, dying is not a credible outcome: Dying is giving up, and hope is refusing to give up. In the health care system of a death-phobic culture, dying is where the health care ends because dying has no place in any understanding of health. We have strategies for not dying instead, and hope is a large part of the creed that informs those strategies. It can make you crazy, being hopeful, and when you are dying in our part of the world it often does.

One alternative is first to wonder our way out of this false choice that we are offered when we are dying. "Hope" is not life, and "hopeless" is not death and depression. Hope is very often a refusal to know what is so, and steadfastly it is a refusal to live as if the present moment is good enough and all we really have. Hopeless is the collapse of that refusal, and it looks a lot like depression. The alternative is to live your life and your dying *hope-free.* If you are willing to seriously wonder about what being hopeful has done to you, what it has obliged you to know and not know, how it has hamstrung the caregivers of dying people and their loved ones who are only allowed to know what they know when they are not with them, then being willing to be hope-free begins to look more like a subversive move toward lucidity. Living and dying hope-free: that is a revolution. The chance to die that way is what dying people deserve.

4

THE QUALITY OF LIFE

Ad men are your best friends, at least for the thirty seconds you give to them before you come to your senses. They know how it is. They've been there too. You're not alone when an ad man has you in his sights. Their embrace is familiar: It is the hug you always wanted from the friend you never really had. They can talk like you wish you could talk. Funny, clever, sage, insightful, and always with your best interest at heart; the ad man's emotional dexterity is the envy of counselors, parents, bosses, and lovers everywhere it is felt. You are the center of the universe when you are being sold. Ad men ask you to buy at retail what they would only buy wholesale; hey, they say, *somebody* has to pay retail. Once you buy, well, that's another matter, but when they're on the sell ad men make a place for you at the table of the Life You Deserve the way no one else does. It's heady stuff.

I don't know who coined the phrase "Quality of Life," but it has the greased feel of the ad man's alacrity about it. It has the power of the quick buy, instantly recognizable, utterly compelling, true. Its coyote wisdom is sleek: It unhinges any dissent in an instant, and it dares you to be a fool and disagree. Who disagrees with fresh air? Who doesn't trust feeling good, except a good Scotsman who knows he will have to pay for it later?

Who won't vote "yes" to not being lonely, except a poet who squeezes his loneliness for the ink of his lines? And who doesn't believe in Quality of Life? Quality of Life is the pitch of pitches that has your well-being as its only concern. In a land where lifestyle is lord of the manor, Quality of Life is where you go to pray. It's the stone you kiss, the pocketed coin you rub, the chant you chant, the rosary you finger, the selfless self of your self-interest, and the least on a long list of your entitlements.

Quality of Life enjoys an unchallenged seat in the small pantheon of goals that professional caregivers devote themselves to providing to dying people. Quality of Life is a known thing to dying people themselves, at least the idea of it. They know it enough to want it. The loving family members of the dying person often set themselves up as watchdogs, keeping a keen eye for any medical procedure, plan, or thought that might compromise their loved one's Quality of Life. And there is the mantra: Not quantity, but quality; add life to your time, not time to your life. Everyone I met on the job seemed to know these phrases, and many used them regularly. Quality of Life might be the only undisputed goal of care in the complex, trying, and mercurial travail of helping someone to die here in the uncertain beginnings of an uncertain century. We could go further without much exaggeration: Quality of Life is the definition of a good death in a culture that sees little or no good in it.

There is a considerable literature that has grown up around Quality of Life in the last fifteen years, in professional journals and in the popular press. There are scales and indexes to measure Quality of Life, to help patients and caregivers figure out where in the project of adding Life to Time they are. There is research contending without qualification that people of enjoying good Quality Life at the end of their lives have better outcomes, although it probably makes better sense to say that Quality of Life *is* the better outcome dying people and their caregivers are after.

Working in the homes of palliative care patients is another animal entirely from working in a hospital. In a hospital you are somewhere familiar. The place probably doesn't reflect anything of your personal style, say, but you know where you are, you know the rules of how things operate, and the patients are about the only thing that changes from week to week. Home visits, however, are often an exercise in managed mayhem. You don't know what people have been told or what they have told each other. Families can live by strange rules when times are ordinary or uneventful, and families can conjure very strange rules indeed when someone is dying at home. The truth is that, no matter how loved the dying person is, few people around them really know how to have a dying person in their midst. It isn't at all like having someone taking time off work because they are sick and hanging around the house. Family life is organized entirely around this thing that some don't believe is happening, around something that no one wants in the house. No matter how strongly they resist the dying of their loved one, families become organized around the looming end of the unwanted thing, the end itself unwanted.

In this line of work you tend to remember some patients, families, and situations more than others. It's not because you liked them more, or they liked you, not because they were clever or affable or sage or fed you well when you came to their house. Usually it's because at that time in your life you recognized something of yourself in what they were wrestling or fighting or being defeated by, just as if you'd seen it before. And sometimes you remember situations because of the sheer unlikelihood that you survived them and lived to work another day.

> The very first home visit I did in this line of work brought me to the stone steps of a formidable house in a neighborhood of formidable houses. I was nervous like I hadn't been in years as I rang the bell. I didn't actually know what I would say to whoever opened the door. Beyond the barest of rehearsed introductions, I had no banter or rap or practiced patter. I wasn't sure about what was on the other side of the door, and I wasn't sure at all what I was there to do. I was alert, but in a quietly despairing kind of way. The person who opened the

door, probably the patient's wife, stood easily six inches taller than me, and being that I was down the steps to allow the door to be opened she stood another ten inches taller still. The door didn't actually open. It was ajar a little, and she spoke to me through a screen. I looked up, way up, and introduced myself to her, and she had no response. I reminded her that I had made this appointment to meet her husband. Still no response. At the end of a string of normal, business greetings, I then asked if I could come in. She told me to wait there and closed the door. Being at a loss, I opened the file to see if there was anything in it that might help this awkward situation. There was something, and it didn't help: I had somehow missed that this very first patient I was coming to see was a doctor, and the woman who wouldn't let me in was a doctor's wife.

After a significant eternity of me not knowing what would come next, she opened the door again slowly and said, "He can see you for a few minutes. Don't upset him and don't wear him out," which I know now but didn't know then is normal family code for "Don't do anything."

If you can remember that scene in *The Wizard of Oz* where Dorothy and the gang have finally made it down the yellow brick road to the gates of Oz only to be examined and then refused and then unexpectedly granted entry by a sentry talking through a hole in the door, then you can get a feel for how these first few minutes on the job were going. I left my shoes on the mat and followed her down the darkened hall to what I now know is the appointed place that most families eventually make for what is to come, what was once a bedroom or living room but now is a dying room. She opened the door and left me there at the threshold. Inside was a small man in a large bed. His look was blank. He looked startled, as if neither he nor I had ever been in that room before, as if neither of us knew why we were there.

When people are in the last weeks of their lives it often happens that parts of them shrink. If you don't have some experience working in hospitals or clinics this can be unnerving at first. Often people don't look sick when they are dying. They look like something is coming in the night and taking small handfuls of energy and body mass and eye light from them. When you meet them for the first time you can hardly imagine how they may have looked when their lives more resembled what they had in mind for themselves. But there are two places in a dying person's body that don't seem to wither and shrink. Because everything else is ebbing, they seem instead to grow. Hands on a dying person start looking huge, like kites on the ends of thin sticks, their boney armatures pressing against the fabric of their skin, floating up above the bed when dying people point or gesture or wave good-bye to you or to your lives. And faces start looking bigger too, as the neck and shoulders melt down, so that you find enormous eyes looking out at you from the pale moon of a face surrounded by acres of pillow.

So that is what I first saw when I came into my first death room. The dying doctor motioned with one of his huge hands for me to pull up a chair. He had the kind of chairs you don't see in people's homes, chairs I recognized from my days going to an Ivy League school, all soft black enamel with gold border and the name of his alma mater in careful, antiqued script. I don't remember now much of what we talked about, but I do remember that he let me know that he was a medical doctor, that he was an oncologist dying of cancer, and that years before he had a hand in helping to organize the beginnings of a palliative care service. I remember that he ended up telling me about the simple things that he was already missing, like being able to chop wood at his cottage, and how it hurt him to lay there and remember what he couldn't do. I remember too, when I finally began to relax a bit and could look around the room a little, something that even in my rookie state struck me as strange: He had saved every name plate from every office in every clinic and hospital and university he had ever worked, and they were all in the death room with him, bronze and silver and stainless steel declarations over and over of his name and his degrees and his accomplishments and his status in the world, reiterations that he was still what he was, that he would die an oncologist, that his competence and mastery would survive what he would not survive, testimonials all to the Quality of his old Life.

Ours is a competence-addicted way of life. "If you are going to work in a factory," said the father of an old girlfriend of mine to his daughter, "be the best factory worker you can be," which made her all but disown him at the time. Many of us refuse to do things that we are not skilled at doing. "Stick to what you're good at" is the recipe we write for success in business, love, living. Learning how to do something in a competence-addicted culture is hard on the ego and mostly undertaken in private, but the something you've learned how to do is the thing for public display. The functional definition of a professional is a person who knows a lot about what he or she is doing and who is answerable for that. We might pay lip service to the idea of learning on the job, but no one wants to *be* the job that the professional is learning on. We want the fruits of their learning—their knowledge—not the process of their learning. For professional people in particular learning tends to be at war with knowing, and knowing has far more cachet at the office. Knowing is what most professional people are paid to do; learning is more a personal undertaking that is brought to the job as knowing. You can find this kind of intolerance for limit wherever you find the new religion of Quality of Life.

There seem to be a couple of recurring themes in the literature about Quality of Life that aren't often discussed. The Quality of Life scales and measures are for me reminiscent of the old IQ tests: They assume a universal relevance and unrestrained applicability, but they are much more a measure of the acculturation of the respondents and the designers of the scales.

Dying people score high in Quality of Life inventories when they are living the kind of life they have in mind for themselves. This is particularly true when they are maintaining or regaining a feeling of competence or mastery, whether in the routine physical requirements of the day or in the existential subtleties of how they understand what is happening. Alongside this expectation of mastery is the requirement of autonomy. Neither of these is unique to dying people, of course, but they are intensely sought after and clung to as basic rights and necessities by dying people and their caregivers. They are the cornerstones of a life worth living when dying is at hand, and they are used as reliable beacons when decisions are debated and made about proposed medical procedures.

Where do they come from, these hoped-for competencies at the end of a life? When was the first time that any of us enjoyed mastery and autonomy in our lives? When was the last time we were masterful and autonomous both? If we can afford to be candid in this, we could be surprised and a little dismayed to find that both questions probably have the same answer. It was not the time of your first steps alone, tipping from one uncertain foot to the other until finally you tumbled into the arms of one ecstatic parent who praised you mightily while the other fumbled to capture the moment forever on film (if you are my age) or chip (if you are younger). It was not when you went to school and were left wailing by one of those same parents who felt aged instantly as he or she walked away from your first classroom, nor was it when you were trusted to cross the street alone, nor when you could finally stay out past ten o'clock.

No, the first time you enjoyed the unequivocal supremacy of mastery and autonomy was when you were fourteen or fifteen or sixteen years old probably, when your body was as young and capable as it would ever be before the incremental ebbing of strength by age began. That was when you glimpsed the world of what could be beyond the outgrown fences of your childhood, when you knew your parents to be the flawed people they were and not the arbiters of the Way It Is, when you knew yourself to be your own uncertain plan, when you were in the full tidal sway of that great North American invention: You can be whatever you want to be.

Of course, there was nothing true about any of this. Your autonomy depended on getting some money from your parents until you had a job, and then it depended on your job. Your competence and mastery lived mostly in the eyes of whoever would grant it to you on the athletic field or in the classroom or at the Friday night party. Filled to overflowing with the feeling that finally your real life was before you, any ability you had to find it or make it or even to imagine that there was such a thing as your real life depended on a hundred things working out just right, and of course they hardly ever do, and if they do it isn't for long. You find out by heading out that way and by things not often going as you wish that life isn't your life, and that your life isn't what you intend for yourself. If you are lucky and have something like a mentor around you when you are still young, you can survive the air going out of the helium dream you had for yourself, and life will take you in tow. The cost for being tutored by life is what you insist life should be and who you insist you were born to be. That is what you pay.

And so it was then that fourteen or fifteen or sixteen was also the last likely time that you glowed with the bottomless certainty that you could finally do what you wanted and that you were utterly capable of doing it. My point in this is to say that the script for autonomy and mastery is written by adolescents, for adolescents. The end of adolescence should be the end of this script, but I worked with forty- and fifty-year-old adolescents every day whose unflinching belief in their entitlement to autonomy and mastery was matched only by their relentless striving to finally get there. This belief in autonomy and mastery is imported whole and mostly unawares by dying people into their dying time. The expectation that this illusion of autonomy and mastery be protected from the vagaries of dying is to me the principal cause of intractable suffering as people begin fingering the symptom rosary of the end of their lives. It is a sad thing that this goes witlessly on and on, but it is an understandable thing given the culturally endorsed mania for autonomy and mastery.

It is a much different thing—and a culpable thing too—when those paid to care for them actively cheerlead dying people to aspire to mastery and autonomy. A legitimate and even a necessary falsehood in teenage years, the illusion of personal autonomy and mastery can be a compound disaster in adulthood and so often is a haunting, taunting affliction in the time of dying.

The psychological secular religion called Quality of Life has an animating creed that is born in adolescence. It is a creed that is informed by the assumptions of health and intactness. The legitimate, necessary realities of dying are nowhere to be found in Quality of Life scales. Quality of Life is measured in terms of how successful you can be at resisting the diminishments that come with dying. Quality of Life sells competence as a balm for the ebbing substance of what dying people not so long ago believed themselves to be. Quality of Life is hostile in principle to the realities of a dying body and a dying heart and a dying self. Quality of Life is the principal strategy in the ubiquitous North American project of Dying, Not Dying.

> After some formal and very pleasant introductions all around, I made some remark about a large poster on the wall of the living room, a very detailed picture of the circumambulation of the Black Mosque in Mecca that is the great pilgrimage destination of devout Muslims. The Muslim patient with sharp eyes and the kindest of manners and faces was honored that I knew

a little of what the picture showed, and we both knew that it pictured something he now would not live to see himself. The mural-sized poster was as close as he would get to Mecca, but I imagined that he had by the time of our meeting prayed himself around that circuit so many times that he likely worked at it at least as much as many of the pilgrims had done.

He was surrounded in our meeting with all the women of his family, wife and daughters and sisters, all of whom you could see were devoted to his care and comfort. He understood why I was there, and he showed none of the hatred for his dying that is so much a part of what I had seen most days in the trade. I explained to him how he could decide what would be done for him after he was no longer capable of making decisions for himself. On this point he became quite adamant in wanting no significant burden for his care to fall upon his elderly wife. His plan was for an uneventful and speedy death. As we discussed the various options for pain control and medical appliances and help in the home, he announced that he wished that we would help him hasten his death when the effort to live no longer made much sense. This is a common enough request, and though there are legal challenges that patient, family, and professional caregivers have to wend their way through, this can often be done, provided that the anticipated time of death and the expressed wish for help in dying aren't separated by too much time passing—the more time between them, the more dilemmas for everyone.

He then told me that he had considered the situation mightily, and he now knew that the point at which continuing to live made no sense, the point at which the burden upon his wife and family for his care would be indefensible, is when he would not be able to make his way up the stairs to the bathroom on his own. Just as he had seen every step of his pilgrimage in his agile and passionate mind, so also had he seen someone half pushing, half pulling him up the narrow staircase, helping him into the bathroom, staying in there with him to see to it that things would go as they should, and helping him out again. He had become a North American in this, where the make or break point for Quality of Life is so often found in the bathroom.

Before anyone dismisses this as ludicrous, small-minded, or Victorian, consider: Our culture places enormous emphasis on success in toilet training in our early years. There are many cultures in the world where children have little or no experience with the trauma of the porcelain throne, but here the toilet is ubiquitous, and so for us the symbolic project that carries so much the nuance of autonomy, control, and mastery is absorbed into how we manage the vision of the void beneath us. When our last weeks are lived partly according to the dilemma of who wipes whom, the sense of regression, the loss of basic dignity, and a feeling a being utterly without competence are acute, implacable, and enduring.

The selling of Quality of Life at the end of peoples' lives is a kind of methadone approach to the dilemmas of dying. The belief that somehow we are in control of our lives as long we agree with how they are going along is the profoundest of illusions, just as is the belief that things go haywire because we are no longer controlling our lives. We are addicted to the illusion that our particular way of being a culture is the natural victory of history, to the illusion that our material sophistication lends us a psychological, even spiritual, sophistication not enjoyed by less innovative cultures, and to the idea that we do and can and must be in control of this thing we call "our life." The film was called *Whose Life Is It Anyway?*, and to me it is not a rhetorical question. Does it have to be "somebody's" life? Or can it be "life, of which my life partakes"?

This insistence on being in control of life is not the creation of any medical system or counseling organization. It is a culture-wide mandate, something medical and counseling practitioners are steeped and trained in along with the rest of us. It is really an *addiction to competence* that I am talking about, part of the inheritance from our hard-scrabble immigrant beginnings on this continent, rooted in self-reliance, mastery over the environment around us, autonomy. It is the shadow side of our *ur*-convictions about limitless possibility and our mania for "be all you can be." If an addiction to competence and control it is, then loss of control, probably traumatic in the short run, could actually signal the beginning of some kind of freedom from that addiction.

What is the goal of being good at golf? I don't play, but I imagine that the goal is to see yourself in your mind's eye making the shot you want to make, or to have some success in those businesses that do business on the golf course, or to justify somehow against reason the expense of playing the sport, or most especially to look fairly effortless when playing. But I don't think there is anyone playing golf whose goal in improving their play is to play less or to finally stop playing.

What is the goal of being good at dying, then, if there is such a thing? Most of us without thinking much about it would probably agree first that no one wants to be good at dying, being the counterintuitive absurdity it would be in a death-phobic culture. We would probably also agree that the point of being good at dying is to "die less," so that less of the time allotted to us would be claimed by dying, to the natural conclusion so prevalent among us that the best death is the one you don't see coming, the one that saves you from dying by happening to you, suddenly, without any sign or significance, like having a heart attack on the backswing at the twelfth hole of your favorite golf course. Our goal in being good at dying is to die as little as possible or not at all, and the second best way of doing that, the only possibility open to people living the last weeks and months of a terminal illness, is to remain in or reclaim control of life, no matter the conflicting evidence or symptom accumulation. The best way not to die in a death-phobic culture is to buy and sell Quality of Life. Quality of Life is what you have in spite of the fact that you are dying. It is the part of your life least affected by the physical, emotional, and spiritual truth of dying. It is the part of your life that is the least reliable teller of the story of what your life is coming to. This mad insistence on competence and Quality of Life instead of Quality of Death is the principal reason you need experts to tell you that you are dying. It is why, in the ending part of our lives, we so often have no idea where in our lives we are.

> Several score of times over the years I have been approached by someone with an addiction who had heard in error that I was particularly good with addiction, asking me to help them, for example, quit drinking. After twenty or so minutes of getting an idea of the history of their alcoholism, I usually propose the following:
> "I will try with you to help you quit this drinking. There are a few things you'll have to do to help get us started, and the first is that you'll stop drinking today. Then I'm going to ask you to..."
> At this point the person has a pained or frustrated or incredulous look, and I don't usually get any further down the list of what needs doing. The person usually says, "I don't think you understand my problem. I'm trying to stop drinking and..." Here I would interrupt the person and say, "Oh yes. I understood you well. You want to stop drinking. So we'll begin with that today, so we can get to the other things that need doing."
> They would typically become more frustrated and say something like, "Look, if it were that easy I wouldn't need you, would I? How can you just tell me to stop?"

And here I would say to them, "But *you* said that you wanted to stop. I didn't say I wanted you to stop."

They agree that this is what they want, but they remind me again that it is too hard just to stop. And I agree with them, and this goes back and forth for a while, and eventually I'll have to say this: "Okay. I get it now. You've figured it out because you have more experience in this than I do. You figured out that you'll keep drinking while you stop drinking. That's the part of the solution I didn't get."

I acknowledge that there are compelling biochemical aspects of addiction, but this story gives you an idea of what insisting on being in control of your life while it is ending sounds like to me. In one of Leonard Cohen's songs, "That Don't Make It Junk," he laments, or maybe brags, "I fought against the bottle, but I had to do it drunk." Quality of Life, as I said, is a methadone approach to the dilemmas of dying in a death-phobic, competence-addicted culture. Quality of Life *is* competence addiction. It is a competence junkie's solution for the addiction to competence, a gesture of impotence tarted up as an accomplishment. Quality of Life sells you control and mastery and competence in the face of something so singular, so personal, and so incontrovertible as Your Own Death because Your Own Death is the largest and latest and last incarnation of what beggars your insistence on control and mastery and competence. Cancer care agencies use the language of warfare and fighting and winning and surviving, because this idea of winning gains a tin credibility for the unchallenged project of being a master in the house of your own life. "Let's make cancer history," they say. What are we supposed to die of, then? Old age only? How old is old enough to die? When are we supposed to die? *Are* we supposed to die? If the raft of your dignity is bound together by the frayed rope of things going as you believe they should, what of this kind of dignity is there left to conserve as the raft of your life plans begins to take on water?

As long as what they call "end of life care" is driven by what we can *do*, we aren't likely to get a good look at the limits of what we can do. This is largely because in principle what we can do, technologically speaking, barely has limits. The limits are imposed by what the body or the person will tolerate, by the cost-benefit analysis of side effects to the desired outcome, by what the family can afford by way of treatment, and not by what we can do in pursuit of that outcome. "What we can do" usually means "what we can do to avert or postpone dying." It almost never means "what we can do to get you to die when it is finally time to die," at least not explicitly. So it is a handmaiden to the expectation and the demand to live. Most palliative measures are decided upon based on how they contribute to Quality of Life. As long as our shared understanding of Quality of Life is driven by unmodified demands for competence and mastery, and as long as our shared understanding of what dying does to us is a pageant of diminishment, dependency, and loss of dignity, then our work at the end of a person's life will continue to be trying to forestall the end of that life.

That is what Quality of Life initiatives, in principle, serve. They don't serve dying. They don't serve the dying part of dying people. The culturally endorsed, culturally enforced addiction to competence is an enormous challenge for workers in the helping professions, and one way of responding to it could be that we regularly ask ourselves whether it is our job to support that endorsement, or to be neutral to it, or is it to challenge it? I know that the prospect of mounting a project of cultural redemption while trying to respond well to the incremental suffering of dying people and their families might seem beyond reach, or inappropriate to what the situation calls for. The only response to that doubt that could have similar gravity might be that we regularly ask ourselves: How is it for the person dying in my care to be dying in a time and place that teaches them mostly how not to die? What can I do, day in and day out, about *that?*

The truth is that "loss of control," the prime obstacle to enjoying Quality of Life, doesn't begin with the appearance of mysterious and troubling symptoms, nor with all the diagnostic testing that tends often to feed the fears of the patient, nor with the Bad News disclosure, nor with the arsenal of palliative measures used and waiting on the shelf. This "feeling in control of your life" is largely a sham. The opposite feeling is a sham as well. We *can* know that life, even our lives, those smaller versions of life, were never really subject to our control, rarely obeyed our demands on them or for them, mysteriously mostly circumvented our best guess of how they should go. The time of our dying is the time for being able to recognize, maybe for the first time, that what was once supposed to be our self-directed life turned into something else. All the things that were bigger than us, and our great wrestling match with them, *became* our lives. We never did control that. If anything, when circumstance and some feeling of security allowed or when desperateness demanded, we tried to keep up with this thing called our life, and on very good days we tried to live as if this were true, as if our lives were life making room for itself in the world. The news of our dying can be the time when we finally shuck off that binding illusion that we were supposed to be driving the bus of our lives because we thought we knew how the thing worked. Before then our lives give us plenty of practice at being good at not being in control. That is a skill worth learning, and worth teaching our kids.

5

YES, BUT NOT LIKE THIS:

Euthanasia and Suicide

It might be true that it is harder to die now than in other times. In the early years of this surely uncertain twenty-first century, after the ages of Enlightenments and Reasons and Holocausts, in the time of Information and Distraction and Epic Forgetting, here in the land of Skilled and Eternal Refugees, in the land of Comfort, where the only ancestry you need to claim is the ancestry that becomes you, it is probably harder by far to die than it has ever been. Here and now, where the business of dying is the Business of Not Dying, where history is written by the victors and the victors are Survivors, where only their stories are told by people who want only winners for inspiration when their time comes, dying is probably harder than it has ever been.

We have bargained for forty years for painless dying, we have spent and are still spending billions on the bargain, and we have something pretty close: pain-managed dying. We have bargained for forty years for good management of the symptoms of our dying, and most of us will die stilled, no need for restraint or murmurs of reassurance. The old nightmares of wild pain and rampaging symptoms are mostly that now: nightmares. And legions of people—not everyone, for there would be a revolution if it were everyone, but enough people—are dying in an unrecognized, low-level, grinding kind of terror that whispers to them when there's no one around, "How's it working for you so far, this almost painless, managed dying? Any questions?"

Nowhere is it written that by virtue of giving birth to someone or raising someone to adulthood or marrying someone or loving someone or having forty years together with someone that anyone knows, or can know, how to care for that dying someone. Nowhere is it written that because you are good at a hundred things and have success and are honestly and justly admired and have grown to a certain full age and have been with that body all those years and seen your share of hard times and then some that you know how to die your own rightful death when the time comes. We don't see much dying, most of us, and some of us see no human dying at all before we die. So the current regime, at least to me, is no surprise.

We aren't taught dying in school. If you think that sex education in schools was an uphill battle, try getting death education into the curriculum. I have, and it should be in the dictionary entry defining "futile." Kids are taught the life cycle, but it's usually the life cycle of frogs. They aren't often taught that it includes death, and they're rarely taught that it includes them. We have no mentors for dying, no National Living Treasures skilled in the traditional arts of dying well. Instead, we have legions of accomplices in the project of not dying, and others in the project of hiding it away. We have just about no tradition of dying well. If you are not born with the instinct for dying well, you have to learn it. I wish you every success in finding someone who is good at it and is willing to teach you. You have to *learn* how to die, or you probably will not die wisely or well.

For those who are relying on instinct as their guide, please consider the possibility that our instincts are now so domesticated, so stupefied by our insistence on being safe and comfortable, so rarely drawn upon and so psychologized that they are more mediated reflex than instinct. No, the sad truth is that there is precious little in the way we live that is useful to us in learning how to die. We come to the time of our dying the way many tourists come to a casino in the Bahamas: thinking that the game is the same everywhere, counting on what we learned about it on the weekends in college, a sweet drink in our hand to steady us, we swagger up to the $1000 table and put down our $5 bet and hold our breath, rank amateurs who believe in the rules and damn the house when we lose.

Now, there is a considerable push afoot these days to bring the debate about assisted suicide into the center ring of health care, medical ethics, law reform, and palliative medicine, which is proper. There are a few jurisdictions in Europe and North America where some form of physician-assisted death is legalized, endorsed, and available. Each of them has their champions and their adversaries. There is a growing body of research looking at the outcomes of chosen and managed dying, and about how the vetting process deals with depression. There are a few famous cases where languishing people have taken matters into their own hands, and there are many more people who have quietly, prematurely died with help. To use the odd language of the suicide prevention business, their suicides have been successful.

The rancorous public debate about physician-assisted suicide for terminally ill people usually centers on the rights of the dying person, mainly on their right to choose when they will die and how. Sooner or later everyone working in the death trade will have to find a way to respond to the dull-eyed, sedated, utterly desperate and strange, neutrally voiced accusation that people who've been asked to die for far too long will make: You wouldn't treat a dog this way. And they are right. We don't. We reserve that kind of treatment only for our own.

For workers in the death trade, the debate about physician-assisted suicide tends to focus a little less on the rights of dying people and a little more on what the exercise of those rights means for those workers. For many, the quandary dying people find themselves in—the prolongation of their dying that comes not from the application of heroic measures but from the treatment process—is frankly not as compelling as the requests dying people make of those workers: They might have a right to die "before their time," but do they have a right to ask *me* to help them do it? The request, you see, changes everything. When a dying person asks you to help them die sooner, you have to have an answer. I have never heard of a palliative care program obliging its employees as a matter of training and practice to know how it is to die. But most every program tunes its employees up on the fine points of the law regarding assisted suicide. Death trade workers *have* to have a position on that, and with the institution's lawyer and medical ethicist close by, they generally do.

The people who object publically to assisted suicide do so very strongly. They are certain that Pandora invented euthanasia and they imagine a time of state-sanctioned premature dying in which legions of people having bad days or bad lives line up for the service. They fear that euthanasia is contagious. They imagine families who have been consigned to the long-term care business by successful medical interventions that left their loved ones alive but inert seizing upon euthanasia as a legitimate solution to their moral or financial quandaries. If these nightmare scenarios are fair and accurate, if there are huge numbers of people who will be herded to the cliff edge by the legalization of euthanasia, if the possibility of dying before "your time" becomes as common and as culturally endorsed as is the real likelihood of dying after your time has arrived, this culture has a far deeper problem with life than the torments over euthanasia display.

Years ago a national magazine sent a journalist to make a small article about the kind of work I do. Someday I will learn that spending hours with a journalist going through the fine points of what you are trying to accomplish doesn't buy you one more lucid clarification than you would've probably otherwise achieved in what the magazine says about you. He was very impressed with one thing I said, though, and the phrase I used became the title of the article. He called me "The Angel of Death." Palliative care workers are a lot like journalists, and sometimes both of them are a lot like prophets: Most of the time they report the news. They rarely make the news. When they are making the news, something is awry.

In this case the journalist seemed to think that I brought death with me when I visited dying people, and so the title meant to him "The Maker of Death." But I was and am a faithful witness to the demands dying makes on all of us, and so I called myself "The Angel of Death." My boss at the time stopped me in the hallway days after the article was published and was very positive and admiring about the accomplishment of "getting the palliative care message out in a national publication."

"But," he said, "Hell of a shame about the title."
"Oh, I don't mind it. It's true enough," I said.
He said, "You didn't say that to him, did you?"
"I did, yes," I said.
"You didn't tell a reporter from a national magazine that you were the Angel of Death, did you?" he asked.
"Sure I did," I told him. "You don't think he came up with that on his own, do you? I told him that, for people who don't want to die and for people waiting for a sign, that's what I am."
"You can't go around saying that," he said. "You can't tell people you're the Angel of Death. It conjures up all kinds of things we don't want to be associated with." I assured him that not everyone thinks of Mengele pointing to the left or right when they hear "Angel of Death," but in fairness to him it is a phrase that doesn't burst with good feelings for most people in our part of the world.

A few weeks later my office phone rang. The weary voice asked for me. She'd been given my name by the friend of a friend who'd read a magazine article in which I was called the Angel of Death, so she thought it was worth a phone call. She was calling about her daughter, or for her, or on her behalf, she couldn't decide. Her daughter had agreed to her calling me. "What about your daughter?" I asked her.

Her daughter had been diagnosed with a progressive degenerative neurological disease. These kinds of illnesses are all the devastation a life should be asked to bear, and more. If there were diseases crafted in hell, they would be those diseases. It devastates the central nervous system so thoroughly, while leaving consciousness and awareness pristinely intact, that a person can watch themselves progress toward paralysis and probable suffocation with precision and utter intellectual clarity, without doubt or uncertainty. If you know anything about these kinds of diseases—and by the end of this story you will—then they probably figure largely in your vision of your own personal, medical, existential hell.

But she wasn't calling because of the diagnosis. She was calling because of the letter. Her daughter had written her a letter, and she asked if she could read it to me. "Before you do, tell me what you think I should know about her," I told the mother.

Well, she was still a young woman, and she'd been living in the family home for a few years now since the disease had made it first too hard and then impossible for her to take care of herself, as it always does. The family was badly rattled when they first got the news, but in short order they had adjusted pretty well and had a feeling of being able to live a kind of normal life together. After learning what she could about the disease, the young woman employed the kind of technical savvy many of her peers have to develop computer programs to help people who'd lost the ability to speak communicate with those around them. She had performed a public service of huge benefit to hundreds or thousands, likely because she treasured the capacity to communicate perhaps above all else and because she'd glimpsed the real possibility of someday not being able to do so herself.

"How long has your daughter been living with this disease?" I asked.

"More than ten years," her mother said. That was an odd, portentous response. Now I knew something beyond what this young woman's mother was telling me. Depending on a host of variables including general state of health, age of onset, and stage of the disease at the time of diagnosis, patients with this kind of disease will typically have a two to five year life expectancy after diagnosis. Her daughter had more than doubled that, which told me that somewhere this family had probably crossed the treatment Rubicon and they had opted for a surgical procedure that kept her alive beyond the norm, maybe beyond more than that.

The letter said that because of the disease's progress the young woman was no longer capable of taking her own life. She had no way of acting on her clearly articulated desire to be finished and done with it. For that she needed the agreement and cooperation of someone else. Assisted living, assisted dying: Probably by the time we were to meet there was no longer any difference between the two for her. She was in hell, no doubt, but not the hell most of us would imagine. Her hell wasn't the loss of autonomy or dignity or control or some kind of dream for her future, though all of those had been truly lost. Her hell was that she continued to have her own considerable intellectual competence. She knew what had happened to her, what had been done to her life in the name of saving it. She knew what it meant. She had put the pieces together, and she knew what she was in for.

The whole course of this disease was an example of how capable she and her family were at problem solving. Now what had worked best for them no longer mattered. The old problem was how to live with what the disease was doing to her. The new problem was how to live with what the surgery had done to her, which was to oblige her to live anyway. The new problem was the sheer passage of time itself. Her hell was the passage of time. Somewhere inside her inert, bound, technology-assisted self, the young woman knew that, better than I did, better than any of us did. It was from that somewhere that she wrote the letter to her mother.

When I met her, that young woman with degenerative neurological disease asked me, using her communication technology, how she could die. That is what she most wanted from me, to find out how she could die. Every answer I could give her ended with the fact that someone had to agree to help her. This was her antidote to the antidote of not knowing. Her health was stable. She lived a particular kind of hell that might be a unique creation of our own time: She couldn't live, and she couldn't die.

When these things are debated in professional circles, it will often come down to something like this: *Is terminal sedation now an acceptable response to profound mental anguish at the end of life?* For anyone who treasures the guidance of the law in these matters, it is a simple answer to an unruly question: However acceptable it may be, I cannot do it to or for someone. For activists in the patient rights or disabled peoples' rights fields, the indignant answer is that no one has the right to judge the worth of another's Quality of Life, let alone to act to end it with the assessment that their Quality of Life isn't tenable. For other activists in the right-to-death business, the answer is just as simple: People unable to act on their desire to die should be helped to do so, as is their basic right as a human being. For the rest of us, though, this won't be simple. It won't be clear. It won't be a solution of one justice trumping the other justices. For the rest of us, we won't be able to tell where "opinion" parts from "right" parts from "human" parts from "monstrosity." The rest of us will have to wrestle the Angel of Death on this one, with the growing realization that our general faith in the health care system and the culture that underwrites it will from time to time deliver people—people we know—to this particular hell, a hell that we'll have to decide upon.

To have an opinion is a right, I guess, in our part of the world, and a sign of democracy to many of us. But to carry the burden of knowing how possible and how impossible your opinion is to act upon, and to bear the consequences of your opinion, those intended and those not, that is the work of a human being. In these matters at least we might think for a moment whether an opinion isn't more of a privilege. In these matters at least we should earn our right to an opinion, and we can do so by wrestling and then in a noble way by acknowledging our defeat at the hands of the contending angels of this terminal sedation dilemma.

You could begin with this simple consideration: The debate on terminal sedation, or physician-assisted death, usually ties "end of life" to "acceptable." People uninformed about the plights of terminally ill people are inclined to say, "Well, suicide is suicide," and not be much persuaded by *when* in the course of a person's life the prospect of suicide is contemplated. People making a case for terminal sedation bind the prospect of helping someone end their life to the fair certainty that this person is at the end of his or her life anyway. The unspoken other half of this position is the view that mental anguish only qualifies for terminal sedation when the end of life is at hand.

For the purposes of intervening to end life, it is the *closeness to death* that *legitimizes suffering*. Ending life is only a credible option when the currency of suffering is guaranteed or underwritten by the proximity of dying. Terminal sedation is the Trojan horse of palliative care, and what it carries in its hollow belly is the culturally endorsed prejudice that proximity to death legitimizes or corroborates suffering because it *increases* suffering. I'll put it differently: The culture that spawned, educated, trained, subsidized, and employs us now binds us to the belief that knowing that *you will die* is as obvious and unworthy as another day at the office, but that knowing that *you are dying* is itself a death-dealing, suffering-engendering monstrosity that any and all have the right to withdraw from. When people defend the right of the patient not to know that he or she is dying, and when people defend the right of parents to forbid their dying child to know that he or she is dying, they are without saying so buying in bulk the conviction that there is no merit, no benefit, no necessity, no moral obligation to know that you are dying, because there is no good in it. There is only more suffering in it. Terminal sedation's acceptability at the end of life is acceptable to its advocates not because people are dying anyway, but because dying, the unkillable killer that everyone gets and no one deserves, is already too hard.

Our way of dying and of not dying—that is what should be under scrutiny in the terminal sedation debate. When we get in line, money in hand, for the weekend seminar called "Learn How to Demand to Live," we have already voted "no" to dying. But in the context of the health care systems of North America, most people with a terminal disease have been living in the shadow of their dying for some time. A death-phobic culture sells More Time to its dying citizens—and not only to them—as an antidote, or a balm at least, to dying. It is a strange twist on the homeopathic ideal, and more so it is an iatrogenic nightmare that dying people cannot be awakened from. Death phobia *sells* bad dying. Death phobia is the child of bad death, and bad death the child of death phobia, and so on, round and round. So terminal sedation is defended in a death-phobic culture as a legitimate answer to the suffering the culture claims is so integral to dying.

The hope of most people I've met on the job is for a long life, and many a vitamin, vacation, and vascular rehabilitation is taken in the name of getting it. When the time comes, most of those same people seem to hope for a quiet death, a dignified death, a painless death, a peaceful death. The dilemma for them and for me is that, being the children of a death-phobic culture, a quiet, dignified, painless, peaceful death is mostly a fantasy for us, because the business of dying itself is a torment, an affliction, a victimization, and a venal injustice. Do Not Resuscitate (DNR) orders, advanced directives, and the rest are designed to wrestle good dying from the hyperactive hands of the emergency response brigade, but those solutions don't believe either that there is good dying, only that there are gradations of bad dying, beginning with the unconscious to the barely tolerable and worsening from there.

If you begin by believing that dying is traumatic, the wheel of sedative salvation is *already* in motion. If you believe that knowing that you are dying, and not the symptoms or the pain, is the real beginning of your suffering, then your real solution is to limit how much you know about how much you are dying. It is not hard to see that when all that can be said about it has been said, terminal sedation is a problem-solving device. But this is less clear: What is the problem that the prospect of terminal sedation is designed to solve? This will take a few lines to answer.

Opponents claim it causes people to die before their time. It kills them, in other words. So here is another dilemma: Once you have had the full benefit of the life extension/death extension scheme visited upon you, when *is* your time to die? The architects of law and ethical imperative in terminal sedation focus heavily on the idea of "hastening death." "Hastening" compared to what, though? Compared to when the dying person would have died had they not been sedated? Compared to when the dying person would have died had they not taken the palliative chemotherapy they were offered?

I have worked with many patients and families with strong religious conviction. Most of them have been thrown into the arena of More Time/More Dying without having been told and without realizing that this is where they are. Many of these families have had to hear their loved one plead for the dying to be over, and some have heard their loved ones plead for their help in ending it. Fenced in and obligated to hang around by hydration, ventilation, and nasal or gastral tube feeding, their loved ones are trying to find a way out of here. One obvious solution is to discontinue most or all of the comfort-giving measures that play a role, however minor, in sustaining their lives. This is what it has come to for many families now: No longer is it a matter of what to do to someone who is dying, but increasingly it is a matter of what not to do to them, and even more acutely, of *what to stop doing to them.* Many families are now being asked to unplug the machine giving nourishment or breath to someone they love in the name of loving them. This is the same machine whose use they were asked to consent to some time before that moment, in the name of loving them.

Some of these religious families defend themselves and their decisions with the belief that God will take their loved one in God's own time, when it is the patient's time to die, and that their job is to keep their loved one alive until that time comes. The harsh truth of the thing is that we have the technical capacity to so alter the course of a person's dying that there is no longer any way of being able to say with certainty or a clear conscience when *is* a dying person's time to die. God's will is at most a variable now, one of several, and God's will is mostly indistinguishable from the will of the family and the health care system in general. I'm not saying that they are the same thing. I am saying that our interventions are so extreme that we cannot find where one ends and the other begins. This is what it looks like.

> When I heard the doctor's voice on the recorded message I knew that he knew that he was in deep, maybe too deep. He was asking for help for his young lung cancer patient and the man's wife, and for himself too. Earlier in the day on a home visit, the patient, who was jaundiced, oxygen starved, and emotionally spent, had waited until his wife was out of the room and out of earshot and then asked that his oxygen and IV be discontinued. The doctor suggested that they have the man's wife in the room for this discussion but the patient refused.
>
> "Why not?" the doctor asked.
>
> "She doesn't know," the man replied. The doctor said, "Well, that's why we should have her in here, so she can understand how you feel about this."
>
> The man replied, "No. She won't agree. I want you to do this without telling her."
>
> It was an insoluble bind: The patient was compos mentis, as they say, clear in his thought and wish, his judgment not seeming to be impaired, and he was sure of his wife's refusal to comply with his wishes. It turned out his judgment was accurate on this point. He was

instructing his physician regarding his treatment, but he was excluding his appointed power of attorney, his wife, from knowing about these instructions. She would quickly recognize this change in the care plan. My assignment was to meet with his wife in order to bring her around to understanding and going along with her husband's wishes here at the end of his life.

The young wife was very willing to meet with me, which I didn't expect. She had a traditional regard for professional people in positions of responsibility and authority, and that's who I was to her. She made room for us to sit amid the clutter of a three-room walk-up apartment. The place was punishingly humid, the air conditioner's broken thermostat circulating instead of cooling the July afternoon heat, and her husband had been asleep for several hours after taking morphine. The couple had recently immigrated from Europe. They had a seven-month-old son. I asked what she knew about her husband's health. She knew that he was seriously ill. I asked whether she had some feeling for how much longer that illness would continue. She had no idea. I asked if she knew how her husband felt about how things were going. She was quite sure that he was exhausted and had had enough of it. I asked her how we together should respond to his exhaustion. She said that she and the doctor had the same job, to keep him alive as long as possible, by any way they could. God would take him if that was God's will, and as long as he was alive, then *that* was God's will.

In most work in the death trade there come times of great delicacy, subtlety, and torment. This is where the biomedical realities of a dying person's body engage the human striving for survival. It is where those who are supposed to know useful things might serve those who are supposed to hope for hopeful things, so that hope might give way to understanding and a good death can ensue. More often it is a time of covert conflict, pseudo partnership, half-spoken knowledge, and deferral to what people seem to want to hear, with the result being a muted, collapsed "long and courageous battle."

In the death trade any discussion about God's will is a torment waiting to unfurl. Leave aside whether there is such a thing as God, or whether God has some purpose for humans, or whether that purpose is discernable in the normal mayhem of human affairs, and you are left with this other, equally hard to manage dilemma: Palliative medicine routinely interferes with the natural course of disease, and in so doing it generates an often predictable series of secondary consequences or side effects. The subsequent need for drugs produces other side effects and the need for more drugs, and so on to the end. This means that palliative medicine is generally the practice of managing the consequences of palliative medicine while trying to keep an eye on the often volatile disease by reading the tea leaves of symptoms—an extraordinarily demanding job. It also means that the way a person dies in palliative care, the arc of their dying, doesn't bear much resemblance to what that arc might have been had there been little or no curative or palliative care afforded them. So, unless we are certain that palliative care itself is God's will, then our ability to discern God's will in the boil of drugs and treatments and symptoms during our dying time is up for grabs.

In the case of that young soon-to-be widow, I had few choices: Agree with her without any evidence to the contrary that her husband will die when God wants him to, regardless of what we do, or prevail on her to question her faith at a time when she is certain it is most true. I did something else, though. I asked her to remember that the respirator and the IV and the morphine and all the rest were there not so much as a result of God's will but of our will, and of her will and her husband's will (a will that had now changed), and of our cleverness with the technology, and that maybe her husband wanting it all to be over was the result of our will too having its way up until now. If any of that stood a chance of being true, then it was probably our job now to keep our eye on the consequences of what we had done so far and try to fine-tune our will so that it served what we knew to be happening. Her husband was trying to die now in spite of, maybe because of, what we had done and were doing for him. What we probably shouldn't be doing, I asked her to consider, was turning away from the results of us having done all we could do when it finally got so difficult, so unclear.

In practice terminal sedation is invoked to solve the problem of family impotence in the face of the intractable suffering of a dying loved one and caregiver impotence in the face of escalating pain when the Quality of Life scores are low and time continues to pass. It is invoked to solve the problem of dying in a death-phobic culture by limiting what dying asks of the dying person. *It is the death-phobic culture's solution to itself for dying people,* meaning that it leaves unchallenged those things driving dying people to suicide while claiming to solve the problems that arise from extended dying. Terminal sedation and profound mental anguish at the end of life are both symptoms of a culture addicted to competence and comfort, a culture unable to make room in its way of doing things for what it doesn't get to vote on. And profound mental anguish is often the consequence of the successful acquisition of More Time, the outcome no one thought of. They both speak of a poverty of real options available to dying people, to their loving families, and to the capable and compassionate people paid and trained to care for them, all of whom were once awash in a sea of treatment choices.

"Profound mental anguish at the end of life" is prose for "heartbrokenness," you see. Dying people, most of them in my experience, are heartbroken people who don't know any longer, if they ever knew, how to be heartbroken. Their hearts were broken by the news of their disease and by how their citizenship in the Land of the Living slipped a little at a time without them having a vote on whether or how that would happen. Their hearts were broken by the treatment options offered to them and by the outcomes of those treatments. They were broken by the confusion, turmoil, and quiet distance-making that befell their families, and they were broken by their own lives having come this. The answer a death-phobic culture has to the heartbrokenness of dying people is *less heart, less brokenness.* That is what sedation and antidepressants are designed for, to compromise dying people's capacity to suffer. This compromise is their great victory, to ratchet down suffering by compromising someone's capacity to suffer.

There *is* such a thing as knowing how to be heartbroken. You cannot treat heartbrokenness or suffering, nor can you manage them nor contain them nor make them less of what they are or must be. You make a place for them, just as you make a place for the things in life that you bargain for and benefit from and approve of. "Making a place for them" means inviting human sorrow to the table as you would any guest unexpectedly appearing at your door at mealtime. These are the rudiments of deep courtesy, and courtesy in the face of suffering *is* the broken heart capably broken. This courtesy, alas, is often the first casualty of uncertainty or torment or strident opinion in a time like ours. Dying people are heartbroken because they are dying, surely, but much more so because they are *our* dying people, dying among us in a place that doesn't believe in what is happening to them, in a place that doesn't know what to do in the wake of what it has done, in a place bereft of the deep courtesy of the heart in times of trouble.

Euthanasia is not sanity in the face of madness. It is our particular madness's prescription for sanity. The practice of euthanasia solves the problem of a particular dying person's refusal or inability to go on, but it leaves intact what brought that person to that impasse, ensuring that others will follow. Opposing euthanasia legally and politically does the same thing. The wisdom we seek by advocating for euthanasia is found instead in learning about suffering. In our time that means learning the inconvenient and deeply sorrowful sort of indebtedness that our way of life has incurred. Wisdom will come from learning the cost of all our entitlements, all the rights we have exercised at such considerable cost to the world around us and to our mutual life. It will come from learning what our kind of privacy and individualism has done to our ability to practice any ceremonies, rituals, or shared understandings of the mysteries of life not utterly purloined from indigenous traditions not yet riven by our poverty on this matter. It will come from learning what those mysteries—including the mysteries of being born and dying—ask of us. We have pursued self-determination at the expense of a mythically mature and binding mutual life, a village mindedness that could guide us in times of such uncharted and radical sorrow. The sudden recourse many dying people and their loved ones have to "supposed to" or "natural" in such times is really them reaching for that phantom limb of a mutual life that has heretofore been so seldom nourished, learned, and exercised. The insistence on the right of euthanasia, strangely, is the vestige of a rarely practiced longing to be gathered into a shared understanding of why we are born, what our life means, why we die as we do. The right to control our own death, tragically, is all that our Religion of Self has left us. Untutored by these considerations, the demand for euthanasia will remain a grim exercise in self-mastery, leaving us, in a phrase of Leonard Cohen's relentless candor in matters of the heart ("Alexandra Leaving"), in full command of every plan we wrecked.

It is in the order of human life that we can learn to die well, but the tuition in our time is dear. A good death is not wrested from the madness of our days by being killed by overdose. The madness moves on to the next house, the next generation. It is purchased instead by very costly learning about what we have made of dying. But this learning must begin well before the crucible of intractable suffering is forged. Wisdom of this order comes from learning grief and from practicing grief. We have lived as needy people for many decades. Our hearts are comfort-seeking missiles, a child's claim upon the world. The language of rights comes from there. Needy or not, the time is upon us to learn the wisdom of being needed people. To do so we will have to learn the eloquence and the human scaled genius of grief, something the latter half of this book approaches. "I can't go on" and "I'll go on" are both true. They don't cancel each other out. Grief is articulate on this matter: Living doesn't always require the ability to live, or the willingness to, and dying isn't the collapse of that ability or that willingness.

6

THE WORK

The palliative care business has in some ways been good to me. I have had the uncommon opportunity to sit in the middle of other peoples' lives and see many of the truest things well before it is my turn to see them in my own experience. I have sat with thousands of the world's truly courageous, outrageous, riven, loving, and grief-addled people, and my job has been to find how they came to be that way. I've wrestled the angel of how to die with people who don't know and don't want to know how to die, and with people who seemed to have been born already knowing. I have sometimes been thanked for it, when the wrestling was mostly over, and I have worked in the business long enough to realize that the privilege of being with people who are dying is almost always its own reward.

The work has taken me many times across North America and beyond as a teacher and practitioner, and I've had the chance to find out what might be unique and what might be common among people who are dying and among those trying to help them die. There are two truisms that I have heard trotted out thousands and thousands of times, spoken as if they are older than dirt and more enduring, truer, and more beyond question than you might imagine. One is that everyone knows they are going to die. This one we looked at earlier. The other is that everyone has his or her own way of dying. This is the one we'll consider now. The singular, standalone, sacrosanct uniqueness of the individual is the banner around which almost all palliative care workers gather in solidarity. It is the organizing principle of all the religious and psychological aspects of palliative care counseling. The uniqueness of the individual is compelling, binding, righteously defended, and vigorously reiterated whenever questioned. It is often enshrined in the mission statements and mandates of all the helping organizations you have heard of or worked for or been helped by, and it is mostly untrue and a useless, bungled, hamstrung idea.

Probably a third of all the palliative care organizations inviting me to speak with them ask me to focus on how their employees might survive doing the work. The request is never explicitly for a survival strategy, of course. They ask for suggestions on how to do the work in a sustainable way, for example, or for guidance on how to achieve and program what is now called "care for the caregiver." But if you listen carefully with your ear attuned particularly to what is not said, you can hear clearly the plea for some kind of hint on how to keep on going despite—not because of—what the work is doing to the people doing the work.

Palliative care workers and their bosses take their instruction about the consequences of doing the work not from their professional affiliations or their employee assistance counselors, but from dying people. This is where most death trade workers learn what they learn about dying: from the travail of dying people and their families. Workers and patients alike take their cues not from guided meditation or from wizened elders long initiated in the ebbing of life but from a dreadful culturally driven understanding of what dying is and means, and what it does to people, and what should be done about it. Dominant-culture North America endorses the grinding apprehension that dying is mostly suffering, loss, and torment, and that compassionate people should do whatever they can to manage, minimize, and mollify the afflictions that dying visits upon The Dying. A number of people working in palliative care speak of dying as "a time of discovery," or "the fulfillment of a person's life," or "a transition, not an end." Very few in my experience are willing to ask a dying person to be fulfilled by their dying, or to thrive in their dying, or to be good at it, or to just transition already.

Instead they sign on for the endurance test that is dying in our time, in their hearts knowing that they will be asked regularly in the course of their working lives to say things and do things to dying people that are rife with futility or the vapor of hope, things they cannot in their off hours believe in. And so those doing the work either hold on for dear life from vacation to "mental health day" to professional development seminar, or roll on autopilot without wondering much what the job is and ought to be. Dying is mostly a test of ebbing endurance for palliative patients in dominant-culture North America, and many people working with dying people endure the work in a similar fashion. Where most of us live, *not dying* is the job of the dying person and surviving this prolonged not dying is the job of the death trade worker.

So there is probably a serious dearth of creativity, individuality, and uniqueness among dying people when it comes to dying and among death trade workers when it comes to working with dying people. Most people, if the truth can be borne, die in a manner akin to the dying they have seen before their own, according to how they lived with those examples. They will die either in the centripetal sway of the deaths they've heard of or been witness to, which are often some form of "bad," or they will die in some kind of headlong flight away from those examples toward a more personalized nightmare. The exceptions to this dark proposition, in my experience, are few. This statement will continue to offend and inflame North Americans, and I don't know how it could not do so. There might be such a thing as a personal style among some dying people, of course, but I don't think that is what is usually meant by the declaration that "everyone is an individual." It means that each person is a snowflake. It means that each life is a singular, never to be repeated thing, entirely precious, whose uniqueness is God given and God intended, and that each death is as standalone, as properly unparalleled in the history of human kind, as a snowflake. I don't think they mean that it is as perishable, and as cold.

In my years in this business I have seen almost no examples of this snowflake idea. I have heard about it thousands of times, and I've heard it defended constantly and assumed almost universally, but I've almost never seen it in the trenches. Recently I was teaching at a large regional palliative care conference, and I was strongly advocating the idea that a good death needs describing and defending and pursuing. At the end of the lecture a woman came to the front of the hall and smiled a half smile and came a little closer and then demanded that I tell her who should be the one defining what a good death is. This is the crux for so many advocates, this frail adamancy that no one has a right to, as it is often said, "push" their ideas on anyone else. It is maybe the lone survivor of that shipwrecked European fantasy that people who came to the New World came to exercise their freedom of choice in how they proposed to live.

"Well," I responded to her, "I just took an hour or two to give you a pretty thorough idea of what I think a good death is. So, I'll be one person who defines what a good death is. I do that all the time."

"What gives you the right to define a good death for anyone else?" she demanded again.

"By the power vested in me by absolutely no one at all, I will define a good death," I said. "You could try too, if you want. You probably do that every day at work, probably mostly by default. Almost all of us do."

That did nothing to slake her fury, and I understand why. She was a snowflake advocate, and she was defending dying people not against their death but against anyone who would propose a good death for them or who would ask them to die well. Just as the Alcoholics Anonymous mantra leaves room in the name of inclusivity for "God, whatever you conceive that to be," so palliative care advocates defend dying people vehemently against anyone "putting their own beliefs" on them. Often with the most compassionate intent they abandon the dying to the vague, rarely discussed, unprecedented, self-directed project of conjuring a personalized dying for themselves and a personalized meaning for it. Because no one is allowed to do so for them. Because everyone has their own way of dying. Because dying in dominant-culture North America is snowflake dying. If everyone does have their own way of dying, each elaborately legitimate and inalienable, then what are those of us working in the death trade who are not medical practitioners doing? Why would any of us be needed at all?

For the sake of not seeming the ideological monster this might make me out to be, I am willing without any evidence or experience to allow that there might be, say, one hundred fashions or styles or ways of dying. If that seems too many you could reduce it accordingly, or increase the number if one hundred seems stingy. Though I don't have many decades in the palliative trenches, I have worked and taught there steadily, with some thoroughness and circumspection, and I have yet to see anything like the full hundred ways of dying. With all the variety of people, with the relentless advocacy of personal preference that many people bring to the project of dying, I should be able to see how personality trumps persistent sameness, how personal style survives the rolling diminishment of the way dying tends to go in a place that doesn't believe in dying. I would think that most of the hundred ways of dying would have been in evidence over the years and would have shown themselves to me by now. In good faith I tell you that I have not seen them. Several, yes, in a good year, but no more.

I would tell you instead that *there are ten thousand ways at least of not dying,* and I have seen each of them, many times. The ten thousand ways of not dying are where the repertoire of personal style and snowflake uniqueness proliferates. We could say that almost everyone dying in a death-phobic culture, give or take, has his or her own way of not dying. That is what I have seen, every day, on the job. That "not dying" is what gives almost everyone in the palliative care field work, and supporting that "not dying" is what exhausts the compassion and devotion that they bring to it. That is where the requests for a survival strategy come from.

The lot of the death care worker is a strange one. Everyone dies on their watch. They are not in any kind of proactive, preventative work. They forge intense relationships that don't last. I remember a new physician, a young man who had joined a palliative care program I worked at, after several weeks on the job stopping me in the hall in a kind of sorrowed panic and saying, with real consternation and no irony, "All my patients are dying," as if he hadn't counted on this as the one incontrovertible outcome of his work. More often than not, family members are relieved when we stop coming to their door or their mind, our faces and voices being harbingers and reminders both of sorrow and amnesia-worthy times. Once in the course of being introduced at a conference, the person at the microphone congratulated all in attendance for being "tireless workers on behalf of dying people and their families," but really there is no task and no worker in palliative care that is tireless.

At palliative care conferences and workshops all over the continent every year, thousands of death trade workers get together to be encouraged and supported in the business of caring for dying people. It is no wonder then that most of the conferences and workshops in this field tend toward being either technical problem-solving events or exercises in not very subtle cheerleading. When the job of caring for dying people is discussed, which is not common, the discussion usually centers on how to improve the quality of the work, or how to measure the efficacy of the work, or how to obtain funding to do the work, or how to survive doing the work. It is rare for workers in this field to wonder in any sustained way what the work of working with dying people has become in our time, or what it ought to be, and especially what it ought not to be. The job itself is always assumed, as are the qualifications for doing this job, and the project mainly is to strategize how to be better at doing a job that is already being done well.

So, about ten or fifteen minutes into my talks and with little preparation or fanfare I will often ask this audience, "What is your job?" Because this is an uncommon question and an uncommon topic for discussion at work, there is usually utter silence after I ask. When a few begin trying to answer, they give examples of what they do each day. It takes some real cajoling for people to be able to focus their thinking not on what their daily tasks are, but on what job these daily tasks are performed in the name of. This is not the obvious, self-evident thing you might imagine.

Eventually the answers will start to come. One universal response is, "I am there to end suffering or to contain suffering." Another is, "My job is to listen." Almost everyone agrees that they are there to comfort. They all agree that they are there to advocate for a patient's wishes and that their job is to be realistically hopeful and positive and encourage the patient and family to be likewise. "Enable" and "facilitate" are common answers. "Accompany people on their journey" is a common answer. Another universal response is "Just be," usually delivered with confounding Zen-style brevity and satisfaction. Asked to elaborate, the advocates of "Just be" expand their answer by half again and say, "Just be human." Over and over again I ask roomfuls of palliative care workers, people who spend thousands of hours every year with terminally ill people, what they understand their job to be, and *I have almost never heard them include any mention of dying or death in their answers.*

Any job has a description and some indication of the qualifications necessary to perform that job well. People working in palliative care can bristle a little when asked to describe the qualifications that enable them to do the job that they have just described. They seem to hear "Are you qualified?" instead of "What qualifies you?" The answers, when they come, tend also to be brief and self-evident. People cite time spent in the field, time spent with patients and families, time spent with coworkers. Some mention personal experiences of serious illness or near-death. Almost no one cites their education as a qualification, or any professional development seminars they have attended. When it comes to that particular nugget of "just being human" as a job description, just being human is usually offered up as the qualification for that job.

So let's wonder about this. You are a nurse working in a fairly large tertiary care facility in a small urban center. You are working on a ward that has some young patients. Your community is not large enough to warrant an institution specialized in pediatric care, nor is it large enough to warrant any kind of palliative care ward. It is the end of a typically long shift, at the end of a typically long work week. You have enough seniority to have escaped the night shift, but not enough to get you on days, so you are getting off work some time before midnight. You love what you do a lot of the time, you put up with the rest, and generally you are glad to be able to work at something you can believe in. Before writing your chart notes, you pass by each of the patient rooms you are responsible for. It has been a quiet night, thankfully, and you aren't expecting much, so you have to stop and double back at the second to last door in the hall, the semi-private room on your left that for the moment has an empty bed on one side and a terminally ill eight-year-old girl from a small town on the other. She'd been admitted two days ago to be treated for dehydration and weight loss, and was waiting now to be stable enough to be discharged home again. Standing quietly at the doorway you can see in the half light from the hall the silhouette of that terminally ill eight-year-old girl, sitting on the edge of her bed, her back to you, staring out the window, the lights of the small parking lot in the distance making a halo around her.

Before you're two steps into the room you've decided either that she has had a bad dream or that she hasn't adjusted well yet to the hospital setting and is missing her own bedroom or that she is experiencing some pain. You say her name so as not to startle her, and you come in and sit down on the bed beside her, facing her while she faces the window. You ask her why she is still awake, since it's so late at night. The girl shrugs, and so you offer her the options you thought of: Did she have a bad dream? Does it hurt somewhere? Is she hungry or thirsty? She shakes her head "no" to each of your suggestions. At a bit of a loss for what to say next, you gently encourage her to think about getting back into her bed, and you say that she needs her rest, and that you can stay with her a few minutes while she falls back to sleep if she'd like you to.

After another few moments have passed quietly, the eight-year-old girl looks at you for the first time with the uncommon calm and clarity so particular to children who have been that ill, the calm and clarity that tells you that there is no pain, there are no dreams, and she says, "I'm dying, aren't I." It has that unyielding, unnerving mixture, half question and half declaration, said in a voice so even, so quiet, so beyond curiosity and fear that all your reassurances wither and stall, and all of your instincts to make things better if only for these few minutes surrender. It is not really any kind of a question at all, but more of a prod, a notice. She wants to hear one adult say the words, and it hasn't happened yet. She isn't asking about what she doesn't know. She isn't even asking something about herself. She's asking something about you and about what you are willing to know, something about your life, something about whether the world is a friendly place and what can be trusted, about how true a true thing can be in this darkened corner of the world that you and she find yourselves in, together for a few minutes, just before the end of a shift, just before midnight.

You've never been that alone with someone before, never that uncertain about what you know. You look into her face, as much as you can bear to, and you remember again what is written on her chart out at the station, below the description of her diagnosis and her prognosis and her goals of care and her list of drugs and dietary requirements and restrictions and the name of the Person Most Responsible, in bold type, so that it can't be overlooked or mistaken or debated: **Patient not to be informed of diagnosis.** Now, what is your job?

This is where all of our ideas about dying and truth and children and life and skill and fear come to pay their rent and earn their keep and prove themselves in the raucous and unregulated marketplace of the way things are. This, among a hundred other scenes of similar, unnerving sorrow in the business of working with dying people and their families, is where we find out again what we believe in, what we can afford to believe in, what we cannot carry and are not up to. When I tell a story like that, and when I ask the question, "Now, what is your job?" the gears of good intent are stripped, and the simple striving for simple goodness has no purchase.

Eventually someone in the room will say, with some verve and more than a little indignation, "Well, my job is to be honest with her."

And I ask, "Why is that your job?"

And the answer will be, "Because that little girl deserves to be told the truth."

I ask, "And what is the truth?"

And that is the question that everyone on the giving end of palliative care and everyone on the receiving end must answer, over and over again, before, during, and after every emergency and crisis and treatment decision and remission and recurrence, every hospital visit and home death and collapse and pneumonia and DNR order and living will and descent into the land of 911: What is the truth that this girl and everyone else in her boat deserve?

Is the truth that our vast med-tech arsenal isn't vast enough, and never will be, to prevent what is happening from happening? Is it that our understanding of life doesn't include our life ending? Is the truth that no one believes that a dying eight-year-old girl is having whatever is usually meant by "a full life"? Is it that she is proof positive that life is arbitrary, chaotic, random mayhem interrupted by seductive periods of nothing much happening? Is the truth that her parents don't believe in what is happening to her, and don't believe in any ability she might have to carry the knowledge of what is happening to her, and don't believe that she can be a child and be dying at the same time? Is it that she will be lost to them, that someday not too long from now she'll be home movies and teddy bears and a room upstairs too hard to visit, that she'll be mostly past tense?

What is the truth that is this eight-year-old girl's right? What truth do the rest of us think we know?

We'll come to some answers to these questions, slowly. First, let's try to answer that question about the job. Most of us feel that wherever possible it is our obligation, whether we are professional or lay participants in the life of a dying person, to end or contain or limit suffering. In these kinds of discussions pain gets most of the attention, and most people seem to have the litigious "pain and suffering" mantra close at hand. Certainly early on in the palliative treatment phase of dying peoples' illnesses they report that being in pain is by far their greatest fear. Drugs and the acquired skill of pain control by physicians have gone far to guarantee that most people will not die addled by pain, but it hasn't delivered sorrow-free or suffering-free dying.

I once heard a brilliant teacher say, "Suffering is the currency of stinginess." At the time this struck me as absolutely accurate and utterly punitive and compassionless. As always when hoisted on the crossbeam of a dilemma like that, I pondered and wrestled the pronouncement for several years, lucky as I was to have a job that guaranteed I would have ample obligation to do so. There is no doubt for me that this culture—at least those of us not in sackcloth and ashes, purifying ourselves for the Rising Up and the Fire—knows suffering to be an affliction visited upon us from without, an arbitrary and indefensible consequence of being born into a body in a world where time grinds away at our energy, purpose, and give-a-shit. Suffering for most of us comes from not getting what we need and from not needing what we get, from the silent and purposeless void that opens up between what becomes of us and what we mean to become. The solution that so many conjure for themselves is to retreat into a kind of small "b" Buddhism, where striving is eschewed, where desire is demonized, where wanting for things to work out is *the* problem in a world that seldom works out, where your expectations of your people and your life are reigned in and minimized to the point where the disappointments—the sufferings—are minimal too.

This teacher saw it differently, I think. Suffering doesn't come from having been born, from being an incarnated someone. It comes from an unwillingness in this culture to recognize how on the take we have been through the entire course of our lives here, how willing and able we are to wring from the world all we desire and require from it, as if that were the reason the world is here at all. To most of us the world is not alive in the way that we are alive, and the world doesn't deserve the consideration that we reserve for living things. We worship in the Temple of Want, and the whole world—not just our small part of it—is there for the satisfaction of that want, just as most of our marriages and friendships are turned into need-gratification machines. When you worship in the Temple of Want your death is an insult, the ultimate, arbitrary frustration of your right to have things go as you deserve until you decide otherwise. The refusal to recognize the trespass that always comes with the gratification of need—that is what "stinginess" might mean.

If you have eaten today, as I have, be you vegetarian or vegan or what, a good number of living things of the world have died to keep you and me alive. Do the math on how many things have died to keep you and those you love alive through the course of your uneven, striving, care-worn lives—not just the things you have eaten, but all the consumption that has occurred in the name of delivering to you what you usually think of as the basic entitlement of living here and now, and all the consumption done in your pursuit of comfort—and you can have some feel for the enormity of how much a one-way street human living in this dominant culture of North America is. The death of living things feeds us and keeps us alive.

And then ask yourself how many people you have known whose deaths when they came fed something and kept something alive that otherwise would not live. How many of us are willing for our death—not our successes or our surpluses or our conquests or our charities, or our good intent or our desire to be benign and take only memories and leave things pretty much as we found them, but our *death*—to be the occasion for something else to live? Not *our* eternal life, not our personal style surviving. Not you and I getting to carry on in some way anyhow. Just the thinner, minor-keyed possibility that only by our dying can *something besides you and I* be fed and have some chance to live. How many of us die in a way that recognizes the extravagant debt that we have piled up by living as we have done? For how many of us is our death not the last violation of our personal volition but instead some just payment toward the debt we owe to what gave us life?

I know and you know that there is a growing understanding among us of the ecological truth of our indebtedness, and of the trespass that debt is a sure sign of. But if we only see this consequence in terms of greenhouse effects and emissions and carbon footprints and reduce, reuse, and recycle, then we'll only worry and react in those terms and try to ease our sustainable way out of that debt. In the manner of our living we might live more consciously, perhaps, and try most of us in our own small ways to have a little less impact on this teetering environment, and that would be good by any measure. It is damage control, though, and risk management by another name. If we come to it that way, then the manner of our dying will fall well outside the ragged edge of our understanding of what it has meant to us and to the world for us to be alive, just as it now does, and our dying will be mostly a matter of our suffering, just as it is among us. Our dying will confirm finally and brutally our grimmest convictions about the arbitrary mayhem of being alive, just as it does: not with a bang, but a whimper.

There might be two kinds of sufferings in the teacher's stony pronouncement. The one comes from this culture's resounding self-absorption and refusal to know the spiritual corner it has backed itself into by refusing to know the debt it continues to gather around itself. So many people I worked with died with the grudge of *being owed something* by life that they now won't live to collect on. Their deaths were a theft and betrayal and rip-off for them, and their families and friends and communities all inherited the poverty, the stinginess, of that belligerent wound.

The other comes from the sudden, unbidden realization that this debt is unsuspected and unconsciously incurred and considerable, that we have lived in a way that has stolen actively, ecologically, spiritually, and culturally from the earth and from our own children and grandchildren and beyond whom we will not live to see grow and love and marry and the rest, and from the children and grandchildren of our friends and of people whom we did not live long enough to meet but probably would have liked and admired. Awakening to this, we cannot but face the realization that we stand a good chance of being heirs that people of a future time cannot be proud of and will not recognize as kin, and the homelessness of heart and spirit that many among us live with during our lives will pale beside the homelessness of heart and spirit that we will live in our deaths. "Remembered happiness is agony," wrote the American poet Donald Hall in the wake of his wife's death. "So is remembered agony."

These, friends, are the sufferings that we propose to soothe in the dying people we are paid to care for. These are the sufferings which are beggared and misapprehended and sedated as "existential death anxiety at the end of life," which are psychologized and counseled as "trauma of separation and loss." We cannot, though nothing seems compelling enough to make us see it, contain, control, limit, treat, anesthetize, or analyze that suffering to the point where dying people do not suffer it, and our continued impoverished take on what is happening when dying people suffer deepens and extends their suffering. The enormous use of sedation on dying people ploughs them under to the point where those of us in attendance can see no further evidence of suffering, and here we can say, "Mission accomplished." In our time, this suffering is quieted to invisibility, and the patient is resting comfortably, and the cost is lucidity, responsiveness, perhaps awareness. Antidepressants and sedatives are tokens of the med-tech industry's elaborate and compelling understanding of the biomechanics of pain and anxiety. In layman's terms, antidepressants and sedatives achieve what they do by compromising a person's capacity to suffer. If you opened a corner store whose sole product promised your customers that their capacity to suffer would be compromised, you'd have lines down the block. We have our equivalent: a booming street business in the sale of dubiously acquired prescription antidepressants, sedatives and analgesics. When we recognize no merit nor sign in suffering, when our ways of living and dying include many days of barely managed impotence, then suffering in the ending of days gives us the feeling of being gutted fish, and it is only affliction. So people in the helping professions and the families of dying people want to end suffering where and how they can.

What should we be doing instead, then? First, we have to stop scrambling to fix. Many years ago I worked with a lot of people whose marriages were going under. Almost every unhappy spouse's solution to the problem that had become their marriage was More Marriage. Try Harder. Do what you once did, but do it all the time now. When every deep thing in life is turned into a problem to solve, then I would say that the way the problem is understood is just about always part of the problem. The afflicted part of you generates a solution for the affliction, and so the solution is an attribute of the problem all along. The problem, if we have to use the word, is in the eye. It is in the seeing, not in what is seen. Habits live in the eye, not in what the eye sees, and there are habits of seeing and feeling that drive every solution most of us have ever come up with.

Most of the solutions we have for people's suffering at the end of their lives are rooted in a grudge match with life and with the body. They serve the conviction that people shouldn't have to suffer, and so the headlong pursuit is for an end to suffering. When this pursuit fails, and it almost always does, the next best solution is to limit or end the awareness of suffering, by resorting to antidepressants and sedatives. We should stop long enough to ask one of the dumb, simple questions that are gold at a time like this: *Will*—not should—*will our people inevitably suffer as their lives end?* If we answer "Yes," then we need a second question: *Are they suffering because they are dying?* If we answer "Yes," this is reflex and not contemplation.

There are few deathbed conversions to a deepened humanity or compassion or wisdom that come just from the fact that there is dying going on. Peoples' ways of dying, in other words, come from somewhere. What causes people's deaths is mostly science, mostly a given. *How* people die is not inevitable, not a given. Dying is not a place where things happen; it is a thing that is being done somewhere. In our case, dying is trying to be done in a death-phobic social milieu, and this phobia tends to drive our way of seeing death. It drives our compelling convictions about what we should do when it comes. A more adequate answer would be that dying people are suffering from the manner of their dying.

The third question: *What is the manner of their dying?* You need considerable breadth of vision and a habit-confounding eye to grapple well with this one. You need a willingness to see the dying in front of you and the dying within you for what they are. Though they are not likely to ask for it, dying people need a faithful witness to their dying, not someone who will banish what is hard and demanding about dying. Dying is hard enough, hugely hard enough in a death-phobic time and place, without that.

Palliative care is one place where euphemisms go to enjoy job security and long life. Faced with a consumer group less than eager to use their services or even to be associated with them, many in the palliative care field find other ways of representing what they do. Hospital-based palliative care workers avoid resorting to "heroic measures" and talk about "comfort giving measures" instead. Purveyors of comfort have to narrow the scope of their work considerably.

Nurses, along with volunteers, stand at the emotional, spiritual, and political center of the work of caring for dying people. Nurses have maximum involvement with patients and families, and with that comes a vulnerability to human frailty. In the many training sessions I've done with them, I always ask nurses working with dying people what their greatest fear is on the job. As you might expect, they tell me that their greatest fear on the job is doing something wrong. When pressed, they don't mean that they fear misreading patient charts or giving the wrong drug dosage and killing someone by doing so. They fear *saying* something wrong. This is astounding really, that with all the technology and drug know-how and the dying at stake, their greatest fear is in saying the wrong thing. It sounds so unexpectedly minor to the rest of us. How would you know, I ask them, if you'd said something wrong? The patient would be upset or angry or depressed, or would report me, they say. There'd be a letter in my file. The dilemma for nurses and for most palliative care workers is that the dying people they are trying to care for do not in the early and middle stages of being in palliative care believe that they are dying. How can you proceed with a plan of care predicated on the fact that the patient is dying with a patient who is as far as they are concerned not dying? You become the purveyor of comfort instead. And you wait for dying people to figure out for themselves that they are dying, or you wait for them to crack. The euphemism that is used is that you wait for them to be ready.

There is a lot of talk in the death trade about waiting for terminally ill people to be ready before they are told too much of anything that has gravity or consequence to it. Many workers bide their time with supportive gestures, encouraging talk, hopeful suggestions about what could be, while in the team meetings the rest of the story—the terminal part—is routinely told. How are dying people to get ready to learn what their lives have taught them so little of? How do they get ready to learn that they are dying? What would it sound like? Would they say, "I knew that"? Would they say, "Fine"? If they cry or moan or throw a chair across the room or curse you out for telling them or go silent, would that mean that they weren't ready? That you'd said the wrong thing?

Comfort giving seems as inoffensive and as necessary as things can get. I have never heard anyone object to the sanctity of comfort giving as a basic obligation of people working in the death trade. I—and this is probably no surprise to anyone at this point—object, strongly. The problem is with the idea of comfort and what it becomes in a death-phobic time and place. Think if you would on what you find comforting. Try to get inside the examples of comforting things and bring your attention to the function of comfort. What is required for most of us to feel comforted? Well, first you need to have some capacity to be on the receiving end and translate some experience in that way. Not the expectation, or the inclination or the need or the desire; only the ability to be on the receiving end of comfort. It is not so inevitable a thing, the ability to be comforted, to recognize something as comforting. It is a skill of sorts, and is not much taught or much practiced in a culture that places a serious premium on self-sufficiency and not letting anyone see you sweat. This comfort ability might not at first blush seem like much of an accomplishment, but any encounter you may have had with someone who refused comfort or was unable to recognize or experience comfort might persuade you that it is indeed a skill.

The next requirement is that you have a track record of being comforted and that you can remember being comforted. What is intended to comfort you will most likely only do so if it resembles what has comforted you in the past. What comforts is what is familiar. Not everything familiar is comforting, probably (though psychodynamic psychotherapists would probably argue you to the ground on this point), but perhaps everything comforting is familiar. If this is true, then it's likely that a new experience by definition has no capacity to give comfort. Take, for example, something like a new pair of shoes. They may be interesting or exciting, they may be revealing or emboldening or even true, but they aren't likely to comfort you, particularly when you crave comfort, particularly if you've been in a hard way for a while.

Think of any tourist attraction you might have been to. What are they selling? A packaged version of the exotic turned into something consumable and familiar. Theme park rides sell the promise of danger, but their lawyers ensure that at most they deliver the illusion of danger. International hotel chains sell the promise of the foreign and the exotic, but all their designs, services, and accoutrement deliver the comforts of home, and home is a generic, dominant-culture North American home where its beneficiaries feel safe. The hotel might be in Dakar, but there is no Dakar in the hotel. Tourism traffics in the illusion of Somewhere Else and the guarantee of the familiar. Tourism is comfort provision, and tourist towns are addicted to comfort the same way that tourists are. Comfort is the crack cocaine of the tourist, just as the tourist is the crack cocaine of those living in tourist towns.

So, how to comfort a dying person who suspects or is fairly, unwillingly sure that he or she is dying? How do you comfort dying people *about* their dying? This of course is a riddle, not a question. Most friends and family of dying people, most paid and volunteer caregivers of dying people, don't comfort dying people about their dying. They realize early on that they don't have much to say about dying that can, without risk of offense or disquiet, comfort anyone in the death room, not really. So they move on to topics that stand a greater chance of being comforting. They talk about what can be done instead of what cannot be done, of what is pleasant or positive or life affirming. They talk about family, about the patient's former life, and though from a vague sense of respect it is not often called their "former life," that life has absolutely vanished in the wake of diagnosis and symptoms. Usually any focus on or serious understanding of dying is sacrificed in order to pursue and secure comfort. All of this usually happens with the active cooperation of the dying person. The value of comfort is never challenged. Comfort is never asked to earn its keep. It is a kept thing.

And so a secret conjuring in the death trade is employed: Dying, if we speak of it much at all, is spoken of in code, in what is mostly empty symbolism, in turgid metaphor, simile after simile rolling off the tongues of the well intentioned. Most people who believe in comfort giving try to turn dying into something that is already known, already familiar.

What is it like? That is how we have to say it in English.

Rapurous phrase makers want to know what death is, but they tell what it is going to be like instead: a ravening bear readying itself for the long sleep; a relentless and parsimonious bargain hunter; a low-grade and unspectacular plague; something that killed the titanic conceit of the West, silently, at night; something that will get you from behind; a modest place only visited but never lived in, never illumined. For death to be death at all, it has to be like something else that we've already known. And there ought to be some comfort in that; this is the bargain we strike.

I had a teacher in divinity school who was an emeritus professor named Amos Wilder (Thornton Wilder was his brother). Amos was pushing eighty or eighty-five years of age at the time, and an upright Yankee he was. He was also good enough to have a few of us over to his house for a very civilized tea every so often, and we'd listen to him tell stories about the old days at Harvard. At one of these meetings a young fellow was admiring Amos's endurance and offhandedly asked him, "Amos, do you feel like an old man?" And Amos answered, "No. I feel like a young man who's got something wrong with him almost all of the time." Getting old, he was telling us, is nothing new. It's more of the same, but with less resilience on his part. I am not eighty or eighty-five, but on some days I can see it from here. I know already that it is not like something that has already happened. Maybe in a time and place that doesn't much honor old men, being old only has merit if it is like being younger, though with a shadow on it. Maybe Amos was comforting himself with the comparison, or comforting the young folk who were listening.

But what in our lives does dying resemble, really? What does it actually remind you of? Nothing whatsoever, is the only honest answer. Dying is so singular, so relentlessly itself and nothing else that we can be comforted in its presence only by conspiring together to cover it with the husks of those former mysteries that we have succeeded in demystifying. Remember the old meaning of "to palliate," of the "pall." Remember the concealment. That is how comfort is achieved in palliative care provided by a death-phobic culture: by sleight of hand.

What is dying like? The realities of dying won't tolerate domesticating similes or comparisons. It isn't like anything. It won't remind you of anything. When people say it is a journey, or it is a transition, it sounds to me like they are saying, "Well, it has the consistency of fish but it doesn't taste fishy. More like chicken." And store-bought chicken these days has no taste at all. Dying is not like being sick, though the sedating language of sickness abounds in the care of dying people. It is not like being sick a long time, not like being sick of being sick. It is possible to be dying and hardly be sick at all. Dying is not like the chicken pox, or a bear, or an iceberg, or like anything you have known.

The young son of a patient who had recently died said to me one day, "I don't want to be a businessman when I grow up." I knew what he said, but I didn't know what he meant. How could he have any real prejudice against certain kinds of jobs at his age?, I wondered. When our time together was over I met briefly with his mother. I told her about her son's declaration and asked her what it could mean. "Oh," she laughed, "that's what I told him about his dad. I told him that his dad had gone away on a business trip." Dying, though, is not like going away on a long business trip, not even to a young boy, not even to a businessman who has had enough of business.

I attended a meeting of the movers and shakers in pediatric palliative care in a big city in the American Midwest. The day dawned beautiful and sunny. I followed the map and found our location, a glass and stone and steel postmodern library with wild, falling-apart sculptures in the front. Waiting to cross at the light, I looked across a finely manicured lawn in front of another glass and steel monolith at a sign informing all that this public park was dedicated to all those who had outlived their oncology prognosis. It was called Survivor's Park, and it was dedicated by the local cancer society to all those who had won their battle with cancer. I thought at that moment: I haven't seen a park dedicated to the other guys, the ones who didn't win. I haven't heard of a national steering committee for them, staffed by them. I haven't often heard in meetings or read in the literature a name coined for those other guys that has the same triumphal ring to it, the kind of name that would make you want to join them, the kind of name that speaks of what they did instead of what befell them, the kind of name you'd want a park dedicated to. What kind of comfort does this park sell?

In the wake of the First World War, there were almost no books or stories written that described the war. It is hardly a thinkable thought now, when books about disasters and calamities are turned out before the ashes have cooled and the waters have ebbed, but we are the aberration. European city streets in what came to be the Roaring Twenties were full of dismembered and traumatized war veterans, young old men who would never be civilians again, but the poets and authors and journalists took years to write anything about them, about what had happened to them and about what they had seen. In a book called *The Great War and Modern Memory*, Paul Fussell tells why this happened as it did. The Great War had no precedent, not in living memory or in cultural memory. The utter scale of the horror, the ordinary horror that after five years it had become, the shredding of European convictions about European civility and progress that the war had achieved, all of this was singular and never before seen, and so literally *there was no language* equal to the task of saying what had happened and no language faithful to the blistering permanence of everything personal, historical, and cultural having been changed by it. Instead there was silence. The moment of silence observed on November 11 at 11 a.m. lasted for several decades as a residual memory of the sheer unimaginability of what had been done in the name of tribalism and righteousness. Recently the last Canadian veteran of the Great War died, which means another library has burned to the ground. The Great War eventually gave way to the Second World War and then became one of many wars, and by now it is a history there is no living memory of. The moment of silence is mostly an awkward antiquity when it is observed at all.

There is nothing modern or postmodern or North American or English-speaking about this language problem. Leo Tolstoy, for example, wrote a book in which the code of "dying not dying" was central, in which the yearning for comfort and the resort to euphemism are revealed for the spell-casting shams that they often are. In the eight years following the 1878 publication of *Anna Karenina* he lived in a pit that today would be diagnosed as part writer's block, part midlife crisis, mostly depression. That period saw three of Tolstoy's children die, but at the end of that time he didn't write a story about dying children. It seems that he fled his children's deaths, either literally by leaving home for long periods during that time, or by a kind of heroic aloofness that would make most parents uneasy:

> All I can say is that the death of a child, which I once thought incomprehensible and unjust, now seems reasonable and good . . . My wife has been much afflicted by this death and I, too, am sorry that the little boy I loved is no longer here, but despair is only for those who shut their eyes to the commandment by which we are ruled.
>
> Leo Tolstoy (translated by Lynn Solotaroff),
> *The Death of Ivan Ilych,* page 21

The novella *The Death of Ivan Ilyich* (1886) shows that Tolstoy, in the aftermath of the enormous success he admitted and the great sorrow he banished, had been visited by the story of his *own* death in the death of his children, a story that trumps cleverness handily. His life and his success up to that point had not in his living of it included the end of it, and the news of the certainty of his death seems to have been a calamity that his plans and his religion wouldn't make room for. With *Ivan Ilyich* he used the grim suffering of a banal, cancer-ridden provincial judge to craft a name for the intolerance that modernity has for dying.

> Ivan Ilyich suffered most of all from the lie, the lie which, for some reason, everyone accepted: that he was not dying but was simply ill, and that if he stayed calm and underwent treatment he could expect good results. Yet he knew that regardless of what was done, all he could expect was more agonizing suffering and death. And he was tortured by this lie, tortured by the fact that they refused to acknowledge what he and everyone else knew, that they wanted to lie about his horrible condition and to force him to become a party to that lie. This lie, a lie perpetrated on the eve of his death, a lie that was bound to degrade the awesome, solemn act of his dying to the level of their social calls, their draperies, and the sturgeon they ate for dinner, was an excruciating torture for Ivan Ilyich … He saw that the awesome, terrifying act of his dying had been degraded by those about him to the level of a chance unpleasantness, a bit of unseemly behavior; that it had been degraded by that very "propriety" to which he had devoted his entire life.… Nothing did so much to poison the last days of Ivan Ilyich's life as this falseness in himself and in those around him.
>
> Leo Tolstoy (trans. Lynn Solotaroff),
> *The Death of Ivan Ilych*, page 103

This is what happens when well people come to dying people in a singsong way, looking to bring a little cheer into what looks to any and all like a cheerless end of life ordeal, visiting, bringing the news of the day, being careful to avoid what is unpleasant. Comforting, in other words.

Not knowing what else to do, many of us handle the alien dying person with the robotic arms of comfort, making as if this were another day in the caravan of days. Comforting, Tolstoy shows us, is lying.

What then of "just listening," and "just being human"? I know that psychotherapists and counselors talk about "active listening," though most of us practice listening as a passive business. "Listening" as a description of our basic job when we are with dying people—active, passive, or otherwise—treads heavily on the assumption that dying people have something they want to say, because they are dying people. Dying people in my experience are no more eloquent than others, and rarely are they more eloquent dying than they were in the more fulsome times of their lives. A terminal diagnosis tends not to give full rein to dying people's imaginations or consciences or memories. People dying in a death-phobic time and place are not visited by an unprecedented inclination or ability to wonder aloud about their dying, not that I have seen. Education and experience in such a time and place robs dying people of any language that could do justice to how it is for them, and it doesn't serve them well for the rest of us to assume that they've been visited by a terminal eloquence. Much more importantly, we ought not to assume that they have anything, eloquent or not, to say to us.

"Journeying" with dying people, though it has all the self-help synergy and New Age affirmation about it our era requires, has a serious limitation that none of its advocates have admitted in my hearing. It is not because the destination is mostly unknown, though that is true, not because the purpose or the ways and means of this "journey" are equally unfamiliar. The truth is that, come what may, you will only go so far on this journey with a dying person and no further. No matter your promise to a dying person or your intent, you will turn off their path and leave them to it, probably without ever saying that you have done so and maybe not being aware that you have done so, watching them head out away from you. Their diagnosis drove an insoluble wedge between you, and they stumbled out onto this path unawares and against their will, and they've been on it for some time before your offer to accompany them. That diagnosis *is* the irreducible distance between you. You'll never be older than your older sibling, and you'll never be journeying beside a dying person on the road to their death, no more than a midwife is journeying with a not-yet-born person in the full grip of contractions.

Could the vocation of "just being human" be just cause and qualification for attending a dying person in their dying? No, I don't think it is. The dilemma here lies in our idea of what it is that makes us human. In the dominant culture of North America, humans are born. Being human is not so much a right in this culture as it is an inevitability. Most of us can't help but be human simply as a consequence of having been born, and something has to go horrendously awry for our membership in the family of human beings to be in doubt or in jeopardy.

This is a minority view in the world, largely an untested view. Most cultures which have survived being modernized, missionized, and mobilized toward participating in this mythic global economy continue, albeit covertly, to practice the rites of human making. These are what anthropologists call rites of passage or initiatory events, and most first occur at the onset of puberty. They do not have as their goal self-actualization or self-affirmation or self-anything. Babies in these cultures are as much loved as anywhere, and their children are prized and protected as gifts from the Givers of Life. But they are just that—children—and they have no capacity for being human as they are. Their childhood is burned off in the crucible of person making during those puberty ceremonies, with the real possibility of failure and death ever present. If all goes well they emerge from those ceremonies as people whose humanity is established, and their ability to carry, defend, and maintain the village culture, deeply embedded in the soil made in every true sense of their ancestors and their deities, is the sign. In these cultures humanity is purposeful and not a goal. Humans are to serve, and their humanity is needed by their world. There is no clause for problems of personal style, preference, or inclination. They are not snowflakes.

We have no comparable person making. We have no comparable foundation in service to our ancestry or our deities. We have no enforced obligation to tether the horse of our humanity to the plough of our culture to harrow up the field of our time on this earth and plant wisdom and sanity for a future time. Maybe some of us will do it. Maybe we won't.

My point is that being born or surviving school or seeing our majority or seniority, none of this makes us human beings. If it is true that humanity is a skill and not a right, then there are very few people among us who are mentors and teachers of the epic skill of being human. That means that our culture is inundated with fifty-year-old adolescents who in their peak earning years are getting as much for themselves and their loved ones as they can, who are waiting for their retirements to serve their communities in their spare time, if they stay in their communities when they retire, during times of fair weather. Uninitiated people do not believe in dying, just as they disbelieve in anything that limits their choices and self-direction and comfort seeking. They will not have their deaths be the occasion for any kind of a feeding and nourishment of a world they haven't seen or invested in. Uninitiated people are the people who are trying to die not dying, and uninitiated people are the people who are trying to help them not die. It has not, on the face of it at least, the makings of an inevitably good outcome for anyone.

Well then, what *is* the job of someone hoping to care well for a dying person? Having crossed all the usual answers off the list, what is left? My answer you'll probably think is a simple one, too simple, but it is one that asks a great deal from all of us. Our first job, and it is the skill that makes all the other skills of compassion possible, is to know death, and know it well, and to proceed through our days as if there is merit in knowing death well. The objection I've heard most frequently is: "How could I know death well? I haven't died yet. If knowing death afflicts the dying person with such devastation, how could knowing it be of any benefit to those who are trying to help?"

Do you have to be dying yourself to learn about it? If that is true it would mean that each dying person, because they have received a terminal diagnosis, has a rapidly acquired and steadily deepening understanding of what dying is and an understanding of how to do it. It would mean that the longer they have been living with their disease, and the longer they have been dying, the more wisdom they have gathered.

Longer deaths, by that standard, should be better deaths. More Time should then be pursued by every means available since it gives the dying person a greater chance of getting it right. And if any or all of that is true, *they* are the experts and categorically more qualified than any of the rest of us to manage the business of dying well. They've no need of counselors, therapists, volunteers, and the like. If you want to know what dying is like, you can do no better than to ask them. But you have very little, if anything, to tell them. If all of this is so, then the "care of The Dying" should be reduced to simple pain and symptom management by the experts in the medical part of dying. The patient already has so much expertise in the human part of their dying. And this is a fairly accurate picture of how things often are thought of in palliative care: Dying people are the experts, they are teaching the rest of us, they know what they need, they'll ask when they're ready, our job is to just be there for them, and so on.

Doing this work for a few years showed me clearly that as a group The Dying have no greater understanding of what dying is or what it asks of them or us, nor any greater ability to teach others about it, nor any greater skill at dying, than anyone else does. If anything, their understanding of death has been stymied by the experience of dying, and they are mortified and defeated by it. If anything, the receipt of a terminal diagnosis itself is another affliction beyond the disease and its arc. With the culturally endorsed death phobia in their background, people who are told that they will die generally suffer from the way in which they are told and will question whether they should have been told at all. "What does it gain me to know?" they ask. "What am I supposed to do with it? How am I supposed to live, now that you have stolen my future from me?" They are clear that knowing they are dying is itself a cause of suffering.

A decade ago I schemed with a physician in eastern Canada to put together a traveling palliative care road show that could go out to smaller communities that are understaffed and underserved. It was my idea to come to the communities where people are living and dying instead of to some anemic ballroom in some homeless, centrally located hotel some-where. The generosity of a private family foundation made it possible. I came a few days early and Tim Wilson (director of the film *Griefwalker*) and I filmed some interviews with palliative patients and their families, and then madly edited hours of film into fifteen minute-long clips to play for the nurses, doctors, and social workers the next day. When I watched those sessions during the editing, I found a few diamonds. This is one.

> We were sitting together in her crowded kitchen, the cameraman, the physician, and me, the seven-ty-five-year old patient and her forty-year-old son. She hadn't baked, but she had bought cinnamon rolls and tea for our talk. We were visiting, she had decided. Everyone was nervous for things to go well, though no one knew how things were supposed to go. Mom was prickly and clever about her lung cancer, downplaying it as nothing to spend a lot of effort on while strug-gling to breathe at the same time, and she kept trying to guess what it was I wanted her to say. The filming and the talk turned out to be harder for her than she'd imagined when she agreed to do it.
>
> About an hour into the meeting, her son asked me a question. He wanted to do the right thing for his moth-er—"I don't want to do anything wrong," is what he said—and went on to describe a fight that they had some days before. As things heated up she had said to him, "You don't know what it's like ..."
>
> "Well tell me what it's like then, what's happening to you. I want to know. Tell me what it's like," he had said to her at the time. It sounded like she hadn't yet an-swered him. Then he looked over to his mother there in the kitchen and asked her again, "Tell me what it's like."
>
> After an awkward pause, she said, "I don't remember that, son. I don't recall that conversation."

Gently he said, "It doesn't matter. Just tell me now. What is it like?"

She said, "I don't know what you want me to say. I don't understand what you want to know." He looked at me then, defeated again, and said nothing more about it.

Mother and son alone together in that small house on a country road in the Maritimes in the early years of the new century that they'd both lived long enough to see, one of them dying and one trying to find a way to know death well and be useful when it comes, and nothing in their lives had really gotten them ready to do what was in front of them. He wanted more than anything to get it right, but he had no belief that there was good dying to be had and precious little experience to help him. He needed her to tell him. She said that she wasn't afraid to die, she just didn't want to, and everything in her manner signaled to him and to us that it was all for not and useless, the talking and the prescribing and the fetching and the mourning. And the filming.

Under it all, she didn't know any more about what it was like to die than he did. Her statement to him— "You don't know what it's like"—was part lament and part accusation. If he loved her as a son ought to love his mother, his love should tell him what it is like. *He* should know, she was saying, even if she didn't. And she genuinely didn't know what it was to die, even though there she was, dying, right in front of us. She had the information of her death, but not the experience of it, and she could not proceed through her days as a dying person having only the information to go by. Dying isn't like anything, the truth be told, so it was a kind of blind spot in the midst of her feelings. She'd no words for it. It was the same after World War I. Nothing like it had ever happened before. They had no words for it either.

If you don't believe in dying, and in the need to be good at it, you will believe that less dying is better dying. By less dying I mean less awareness, less presence, less evidence, less to do. I appeared once on a live phone-in television talk show together with a palliative care physician and a writer of a book about grief. This is my favorite kind of caper, where there isn't much possibility of deleting, editing, or censoring. You can really get things said and sort out the consequences later. The host of the show had a very canny opening gambit. As soon as the introductions had been made, she asked each of us experts how we would like it to be when we die. The physician went first, and said that, while he hadn't really thought about this much before now, he hoped he didn't die like doctors tend to do, querulous, obstreperous, argumentative, angry, and noncompliant. He hoped that he died calmly and quietly, with close family about. And he hoped he died quickly. There were murmurs of assent all round. The author was next. She hadn't thought about it much either, but she wanted to be peaceful, easy for her friends and family to be with, and she wanted not to linger. The murmuring approved and understood. Then the host looked to me from an off-camera angle, pleading for a little variety. I was able to oblige.

"I've thought about this quite a bit. It comes with the job. I believe I would like things to be as messy as possible."

Silence. After a moment the host said, "Messy?"

"I don't mean with body fluids flying, that kind of messy. I mean that I want it to be a knowable, doable thing. I would want the people around me to have to do something. I want us all to have work to do." Still no murmuring.

Caught off guard by the question, the first two guests tipped their caps in the direction of calm, quiet, torment-reduced exits. Their recipe for good dying is less dying, as I would say it. They were more than ready to enlist friends and family in the project of less dying, in the name of there being no undue suffering. I have seen this happen too many times to count, and it almost always ends in everyone conspiring to under-report pain and torment, under-respond to pain and torment when they are evident. They follow that lunatic incantation, that free advice that is doled out when the news of a terminal diagnosis is given: It used to be, "Go home and get your affairs in order," but we are far more humane these days, and so now it's, "Go home and live as normal a life as possible, under the circumstances." It's a recipe for less dying in the face of death. It prescribes seduction as a treatment for anxiety, despair, depression, and terminal agitation. What we want is lucidity (although not too much of it), painlessness, an easy go of it. What is stolen is sorrow, grieving, knowing. That is how less dying is bought, with terminal sedation or with less knowing about dying.

> This is an example of how it works in practice. I had recently joined a home-based palliative care team made up of nurses, volunteers, a coordinator, a physician, and a psycho-spiritual counselor. Being new on the scene I thought it wise to get the lay of the land of how things worked, how decisions got made, and the like. After a couple of months I risked it all. I'd noticed that the nurses automatically saw every patient, as did the co-ordinator. I'd noticed that the doctor saw every patient too. So in the weekly meeting I said, "I've been seeing what I figure are the patients in the worst shape, physically and emotionally, while the rest of you see every patient. How is it happening that way?"
>
> The physician replied, "Well, there is only one of you, and as a scarce and valuable resource we keep you for the patients who need you most."
>
> I appreciated the compliment that was intended, but I caught the scent of something else. "But aren't there some other criteria that you use that determine who I see?" I asked.
>
> The physician thought for a moment and said, "Well, they do have to agree to see you." That is what I thought I had sniffed in the wind.

I said, "When you go to a patient's house, and you are discussing with them what kind of care they will receive and how things will go, do you take out your prescription pad and ask, 'So, what would you like?' and take dictation from them?" Well, of course he didn't. "And why not?" I said. "Because your training and your experience are worth something, and they guide your actions, right? And you don't assume for a minute, do you, that just because the patient is the one with the disease it means that they know what drugs they need and what is good for them? I know you don't do that. You don't leave it them to decide on what you know about. So why do you do that where what I know is concerned?"

I give enormous credit to that physician and the others on that team. That discussion prompted quite a struggle to rethink how we all did our business and what kind of business we were in. As the care of The Dying has grown as a specialization over the last twenty years, so has the practice of a principle in health care called patient-centered practice. This way of working was developed as an antidote to the old hierarchical, "paternalistic," top-down power relationship that had prevailed between patient and professional caregiver. It enlists the patient as coauthor of a treatment plan, reconfigures the patient from a needy supplicant to a consumer of a service, and gives credence to the patient's experience and way of going through their sickness and death. Subtly, it shares some authority and responsibility for how things go between caregiver and patient. When it comes to doctoring and nursing in the death trade, when it comes to the science and the body and the drugs and the decisions and measures taken, doctors and nurses know best. The medico-legal community insists that this be so. But when it comes to dying, to the maze of sorrows the likes of which they had never known before, no matter how much experience all of us have, suddenly The Dying know best, and what they want for themselves—and what they don't want—has a gospel ring. Where does their expertise come from? What death wisdom do they have that automatically derives from their diagnosis? Why do we think that dying people know what they need and treat them accordingly? In practice, patient-centered care means the patient's understanding of what makes them suffer checkmates any caregiver belief that good dying requires knowing that you are dying. That is where it leaves us all: stymied by the patient's fear and inexperience with death, inert because of the caregiver's fear of saying the wrong thing.

My point is that you have to know dying well to qualify at all to work with dying people. You *can* learn dying from being with dying people, but you can only rarely learn it *from* them. Though well-intended people working in the death trade regularly praise dying people as their greatest teachers, dying people are typically busy trying to figure out how to die, most of them in the undertow of the death-phobic aversions that predominate at dying time. They are not teaching, nor are they trying to teach. The most accomplished among them are struggling with all this. In a death-phobic time and place you cannot as a given learn what dying is or what it asks of us all from their tuition. You could learn, by deduction, from their example.

It takes some real living to learn the difference between courtship and seduction. This culture swims in one, struggling in its undertow toward the mirage of the other. Seduction is finding the ten thousand ways of stealing something from someone for yourself without them knowing that you have done so. Seduction needs coercion, sleight of hand, distraction, and a keen nose for weakness. Courtship is finding the ten thousand ways of giving something to someone that they need for their lives, without recourse to asking them what it is they might need. Courtship needs slowness, elegance, discernment, some cunning in the name of life, and a well-cooked heart. Both are skills of a sort, but one leaves rupture and vacancy as evidence and the other gives with a deep respect for the need or the struggle of the recipient.

And so you cannot ask dying people what it is like and then take dictation, for two reasons. First, it is an act of sloth to do so. More, while there may be no seduction of the kind I have described, no stealing in asking them what it is like, there is no courtship either. And caring for dying people is supremely a courtship and must be. Second, it presumes something that almost never holds: that dying people know what it is like to die and that they have the language to tell you about it.

Knowing death well doesn't mean knowing the dying person well or knowing what their opinions and their feelings are. Knowing death at all is a much more demanding business than that, and we will have to pay the tuition not from how learned we are but from how much we still have to learn. Life, as I said earlier, is not "the human life span." Life is by every measure a bigger thing, a more devout and devotion-inspiring thing, a truer thing, than the human life span. Life is that of which the human life span, for a while, partakes. Our secular humanist religions will not tolerate it, but let us be humble on this point: *Life is not a human thing.* It is what gives us the opportunity to be human. It is not the stage upon which we play out our humanity or our lack of it, though merely players we surely are. It is the play. And the play's the thing.

Some people these days are reading books that describe the "inner lives" of domestic pets, but these are stories inflected hopelessly toward the human. The very fact that the animals are house animals means that their "inner lives" have the human at their centers, that their nature has been subjugated by centuries of domestication to human need and comfort seeking. What of the inner life of a stone? The inner life of the wind? What is the inner life of the mountain on one side and the river on the other that cradle the farm that is my home? Would those be the stories of how any of us *feel,* or how we *see* things, or how we *want?* It wouldn't. We have religions that sanctify all sentient beings, which is good for the sentient beings they have in mind, but this still ties "life" to having eyelashes or a central nervous system or a pulse. We are denying this quality of sentience to mountains, rivers, the air, the ground, and all that sustains us at our considerable peril and to the demonstrable corruption of the world. We should rather at least consider that mountains, rivers, the air, and the ground are all ways life has of being sentient. The realization and the humbling power of knowing that life is not a human thing could go a long way toward making us human.

And so *neither is death a human thing.* Death is an epic mystery that will mean more than we can possibly mean by it. This is why slaughter, murder, pogrom, war, and ethnic cleansing are all the monstrosities they are—not because they end human lives so much as because the perpetrators take into their untutored hands one of the great mysteries of life unawares and violate it to make it serve their ends. Death dealt by people is Jacob's ladder climbed, the Holy of Holies torn open and nothing found inside. It becomes Death the Destroyer of Worlds, the act and the consequences too vast for humans to carry. Just as a theme park mountain is not a mountain but the slander of a mountain, and a slag heap not a mountain but the end of a mountain, so our capacity to kill each other or ourselves is not the natural order of things playing itself out, no matter how common it might be in our history and in the papers, no matter how much we are inured to it or numbed by the horror of it. Instead it is a rupture that will not let life live according to its nature.

The dying and death that are the subjects of this book are not the dying and death of murder and mayhem. I am writing about the kind that we can see coming, that we know about—at least the medicine and the mechanics of it—long before the final hours, the kind that comes about because we have been born and because we live. When I say "know death well," I mean that we must know how singular and nonhuman death is, how it is a knowable mystery not much known by our culture, how for all its ubiquity it continues to be dreaded and entered into as separation and loss and a miserable shock. If we are going to do anything more than remind dying people of what they no longer have and can no longer do and what they will never be again, we must know how it is for a man or a woman in the course of the ordinary business of getting dressed or washed to see or feel something they have never seen or felt before, and how it is for them to wait for the doctor's appointment, and wait for the appointment with the specialist, and for the test results, and to be asked to come to the office because they will not tell the results of the test on the phone, and wait for that appointment. We must know how it is for that man or woman to sit in the chair in the office that countless other people have sat in and have someone take away whatever is left of their frail feeling of well-being with the news that this is not curable, and how it is for them to be rushed then into a technical and encouraging discussion of how it might be operable and treatable, before the news that it is not curable has even cooled enough to take some kind of shape inside them, before it has turned from news into knowledge and from test results into the rest of their life. We must know how it is to stumble out into the daylight with nothing, not the sun or the street or the noise or any of the faces, none of it having survived the news, and the twin misery of every compassionless thing proceeding just as it has done. It is the same kind of mysterious timeless time you spend in a matinee movie and then walk out into the same daylight, as if nothing has happened while you were inside, as if there were no news, as if life was still life. We must know what it is like for that man or woman to look down at their body as if they had never seen it before, as a blighted thing, as an old friend that has quickly turned from acquaintance to adversary to enemy to assassin, all in the space of a few endless minutes. We must know how it is for that man or woman to surrender their clothes for the clean-pressed blue backless gown and the soulless paper slippers of treatment and palliation, to carry their valuables in a paper bag with them down the endless terrazzo hallways of med-tech doing all it can do. We must know what *If you can, you should* does to a person.

> A woman I once knew, a famous writer and counselor and ally through her life's work to tens of thousands of suffering people, was diagnosed with cancer. She experienced most of the same devastation most of us do, she was offered the same treatment regime most us would be offered, and she hoped for the same thing most of us do in a time like that. Her husband told me that he insisted on taking her to her appointments even though she assured him that she was not really sick at all and quite capable of driving herself. One day, as they parked at the clinic for the third or fourth chemo session, she turned to him and said that she was going to this appointment alone, and that he would have to wait for her in the car. She explained, gently but with

the fierceness that is part of her stock in trade, that he was compromising her chances for remission.

He was stunned, wounded. She said that his desire to protect her from hurt and cancer and stainless steel machines meant that he was demonizing the drugs and the people that she was going into the clinic to be with for two hours, and that if she had any chance at all of getting some remission from this cancer it meant that the receptionist and the lab people and the orderlies had to fall in love with her and she with them, and that his presence was getting in the way of that happening, and that if he loved her as he said he did he would stay away from this love affair she was trying to make and wait for her in the parking lot. We have to know the sound of the passenger door closing and those footsteps walking away. We have to know the quiet of not being able to do much more than wait, the awful ordinariness of that. We have to know something about having the person pushing you down the hall in a wheelchair somehow fall in love with you, or trying to have it so. We have to know what all of that is.

And further, we have to know the terrible seduction of dying not having to die, of being inundated with friends and family who cheerlead their loved one into the attitude of health, the positive outlook, the hopeful countenance, who enforce the banishment of any and all who would speak of dying when dying is at hand. We have to know how it is for dying men or women who are not allowed to know they are dying as they die, though throughout they know, how they have to maintain that secret awareness that masquerades as a fear alone, and how their job as someone's parent or child or spouse now includes not dying, and how not giving up is the only show of love and commitment tolerable to those who love them. We have to know how impossible it feels to refuse a treatment that will give them more symptoms and more pain to go along with their More Time. And we have to know how it is for families who have relied heavily on the med-tech miracles to keep their loved one alive to finally be asked to consider withdrawing that same technology and how much that will feel to them, years later, as though they were being asked to decide that their loved one should die then and there.

Knowing death well means knowing how and what it is to die now, in our time, and here, in a culture we have grown accustomed to and mostly believe in. It means knowing death not as an intra-psychic event trans-formed by the psyche into another attribute of personality or neurosis or repetition compulsion, but as a cultural, political, spiritual event that demands of all of us on both sides of the canyon of dying a cultural, po-litical, and spiritual intelligence, savvy, and capacity. Snowflake advocates might demand at this point, "Well, whose death is it, anyway?" and the only answer worth a damn, the only answer that gives the rest of us some way of being human in the face of it, is that it is the culture's death, one person at a time. I don't mean that each person's death is the death of the culture. I mean that the culture renders each death unto the one who is dying. The culture gives us our ways of dying, gives us the meanings and meaninglessnesses we wring from it, forcing upon us the repertoire for dy-ing. I do not use this phrase "to die not dying" to describe a psychological reality or a facet of individual style or psychology. I mean by it the myriad schemes of refusing to die that are this culture's *ur* response to dying. If we are to know dying well, we have to know what the culture has made of it. We have to know that our society is fundamentally death phobic. We have to know that the culture is to be found in the newspapers and the op-ed pieces, yes, but just as fully and intractably at the deathbed, in the home of the dying person, in all the professions that would serve the dying person. You should expect to find a culture's beliefs defended in those places where they are challenged, and the care of dying people is one such place.

Knowing death well costs those willing to know of it a tremendous amount. It costs all of us our well-learned and polite deference to the personal stylings of a dying person who will not know they are dying and will not die, surrendered in favor of an unknown deathbed etiquette and an uncharted job description. It costs all of us our fairly safe place in our professional identities or our identities as friends, coworkers, uncles, grandmothers, or neighbors of the dying person. It costs all of us our belief in only doing what we're good at. It costs us our deference to agency mandates and mission statements when mandates, statements, and professions leave this culture's death phobia intact and unchallenged. It costs all of us our friendly neutralities and loving, uncritical support of the culturally endorsed hatred and fear and refusal of dying when it comes to our friends and family members. Friendship is not the quality of how friends feel about each other. Even in deep and enduring friendship we know that those feelings are inconstant. Friendship is better honored by our willingness to risk the friendship itself for the sake of the friend. That is what being the friend of a dying person asks of us, a massive achievement, and that is what it does to us. When a dying person sees their dying coming from a long way off they might say, "There is no one on the road. And there is no road." If you are his or her friend, you begin by saying, "Amen."

If you carry these things with you and you let them be known, you will have people who will hold you in some esteem and ask that you attend their patients or their loved ones or their own deaths someday, and many more who will be uncertain, edgy, guarded, or hostile. These are the ones who would defend dying people against you and what you know. But you know death well not to be forearmed or defended or inoculated against mystery or suffering or fear or resentment. You know death well to be *able*.

Once I was asked to teach these things in a big city hospital. The one inviting me had colleagues and people she answered to, and she was apologetic when she said that they had requested a preliminary meeting with the education committee wherein I could give a demonstration of what I would teach them about. "They're thinking of an audition?" I asked, and she, with some embarrassment, agreed that it came to that. On the day in question I presented myself. Way up in the tower of the hospital, three people sat facing me: two palliative care physicians and a visiting medical ethicist from the U.K. Sitting there I knew again that advocating for a good death in a place that doesn't believe in dying means that these are not ideas to be explained so much as subversions to be administered. So, instead of talking about what I might talk about at a teaching event for the hospital staff, I did what I would do at the event. I told a couple of stories. I asked them to see their jobs differently by holding up the difference for them to see. After fifteen minutes or so, the two physicians said that they were keen to have me talk with the staff, but the ethicist was holding out for more. After some silence I said to him, "Well, friend, I've sat here working for the last fifteen minutes, and your colleagues have voted. Let us hear from you. What do you say to all this?"

After a pronounced pause he cleared his throat and said, "Yes. Well, this is all very interesting."

When someone calls your life work and your passion "interesting," you ought not to feel complimented, I don't think. This is the damning with faint praise you've heard about. He went on: "This is all most interesting. But I wonder what it looks like, practically speaking."

"You mean," I asked him, "Do I know how to do what I'm talking about?" He protested that he was only curious, but he was doubtful too. And so I explained myself this way.

"I don't know how it is where you come from, but I will guess that it is pretty much the same as it is here on this point, since we got most of our stuff from you. Here, when people say 'I love you' to each other, there are some things in there that are not as noble as we'd like. For many of us, much of the time 'I love you' means 'I love how I feel when you do what you do that makes me feel that way.' The first thing you see with this is that love is something I feel, an inner state of some kind that is mine. Like all feelings, the love feeling would be inconstant. The second is that it is a provisional thing. I'll take all the credit for being able to love you, but my ability to love you depends on what you do to make it happen. Especially it depends on you remaining loveable. That means that I love mostly what is loveable about you. That's my skill.

"And, at the bottom of it all, it means that you have to stay put long enough to do those things that make me love you. You have to stay around, to give me the chance to do it. We say to the person we propose to love, 'Listen, now. As long as you are as lovable as you are in this magic moment, I'll love you, no problem. Don't let that change, though. My skill will be up for grabs if you do. If that changes, well, my ability to continue to love you could be up for grabs.' It is a kind of reaction, this love. Not the greatest news for people just trying to make it through the matrimonial maze. But even more so, a lot of people love each other based on the shaky assumption that they will hang around long enough to do the loving and the getting loved. Not many go into the love business with the end of that love firmly in mind and in view. Fewer still are those that plan the end of their love. They'll hesitate if they have any sense that the one they're trying to love might not be in it for the long haul, or that the deal has changed, or that one of them is heading out of town and out of sight without waiting for the other one to get ready or agree or even be aware that this is what is happening, and must happen, and will.

"Now, all day long I meet people who are dying, and who are on their way to losing someone they've known for a long time. They've never done anything like it before. They don't want to have to do it, and they don't even want to be able to *learn* how to do it. Mostly they hate the whole enterprise. And that's my very promising job, to find a way to oblige people to learn something they don't want to learn and to learn it well and to learn it soon. I have to teach people how to love someone who's leaving, not someone who's staying. Nobody wants to learn to love like that, but that's what I have to do. My job, pretty much every day, is to persuade people to love someone who is leaving when almost everything inside them is screaming, 'Run!' or 'Give up.' And every day my job is to oblige that one who is leaving to do so loving the life they're leaving behind and everyone they've loved in it. That's the lion's share of the job, to get them to love someone and something as if it will end. Is that practical enough for you?" He agreed that it was. The vote was unanimous.

That is one example of knowing death well as a job description. Here is another. I've done most of my work in the death trade in people's homes, not in their hospital rooms. Without the structure of an office, a receptionist, a waiting room, and an invariably delayed appointment time, I had to develop an ability for improvisation, spontaneity, and hanging by a thread with no visible means of support. I was always in their world, and when I was working well it was impossible to forget it. You can't learn how to be nimble that way from books or in classrooms or in role playing with simulated patients, not really. Learning begins for real on the street in front of the patient's home.

When I was training new counselors for this work, I would bring them to the front door, and we would stand there. Then we would stand some more, and eventually the new recruit would start feeling uneasy.

They might say something like, "So, what are we doing?" They might ask, "Aren't they going to think that we're strange, just standing on their front porch?"

I'd say, "We're already strange to them. Look what we're doing for a living." Or I'd say, "Well, what are you doing?" and they would answer, "I'm waiting for you to ring the doorbell so we can go inside."

I would say to them, "Not yet. It's too soon." They would say, "Too soon for what?"

I would say, "You're not ready to go in there yet."

A little perturbed by now, they'd say, "How can I get ready standing on their front porch?"

My answer would be, "But this is how you get ready. You see, there's no death out here. It's all in there. There are cars and cats and kids out here, but no death. Do you remember me telling you that the hardest part of this job is knowing death well and that you can't do the rest of the job without it? Well, we're getting to know death well by standing here."

They would say, "But you just said there's no death out here. How can I get to know death well if it's not here?"

Then I could tell them. I would say, "You feel that nervousness running through you? That's life running through you. You're about to go inside there as a living person, and that nervousness, that strange kind of excitement and that desire to be helpful and to do the right thing, they are all signs of life. If you go in there with all of that you'll swamp that person who's trying to die or trying not to. You have to leave your nervousness out here. You don't go in there as someone full of life, as a reminder of everything that person inside is losing or has lost already. You go in there prone to their dying, as a midwife. *You* are the one subject to change without notice."

Knowing death well is not preparation for doing the job of caring for a dying person: It *is* the job.

I said earlier that dying is not a human thing—nor is it an inhuman thing. *Dying as a human being is a human thing.* Knowing this and carrying yourself as if it were so is mythically difficult. Knowing is the burdensome task. Knowing that dying people are dying in the care of a death-phobic culture, knowing what dying people will be subject to in the name of good care, whether you are there or not, you and I and any caregiver stare down the double barrel of how it is and how it could be: Either you will endorse, support, practice, and perpetuate the death phobia of the culture by visiting it upon dying people in the name of caring for them and supporting them and in the name of giving them what they say they want, or you will challenge, subvert, derange, and bleed the death phobia of the culture by asking dying people to die in an uncommon way.

If you choose the second path, you may for the rest of your working life have some kind of position in the death trade, selling what almost no one wants: a human death. That position will probably end calamitously. You will be a comedian away off in the wilderness or the bush, telling jokes to no one, with no way of knowing if they are funny, or if they are jokes, or if you are a comedian. You will be a spiritual activist when almost no one around you will acknowledge or recognize anything spiritual in what you are doing. You will be a grief monger with a stall in the strip mall of distractions, feel-good bromides, and Anywhere but Here holidays. You will be a teacher of the skills of broken heartedness in a place that grants doctorates and big paydays for being fine and staying the course. You will be an apostate in the Temple of Want. You will be a midwife at the end of a person's life when those who love them will demand that you bind the legs of life together and stop what is trying to be born from crowning until everyone is ready. Mostly—and this is one epic achievement of a human being—you will be a faithful witness to the hard truth that it is harder to die now, with all of our medical pain and symptom solutions and psychological technologies and New Age affirmations, than it has ever been. You will be a faithful witness to the labor necessary for a dying person to die well. You will not blink when it costs you so much to see how hard it really is, or you will turn away for a while and then turn back, I hope. You will be able to tell some of the truth of how it is when the exhaustion of dying not dying might incline some dying people and the people around them to wonder if it is worth it. You could be the one who says that it is and lives accordingly. You could be useful when death comes. That is the job: to know death well and to be useful when it comes.

And that is what an eight-year-old dying girl sitting up in her temporary hospital bed just before midnight looking out the window on the darkening world deserves. She deserves a faithful witness. Yes, she deserves the truth. The truth is that she is dying in a death-phobic culture that doesn't believe in what is happening to her. The truth is that just about everyone around her doesn't believe that her dying is a part of the natural order of things or that life includes her eight-year-old death. The truth is that everyone knows what is causing her to die, and no one knows why she is dying. The truth is that almost no one will know what to do with her and for her in the months and years after her death, that almost no one will imagine that she would need anything from any of them. The truth is that almost no one knows how to talk to her, nor does almost anyone know how to answer the question she asks, sitting up in bed minutes before midnight. And the truth she most deserves from the older people around her is that all of this can be different, that it must be different. The truth that she most deserves is not that it is her birthright to live to seventy-eight years and a few months, nor to be free of loneliness or pain, but that it was her birthright to have been born into a sane culture that knows how to care for her now not as if she will be around for decades, but for months. She deserves a few trustworthy adults initiated into the mysteries of the coming in and the going out of things who can sit with her in the night not in rancor or blunted, tranquilized misery, but in wonder at the hard-to-carry mystery of how life is, who can bear witness to that mystery and to her life, who instead of agreeing or disagreeing with the mystery of how life is can say yes to it anyway. What a dying eight-year-old girl deserves from life, I cannot say. But this is something of what she deserves from us.

7

SO WHO ARE THE DYING TO YOU?
WHO ARE THE DEAD?

If you are a teacher, your blessing can come in the shape of someone willing to ask you the simplest of questions. The simplicity will make you wonder again about all you have known and taught before that moment, whether it is still true if it ever was, whether you still know it, whether it is still a needed thing in the world. If you think well of a teacher, ask that teacher the simplest of questions. This can be hard on the ego, if you are the student. The more schooling you have, the harder this will be, since simple questions in a culture that trades on easy competence make you sound simple, as though you don't know enough even to ask confounded, pretzeled questions. But simple questions are great achievements. They have a good mixture of humility and wonder.

Our willingness to wonder is where mystery goes for shelter from the steady attack it endures from our demand for information, clarity, and certainty, and from our rarely questioned right to know what we demand to know. Wonder serves mystery with grace and a humble approach. Resolving mystery is like dissecting someone you love to find out how they got so loveable. You might know something you didn't know before, but what you loved gets lost in the inquisition. Malidoma Somé, the Dagara writer and teacher, has written that in his language there is a word, *yiel-bongura*, that is quickly and inaccurately translated into English as "mystery." He says that this word more accurately should be translated as "that thing which your knowledge cannot eat." Here is an indigenous understanding of understanding, and one our culture must learn: Mystery must have a proper place, a fundamental place, in learning.

Anishinaabeg culture has a similar kind of understanding at the center of its theology. The Jesuit black robes of the seventeenth century readily and monolithically translated *G'tche Manido* as "God," but its truer translation instead is "Vast Mystery." It is not the adversary of our intelligence, nor its opposite, nor its prey. When our education is a good one, mystery sits on the throne of our well-crafted intelligence, and it is the proper limit of our intelligence. Mystery is the place where we can finger the ragged edges of what we know and begin to make peace with what we will not know. It is in the nature of mystery, after all, that the more we know about it the more mysterious it becomes. Simple questions can get many of us there, seated on the ground at the foot of the throne of our intelligence, gazing up into the eyes of unknown things that serve us well by being unknown. Mystery survives our knowledge, and knowing that is a great thing.

> I had spent the better part of an hour at a hospital teaching event with a small group of palliative care physicians, and they were extending to me the cursory courtesy of seeming to attend to what we were discussing. This is typically a tough crowd to try to wonder aloud with. Their education predisposes them to cramming, to reducing things to memorable patterns of information, and their workloads don't tolerate much imprecision. They had some elaborate objections, other ideas, and not many questions. With only minutes left on the schedule, a doctor in the third row raised his hand and asked this:
>
> "I agree with you about this death phobia idea. I've seen it many times. It has buggered up a lot of patients

and families I've worked with over the years. My question is, When did it start?"

I asked him, "Do you mean when in the disease process does it begin? Or when in a person's life does it begin?"

"No," he said, "I mean when, at all. I mean, when in human history did this death phobia come about? How did it happen?"

I know he didn't feel brilliant at the time, but this physician's question is to me a brilliantly wondered thing. Right there in the question lives the possibility that death phobia is not inherent in being human, not inevitable, not a consequence of having been born and living into adolescence or adulthood. He may have been wondering for the first time in his work and maybe in his life how the fear of death came into the world, and whether it must be so.

Do we believe that those who fear death fear it because by the time they start thinking about these things they have lots to lose? If so, we believe that fearing death is part of being successful in life. Because they love being alive? Then we believe fearing death comes from attachment to things and people and the plodding sequence of our days. Because they were born? Then we believe it comes from having been born, and so all people should—must— fear it. Do those who fear death fear it because they are dying? If so, we believe it comes from knowing that you are dying, or that you will die, that it must be the affliction of all people willing to be wise in this.

Our dilemma here is as simple as the physician's question. If we go by any of these answers, it would follow that everyone fears death, and those who say otherwise are either spiritual geniuses, or not inclined to introspection, or lying. But anyone who has worked in the death trade for any length of time knows that there are dying people who do not fear death, thoughtful people not prone to the rampant death phobia that passes for prescience among us, who at the news and the immanence of their death are curious and sad and reluctant and disappointed and mystified, but not drawn and held in the undertow of a low-grade, grinding, unarticulated, and dusky terror that is the death phobia of our culture and one of the certain ways by which our culture can be recognized by outsiders. If you have traveled a little in the world, you know that there are places where people's way of life is so radically different from our own that we have a hard time believing we live in the same world at the same time, and one of those differences is in how they die. It is another thing with them, entirely. So we cannot kill off the mystery and the misery of *our* death phobia by accusing all in the world of that affliction. If being afraid to die is not a consequence of being born or knowing that you are dying or being human, then where does it have its beginning? How does it make such a sure and undisputed claim upon our imaginations?

It isn't a hard case to make, that the dominant culture of North America has a death phobia. I have had something of a working life because of it. Fear of dying stalks hospital hallways, of course, but lifestyle advertising is rife with it, parenting carries it along, the fitness workout industry is carried by it, and so too the insurance business. It is usually unspoken, but fear of dying is traded on and counted on. This culture has been very fond of the idea of "natural" for more than forty years now. "Natural" is used to sell shampoo, investments, retirements, lawn care, and funerals. "Natural" is sold to you and me and our children as "good," "wholesome," "your mother would approve," and "the Earth will love you for it." But "natural" also means "naturally occurring" or "not tampered with," as in "left alone, that's what will happen." Some use it to mean the inherency of something, as in "comes with the territory."

How "natural" is it to be afraid of dying? If it is natural, that should mean that everyone—or everyone who is following their nature, or everyone who is sane—should be more or less afraid to die, or prone to it. It should mean that being human and being alive means being afraid to die. Or it will mean being afraid to die once you wise up to what is coming.

Our infants don't seem to show any fear of anything. It doesn't seem natural for them. Our children are afraid of strangers and of falling down the stairs if they have done it before, but they don't seem to be afraid to die. Psychologists and those persuaded by them say this is because children have no capacity for a sense of the finite, or of finality, but I don't know how true that is. Most grown-ups I have seen in action proceed without much of a sense of finality either, but they have the ability to fear their deaths, and they do. After what I've seen, I doubt that fear of death comes from the ability to understand finality or that it comes from *any* ability. Fear is many things, but a skill it is not. Uninitiated adolescents—almost *all* of our adolescents—are occasionally drawn to the idea of dying as a solution to their jittery insubstantial selves, to their uncertain future in the world, but there doesn't seem to be a lot of death fear that drives them there. It doesn't seem to be natural for these younger people to be afraid of death. Our adults, on the other hand, are the carriers, the acolytes, the mongers of death fear. Evidently something happens on the freeway from adolescence to adulthood in our part of the world. Or, maybe something doesn't happen. It might be that you have to *learn* to be afraid to die in that gap, in that blind spot where something didn't happen.

Poke around in the growing literature about dying and death, and two kinds of answers to the doctor's question start showing themselves. The psychological books teach that the cause of death fear is the growing awareness of frailty and impermanence as people come into their adolescence. Writers who are fond of "attachment theories" as the bases for a healthy emotional life argue that close relationships teach that kind of anxiety, that *having breeds the fear of losing.* The greater exposure people have to dying, which the psychological literature calls "loss," and the more they have to lose, the more they have to fear. It makes sense, and it probably isn't true.

During the last century North Americans had a steeply diminishing exposure to dying people and dead people. There are more people here than ever, but there is far less dying going on for people to see. Hospital deaths have grown more common over the last fifty years, and as our populations continue to head for the cities to live out their lives and deaths, hospital deaths will be for most the only kind of death they might know about. The funeral industry remains a bona fide moneymaker, and we will pay the undertaker well to do the work of caring for our dead. Between the hospital and the funeral home, there's very little for the average person to see or do where dying and death are concerned beyond signing forms, making calls, paying bills, getting a nice suit, and making his or her way through bad traffic to get to the funeral on time. The pervasive fear of dying in the adult population of North America doesn't come from seeing more dying as people get older. It comes, partly, from seeing not much dying or much death at all as they get older.

The spiritually inclined books on the subject take aim at "attachment" too, but also at the materialism, distractedness, and faithlessness of modern times, the inability to be mindful, the waning of "family values," not learning the five stages or the twelve steps, all kinds of things. They say that fear of dying is in the culture because of what is missing from the culture. They say too that fear of dying has become so pervasive that it is in the fabric of daily life. This is compelling too, but untrue. Until now I've used the expression "death-phobic culture." Now I will offer you a different understanding. We don't achieve much by decrying the obvious, that ours is a culture where the fear of death is common and adamant, but it is going to help our understanding to hesitate in declaring this a death-phobic culture. As an overture to the rest of this chapter, consider it possible that *where you have culture you do not have death phobia.* The fear of dying is a sign of something gone profoundly wrong, not personally but culturally.

We have a high and rising cancer rate in North America, but we cannot say that cancer is a cultural value of North America. Cancer and death phobia are *norms* of the culture, in the sense that they are common. No one would vote for them, no one defends them or advocates for them, yet they proliferate. No one approves of them, no one wishes them on their children, no one believes in them, and yet there they are, at least as pervasive and as persistent as they have ever been. Mysterious.

And we have an aging population, but we cannot say that the proliferation of old folks' homes is any kind of a sign that our culture honors our elders. Old folks' homes in every city and town don't mean that we love our elders and give them an honored and carefully maintained place among us, any more than the proliferation of self-storage units outside every town and city is a sign that we love our stuff. No, death phobia is an elephant in the hands of blind men as long as we keep saying that it is an attribute of North American culture, or any culture. It is truer to say that death phobia happens when something happens to the culture. Death phobia happens when culture doesn't happen, or when it is imperiled in a fundamental way. Death phobia, I am asking you to consider, is not culture. It is anti-culture. It multiplies wherever culture is under attack, especially when it is failing from within. Death phobia is a syndrome at war with culture, and where I work and live it is prevailing. *Death phobia begins to metastasize whenever our ability to make culture, to be deeply at home in our skin and in the world, has gone missing.* This is the idea we'll pursue now.

Looking for Home

Somewhere around the age of twenty I looked up one day and said, "How do I know that there's any such thing as Europe?" This is *the* coming-of-age question for many of us here whose deep ancestry cannot be found in North America, I would say. It is the local way of asking what Rumi asked eight centuries ago:

"Who am I? And what am I supposed to be doing?"

He answers himself with mystery—this is genius, to answer your yearning with mystery—and his answer is true historically, culturally, and spiritually for us too:

I didn't come here of my own accord,
and I can't leave that way either.
Whoever brought me here will have to come
and take me home.

Rumi (translated by Coleman Barks), "Who Says Words with My Mouth?" in *The Essential Rumi,* page 2

Where that home might be—*what* home might be—is the secret garden the North American psyche has heard about from others but not much lived in. Home: This is the beginning of the answer to the doctor's question about where the fear of death came from.

That day, when I was teetering on the edge of the culture I had been born to, I took on the job of finding out for myself if there was such a thing as Europe. The first consequence of taking on that assignment was that continuing with school was suddenly goofy and out of the question. I stopped going to the library. I went to the airport. The initial plan was to go to Spain with a Turkish-Polish-American dancer I was very close to. She was named after a Eurasian mountain range and had that same dark, epic beauty. I had given my heart and mind to her during the school year. During that summer, by an authentic Dear John letter, she gave them back. This dancer, I know now, had the scent of Home all about her, as women usually do for men, and this woman was in her name and her dark eye the great Somewhere Else for me. But all I knew then was that I was wrecked, disconsolate. The devastation was thorough: A week before the scheduled flight, I had no reason to stay and even less to go. But there was a plan, shredded as it was, and the plan, minus that beautiful woman, prevailed. With my reason to leave gone, I went. I ended up in a world of hurt on a charter flight wrangled from a friend's travel agent father with 212 seniors who, certain indeed that there was a Europe, were bound for a Mediterranean cruise.

Bad weather grounded us in Seville. Tour buses got us lost in villages with more dogs than people in mountains that looked like the backs of old men's hairless heads, mountains in every way older than anything we had where I lived. In a gust of diesel we thudded into Malaga and pulled up to the boarding ramp of what looked to me like a seagoing condominium. Everyone had a "we're all in this together" feeling from that bit of adversity and, because I was the only one with a guitar and without matching luggage, they started working on me to extend the caper and stow away with them on their Greek luxury liner for two weeks. One old guy in particular kept leaning across the aisle of the bus and advising me, "Don't sweat the small stuff." I didn't think being busted as a stowaway on the high sea was small stuff, but my heart was still a piece of coal and my instinct for self-preservation was cashiered by the dancer's not finding me worthy. By sundown I was on the ship, secreted in a luxury suite and surrounded by mostly raucous old Jews from the Detroit area who counted among their recent and highly successful seditions raiding the bar fridge of an unoccupied room and persuading me of the obvious merit of hitting the high seas in their company. Crimes without victims were victories of a kind, and we all decided that we were winning. Minus my dark eyed ex-companion, with the wreckage of my plans now wrecked too, a North American kid on a cruise ship in a port town somewhere in the Old World, I was sweating nothing at all.

I kept my head down for the first day, sleeping on the cabin floor of one of the legitimate passengers, and all seemed well. On the second night, wonder of wonders, we received an invitation to dine with the captain. This wasn't to be missed. With my eating companions well decked out in good cruise wear I stood out a bit, but a good time was had by all. Many times we toasted the captain on his fine hospitality, and more so each other on our continuing larceny and hustle. Later that night, carried along by the pirate bravado of successfully violating the rules of international law and travel, a dozen of the my golden age coconspirators and I had quite a sing-along in our hideout while the ship slipped out into the black-sliver Mediterranean, bound for Gibraltar. All was exotically well, but most of the next day, moored at the foot of the famous Rock, I was haunted by the gloomy certainty that my luck was running on fumes. I saw myself in chains below decks, taken into serious Interpol custody in Sicily. Providence assisted in me reacquiring my passport from the purser's office. I had been midwived into the Old World by wily, purple-tint, creaking immigrants to the New, and I liked them tremendously for it and still do. All are dead now, I'm sure, and I remember with great fondness their willingness to have me. A half hour before she was set to sail, and without telling my recuperating companions and giving them a chance to talk me out of it, I bade my silent farewell and made my uncertain way quietly down the pleasure ship's plank by moonlight and into the arms of the true reason I was in Europe and the good reason that I was there alone.

Gibraltar is like so many crossroad places, especially end-of-the-road port towns, built on everyone being there by accident and no one planning to stay. It is layered up in an epic Iberian, Carthaginian, Greek, Roman, African, Muslim, pirate, Christian, slave-dealing, English, Moroccan mystery/history stew. The townsfolk lived and did business in what would in North America be national historic sights and treasures. Within a day I had found an old pension I could afford, and within another I had a job, having misrepresented myself as a soundly qualified stone mason to an English engineering firm refurbishing a nineteenth-century building on the main street for an upscale retrofit. I was thrown in with a good-humored band of red-haired and freckle-faced Moroccan Scots Spaniards who rendezvoused at sunup by the old casement walls to be driven to the job site, holding on for life, by a one monocle-eyed, ex-military, Bermuda short-sporting Englishman on the flatbed of an old Fiat truck. By the end of the week, I had a gig in a second floor bar called the Lizard as the only New World guy in a house band made up of Moroccans (one of them the same guy who kept stealing my tools on the job), Spaniards, and Algerians playing American folk music on instruments that were never made for that job. I netted three or four hours of sleep a night for weeks, running with an international brigade of hooligans who like me had washed up in Gibraltar homeless, hopeful, and keen. With a shredded plan now magically reconstituted as a moneymaking adventure of the first order that seemed like it could go on for a good while, and life blowing wind into my sails, my heart slowly began to find its legs. There *was* such a thing, I thought, as Europe, if this was Europe.

One night at the Lizard, between sets, a Mexican guy from Texas invited the band for a night on the town. After the limited carousing that the one main street of Gibraltar allowed, we watched the rising sun dance up in the Straits from the ruined Roman fort up high on the Rock as the fabled hooting monkeys of Gibraltar watched us. It turned out our new friend, Rudy, was a crewman on an eighty-five-year old Danish ketch, and we ended up crowding around the teak beauty's galley table for breakfast, riding the harbor eddies and lying devoutly to each other about our lives back home. In keeping with general trends, a few days later I was being auditioned by the boat's captain, a wispy bearded Frenchman with black eyes who had just come out of the desert after living with Bedouin for six years, with a view to joining the five man, one woman crew as an able-bodied seaman to take the good ship *Lova,* which still had its original cannons rusting in the bilge below decks, to Malta for refitting to suit the carriage trade. Badly overplaying my sailing experience—I had only once sailed a one-person Sunfish out to the middle of a small lake, and had to swim back in, towing the boat by a nylon rope between my teeth—I got the job. The good captain requisitioned the crew's passports for divination purposes, the second time that passport wrote something of my fate. Using birth date numerology, the Kabalah, and I don't know what Berber mojo he'd picked up in the desert, he did a lot of silent calculating, and then gravely announced to us as follows: The voyage will have many events.

A week later I was riding the bowsprit on a midnight crossing to Ceuta to fill the ship's stores at the dawn market, dolphins riding the cresting waves below me and the half-moon dancing phosphorous in the surf. The Jews from Detroit, the expat hotel owners, the one-eyed English renovation boss, the Moroccan job site tool thieves, the Straits straddled by Hercules himself, most all of what I had known to be true, all of this was in the darkness to the west, behind me, and I was bound for somewhere east of anywhere I'd ever been, into the Old Time. My plans were gone. I knew for certain that Europe was there, and I was alive.

The main event, it turned out, was the wrecking of the ship. I was a week with an epic, relentless, dawn to dusk to dawn seasickness. It was so constant that at first I was sure I would die from it; a few days later I was afraid that I wouldn't. Miraculously, on the seventh morning I woke up utterly cured, sea legs at the ready and thinner but able-bodied. Through all of the next day the wind steadily freshened, I scrambled to pick up my end of the work that my mates had taken on during what to the French captain was my shameful infirmity, and the ship skidded finely on course, leaning with old-time windblown majesty into the waves. Bound we were for Malta, ancient as dirt for a North American kid and waiting for us. The amateurs on board—and we were the lion's share of the crew—were thrilled at the speed after a few days of the doldrums, but the ex-Royal Navy man among us, who looked entirely like Ernest Hemingway in Idaho, handsome and at the end of things, who took nitroglycerine for a bad heart, had a sense that the seas were in for a change. His line was, "Everything's happ'nin'." He'd use it just for punctuation most of the time, but when a day later waves began to multiply, his pronouncement had something Old Testament-sounding in it. By midnight everything not tied down below decks was on the floor and the rigging was moaning and thrumming the low drone of what could not be outrun. By dawn, if dawn it was and not the endless twilight that it soon became, we were in a perfect storm.

Sea storms are measured in units of gale force. There was a little handbook on board that described the conditions as the weather worsened, and it divided the mayhem from Force 1 through Force 15. Accompanying the descriptions were photographs, but only up to Force 11. The other four chapters were in the book, I guess, for the sake of knowing what was wrecking your boat, what was coming to get you. The morning hours had us in a Force 11 gale. The waves crested at forty feet; the little grandchild waves that clung to the belly of the big ones were bigger than anything I'd ever seen that could move on its own. When the ship was in the trough, the wave tips were as tall as the main mast. The main sail was in ruins from the wrenching winds, and the rudder twisted in the boil like a broken arm, sheared from the steerage. The ship groaned in the blow. The planks below decks began to wrench open from the wind's torque and take on water. The bailer—a brass tube from the deck to the bilge with a leather-collared plunger as old and frayed as was the ship below the waterline—split and failed. To stay afloat we had a bucket line and hand bailed from the greasy diesel bilge where the old cannons rusted and who knew what else washed around, up the steps and into the roar. The shortest person was sent down into the diesel to start the bailing, and there I was. We had a little radio on board that, a lunatic arrangement that is ludicrous now but was mind-boggling and cruel then, could receive but not transmit. As the morning wore on, between bailing sessions we sat, or we held on to something in a sitting position, and listened to the ship moan and wrench and shudder. And we waited. Our Royal Navy man told us as the storm found its keening pitch that he'd been sunk a few times in the war, but he'd never been in anything as bad as this. No one said as much, but by noon it seemed likely as not that the ship would be in pieces by dark. By three, under a clear blue sky, for the first time rogue waves began to pound the deck above our heads. There were times now that the ship was under water, the beginning of something more certain. Somewhere in there, we began to consider dying.

You could see it. Each of us began fixing ourselves for death. Each of our faces clouded. Most moved off to sit by themselves, something I remember as so sad and unnecessary now, but then it seemed grim and proper. Our young and untested camaraderie didn't need laughs to endure, but it did need a future. Without it, the instinct to be together leaked out into the boil and was gone. Being too close to one another threw each of us off the scent of what was coming, and strange as it may sound to you, none of us wanted distraction from it. There was early on a feeling there among us that if we concentrated well on what was coming we could somehow do something about it. But as it came on, our approaching deaths drove us to aloneness. Some of the crew slipped away, sitting there, broke the deal they'd made with their plans, floated alone on the raft of their never-to-be-lived life. They were catatonic. Some saw their names in their hometown newspapers, their picture in the church, flowers. I saw my mother disconsolate for most of the rest of her shortened life, no body to bury. I saw the unexpected end of everything. As the sun found the heaving horizon line and darkness came, six were below decks and bound to the deep, none but one a sailor, all without strength to fight the wind, all wondering what More Time would do to them, none any longer knowing what to wish for, all homeless on a sea that awaited us.

No one died the death we feared on that voyage, as things turned out. The storm grew weary, blew itself out and ebbed away, the seas kept heaving, but their appetite for our masts and sails was sated, and by dawn we were left alone hundreds of miles off course to limp into the port of Palermo with the rudder in pieces. Promptly we were arrested by the Guardia on suspicion of being incompetent boobs who had gotten into some real trouble in the course of running drugs or guns in or out of the eastern Mediterranean. Interpol got involved. After what we'd seen in the seas, the stern faces, the epaulettes, and the Uzis of our captors didn't mean much to us. After what we'd seen inside of ourselves and our lives, and inside of each other, being safely and strangely on land didn't mean much either. Within a day or two of our passports being returned to us and without much in the way of ceremony or testimony, we scattered north and west, as Europeans have done for many centuries. I learned later that the *Lova,* addled by the storm, after keeping us from the sea those long, driven hours, was deemed too expensive to restore and was scuttled for the insurance money.

Some other kind of dying instead had planted itself in me in the weeks and years after that autumn on the Mediterranean, a dying that began to deepen my understanding of what it could mean to be alive. Though this was not the first time I had seen the likelihood of my death, or tasted the certainty of the thing, it was the first time I had been held by the fear of it and by the vast and solid longing that it not be so. It was the first time it had been planted in me that dying and an instinct for home somehow nosed each other, were somehow not opposites but twins, that where one was the other was close at hand. That is where I first saw something that became the overture to my working life and is a theme for the rest of this book: Whenever you go looking for home, you will find death on the welcome mat.

Could I Be from Somewhere? Stories

TIBETAN PRAYERS Years ago I was approached by a woman who became a mentor for me in the death trade. I was working in the hellish custody and access industry at the time, helping to determine what was to become of children whose parents were more than ready to dismember their kids Solomon-style to get a little justice. She proposed that I take on a group of men who recently had someone die who was close to them. Typically it was their wife or girlfriend who had died, and their ability to be at home anywhere again was in real doubt. "What would you like me to do with them?" I asked. She explained how the counseling and medical staff at the hospital, mostly women, were unnerved by them and at a loss as to what to do. "Why are they afraid of them?" They found that the men tended to divide into two groups: Those who'd become bellicose, obnoxious, and aggressive were hard to counsel, and those who'd become remote, cool, and monotonous were eerie. "Just take them on," she said. I took the job and got a list of names and phone numbers. Not one of the men was keen to meet together, even once, when I mentioned that there'd be no women present. After the fourth cold call I hyped the idea by saying, "But this will work out great for you. It's turning out to be a group for men who don't want to be in a group for men." Eventually about eight men agreed, and we started with no clear idea of what we were meeting to do. But early on I saw that they had opted for anger or austerity because they didn't want to be sad and didn't know how to be sad and didn't trust sadness. So it became a place where men learned sadness, and heartbrokenness turned it into a skill instead of an endurance. Sad school was scheduled to go about eight weeks, but at their urging it lasted eighteen months.

During that time I came across a documentary film about Tibetan Buddhist practices of dying and funeral making. One of the compelling things about it was the minimal narration. In its place was a voice reading passages from *The Tibetan Book of the Dead* to illuminate the scenes. In a brilliant piece of casting, Leonard Cohen was the voice. I wanted the men to see this film. It followed the death of a middle-aged man—"Polten Tsering," Leonard intoned repeatedly, making this name sound, as Leonard can, like a prayer itself—and the month-long rituals performed by monks that ended in his body being cremated on a small pyre in the village square. Though it was long, I played it through without a break. After the credits the room was silent for quite a while. The men sat with their arms folded, looking at the floor, just as they'd often done in the first few meetings when no one knew why they were there. Finally the youngest, a man who'd recently watched his twenty-six-year-old fiancée die in her hospital room from a graphic catastrophic bleed, who'd endured a lot of sorrow in his short life, cleared his throat, looked up at everyone, and in a voice that mixed confusion with confession and turned it into mourning said, "I feel like I come from nowhere."

That feeling is the soundtrack of dying for many people in North America. Feeling like you come from nowhere can happen when the living and dying you've seen so far seems nasty, brutish, and short to you. It can happen that way when you've no teacher for grieving and sorrowing, and no initiation to bring you into the fellowship of human beings. It can happen because an initiation-free adolescence, in hindsight, is its own kind of nowhere, and because initiated humans can make you feel like you *should* be from where they're from, that something vital is missing if you aren't. The men in that room that evening felt a yearning suddenly to be Someone, from Somewhere, because they'd seen for the first time that such a thing is possible, and even necessary, in the world, that such a thing often shows itself when human dying is in the room.

HINDU HOLY MAN A boy of East Asian descent was admitted to the hospital with seizures. He had previously been in good health. Diagnostically he was a mystery, and shortly after his admission he began to seize continuously. As the days passed he deteriorated. His brain was being damaged to such an extent by the seizures that it was very likely that, should he live, his impairment would render him incapable of communicating and in need of constant and intense care for whatever constituted the rest of his life. There was very little the hospital staff could do medically, beyond sedating him to a point where he wasn't seizing visibly and keeping him hydrated, fed, and ventilated. His life drained away, unexplained.

A week or ten days later the care team approached the family in a gentle way with the suggestion that it seemed less and less likely that their son would be able to survive even the withdrawal of the life support he was on and that everyone had to begin to try to wonder about the purpose of maintaining him on life support. They were surprised that the hospital staff had taken so long to recommend withdrawing life support. They realized that the technology had its limits. They had contacted a holy man in their home village and wanted their son kept alive while the holy man made his prayers and divinations. They were hopeful that the end result could be a cure from a distance. The care team agreed to continue the present course.

To most people on the team this was another case of the understandable but futile persistence of Old World, pre-technological religious conviction, at war with irreducible, inevitable human frailty. Working in a multicultural environment, it was a common experience for them. Situations like this escalate readily into nightmares: Families harboring the resentful certainty that the hospital could do something but won't, the care team hamstrung between family traditions and the life-support technology that, once applied, can only be withdrawn with the harsh knowledge that the patient must die as a result. Quietly some probably hoped that the boy's timely death would solve the impasse. But he was, as it is said in situations like this, otherwise healthy, and with the life support in place the boy was unlikely to die. He could not die.

A few days after those talks, the family reported that the holy man had discerned the cause of the boy's affliction and advised the family to take certain measures that might reverse, at least to a livable level, his misfortune. In addition to recommending herbal remedies from the old country, the holy man prescribed feeding the family's ancestors. The problem, he told them, was that since the family's emigration to North America no one in the village had continued the proper rites and ceremonies at their clan's gravesite. No one had left money enough for the graveyard to be maintained. The result was that the unfed, uncared-for ancestors sought solace and sustenance as they had, from the boy who soon was continually seizing. One solution was for some family members to return to the village and sponsor ceremonies to restore the health of the ancestors. Whether the boy's health would be restored was uncertain, but the health of the ancestors was mandatory to establish the health of the living.

I was asked to join a meeting of the care team. The stated purpose of the meeting was to find a way to give the proper amount of regard for the family's religious convictions while obliging them to face the real inevitability of having to make a decision about the life support. The boy's current status, the parents' understanding of it, and the recently obtained diagnosis from the family's holy man were all discussed. After a moment of strained silence, the conversation went directly to how to overcome this most recent obstacle and to getting the family to a workable position on life support. About then someone said, "Well, I'm sorry, but I do not accept a God who punishes children. That is it." She wasn't dismissive. She was angry, and she called down the whole Hindu pantheon in her anger. The doctor chairing the meeting said to me, "You're interested in this sort of thing. What would you say?"

For this family and their holy man, God didn't appear anywhere in the story. The team seemed to need God showing up to make sense of what the holy man recommended, but the family did not. This was a dilemma strictly between the living and the dead. It was part dereliction of duty, part soul-forgetting brought about by chasing the dream of a better life somewhere in the West. The kind of remedy the holy man offered was also practiced on this side of Europe, in places not far from where we were sitting. Most of the team believed in the principle of what now gets called "cultural humility," but the breaking point was that no one in attendance believed in ancestors, hungry, angry, abandoned, or otherwise, who could influence events in the present, let alone be the root cause of *status epilepticus*. The holy man was talking about the dead in the present tense. No one on the team was going to do so. Everyone was from Nowhere, staunch monotheists. Because a holy man from Somewhere had shown up with a story that bound the living and the dead, a story whose central lament was the loss of home, the general response was to consign the family to Nowhere too, where the living live alone and the dead are God's business.

IRISH PSYCHOLOGIST I was asked once to see an old lawyer who was dying slowly and painfully and putting his adult children through epic misery in the process. It turned out that most of his concerns were legal—who would inherit what, what would become of his house, and the like—and when he saw that I wasn't legally inclined, he thanked me for the visit and showed me the door. Ten months later one of his children asked that I come to talk with them as, finally, their father lay immanently dying. There were four, all professionally trained and inclined. After an hour or so of guiding them toward helping their father die well no matter their feelings about what kind of a father he'd been to them, his death now very close at hand in the next room, I said my good-byes and headed for the door. As I put my shoes on the youngest son, a psychologist, asked if he could have a private word with me on the porch outside. Once there he told me that he had to his dismay found that all his training about the psychological life was proving to be all but worthless to him and his siblings now that death was in the house. Then he asked if I knew of anywhere he could go to meditate and clear himself, being a Buddhist practitioner of long standing.

I answered him, "Your name's O'Flynn, isn't it?" He nodded. I said, "About one hundred and fifty years ago there was in a silent throng a woman, old by the standards of the day, standing on a stone pier in the harbor at Cork. It was probably close to sunset, coolish from the sea breeze coming landward, and she was standing there in her homespun dress and coat, waving her best scarf from side to side, neither fast nor slow, a flag of certain sorrow, a rhythmic good-bye. On the stern deck of the creaking scow, a crowd of a hundred or so, all leaving, all sailing to God knew what, among them a boy of about nineteen years, trying to pick out from the crowd his old mother waving her last and only good-bye to her youngest. That boy of nineteen is your great-great-grandfather, bound because of famine and all for this country before it was a country. That old woman is your great-great-great-grandmother, losing her youngest forever though he was still so much alive. And that old man upstairs in there, dying, is their son, you see, your father. And you are son to all of them. There's your meditation. You go out in the backyard and make the sound that she made that evening there on the docks in Cork. That's what's happening in there again. Make that sound for their son, your father, sailing off in the cooling evening of his life. Make that good-bye for him, and for them."

ENGLISH CEMETERY Though there is a big portion of my family that has gnarly, knotted roots in England and some in Ireland, I myself have a Mediterranean leaning instead and have never had any desire to go on the old pilgrimage. More than that, I had a pretty strong aversion to visiting even for a short time, even for a stopover. For many years I would make no plan that brought me to England. I joked it was because of the food, but I never really knew why. Fortunately, as I've grown I have acquired a little understanding of these stands that I make. I respect them enormously and then, playing the understanding spouse to my adamant self, leave a little room for things unfolding differently even still. Over the last few years I have met some fine people from England, and the opportunity to be with them made teaching at a palliative care conference in Wales seem like something I could manage. After the airport mayhem in North America, customs in Cardiff was sweetness itself: One older fellow with crimson cheeks leaned against a pillar and took your written declaration, asked after your health, and wished you a fine visit. He, or his demeanor, is probably long gone now.

I was at a conference at a university, teaching about caring for dying children. The audience there was from all over the U.K., and some were from other places in the old Commonwealth. They were respectful, attentive, and the like, but there wasn't much juice flowing. It was an event that, having come so far, made me feel emptier and drier than when I got there. My host, who was in the funeral business, offered to organize a public talk for me at a local Zen retreat center on the night before I left. Even though my old prejudice about the English was prevailing at the time, I agreed to give it a try. There wasn't much time to get the word out, and he advised me not to expect many people.

After driving in rural England for a week, I stopped trying to make out the hieroglyphic highway signs altogether, and the sheep lanes that passed for roads became a terror whenever there was oncoming traffic. So the afternoon of the talk, my wife and I walked miles through the villages in the rain, in withdrawal from the gas pedal. These were places choreographed by the Industrial Revolution: factories down by the river, worker's housing hugging the factories, homes of the factory owners and managers up on the hill, the old glacial and ancestral shoreline. In one of these villages we followed a lane down to the skewed iron gate of a churchyard. The small and proper and severe stone church was built into the hillside, and it was surrounded on three sides by a cemetery. The stones were shoulder to shoulder almost on top of each other, many of them heaved up by tree roots or toppled by time passing. There'd been no new graves for a hundred years or more. There was gray stone upholstered with gray papery lichen and a stone wall keeping the graveyard from the Renaults and the roaring lorries beyond.

The moment we passed through the gate I heard a murmuring woven into the rain. The air was thicker, and the gravity there made a truer claim on us. We slowed our pace, and the farther we walked the more crowded the place became, crowded with what was missing, with what had dissipated. All was forlorn. That piece of ground had the presence of what was absent. It was a place of mourning that was itself not mourned. The cemetery was on the edge of a large town, with a busy main road on the other side of the stone wall, but the cemetery and the people in it seemed utterly forgotten. The dead were still there. It was the living that were missing. There were no plastic wreaths, no pebbles on the grave-stones, no manicure of the plots. The living, the ones who might have remembered those who had gone into the ground, had vanished into their lives. A good number of them had fled to America, become Yanks and Canucks and Caribbeans, *become America.* America is a hole in the collective memory, the fortune seekers forgotten, their leaving breaking the web of memory binding the living to the dead of that little cemetery. Standing there in that air thick with old sorrows, I was following down the scent of some kind of answer to the doctor's question about where the fear of dying started and how it had come so relentlessly among us, and why I'd never wanted to come.

While we didn't stay long in the cemetery, the desolation of the place stayed with me all through the afternoon. That evening we were driven by our hosts, thankfully, to a picture-perfect reproduction of a Zen temple in the English countryside, an amazing thing to see. I had lived in Kyoto years before, and it was not a stretch to imagine myself there again among the carp pools, the Zendo halls, and the bamboo gardens. They installed me in the speaker's chair at the front of the hall while people came through the door in ones and twos, and after ten minutes I stood at the ready. As often as I tried to begin, that's how often more people came in. In twenty minutes the room was full. As has happened so often before and since that night, the word of mouth advertisement of a discussion about dying was like the rumor of a free meal: People don't know they're hungry until the food shows up. My undertaker friend was very pleased and he beamed and gave me the thumbs-up from the back row. I began by announcing that we'd the giddy good fortune of an evening together without limit to our thought, and asked what would they like to hear about. No response.

I asked them what brought them there. Nothing. I asked them how much they wanted, how long they wanted to sit together. Finally a man in front said, "Oh, I can take in about ninety minutes, tops." It was as if we were talking about food, about consumption, not about wonder.

As it happened, the willingness of the English folks to stay with the hard themes of dying and history, gradual and guarded as it was, made me want to reward them with more to consider. They seemed to forget that they only had a ninety-minute limit, and after a while we were enjoying each other, and I didn't want it to end. I talked for four hours, and when I stopped we'd made a fine beginning of an approach to a possible introduction to the business of caring for dying people—a good achievement for four hours' heavy labor. We hadn't made much of a path for learning about caring for the dead, but it isn't something to be done from a standing start in one night together.

It was minutes to midnight, and most were overwhelmed and bleary. I asked if there were any questions or comments. The first person to raise her hand was in tears before she got a few words out. She sobbed, and the night grew a bit colder and lonelier, and her grief rang through the room as if it were the clapper in a wooden bell, painful to all. She told how her father had died some months before, and how she'd thought that by the standards of her place and time she had done well by him at the end of his days, but she'd begun to realize during the evening that many things were left undone and unsaid for him. The story tumbled out of her, raw and abrupt. It was a kind of confession. Silence is a respectful response to confession, and I let the silence that followed her painful story go on a long time, and when it was clear that she didn't know what else to say, I said to her, "Well, that's a very hard thing, to know that it should have been different for him." She looked at me, tear stained and blank, waiting for me to do or say something else. After another long pause I said, "Do you have something you want to ask me about all that?"

She wiped her face with her sleeve and then asked, "What should I do?"

It's always hard for everyone at moments like that. So many people have seen talk show therapy sessions now, and their expectations come from the "fix it fast" school of public suffering. Most people in most audiences I've been with believe without saying or being aware of it that being upset is a kind of noble labor and that it should be rewarded. For most of us in the West, a public expression of pain or confusion is a problem for the listeners or the experts to solve, as if the hurt has an automatic request in it to have the hurting end. I've never been persuaded by this, though. You learn from working in the helping trades that hurt has to find its words as well as its voice. Hurt has to speak its name and find a language that does justice to what has been seen and endured. People can hurt well, meaning that they can hurt toward a purpose. They can hurt for some reason or merit beyond how it is to hurt and be hurt. Saying more when you think you've said enough is one way to begin the labor.

So I asked her, "What should you do about what?" From that moment on the crowd went from being concerned for her to being uneasy with my failure to fix things before the things had a chance to be said. They wanted me to put an end at least to the raw anguish she felt, by reassuring her that a renewed intent to be more mindful of these things would inevitably be comforting in the coming months. But I wanted something else, for her and for them: I wanted the woman's father to hear from her about all this.

She answered me this way, "What should I do about everything I didn't do for him when he was dying?"

We were all on familiar therapeutic ground: There was a problem, and now there was a request for a solution, and next should follow the solution reward. They looked back to me, relieved that the ordeal would soon become some kind of feel-good story. I asked her, "What do you want to do about it?"

Up until that moment everyone in the Zen temple hall seemed to be wearily but happily together in the project of getting something out of my talk, but now they wanted me to cauterize the wound. It was looking like I wouldn't do so. Most of the people fixed their eyes on me, and it was obvious that they wanted this exchange to end. The woman answered, "I think I should forgive myself. I should do that first."

Ah, self-esteem. You know what kind of appeal self-esteem has as a goal in therapy and in life. We had started talking about a dead man, someone's father, but she and the crowd were on more solid and familiar ground now in the land of self-help. The real problem wasn't what she had left unsaid and undone at the time of her father's death, and after, not that night. It was the woman's feelings of unworthiness and inadequacy, and the solution was to encourage her and lead her down the road to self-forgiveness. Her father's death was the place where she could feel good about herself again—and nothing else. Whenever that preoccupation with self-esteem and self-help takes charge of the proceedings, there are always other things, usually things that have nothing to do with the self and its comfort, that get covered by the pall of getting on with your life. After a long while in the death trade I have grown an ear for what is no longer being said and an eye for what has slipped from view. So I asked her, "If you forgive yourself, what good will that do your dad?"

I know there are people there who still think I was insensitive, utterly without empathy and all the therapeutic rest. It probably sounded that way. But I wasn't doing therapy, not there and not anywhere where the big things are at stake. I was saying something about the living and the dead, which is what the people had come to hear something about. This woman's hurt was true, of course, and she had done us all a noble service in beginning to grieve out loud. Her "road to recovery," perhaps learned while watching talk shows or reading the "be all you can be" literature, was to employ the hurt to stop hurting, to feel better, to carry on, and there's no blame in that.

But carry on with what? With a way of living that will with fair surety deliver her to the same place of self-loathing the next time someone close to her dies, that's what. Or worse, to a place of "resolution" where she accepts that she can only do so much when someone is dying, or worse still, that she vows to protect her dying friends and herself from their dying. This is all psychology and self-help. Her dead father had in the few months since his death become not much more than an occasion for her self-actualization, her self-soothing. That's what he was now. Not believing in sorrow or grief, and not believing really in the dead, she was looking for an end to the sorrow by ending her father's enduring presence in her memory.

The therapy solution is the acceptance that her father is well and truly gone, and it is achieved *by beginning to live as if he is well and truly gone.*

All that was left of him by that night was how she *felt* about him. All of this is driven by the language of "loss," and loss means "gone," and gone means "you're on your own, baby." The woman in that hall that night was on her own too. She didn't lose her father by her own neglect, treachery, or Electra complex. She inherited the program of losing the dead as a psychological obligation to her own restored mental health.

This whole way of thinking about the dead—or of not thinking about them—is hugely compelling these days. It is no wonder that she was under its sway. But I was asking her to allow some other possibility to arise, instead: Why does your father become "how you feel about your father" after he dies? Why does his death extinguish the obligation you have to him so that the whole thing shifts over to the obligation you have to yourself? Why does his death convert "what he needs from me" into "what I need to do for myself"? Why do you *give up* on him so easily? Why, when he died, did you lose him? And this is the standard way we have of grieving in the West, a psychological way, as if grief were a tidal pool of inner events, the lost one a pebble dropped in that pool, the ripples another occasion for working out our feelings. For most of us grief is entirely an interior event, exclusively emotional, cathartic in purpose and resolving in outcome, the dead a prop in the pageant of our recovery.

Sometime in the course of that long day I saw something enormous about Europe and something about where I had more truly, more deeply come from. This realization came to me in the graveyard, and then again in the Zen center, just as it had come to me countless times in working in the death trade. This sense I had in Europe that you cannot find anything that isn't "of humans," anything that hasn't been trodden, heaved, ploughed, cut down, squeezed, burnt, and taken by humans for longer than anyone can bear the memory of, is everywhere you go. There is almost nothing that I know as *wild* there. It is as if people over the centuries have left no place for the world in their world, no room for it in their millennial struggles to eat and feed their children and live. It feels like there is only a human world there.

I understood then something dark and mostly untaught about the early history of the thing that has become dominant-culture North America.

I caught a glimpse of something that Europeans fled when they could buy, borrow, or steal the steerage and had gathered on the piers—or been driven there—and sailed. No matter how many they were, they were too many. The whole place had been made in a human image. The spirit of the *place* had long ago been swarmed and ploughed under. The land had been turned into a setting for human life, with no life of its own. The tragically false idea that there was land for the taking across the waves that was free of people and free of history, a place where you could reinvent your identity and craft a nobler history for yourself and your kin, must have been intoxicating to the European of the time to a staggering degree that we now are heirs to but cannot imagine.

I understood something else. That corner of Europe where I had been all that day was full to overflowing with dead people, with their palpable, disregarded presence. In that cemetery far from home on that rainy afternoon, and in that perfect Zen hall in the English countryside with strangers who were bound to me by DNA and by the Atlantic Crossing, in that woman's bewildered sorrow, the dead were with us. With no promise of any kind of welcome, still they were talking. The neglected and abandoned and forgotten dead of that place, who have kin scattered all across the Americas and in every land with a recent history of empire and conquest, in a language the living of that place do not seem to know, were pleading for presence, for some kind of standing among the living, to be remembered beyond the living memory of the kind grieving daughters have of their fathers. The dead there, as the dead do everywhere they are left behind, longed to be claimed by their heirs, by the people hurrying to work and looking to forgive themselves, to be carried for a while by the living, not to be gone, not to be lost. They were whispering something of why it is that we fear dying as we do.

CREE SCOTS Where I live and work, there is no such thing as "the dead." There are the dearly departed, family members we once knew, whose voices we remember, whose graves we can visit if we remember to, if our family has the now somewhat antique habit of going to the cemetery, if we have a crisis that drives us unexpectedly there. There are vague great-grandparents from the old country who we suddenly claim when an old tribal allegiance rears up while watching the Olympics or when reading of the latest travesty that old religious or tribal prejudices unleash "over there," on the other side of the world. But we have no dead. Try using the word in casual conversation and listen for how people will stay away from it. Try using it in the present tense, and watch how everyone will think Ouija boards and fake séances and wonder what you've been reading lately. The dead are like the Shroud of Turin: Wouldn't it be something if it turned out to be real? The dead are a rumor, the way we live.

My wife is from a huge, rollicking Quebecois family with an itinerant history in America going back almost four hundred years. The cast of genuine characters is long and extravagantly remembered whenever weddings and funerals bring them together. On a visit to the ancestral homestead a few years ago, one of her wild uncles proposed a road trip. He was delivering new diesel trucks to customers in a Cree community on James Bay who were temporarily flush with cash payouts from the provincial government's hydroelectric scheme. We would all drive different vehicles, get them there unscathed, and see some country. The drive turned out to be about ten hours of muskeg and fifteen-foot-high black spruce as far as the eye could see. We had a lunch break on the shores of a thundering river that had given the community its English name, knowing as we sat there that the hydroelectric scheme would within two years choke that river to slow, trickling extinction, and with it the millennial relationship the Cree had lived with that old power would be gone too, in the name of progress.

We checked into the only hotel in town, delivered the trucks, and had the early evening to walk around and get the road drone out of our bones. I knew something of the recorded history of the place. The community grew up around a Hudson Bay Company trading post that had been there since the mid-1600s. The old storehouse for the trading post was still standing down by the waterfront, though the company had left the community a generation before and there were still hard feelings among the older folks about the one-way benefit of that trading history. I was poking around the storehouse in the fading daylight. Coming around the back of the building I saw something I'd seen nowhere else in the community: grass. It was green, knee high, and hid a mostly tumbled-down chain-link fence. I stood there for a long time. This lumpy little patch of ground had a strong presence to it.

The next morning I asked the lady pumping our gas about it. "Oh," she said, "that's where they are."

"Which 'they' do you mean?" I asked her.

"Oh, they put them there, those company people, in the old days. They didn't ship them home. They just put them there in the ground, behind the store."

It was, as I thought, the burial plot for those Orkney and Shetland men, many of them young, who died in the service of the Hudson Bay Company, who would not see their homes again. There were two other cemeteries in town, both of them church cemeteries, the grass cut and the fences standing. There are quite a few people in town whose hair is browner than it is black, sometimes even a little red tone to it. We and a few government types in for negotiations were pretty much the only white people in town that day, but there were quite a few shades of brown and beige in the faces of the people we met. Most of the people were nominally Christian. They got married and buried by the church.

That word lingered for a long time in the air while we were getting gas for the trip back south: "they." Unclaimed and unknown by their heirs, unknown in name by those who were hearing the thunder of the old river for the last time or who were going to the store for white bread and canned vegetables, their bones long gone to dust. Exhaust fumes lingered in the long cemetery grass. Shiny diesel trucks raised clouds that dusted the morning air. The drivers were, for a time, flush, and their father's father's father's grandfathers lay under the grass. How many times has this happened, that heirs turn away from their dead or are deprived of them by war, conquest, calamity, or flight? How many unwelcome ancestors are there? Is this the unauthorized orphan story of the Americas?

The Bone Yard

Archaeology and human genetics studies over the last twenty years have given us some good information with which we can imagine the first movements of humans across the earth. Many can object and probably still do, but it is hard to refute the likely story that we are all, blue-eyed and red-haired too, scatterlings of northeastern Africa. Likely too is it that humans trickled out of Africa in staggered and distinct waves over the ages and that we didn't all follow the same path across the epic and endless face of the world. The jangle of our differences has been with us at least since then. Our millennial movements don't make much sense if you look at a flat map, but they start to if you can find one that charts wind and ocean currents, mountain ranges and river flow. Until fairly recently we have always brailed our way across the skin of the world, I think. We all had the requisite dexterity of spirit to achieve such a thing.

The earliest wandering seems to have skirted the Sahara and flowed south, or east to follow the coasts of what we now call Saudi Arabia, Persia, India, Southeast Asia, and Indonesia, coming to rest in Australia and New Zealand, and by some extraordinary courage and calculation in the Pacific Islands. Another wandering seems not to have followed ocean shorelines. It followed rivers and mountain ranges instead, heading north and east: Anatolia, the Caucasus and Crimea, Black Sea and Aral Sea, the Pamirs and the Urals, the Steppes, Mongolia and Siberia, Japan, China and Korea, and perhaps to the Americas. Perhaps there were always people in the Americas. Each of these long treks probably spiraled out into other wanderings that became other peoples. The last or close to the last wandering seems to have covered the least ground: north and maybe finally, inevitably west, hugging the north coast of the Mediterranean—Greece and Italy, Hungary and Poland and the Baltics, Scandinavia, the caves of Gaul and the German forests, Iberia, Britannia, Eire. All of us, unless we are of the tribe that stayed in east Africa, seem to have most of our history in one of those treks, and to those wanderers we owe our cultures. All of us are what and how and, for the most part, where we are because our ancestors walked.

The first great mystery: Why did our people's people's people wander as they did? What got them going? Climate change and catastrophe are the most common hypotheses. Of course, this is the prejudice of sedentary people showing itself, disguised as contemplation. To most of us, no one who could choose otherwise would wander. Climate change might have started us wandering, but Africa to Australia is an awful trek by foot to get out of the rain or the heat, or to find them. Most of the theories assume that the humans who moved were driven out of Africa, and driven I guess all along the way until they ran out of running room before they ran out of reasons to run, until Australia reared up on the horizon as the dead end.

I call the great peregrinations "wanderings" because I doubt that those people were forced to move. I think, instead, that they obeyed. I think that their early, faithful bargains with the natural world, rooted in the indigenous capacity for intense observation and for a way of living that required little accumulation, forged a keenness in those people for knowing themselves—and wanting to know themselves—as kin to what surrounded them. Their ways of life I think must have been *collaborations* with the places they lived in. Their movements weren't flights, they were followings: As the wind and the water and the animals went, so must have gone the people. Etymologically, "obeying" means to be in the manner of hearing, of listening, and that's what the wanderings seem to me to have been: listenings, probably the conjurer of all human faith and all our senses of home. Those ancestors obeyed the ways the world has of being itself—weather, water, elevation, the grasses, and the animals—and so they moved. These were not flights away from something savage and inhuman or toward some kind of heaven that would finally be friendly. Their home was their way of living, and obedience was their life, and moving was their obedience.

I know that this sounds dreamy and fantastic to all those who have only lived a sedentary life. It is a hard imagining for contemporary people to manage, that there were and are humans whose way of moving across the face of the world doesn't have efficient, straight-line destination as its purpose or in its language or its ontology. The early wanderings of our people's people's people might have been mimetic instead. Theirs might have been a way of moving with the world, as the world moved. In gross, observable form this refers to gravitational pull, tidal sway, solar and lunar comings and goings. But more subtle and local are the whorls of wind, the tilt of the landscape, the convection of water up the mountain's face as mysterious mist and down the river arteries again as the life-blood rain. The story they would tell their children was of a mountain's longing for a river. Wandering people, with and without grazing livestock, have moved and, where sedentary peoples have not prevented it, still do move like that. There are wars of attrition still waged against them, today in Mongolia and elsewhere in central Asia and in the Amazon. But this would be how they knew themselves to be at home, that they recognized in their wanderings the nap of the world and followed it, as your hand follows the grain of a hickory axe handle when you rest from wood splitting or traces the downy eddies of a newborn's head when you are carefully trying to find out who is this young one who has come among you.

This idea that you wouldn't move unless you were *forced* to comes from a way of life, an accumulating way of life, which bargains for self determination and dreads involuntary movement and regards it as a loss, as a disaster. The disaster hypothesis I think comes from peoples who have loss—homelessness—in their foundation story. Those peoples, the ones with too much to lose by wandering and by obedience to the world, are the peoples we are coming to. They are who many of us in North America come from.

There is a lot of difference—and a lot of human history swells out of this difference—between not moving and refusing to move. In the early going, each subsequent wandering wave of humans probably found other humans and so kept going. The origin of the nomad, by this way of thinking, is not in *their* wandering, but in the eventual choice of some other people to stop wandering. When hunting and gathering gave way as it did to cultivating and accumulating surplus in some places (and "gave way" is a very neutral way of rendering what happened), in Mesopotamia certainly, wandering gave way to settling and clans gave way to urban sites. The earliest urban sites seem to be where people first gathered on the basis of needing things from each other—trade and its spawn, commerce—rather than on the basis of kinship. Those who continued wandering, bound by kith and kin to those lands left them, "became" nomads to the settled peoples. Those who stayed put set about altering the places they settled in to accommodate and complement their sedentary ways. From that point on they probably wouldn't have moved again unless catastrophe—natural or man-made—obliged them to move.

So, there are worlds of difference between wandering and fleeing. The difference doesn't hover around preference, not at all. Wandering is a way of being at home in the world that doesn't require forty acres and a mule, and fleeing is a way of losing your home, your forty acres and your mule, and being driven across the face of the world. Only the second kind of human movement is prompted and perpetuated by crisis. Disasters of nature inspire involuntary awe in those who witness them because their magnitude dwarfs human plan and achievement. When earthquake, tsunami, or drought have come upon a place, still in our day a common enough thing in many places, they have made many peoples homeless at different times and forced them to find a new home. Chronic homelessness, though, *homelessness as a way of life,* is not the consequence of natural disaster. It is the consequence of disasters perpetrated on humans by other humans. Natural calamity pervades; human-made calamity pursues. Natural calamity renews the obligation for obedience to the world. Humanly wrought calamity prompts flight through the world, and that flight more often than not is eventually christened as a "way of life."

Probably the most common and the most thorough calamity visited on humans by humans is enslavement. As a social institution, as a way of making war and writing history, as a business, it is an ancient thing. Where villages have swelled to empires, they seem always to have done so riding the backs and the souls of slaves. Slaves chained to a foreign piece of ground and to each other, doing someone else's work, aren't the only kind of slaves in human history, nor probably even the most common. In institutionalized slavery, human beings are stolen from their homes and their kin, but they are also stolen from themselves. Every slave owner in history has known that a slave is a slave first in the mind. Enslavement of the body and its strength for forced labor comes second. Slavers only sometimes steal the slave's home. They always steal the slave *from* his or her home, and they always steal the slave's ability to be *at* home.

The horror of slavery is this: You can sit beside a slave, you can speak the same language, even obey the same laws. You can eat the same food. You both can weep and love your children and miss your dead. But you are a human being, and he or she is not. Slaves are property, and human beings are property holders. The power of slavery to corrupt a person's capacity to know themselves as worthy, as belonging in the world, as made by the Makers of Life, is beyond reckoning, and this is comparable only to its power to corrode the ability of slave owners or of those who live off the avails of historical slavery to honor their ancestors or to know themselves as coming from honorable people. It is the undoing of humanity, nothing less, as we are about to see. It is the ushering in of oblivion.

If your people have been slaves for so long that no one among you has a living memory of your home, then your people have lost not only their freedom of worship, of movement, of language, and of custom. They have also lost their ability to be at home, no matter where they are. *That is their real, enduring enslavement, that they cannot know the ability of being at home.* The horror of this theft is unimaginable for any who have not known slavery in their lives or in their ancestry. For those who have, the horror is, though subtler in less troubled times, haunting and compelling and inescapable. Please consider this: Most of us whose people found our way to this place and made it North America do indeed have this enslavement in our ancestral past. Alas, look deeply into the story and very likely you'll find ancestors on both the perpetrator's and the victim's side.

As many people and peoples there are who have been enslaved in the dark record of human history, there surely have been many, many more who have fled slavery. We could say that those fleeing enslavement make up another great wave of human movement over the earth, radically different from those who came before and after it. Those countless peoples who have taken flight to avoid the master and the manacle, who kept running and bequeathed that fugitive status to the grandchildren not yet born as their new way of life, those peoples have taken the manacle inside as part of how they know themselves. This flight-as-culture, this is a spawn of slavery. Fleeing slavery, when the consequence is the loss of a home place and when that flight has gone on long enough, turns into the loss of a *capacity* for being at Home.

Running from "the man" doesn't often foster people's capacity for being at home somewhere else. Anthropologists who study the wretched consequence of conquest, language loss, and ethnic cleansing say that it only takes two generations of rupture to sever the chord binding people to their ancestors and their ability to be at Home. The grandchildren, with no lived or recounted memory of any ancestral home, know nothing of Home—nor do they know *that* about themselves. They don't know what the elders are talking about, if they are still talking about what was left behind, and they don't often know much of the language the elders are speaking when they do. What the grandchildren know is flight. That homelessness in two or three generations can turn into an inability to be at home, and that inability to be at home can become a kind of "unculture." As a wretched formula it could be said this way: *In the first generation, trauma. In the second generation, God.* Subsequent generations, as a way of coping with the loss of what they know not, enshrine their lostness as a kind of freedom. They deify what dispossessed their ancestors. Homelessness *has* become what many people have instead of a culture. This is the archaic, ancestral truth of any society made fundamentally by mass migration. This is also an early, foundational history of the place we now call Europe. The history of this thing we call the West is full of this story.

Ah, but what about human ingenuity? What about the indomitable human spirit that overcomes when it cannot overwhelm? We know that people for millennia have rebuilt homes, reestablished villages, and reconstituted ways of life following a period of crisis and flight. Is this the same thing as reclaiming the ability to be at home? Not initially and not inevitably, no.

Being at home in a given place means *learning*. It is only coincidentally a "feeling". Specifically it means learning the ways that place has of being itself: This is what I mean by obedience. It means having an enduring recognition and knowledge of a specific place and finding your clan identity in that endurance. And there is something more, something unsuspected and fundamental that the doctor's question has been leading us to. Being at home in a given place means recognizing the rocks, the plants, the winds, and the waters and stars of that place in your own body, and your body in the rocks, the plants, the winds, and the waters and stars of that place. It means more than having memories associated with a given place. *It means learning again how you and those you love and admire,* in every physical, metabolic, chemical, mythical, and spiritual sense it can be meant, *are made of the things that make the place you belong to.* That is the alchemy of belonging. This is where home comes from.

This learning of home is what informs the indigenous creation stories that are on the syllabus of every comparative mythology or comparative religion class, and it is what enables an indigenous person to point to a particular cleft in a rock or a particular blue lake in the mountains and say, "My people came to this earth from there." They mean it in every sense that it can be meant. Those of us without the ability to be at home might guffaw when an indigenous person means that his or her home and ancestral origin place is right over there, in the right of way of that highway overpass we are proposing to build, or in that grove of trees temporarily delaying the addition of another nine holes to our golf course. Usually we do guffaw. Or we turn it into a symbolic story, an allegory, a metaphor for being born. But here is the scorpion's tale: Symbols and allegories are homelessness remembered, in truth. Symbol and allegory are the syntax of homelessness.

That kind of learning one's home place does not happen by a feat of imagination or fantasy, or by socialization, or by the transcendental yearning for things to be different. It happens by an act of interment. You plant your dead in your home place, and the bodies of your dead sustain that place. The same place that once fed them feeds you now as food and water and air and ground. Time goes on, life is lived, and then you can recognize—meaning *know again*—your dead in the grass and the animals and the water and the air—in the *nature*—of your home place. *Being at home is not a feeling,* any more than your dead are "how you feel about them": *Being at home is a skill.* It is a skill of recognition and belonging, the skill of inextinguishable obligation. Obligation: not *"to owe,"* but *"to be bound to."*

Brother Blue and Martín Prechtel, each in their way, have taught us this idea well. When people say something like "all my relatives" at the conclusion of a ceremony, it is this kinship they are recognizing, a kinship with all that belongs to the place they belong to. Being at home is knowing your obligations to your home and proceeding accordingly. Being at home is a competence born of deep knowledge of your belonging to and your obligation to all that has been and will be for that belonging. That knowledge includes—it *requires*—knowing where the bones of your dead are, and knowing where your dead feed the life that you are learning to obey.

To say it again, this isn't symbolic. It isn't a metaphor. It is not metaphysical. It is *physics,* the ground of metaphysics. It is biochemistry, ethnobotany, spiritual ecology. Taken all together, it is ancestry in this world. Being at home is having kinship with the place where your kin live and have lived and cooked and loved and suffered their sufferings and known their Gods, the place where they died and were gathered in. You are woven into belonging to a people by belonging to a *place.* This is what "indigenous" means, etymologically: to be born inside. "Indigenous" answers the question, "who?" by being able to go and stand on a certain "where."

Home is home because it is where your people's bones lay, both those you come from and, as time goes on, those who come from you. You have a people to belong to because you all have the bone yard in common. The bone yard feeds the place that feeds you and your people. So you and your people, when you *are* a people and know yourselves to be so, are nourished by your ancestors, in the food chain, in every sense that this can be meant. Being on the conscious, ritually remembered receiving end of that arrangement plants a knowledge of deep obligation in the middle of your identity at the same time as it plants you in a specific "somewhere."

When you know yourself to be at home, *you are who you are bound to.* In gratitude, in awe, and in the good symmetry of how it is when nature and human nature recognize each other well, you and your people feed what has fed you all along. Your life simmers in the cooking pot made of the clay of your family line, suspended over the fire of your labor in trying to live well, hanging from the sturdy tripod where your Home, your People, and the Gods of your Place meet. The willingness to know the truth of this, to live as if it was so and is still so, that willingness keeps the human world alive. It does so by keeping your ancestors and their memory alive. By remembering all the old stories and by telling them to the young among you, by respectful, sustainable human ways of living, you keep that small part of the world that is your home alive. This is the great ellipse of being human and knowing your obligation to life. In time, you learn what your death will mean. And in a little more time you become one of the ancestors you once nourished. This is the *arche* of human life, its real foundation. This is the warp and weft of home.

There have been peoples in this world—some of their stories are known today, and some are still living as a people—that were entirely willing to die in the name of Home, and especially in defence of their ancestors' bones. Most river valleys and plains across Asia and Europe, the Indian subcontinent, and the Americas have seen that happen many times. Herodotus is known to moderns as a Greek writer who died circa 425 BC. He left us a book whose title is usually translated as *The Histories.* From him as much as from anyone more our contemporary, Western people have a very limiting understanding of that from which their history is made. His stated purpose in this book is to see to it "that the great deeds of men may not be forgotten … whether Greeks or foreigners: and especially, the causes of the war between them." History for Herodotus is the story of who fought whom, and why, and who won: From these events all else flows, and the history you and I learned in school was mainly that same history. He saves a few pages to describe a nomadic people known to us as Scythians, though they only warrant the pages because they were invaded by the Persian king Darius, following his conquest of Babylon, that same Darius who is a shadow figure in the Jewish Testament. The Scythian homeland lay to the west and north of the Black Sea, the area through which the great wanderings of people passed to come to what we now call Europe.

Darius's bone of contention with the Scythians was that they would not stay in one place long enough to meet in slaughter. He noted, as a committed agriculturalist, urbanist, and imperialist, that their real lack of civilization was most naked in their incessant movement and their failure to build cities that could be sacked. He also made fun of their habit of wearing pants. Though the larger Persian army occupied vast stretches of the Scythian lands, Darius's only satisfaction lay in conflict, victory, and enslavement, and so he pursued them. The Scythians, for their part, seemed generally unconcerned with the Persian occupation and continued to wander across their plains not as an army but as a people, in felt-covered wagons, apparently living with the faith that, as long as people moved, there was enough land for everyone. It is a story familiar to the indigenous peoples of the Americas.

Finding no end of this, Darius at last dispatched a rider with a message for Idanthyrsus, the Scythian king.

> "Why on earth, my good sir," the message ran, "do you keep on running away? You have, surely, a choice of two alternatives: if you think yourself strong enough to oppose me, stand up and fight, instead of wandering all over the world in your efforts to escape me; or, if you admit that you are too weak, what is the good, even so, of running away? You should rather send earth and water to your master, as the sign of your submission, and come to a conference."
>
> Herodotus (translated by A. de Selincourt),
> *The Histories,* page 312

Darius is of a culture that learned well by flight until they were strong enough to fight that the only reason people move is to run. You see, it is a very old story. He cannot see the wanderings of the Scythians in any other way. Yet there is an old understanding of the bond of land and culture in the terms of surrender he offers. He demands that the Scythians hand over—literally—their dead, in the form of earth and water, as a sign of their submission to enslavement. The Scythians were different people, with a different understanding of what is at stake.

"Persian," Idanthyrsus replied, "I have never yet run from any man in fear; and I am not doing so now from you. There is, for me, nothing unusual in what I have been doing: It is precisely the sort of life I always lead, even in times of peace. If you want to know why I will not fight, I will tell you: In our country there are no towns and no cultivated land; fear of losing which, or seeing it ravaged, might indeed provoke us to hasty battle. If, however, you are determined upon bloodshed with the least possible delay, one thing there is for which we will fight—the tombs of our forefathers. Find those tombs, and try to wreck them, and you will soon know whether or not we are willing to stand up to you ..."

"The mere suggestion of slavery," Herodotus wrote, "filled the Scythian chieftains with rage."

Ibid.

When people are driven off their home place, those ancestral bones usually stay put. When people are in flight they have not the leisure nor often the ability to dig those bones and pack them along with whatever household things they can carry. Houses can be rebuilt farther down the road, material culture can be reassembled, and something like daily life can be made again, but the bones of their ancestors are lost. For people who have once lived the life of being at home, this is hardly bearable. Perhaps it isn't bearable, finally. Perhaps modernity is not much more than the unbearable drift from a home place. Perhaps it "looks like freedom but it feels like death. It's something in between, I guess. It's closing time." (Leonard Cohen, *Closing Time*)

This has happened to the ancestors of most living at this moment, over and over and over again. This has been done to people by the ancestors of most people living at this moment, over and still over again. We have both of these stories in our Story, and we cannot by claiming the one be ever free of the other. This human grief is in history's caravan of sorrows. You see that grief in the particular shape of the back of your grandfather's bald head, or in your newborn's wide nose or in the whorl of their hair. You know it as the rightful but usually unclaimed inheritance of the people you love and call family and so the rightful inheritance of you yourself. It is good to stop for a while and ponder that.

It is very good for us to wonder whether this story, the loss of Home, has happened to our people, and so to us, and whether we have stolen Home from people when we stole people from their Home, and whether in our comfort-seeking way of life we continue to do so, and whether any of this matters a damn. I assure you that it does. It has appeared at almost every deathbed I have attended. Most people die awash unawares in a grief that is much older, more enduring, more trustworthy than anything else they might regret or resent in their last months or days.

The inside lids of many Egyptian sarcophagi have the star body of the God with hands on one horizon and feet on the other. This is an apt way to understand who parents are to their children. They are the vault of their child's heaven, the firmament of a child's life. When they separate, the world's body is rent, limb from limb. The young one has no way of gathering back together what is scattered. To survive this catastrophe at all the young one has a terrible bargain to make with the way things have come to be. The longing for the one who has gone is not bearable for long. It is that longing that is sacrificed in the name of going on. For the child, the loss is insoluble; the missing parent cannot be called home. But the longing itself is something else. The longing is a problem that can be solved, though the collateral damage is severe. The longing can be abandoned and forgotten, in the name of not dying of sorrow, and most often it is. The absent parent might be visited, but is less and less longed after when he or she isn't there.

And so it has been, probably, for whole cultures that have been driven off their land and had their home places stolen or violated. Surviving requires heavy adaptation and considerable amnesia—"displacement," the psychologists might call it. Cultures in flight might not have portable homes—those are usually for nomads—but their yearning for home travels with them, uprooted and dangling, uncertain and unplanted. To survive that flight, with the home place gone, just like the child whose parents have parted, cultures in flight have to radically alter their idea of home, and they do. For them *home is a place no longer; it is a state of mind.* The internalization of "home" is a hallmark of homeless culture.

That is the empty victory of a traumatized culture in flight, making a metaphor of home. People with this trauma go to psychology so as not to have to go to history and culture. People with this trauma think of home, when they think of it at all, as an interior, psychological feeling that they are on the receiving end of. Doesn't this sound much like what became of the English woman's dead father? He became a feeling, an interior event she was on the receiving end of. This interiorization of home might sound to you similar to the capacity for home which the nomad has, but there is a fundamental difference: The nomad wanders at home, while the traumatized person flees the loss of home by coping, and coping turns home into feeling homey. Ikea makes a lot of money—a *lot* of money—from that difference.

It is a reliable mark of indigenous cultures that *their Gods live on the same land that the people do.* That kind of neighborhood is really unthinkable for someone who has grown up in a monotheist culture, but it might be a root condition for indigenous identity. Try then to imagine something of the utter calamity that awaits an indigenous culture fleeing slavery and mayhem: Their Gods become homeless too. It doesn't take long in the pageant of coping and surviving for displaced people to begin thinking of their Gods as the Gods of a people, *not of a place.* That is how Gods become homeless.

When I learned about imperialism at school I was taught that proselytizing was a natural and inevitable part of the program. But it is good here to wonder, Why would military and commercial conquest include God conquest? Do the winners plant their Gods in the newly conquered land, giving them a new home?

They do not. They claim the new land for their Gods, but they do not uproot their Gods and bring them to the new land, not really. They are extending their Gods' dominion, instead. There is no God but God, as the saying goes. It always seems to be that with omniscience and omnipotence comes omnipresence. These are not Gods belonging to a particular Somewhere and happy to stay there. The missionizing Gods are the Gods of Everywhere. Remote, unlimited, never really incarnated: These qualities give them their sophistication. This homelessness of the Gods—them not being of this world—is fundamental to the missionizing project, and it happens that the one-God religions and nonreligions that dominate the missionizing project in the modern period are each of them religions of homeless Gods, claiming the fidelity of homeless peoples, belonging to nowhere and no one, marauding the countryside, breeding homelessness by selling conversion.

When Gods are homeless, there is great danger afoot in the world. There is, I think, a trauma of dispossession and displacement lying at the root of every religious tradition that has obliged its neighbors to take its God. Missionizing cultures force homeless Gods upon the world. Homeless Gods are the necessary precursors for the idea that there can be and should be a God of all peoples, no matter their home places. Of course, missionizing cultures don't think of their Gods as homeless. They think of them as universal. They make a boon from a malady: The world is not a fitting place for their God. It is their God's footstool. A homeless God is for His or Her adherents One who has never lived in the world, who floats above the world with a remote regard for the chaos He or She bestows, seeking dominion.

When European missionaries disembarked after the military had made the conversion business a little safer in the "New World," they proceeded without hesitation as if their God was the God of all. In the early days of that sorry saga many indigenous cultures responded, "Well, that's your story, and it clearly has worked well for you, but our Gods gave us a different understanding."

Missionizing cultures responded, "There is no other understanding."

"Different understanding" isn't tolerated by missionaries. It is a thought that cannot be thought by them. At the root of that rigidity and relentless and unreflective absolutism you will find an ancestral trauma of flight and homelessness, exported to the world as enlightened monotheism. Indigenous people have often responded initially with a qualified embrace: "You and your God are welcome, but neither of you is from here. Neither of you belongs here."

At one screening of *Griefwalker*, a documentary film about my work with dying people, someone of European origin argued yet again how native North Americans had originally made their way into the New World across the Bering land bridge and that they weren't really from here at all. I asked her why she defended the theory so fiercely. This was her answer: Since no one is really from here, anything goes, and there is no theft or trespass. And then an aboriginal man said, "Yes, I've heard this many times. This is your story, but it isn't our story. Just because you don't come from here doesn't mean nobody does."

In the old days at least, the missionaries used to take pride in not being from here, but things have changed a little. A few years ago Sharon Butala wrote a book called *The Perfection of the Morning*. One story that has stayed with me described her riding across the prairie ranch where she lived and coming upon unfamiliar stone formations in the skimpy grass. After pondering and reading and consulting with Blackfoot elders from a nearby reserve, she recognized the formations as tepee rings and medicine wheels, and realized that her ranch sat on a much older home of a much older people. It was then she saw something. About the religion and the culture that had given her life she admitted: They just don't belong here. It doesn't mean that they shouldn't be here, not necessarily, but it does mean that they aren't from here, and never will be.

When the people are homeless, and their Gods follow suit, what becomes of their forbears? How does this massive calamity change the way the living are with their dead? The same coping strategy adheres, the same adeptness for losing, the same capacity for amnesia, the same penchant for crafting marvel from mayhem. The ancestors of people in flight are not remembered as people buried in a particular, lost place. They become utopian spirits instead, ancestors with no place and no need of a place, as adrift as the living, neither of them with any devotion to the old home ground. Torn from its root, the lived truth of ancestry starts to look a lot more like a more sophisticated *idea,* like an option. The old obligation to maintain your ancestors turns into a hokey anachronism, an embarrassing superstition. Ancestors are notions, mostly, and are no more in need of being fed and cared for by the living than the old bone yard is. The homeland and the old people: both remote, both adrift, both unnecessary. The dead are those about whom you have the odd thought, to whom you owe nothing but a vague gratitude when it stirs, gone with the wind.

Once this has gone on for a few generations, the only place you have any allegiance to is the place you pay a mortgage on. The world—not itself a real home for anything or anyone—needs nothing from you. It is only a place that you go to get your dietary, recreational, and lifestyle needs met. Sounds familiar, doesn't it? The dead are a place inside you that you go to for solace or self-assurance. There is no reciprocity of obligation because there's nobody there. The ritual and ceremony of caring for ancestors, if it happens at all, if we can even any longer use that expression, is mostly an interior event, a symbolic exercise that can be done anywhere, anytime. Cultures that have endured this kind of long-term trauma and made it part of their identity tend to develop a sense of the natural order of things that has been emptied of Gods and ancestors, where human beings occupy the vacated center and always have. The God Who Has Fled: That is the honorific title homeless cultures bestow upon their deity. When you're trying to survive you turn malady into a coping strategy and loss into culture. The outcome for the living is the cult of autonomy, the cant of self-sufficiency, the code of lonely multicultural cities. The outcome for the living and for the world is palpable, and evidence of it abounds now. The outcome for the dead is, mostly, unknown to us.

The Garden

Whether North Americans claim the Genesis story as their own doesn't determine much; the Genesis story claims them, and has done so since well before the first Europeans, scatterlings yet again, fleeing poverty, persecution, and slavery, and bringing it all with them, arrived here by accident and avarice and imagined it an empty place waiting for them. Whether or not the majority of North Americans believe the Garden ever happened, or believe that it is someone else's story, or that it has any consequence for their lives or should, the Genesis story remains curled around the brainstem of the culture that has grown up in the wake of the European invasion of North America. Not believing in stories does not often prevent them from being in your life anyway. You can know things without believing them and you can proceed accordingly, and most people here know the rudiments of the Genesis story without even knowing where the story comes from.

The Genesis story is, among many other things, a story about how good things used to be. It is a backward-looking sigh, saying: It was so good then that we didn't know how good it was. It is also a story that claims to describe and explain the entire history of the making of the planet, the creation of the conditions that could sustain life, the installation of every living thing in its proper form and place, and, as the centerpiece, the conjuring of the first human being from dirt. But the story didn't come from a general "anywhere" and it isn't universal; it came from a very distinct somewhere.

From the beginning of the story there is a lot to learn about the people who carried it, told it, and eventually wrote it down. It was rendered into its present form by people who were cultivators. Their story says that at first,

> *there was no man to till the ground . . .*
> *and that when their God made the first human*
> *the Lord God took the man and put him in the garden*
> *of Eden to till it and keep it.*

Genesis 2:5 and 2:15

Their culture was gathered around the first gifts of their God: dominion over the plants and animals of the world. There is nothing in the story that remembers a hunting, gathering era that predates cultivation. It says that the world given to them was neither semiarid desert nor savannah, but a garden. And there was no one there before them. The Edenic life is not wandering in obedience to the winds and waters. According to this story it is living an agriculturalist's life. The mythic home of this culture is the garden. The mythic origin of the culture is in husbandry, and it came from the power to name the animals and the plants they fed upon.

When a culture's creation story includes power over plants and animals, it might signal a lingering memory of a time when that wasn't so, a time probably when people were prey as much as predator. A culture that survives by cultivation is probably one that has passed through the period when humans competed with animals for food. Cultivating cultures through close observation and trial have achieved a considerable capacity to manipulate pollination, germination, fertilization, growing season, and, probably most significantly, plant genetics. It is not a culture that takes the natural world as a given. Acting on the founding principle that the garden is given to humans, it grapples with what it finds to get more from the natural world. Cultivating cultures are not as a rule "at one" with their environment, but more often contend with the field and the weather as adversaries, just as the story foretells. Many of these cultures traffic in power, and enthrone power as the first condition, the first relationship of human and nonhuman. They are also cultures that have come to a stage of sedentariness and some scale of urbanization. The processing and distribution of food typically requires an infrastructure of sorts, a moderate concentration of people in one place, each of whom is looking to produce surplus, and a means of keeping track of who owes whom. They are cultures with a lot to lose.

The Genesis story tells how it was lost, how cultivating cultures trafficking in power and homelessness got that way. A combination of curiosity, aspiration for a certain kind of knowledge, and the cunning of the nonhuman adversary was the end of human presence in the garden. The garden remained—the story does not say that it was destroyed or closed down—but the people were exiled:

> *Therefore the Lord God sent him forth from the*
> *garden of Eden, to till the ground from which*
> *he was taken. He drove out the man.*

Genesis 3:23

No longer able to gather food at will, the first man and woman end up in the grinding work of cultivating impoverished ground instead of gathering from endless bounty. The ground is cursed and unwelcoming. Field work is toil, futility, and the iffy possibility of meagre return, a liminal existence. The farmer will war with the shepherd (Cain and Abel), the victor doomed to be "a fugitive and a wanderer on the earth" (Gen. 4:12), a terrible outcome indeed for a sedentary culture.

Losing home and then stumbling out into the world is this culture's foundation story. And here is a detail that is fundamental to everything I've been describing: Prior to that exile, life was eternal; *after the banishment, humans are frail and murderous—and mortal.* The natural disasters will come later, well after losing the garden. The first calamity visited on humans comes from God, the second humans inflict on each other. *The loss of home,* the story says, *is the beginning of death.* That is how human death comes into human life, in humans being driven from home.

So the story of the origins of humans in Genesis is a story of homelessness. Homelessness is the origin of human life in the world and it *is the origin of culture.* It is the beginning of physical frailty and the origin of the mayhem that humans have visited upon each other ever since. This is the story's whispered refrain: The world as it is is not your home. Your home is Somewhere Else. You are at your best when you are in the world but not of it. The human experience of having a lot to lose and then losing it turned into a story of the cosmic drama of trespass and punishment. This is the story that was so recognizable and so readily taken up by homeless black slaves stolen from West Africa to work and die in the Americas, which for the sake of survival became the gospel music that is now so beloved from a distance and so poorly understood by the ancestors of their slavers.

Let's pause for a moment, right here. Consider how disturbing this could be and how relentlessly sad it is to realize that the foundation story of the West, the story that still has some gravitational claim upon what remains of the mythic imagination of modern dominant-culture North America, knows the loss of *home*—not the loss of *life*—as the beginning of death. Consider how many times in human history people have been driven away, how much heartache there has been that was turned from affliction into culture, how many times the dead were abandoned to their own devices when the bone yard was ploughed under for grain or vineyards or parking lots or suburbs. Consider how many unknown bone yards you and I have driven through on our way to the corner store for bread, or how many are under your house. And then consider how we who think ourselves the victors of history think of this pageant of flight as inevitably leading to us prevailing in the world today, as if the story of homelessness and death and the loss of ancestry is over now for us and we are on the other side of it all, as if we are at home here, where we now find ourselves after our people fled what they fled—*as if we ourselves are not still fleeing.*

So this belief that the dead are essentially not the business of the living has a long history. The abandonment of the dead is a reaction to the calamitous loss of home. It is a trauma that when institutionalized as a culture is still no less a trauma. As our history has gone along you can find this trauma wherever you can find monotheism. I am not saying that abandoning the dead to their fate is a tenet of monotheistic religions. I am not saying it isn't, either. I am saying that the belief in a single omnipotent deity seems to have translated for most believers into an unspoken certainty that the deity's relationship with the dead eclipses and obviates the living's relationship with the dead. When that happens, "let the dead bury the dead" is not far behind.

Christian missionaries, to take one well-documented example I know something of, made it their business from the outset when converting "tribal" peoples to disturb and then to rupture the old reciprocating relationship between the living and the dead, not by arguing against the feelings of connectedness to the recently departed but by ridiculing or interfering with rituals which are rooted in that relationship. Across the Mediterranean world and then again in the "New World," missionaries dismantled the relationship with the dead by calling it misguided, uninformed, and backward, and where that didn't work they called it dangerous, arrogant, backsliding, and devilish.

Augustine, for one, *recommended* loss of ancestors. He did so by ridiculing indigenous burial practices, and by re-directing the care of ancestors toward the care of the poor instead. The dead, he advised, couldn't be helped by the living. What Augustine is doing here, and what all those following in his stead continue to do, is trafficking in the trauma of homelessness and ancestorlessness. The argument sounds sophisticated, but to me the loneliness of it is unmistakable. When the rituals of burial are slandered as nothing more than empty, expensive gestures that were done for the good of the living (as they so often are today), the dead are already gone. Without benefit of what we have, a systematic psychology, Augustine and the new religion he was helping to grow were yet able to turn the dead into an interior reality only, by shaming care of the dead as backward and unsophisticated. The English woman in the Zen temple is Augustine's spiritual and psychological heir. The inheritance cost her her dead father. "I lost my father," she said, and she spoke the truth.

From homelessness comes heaven. Wherever you find people advocating for heaven and trying to get you ready for it, you find people who have given up on the world, and particularly those who have given up being at home here in the world. All that heaven is has gone from the world. Heaven *means* that this is not your real home. Heaven is anywhere but here. Since the world's domain is the present and the past, heaven is always something the living must prepare for in the time to come, not a life they can live now.

If heaven really is the place where every needed and longed-for thing resides, then people who are at home *are* in heaven. If heaven is where friends and family go when they die, then people who are at home and know where the bones of their dead lay *are* in heaven. If not, then heaven is both a creature and a comfort of the homeless. It is an attribute of homelessness. Celestial heaven makes no sense without the loss of home to justify it, in the same way that salvation makes no sense without sin to justify it. That kind of heaven has no attraction, no compelling promise, no necessity for people who know themselves to be at home and who live accordingly. You have to sell the idea of homelessness first in order that the need for heaven has some place to roost, in order that it can make a home inside someone. You have to make people homeless in order for a homeless religion to be able to make a claim upon them.

When the preaching of Jesus became the preaching about Christ risen and began its extraordinary metamorphosis into what the world knows as

Christianity, it quickly slipped the cultural confines of Jerusalem, initially at Paul's insistence, and spread rapidly westward along the dying trunk and limbs of the Roman Empire. As it has been with all empires, the Roman Empire was built according to a program of conquest, dislocation of populations, and institutionalized slavery. Christianity found its early and most earnest advocates among the slaves of Roman cities and large towns all around the Mediterranean. They were neither citizens nor humans under the laws of the Empire. They were landless and homeless, and they recognized the Genesis story in their own. Heaven had a clear and compelling appeal for them, as it did later for slaves in the Caribbean and the southern U.S..

This history of homelessness, running from the manacle and the man, losing the dead, all explained and compensated for and legitimized by a new religion, this is the foundational history of the thing that was to become Europe. Before the Muslim incursion from the south, this is how Europe was being conjured and converted. Hundreds of years later Europeans fought the Muslims with this homeless religion in hand and then purified southern Europe by reinforcing the religion at the point of the sword and the heat of the cleansing flame. Knowing this is fundamental to being able to answer the doctor's question about where all our torment about dying came from.

And so we come to the roots of now, the roots of "the new world". North America is European. It has always been European. It was made by Europeans, according to their image, and it remains so. North America was dreamt, conjured, built, slaved, and bled into existence by Europeans and their servants. It was not a *place;* it was a *reaction.* It was empty and free, a blank page on which could be written their demands, their fantasies, their entitlement to the kind of life they'd never themselves known. The real efficiency of the Europeans was not their mad capacity for building, expanding, and multiplying across the depopulated fields and forests of the Maritimes, New England, Virginia, Florida, Cuba, Haiti, Guatemala,

Mexico, Peru, and the rest. It was their capacity for imagining themselves no longer to be European. It was their capacity for believing that they were making a New World by leaving behind all that had caused them to flee the Old.

Europeans didn't migrate or wander or sojourn or gather here. They fled here. They didn't come to the Americas; they ran from Europe, from the thousand landless, homeless, feudal miseries that together were their days. They ran not so much to give to their children what they never had as to not have to inherit what their parents and grandparents bequeathed to them. This fantasy of energetic, optimistic people seeking the freedom to be their own true selves, freed from the old feudal constraints to prosper and multiply in natural contentment—this is retroactive PR, selling to us a history that never was. Homeless people fleeing slavery, with little or no capacity for Home, with a homeless story of homelessness at the center of their religion—*they* made America. And from them and from this most of us, and certainly most of our institutions, are descended.

This loss of home is what the indigenous peoples of this continent saw get off the boats and drag itself through the forests and valleys and hillsides of the East Coast and build towns and restlessly keep going farther west, obeying the flight that began in the east, back across the ocean. It flooded across the great rivers and relentlessly across the plains, and all the rest, slouching toward Bethlehem, hankering after Jerusalem. This is what you can see in the old immigrant photographs, where that strained, haunted, homeless look is the same in the faces of babes in arms as it is in the faces of the parents and grandparents holding them. It is from them that we learned our fear of dying, of the real possibility of being lost because we die. It is to those particular dead, and their place among us, that this book now must turn.

8

DYING FACING HOME

Cities are tough places to get people to stop making money or running from the boredom that haunts them long enough to wonder aloud with you about things that could be important. My job gave me a regular chance to do this. I was able to poll people informally, and in one way or another I'd ask them, "Could you tell me, please, what happens to you when you die?" I don't know many people who give some of their idle hours to wondering what will happen to them and the people they love when they die. I've met a great many who are tormented, terrorized, or hamstrung because the rolling sea of their fear is so great and the groaning barque of their wisdom is so small when it comes to this question of what happens to us when we die. I wish otherwise for all of us, but there it is.

About three or so of every ten people answered as follows: "Well, when you die, that's it. There's nothing else. That's the end of it." Another three or four said: "Ah, nobody knows. You can't know anything about that from here," which for its edification and influence on how we proceed with our lives amounts to the same thing. Almost three-quarters of all the people who answered this question had nothing much to say about it. Ask about trade deficits with China, ask about global warming or what watching television does to preschoolers and you'll have no shortage of answers and opinions. But ask about the one thing that every person will live to see, the one event that no one will miss, the single most constant and trustworthy proposition beside which all others falter, and three-quarters of us seem to draw blanks. This is a sad thing to me, that after sixty thousand or more years of wrestling this very question as homo sapiens our contemporary selves have managed to generate only that much wisdom and insight into what has become of many of us and will become of the rest. And that passes for sophistication.

This isn't a question about what people "know," in the usual sense of the word. It's a question about how they live with what is so. It is a question about what kind of room they have made in their plans and their achievements for the plain certainty of dying. Ask ten people living in small villages in intact cultures the world over and you will get hours of maps, schemes, topographies, and moment-by-moment descriptions of what happens to them when they die. You'll get answers from toothless grandmothers, their overworked children, and their dusty, noisy grandchildren. Cultures that are "underdeveloped" in their technologies, buildings, and comfort-securing schemes tend to be highly developed in their mythologies, cosmologies, and understandings about how things work together to make life. Here though, where buildings can't be distinguished from monuments and where comfort is there for the taking, people's attention can be wrangled by catastrophes present and pending but their imaginations can't be very much engaged by ordinary mysteries. "When you die, that's it" and "Nobody really knows" both come from the same withered imagination and abandoned capacity for storytelling and myth seeing.

Well, we have three more people to hear from in our survey. Every time, their answers divided like iron filings on magnetized paper into three themes. The first: "When you die, you know everything you didn't know when you were alive." I've heard many people describe the newly dead that way—"Well, now they know"—as if dying solves the inscrutable mysteries of living, revealing all that was hidden. Dying gives the dead an overview that utterly escapes the living, so that story goes. Most people who have anything to say about them will readily allow that the dead have become aware, just from dying. All of us who have had a favorite grandparent die and have the clear sense thereafter that he or she knows exactly what we are feeling and doing every moment knows that what this really means is, "When you die you become an omniscient spiritual genius."

When I was about ten years old, my grandfather was to me emperor, sage, and force of nature. He was possessed of a handshake that could devastate my knuckles. He had a full set of dentures, upper and lower, and could slide them out and reel them in at will in delicate social situations without anyone but me seeing. He was manager of the only skating arena in town, which in those days made him potentate over all he surveyed, easily eclipsing any elected official and many of the town's well-to-do. When we walked together down the main street everyone greeted him by name. He traveled with a massive key ring jangling from his belt loop that came as sign and seal of his office, and I believed he knew every townsperson and every secret place in the catacombs of his empire. He wasn't a big man, but he had an easy way with the town toughs that kept the arena windows intact. There was no one else to be, when I grew up, but him.

When he died, which was unthinkable at the time, I was numbed and disbelieving. A few months went by and somehow his goneness started to become a ragged little corner of my life. A certain day came when I was thinking big thoughts: My grandfather gone, the world pretending to roll on as if there was no difference, nothing as it once was and no promise that things might one day be whole again. As can happen when you are young and thinking big thoughts that no adult could ever join you in, I was absentmindedly picking my nose, which seems even in hindsight a natural part of deep pondering. And then I stopped, and assumed a more hygienic pose, listening carefully. In that moment I knew without doubt that my grandfather was aware enough of me to disapprove of the nose picking, just as he knew everything else I was thinking and doing. He had become, even more so in death, a spiritual genius.

The second theme that shows up if you ask people this question: "When you die, there is no more suffering, no more pain." Look in most every cemetery and find the two words that show up over and over again on the gravestones: peace and rest. These are the code words for "no more pain and suffering." What this culture is trying to provide the elderly in rest homes they find, it seems, in death. Having shed their bodies, the dead lose the frailty that goes with them.

The third theme: "When you die, you have no yearning or longing. When you die you are free from the strivings of life. You've no wants, no needs, and especially no need of the living." We carry ourselves in this culture as if the dead have just by dying achieved something that the living strive for but cannot find: a thorough, austere, and utter self-sufficiency. The great reassurance that family members of a person recently died spill upon each other at the graveside or at the wake table is that their loved one is no longer embroiled in the cauldron of trying to love and be loved. It is not that we believe that the dead are now entirely and finally loved. It is that we believe that the dead no longer need love in order to be what they have become.

Any longing flows in one direction only, from the living toward the dead, and we are in some sorrowed way relieved to know that, of the two, we are the ones who suffer "the loss." They are already in a Better Place, a place that does not include arthritis or debt or lousy neighbors or sorrow—or us, or our longing for them. Push this a little, and you can hear plainly the belief that when you die you graduate from any ensnarement in human affairs, and this includes the ensnarement of reciprocal need or yearning. It means that when you die you don't miss anyone, you don't need anyone, and this is good for you. It means that from the time of death, any missing, any longing, any yearning for a sign or news that all is well goes one way only, from the living toward …

Well, this is the question for our grieving people, isn't it? Where does our missing or our loving go? What consequence does it have, and what purpose? The counseling business has answered these questions without equivocation: Good grieving is time limited, beyond which it is abnormal or pathological, or at least not good for you, and your job as a grieving person is after a seemly amount of time to stop grieving and, as it is said over and over, get on with your life. Because there is no one on the other end of your grief. Because your grief is *your* grief.

I know that many will disagree that this is a widespread belief. You could offer up an example of the strength and persistence of a bereaved person's love for their dead spouse, which many have felt and many more have witnessed, as evidence that belief in the need of the dead to be loved is strong among us. It is true that many people long to be buried beside their life partners and are sure that they will be reunited somehow after death because they found each other and managed to stay together throughout their married lives. I haven't heard the same belief among the unhappily married, for example, or among the divorced. Overall, this probably comes from a hope that our longing for the dead, when it isn't extinguished by the passing of time, is not unrequited.

You would probably agree that being loved is crucial to becoming and remaining a healthy, vital human being. We can point to people we know who have not been well loved either early in life or in their adulthood, and we can see the devastation that comes from it. But who among us believes with the same certainty and conviction that a dead person needs to be loved by living people in order to be a healthy, vital dead person? Who among us believes that the well-being of the dead, whatever that might be or whatever form that might take, requires the active participation of the living to initiate or maintain it? Who carries themselves from day to day behaving as if this were true? Who among us carries themselves as if there were *such a thing* as the dead?

People with deep religious conviction often believe that praying on behalf of the dead can benefit the dead. But all these are prayers for the involvement of intercessors. People who are praying for the dead are typically a kind of Greek chorus praying on behalf of someone. They are not usually praying *to* that someone, because that someone and their welfare are not in the hands of the praying person. What becomes of the dead, in this culture's way of doing things, is between them and whatever or whoever awaits them, not between them and those who long after them.

In North America we are living in a time when overt and public acts of worship are rare. People's ability to speak clearly and deeply about their understanding of the Divine is underdeveloped at the same time that many of us now can manage extravagant articulation regarding the merits of the latest smartphone. In my job I have paid careful attention to the general beliefs about God or about the Sacred that people bring to the experience of dying. It may surprise you, or it may not, but most people seem to have a sense of God or the Divine that matches up, theme for theme, with their understanding of what becomes of the dead after death. There is an eerie resemblance between our way of knowing the Divine and our way of knowing the dead.

Neither is pained by a body nor by any traffic in human affairs. They know of it but have no presence in the daily grind of the living. Neither yearns after us or misses us. They are mysteriously completed and self-sufficient. Both God and the Dead know all that we do not. Both God and the Dead are above the fray. Both God and the Dead are austerely, sublimely, perfectly themselves, with no need of us.

> The other night I heard a preacher on the radio who was also a doctor and a scientific man. His rap was about how powerful God was. He was giving some practical examples of how to understand that power. He said, "If the head of a pin was heated to the temperature of the sun's surface it would kill all living things in a thousand kilometer radius. And God can swallow that pin." That sort of thing. Example after example tumbled out of him. His tag line at the end of every vignette: "Do

you think if God can do that He needs your help? He doesn't need your help." The thrust of the whole thing was not whether God is powerful enough to help you out no matter what your problem is. It was that God is perfect and complete and doesn't need you. That's power, in a place like ours. I guess the preacher meant that to be comforting, somehow, that God was fine no matter how we were doing.

Most people who acknowledge a belief in God would not likely make a case that God's well-being depends on their belief or obedience. It just doesn't sound Godly. Oh, there are Commandments, but these are obligations that flow in one direction only. God can remain God without human compliance or adoration. And in our way of doing things and not doing things, the dead can remain as they are without the love of the living. God will be God no matter what we do, and God's ability to be God—God's health, or Godness, we might say—depends not a whit on what we, the living, might do or fail to do. And this is equally true of our Dead: They need nothing from us to be themselves—if there are such things as the Dead. Who are the Dead to us? The Dead are gone. That is what they *are*. What really binds them in the horizontal imagination of contemporary people is that *both of them, God and the dead, are gone.* They meet Somewhere Else, not here, not now, not among us.

And so we live with no obligation, no duty, no purpose where our dead are concerned. Every day we turn away from our dead. They're not really our dead at all, anymore. They're *the* dead instead. Think of every funeral or memorial service you have been to: How many times were the dead spoken to, instead of being spoken about? Not often, probably. How many times were the dead beckoned and courted and invited into the event, and how many times did you carry yourself as if the dead were there? It isn't likely that you did. How many times was the ceremony *for* the dead, and how many times was the ceremony conducted as if all of you figured enormously in how it was and was to be for the dead? Alas, certainly not often enough for them or for us. Why do we do our memorial services in the way we do, without the dead? Because we speak of dead people as we do. *Because of our language.* That's why.

Think of how you feel when you lose your car keys: frustrated, inattentive, careless. How do you feel when you lose your wallet? Inadequate, miserably incompetent, and capable of considerable self-hatred about it all, especially given the exquisite mayhem of trying to cancel and replace everything in it. That is how we feel about losing our wallets. Yet without hesitation, without wonder or challenge or any question at all, without feelings of inadequacy, carelessness, or self-hatred, we lose our dead.

That is what we say: I lost my father last year, or, I lost my husband to cancer. It isn't just a word, friends. It is not in any way a synonym for "died." Losing is not something that happens to you or your dead father or husband. Think for a moment about the language. When you say, "I lost my wallet," you are not describing what your wallet did to you. You are describing what you did to your wallet, and then how you feel about yourself for having done so. Losing your dead loved ones is the same. Losing is something you do *to* them. When someone says that to me, that they lost their wife or their child, I ask them, "Why did you do that?" When I tell that story people usually laugh, because on the surface of it the question makes no sense. But it makes huge, unalterable sense when you realize that "dying" and "losing" are not synonyms. One is what the dying person does, the other is what we do to them. Why do we do that to our dead? Why do we say over and over that we have lost them, as if it were as inevitable as taxes and weather? And then why do we proceed to lose them over and over and over again?

The answer to that question is in our history as a culture. The answer is in our ancestral homelessness and in the homelessness of our ancestors. Listen to how people speak about them around you, or how you speak about them. Almost universally we call them "the ancestors," not "my ancestors." Ancestors are not family, and in North America there are for the most part no ancestors in the cemeteries we might be able to visit. Family are those whose voices we heard, whose faces we knew, whose names come easily and sometimes painfully to us after their deaths. They are the ones in the cemeteries.

Ancestors, no less our people, no less our kin, are the faceless, nameless, voiceless multitudes—yes, multitudes—we never knew, never suspected, and it is to them that we owe what it is about ourselves we cherish and claim and betray and deny. We are heirs to the flight from homeless misery that brought our ancestors to the Americas, and we are heirs to the homelessness they brought with them and to what was done to the peoples already here in the name of that homelessness. When we make no place among us for our ancestors *and their homelessness,* we have compound homelessness for an ancestry. It visits us every time we begin speaking of the dead only in the past tense. This is the epic isolation of dominant-culture life in North America. This is the proper answer to the doctor's question in the preceding chapter about when and how our fear of dying came to be. Our fear of dying came into the world before we did. It was conjured every time those we descend from ran, every time they left their capacity for being at home behind, every time they were unable to visit the old bones, every time they forgot where those bones were. It is not universal, but it is a constant in every culture built by waves of calamity-fleeing immigrants who have lost the bones of their dead.

Dying is mostly seeking, running your hands across unfamiliar things, not being able to see them but feeling them clearly and knowing certainly that they are there, trying to figure out what is at hand. Dying people often said to me, mournfully, about nothing in particular: "I don't know what to *do.*" But a better way of saying what they meant with this lament is: "Something is mostly coming, and it is mostly here too, elbowing everything else out of the way. I don't know which way to face." In the early days of diagnosis a dying person has as his or her new purpose in life to be "anywhere but here," to know "anything but this," to go after that fugitive running down the street called My Normal Life. But in the last days there is more often a feeling of "this, and this only." When older dying parents in their last days or hours mysteriously stop wanting to see or talk to their adult children this makes for a lot of heartache, but what is really happening is that the dying person is distracted by the sorrows and grief and familiarity of the living from the epic project of setting his or her face in some other direction, in a way that finally *obeys* what is happening. They no longer face those who have come from them, but face instead—or try to face—those from whom they came. That is the instinct, to begin dying toward their beginnings instead of living for what they have begun. But the instinct is hamstrung when, after generations of immigration, flight, and amnesia about ancestry, a dying person isn't sure at all from whom they came, or where home is to be found or faced. This is where the lament about not knowing what to do really comes from.

The great fear that dances across the faces and the families and the medical charts of dying people with the news of death coming is the fear of rampant pain, but with good medical management it rarely is an enduring fear. As the dying proceeds, the unthinkable emerges from the mist: Dying people are very often entirely mistaken about what they fear most. It is not the pain. It never was the pain. The more energetic and resilient fear by far that I have seen is the fear that the rest of us, the living, will after some time and adjustment be able to live our lives, that the end of the dying person's life doesn't end much else after all, that the living will continue to be the living and be able to proceed as if the dying person is past, done, over, in some way as if that person had never really, enduringly *been*.

We are sometimes able to realize late in life, often only then, that the real substance of our lives is contained in its witnesses, that our life is tangible in how it is to others, in the relationships we were part of. We are real, in other words, to the extent that those around us grant us our reality and we theirs. Think of how we do our business where the dead are concerned, how most of us live our lives with them and without them, and ask: How *real* are the dead—not only real to us, but real at all? How real are they, the ones we claimed to love and cherish and carry forever in our hearts? How real can they *be* if the dead are gone, or lost, or in the past tense? Dying people intuitively begin to understand that their reality is pending, that their citizenship in the land of the living is tenuous and ebbing, that they are even now beginning to join that faceless, nameless caravan of the Lost and the Gone, heading out of town. They can feel it in the strained etiquette of conversations about how they are faring. They see that the living have already made for them a separate place, emotionally and spiritually, to live out their days. They are, with the shadow of their dying upon them, no longer part of the plan We the Living have for ourselves. They are on the Lost Nation highway, even now.

And they begin to recognize and remember, probably for the first time, that when it was their turn and they were the living and they buried friends and grandparents and parents, they were able without much thought or difficulty to get on with their lives, as they say, and start talking about the ones they buried in the past tense. They were able eventually to turn away from the dead and were rewarded for it by being treated by their friends and family as fully recovered, as healed. Our bodies know how to die, but we have little or no idea how anything of us could survive the amnesia that seems built into our history and our memorial practices.

In my experience, people working in the death trade really pour their heart and soul into The Dying. When they talk about burnout in this business, they are not talking about working too hard or for too many hours and not taking enough holidays. They are not talking about the constant exposure to human suffering, frailty, and inevitable death, which most people wrongly imagine is depressing. They are talking about the cumulative effect of directing all of their experience, compassion, and know-how to benefit a fellow human being and, within minutes to hours of that person's death, having to transfer all of that to a new recipient. The Dying are the reason for the death trade. Who are the Dead, though?

I once sat with a group of palliative care physicians discussing this question of burnout and the fugitive sense of purpose in working in palliative care. I asked them,

"Who are The Dying to you?" Their answers were quick, certain, noble: The dying were the reason they got into medicine, the reason they come to work each day, the welcome opportunity to be useful and to do something about suffering in their corner of the world. Then I asked them, "And who are the dead to you?" There was silence, and a lot of it. Some claimed not to understand the question, some were stymied at the unsophisticated naivety of the question. Some thought it was a trick question. I had to prompt them several times to respond to a question most thought was rhetorical, nonsensical, or unanswerable.

This is frequently what happens if I begin talking about the dead. The recoil is almost instant, the intolerance is manifest. People are often embarrassed for me that I've begun talking naively about gas, shadow, antique delusion, and about the understandable and desperate projections of the bereaved (all synonyms for "the dead") that are palpable and beneath the intelligence of us all. Without it being said aloud you can hear the defiant refrain of the rational enlightenment anthem: There are no dead. There is only how we feel about the dead. I think some recognize without wanting to that because of training and education and acculturation and attrition The *Dying* are people to them, and the *Dead* are ideas or notions or propositions or personal beliefs. When a person dies in our culture, they take on the same status as the unborn: hypothetical. My wife asks me regularly to stop talking about the dead when I'm teaching. She says I lose credibility instantly when I do, and I imagine she's right.

The Dying and the Dead, we must, finally, recognize, *are the same people,* separated by a little time and a little breath. They are the same people. But among We the Living they do not qualify for the same concern, the same attention, the same insistence that they should eat, to keep up their strength. They are gone.

Well, this is theology at work, not personal inadequacy or frailty or hardness of heart, and theology has history. In the hole in our culture left by the Dead and by Deus Absconditus we plant our theology. The history of our theology is the history of this kind of homelessness, as victim and perpetrator both. Those of us who have inherited something of the culture and the history of the Book must know that the banishment of the ancestor is monotheism singing its one and only song. There is one God, there are no Gods; there are no spirits of place, only special places in a world which is not your home. The Dead, if they in any way exist, are consigned not to the fellowship of each other but to the care of the one God. The care of The Dying is the repository of our best technology and our best intent. The care of the Dead, if there is such a thing, is none of our business.

It is one thing to try and keep the memory of your beloved spouse or parent or child alive as you live through your days. It is another thing entirely to try to keep close an ancestor you have no living memory of, no information about, no felt connection to. While many of us in our dying time can draw some solace from believing that we will be remembered, hopefully for a good while, by a few people who thought well of us, all of us are fairly certain that we are destined to disappear, and in short order, that all we have known will be forgotten, because we perpetrate the disappearance of those who are no less so our people. The bluff and the bravado I have heard among The Dying about "Whadd'ya gonna do?" does not hide that fear of disappearing very well. That is the root dread of dying people, as I have come to know it. It is an inherited dread, and it comes from an inherited poverty that is rooted in certain historical experiences of those who were once our people.

The death phobia that I have been teaching about for many years now is not a product of our humanity. It doesn't come from being born. It doesn't come from knowing that you are dying, or from not being positive enough, or from too much attachment or from not enough. It comes from certain kinds of experiences, and from how those who were once our people tried to live with the aftershocks of those experiences. Our fear of dying is an inherited trauma. It comes from not knowing how to be at home in the world. It comes from having no root in the world and no indebtedness to what has gone before us.

It desperately needs to be healed. We need to be healed. They—our Dead—need to be healed. The Living and The Dying are the ones who can and must start that healing. I have taken most of this book to try and give us the beginnings of a shared language and a shared understanding of what we all face in our time when dying makes its guaranteed appearance among us. To do so I have had to spend an awfully long time talking about what is wrong and how it has come to be that way. Now I think I can begin to talk about what we can do about it, and what we must do about it. How we are with our dying is how we are with our dead. Caring for The Dying *is* carrying the dead, when it is done well. That's where we go next.

9

WHAT DYING ASKS
OF US ALL

Everybody Knows?

If there is going to be good dying for us and for those we love, then we and they are going to have to learn what good dying is and what it asks of us, and we are going to have to learn how to fashion it from our good intent and our old poverties. This can all be learned, and it can be done. That is the good news, that it can be learned. The other news is that we as a people are generally not too big on learning, or haven't been for the last century or so.

A competence-addicted culture happily amasses labor-saving devices, time-saving gizmos, and comfort-giving technologies. It signs up for self-improvement and self-actualization. It puts a high premium on knowledge transfer and skill acquisition. It resists learning, though. This is probably why: Knowing is generally hostile to learning, and learning is enormously expensive. You could say that knowing is a way of storing all kinds of things for the proverbial rainy day. The internet is full to bursting with this kind of thing, tons of bits of information all carrying a little orange tag that says, "You need to know this, or you will. Add to basket." Learning doesn't go about its business the same way. Learning wonders rather than accumulates. Learning wonders about the things we claim to know and about knowing at all. It wonders if knowing is all it is cracked up to be. Learning is subversive. What it asks you to pay in tuition is most of what you had thought was true, and what was necessary, and what was enduringly so. Especially it asks you to fork over most of what you thought you needed. To learn you have to trade in your comfort and your certainty for wonder, and wonder when it is fully employed and in good working order generally won't let you build a new religion upon it. The new religion will get wondered about, and pretty soon, well, you're asking the religion to earn its keep and the old certainties will start to slide and the dogmas won't hold. This is very good news.

So learning is first and foremost hard labor for human beings—a very noble hard labor. People who are good at it tend not to carry a lot around with them. Instead of being bloated with acquisition and padded certainties, people who learn have parted with much that was important to them, still more of what they thought they needed, and their penchant for wonder keeps them trim. They are much like nomads whose real wealth is measured by whether they can wear all their riches at one time: If not, their wealth is of a middling kind, but if so they are to be honored and learned from. Some people can put their most treasured, most valuable possessions, acquired at great cost while knowingly incurring great spirit obligation to the world, in their casket. For some there is no casket big enough for that obligation, let alone for the body that incurred it.

Learning isn't a product. It is measured not in what you drag home, but in how you walk. Learning is a skill. Like all real human skills, you will not live long enough to pay for it entirely. You will die still indebted for the skill of learning that by good fortune and some persistence when it no longer made sense you learned. Dying wise is a learned thing, a costly thing, and, for all that, a precious thing. Dying well is in the same way the beginning of paying the obligation to life you gathered up in living.

Imagine this if you would: You are kibitzing with a few acquaintances about maybe making a big financial decision or quitting smoking, or doing something risky, and you are fretting about whether it will work out well and how much sense it makes to even think about doing it. Someone says, "Well, everybody's going to die." What happens to you, to your imagination, when someone announces this as a kind of painful, obvious victory over the vagaries of life? Do you feel reassured? Do you feel encouraged to go ahead and live deeply and well? Do you sit back in your chair and sigh, "Well, thank God. I wasn't sure about that one. Sleep'll come easier now"? Does it pave the way for peace of mind? Does it feather the nest of your dreams for your life? Does it help to get the priorities straight or to give you a compass with which to chart the path through the rest of your days? Or does it help you feel better about the life to come for your spouse, or your children, if you are blessed to have either or both?

It does none of this for most people, so far as I have seen. Most of the time most of us will agree with the pronouncement without debate or rancor, without hesitation or melancholy. Most of the time, when people say "Well, everybody's going to die," nothing much happens. And this is the great poverty of our common days, that when the story of the ending of our days is told, nothing seems to happen. But it should. Something should happen.

You might say, "Well, it *is* a bit of a conversation killer. There isn't much to say about it." You might say, "Nothing happens because it's not news to anyone. Everybody already knows this, so why would they talk about it? What do you expect?" I expect that if most of us really know we are going to die there should be some kind of indication in the way we live that we know this to be so. It's not a piece of neutral information. It's not like knowing the color of the placemats on your kitchen table. It should have some kind of consequence, knowing this about the number of your days. We should see some kind of sign in the way most of us live that most of us know we won't go on forever. I don't think we do see a sign that our death is a known thing. We see all kinds of signs that our death is a feared thing, which makes for the kind of culture we have made.

Compare it to the fairly inescapable news about global warming and climate change. You could debate the rate of change or the location of that change. Some still want to chalk it up to poor record keeping or short-term climate memory or Greenpeace propaganda or liberal fudging of the science. There's money to be made from just about any fear or mayhem, and so far global warming is no exception, so there will be cynics on that side of it too. But for the rest of us who are willing to know that such a thing has come to pass, what possible sign could there be that *we know for real* that the climate is changing? It might change the way we live. We might worry a little, or have some vague concern for our future. We might change our buying habits or driving habits, and there are some signs that we are. There might be some defeated shrugging of the "Whadd'ya gonna do?" type. There would be something that showed that this news has happened to us. That's how you would know that you know it.

Depending on where your people lived a hundred years ago, the chances are good that through the course of their lives and from a very young age they saw a lot of death. The opportunity to see it came mostly in the home, and that is because home deaths were the norm a hundred years ago. Since then, three trends have kicked into high gear, and they have changed everything. One was the increasing medicalization of the care of dying people, which took the lion's share of the hands-on work away from family and friends. Though the current model of care is called patient- or family-centered care, the families in a hospital setting are echoing the drama of a hospital death without influencing it much. Beyond augmenting what the harried and overworked ward nurse is capable of, there isn't much for them to do. Now we are living with the beginnings of a reversal of this trend. Many jurisdictions in North America can no longer afford the ballooning health care expense that has for a generation or two been lavished on the last month of life. Health budgets are making early discharges and home deaths a little more common than even a decade ago, and without much experience families are obliged to welcome home this loved one who has become a patient, a sedated stranger, and care for them as best they can.

The second trend was the growing inclination—often it was and still is an insistence—for people to die in hospitals or chronic care facilities. Dying at home became a poor person's option during the twentieth century. These days, though, there are small signs of change; most people are trying to crowbar caring for their dying kin into a schedule already full of work and parenting obligations and plans for the future. The hospitalization of dying people happens not usually because the symptoms are too complicated to manage at home but because the family members *feel* overwhelmed. They can't afford to let dying change their lives. That feeling comes from not having much experience with caring for dying people.

The third trend is the almost total legal, political, and moral ownership of postmortem arrangements and events and procedures by the funeral industry. In most jurisdictions there is legislation guiding the handling and disposition of the body, and that legislation delivers the body directly into the hands of the funeral people. It is a legislated monopoly that promises to serve the bereaved by guiding them through a difficult time and does so by preordaining any important decision making. We are obliged to leave things to the pros. I know many people now who are outraged at having no real choice regarding the disposal of their body or the body of their loved one. They recognize nothing in the services or products of the funeral industry that is sympathetic to their concern for the earth or for the loved one who is alleged to be returning there, and they are planning covert burial rituals that ignore the funeral parlor, the cemetery, the cremation chamber, and the law altogether. May this civil disobedience continue. There are alternatives that are showing themselves in the industry, and they might be a signal that real change is coming (the Death Store in Maui, which sells whatever you need to bury your own, is one I know about), but funerals are not substantially different than they were a generation ago. Many funeral directors have turned themselves into event planners for a ceremonially impoverished clientele, but this may not signal a change of conscience on their part.

Taken together these things have had enormous consequence that has visited probably every family you know of. All our technological sophistication and psychological theorizing about traumatizing kids and delicacy of manners and legislation about the disposition of the body have insulated us unintentionally from how it is to die and to be dead. Dying and death are witnessed by the living from a long way off. Dying people are handled mostly by the robotic arms of health care systems and treatment protocols and professionalized competence, and not too often by the people who have grown up around them and love them and know them well. Instead of hard-earned wisdom about dying and what it asks of us all that comes from a lifetime of seeing it and smelling it and being a faithful witness to it and grieving it, we have premature opinions galore about dying that come mostly from rumors and horror stories and undigested compilations of Native spirituality or Eastern mysticism. We have massive technical sophistication for managing The Dying and a serious mythic poverty in knowing dying, and most of us stagger under this irony. How we are with our dying and with our dead, and how we ourselves are likely to die, is the sum of what we haven't seen and haven't touched and don't know much about. That is the meaning that we now often find at the end of our lives: a hole, a crater, where our life and our skill of living used to be.

Imagine if your understanding of what your job asked of you day in and day out came from doing that job less and less. After a while your job would mostly be made up of what you thought it should be instead of what it asked of you, of your feelings for and against it, of your aging and thinning memory of what it was like to do the job, whether you approved of it, and so on. The essence of your job would disappear under the burden of opinions you had about it. This is what C. S. Lewis so elegantly described in his book *A Grief Observed*, how he began to understand in the wake of a loved one's death that as he struggled to keep her present by gathering up all his memories of her, so she began disappearing under those memories, until that was all that was left of her to him.

How then can we possibly feel able, when dying comes to call? How can we ever have a real knowledge about dying that can serve us and those we love when we have so little experience with it, so little chance to learn it? Because of this recent history in our part of the world, the inevitability of our death *is* news itself. For the young among us their deaths just aren't possible, or likely, or necessary, or just, not to them nor to the people who love them. When other people, especially grandparents and others that were deeply cared for, begin to die around them it is news of the hard kind and it hurts, but it happens "out there," to *their* bodies, to *their* lives. Someone else's death rarely brushes up against our own. The fact that most of us don't plan on it, don't see much of it, don't live as if it is true, are staggered by it—that is all the proof you are likely to receive or require that your own personal death will come to you out of the blue, where all the news comes from.

When we traffic in this sleight of hand that says, "Everybody knows they're going to die," something does happen inside us. It has a subtle but devastating impact on our imaginations and on our ability and willingness to think in certain big ways. It turns dying into an inevitability in which we've no meaningful part to play. It is something that will befall us, something that we are utterly on the receiving end of. It also turns dying into an endurance test that is emptied of any possibility that it could be achieved instead of endured. When that happens to our imagination, our own way of dying can never really be something that we could be proud of, or something that we could leave to our children knowing that finally we found something for them that won't end up in a yard sale some place, something that the moths won't eat—maybe the only thing the moths won't eat.

So please consider this: We don't say that all of us will inevitably live just because we are born. Whether we live or not depends on all kinds of things, including our stamina, curiosity, willingness to know difficult things, and courage. Whether or not we will die doesn't depend on our diagnosis or prognosis. It depends on stamina, curiosity, willingness to know difficult things, and courage.

Enough

I don't know if I achieve much for you or say much to you if I say that ours is a culture that doesn't do too well at not doing too well, but I hope this might be apparent by now. As I said earlier, ours is a competence-addicted culture, and savagely so. I know it sounds strange to put these two words together, since competence by definition is supposed to be a good thing to be, and being "addicted" is far from that, but there it is. We all know the mantras: *Be all you can be. Maximize your potential. Your only limitation is your imagination. Just do it.* Do you see how fierce it is, the intense aversion so many have to being ordinary or average? Remember how you were graded in school not according to how well you did but in relation to how well or badly everyone else did? The Holy Percentile. There are antiaging shops and seminars everywhere, if you have an eye for that kind of thing, and they extend the competence addiction to include defying even the proper and noble signs of time passing through the body. Looking your age is good when you're young, but only then. Ever after the standard compliment goes to your failure to comply with the passage of time. Growth rings are for trees.

Being *good* at hurting, or suffering: What would that look like? We know what we think it should look like: Anybody in the room with you would have a hard time knowing you were suffering, and not because they were insensitive or didn't know you well. Being good at it for us tends to mean that the effort is nominal, that "I know this already," that "I'm driving the bus." So suffering well in a place that doesn't believe in suffering means less suffering, controlled or contained suffering, suffering that doesn't color everything else, barely visible suffering, suffering with manageable consequence that doesn't include more suffering if possible. Competence is the opposite of struggle, in other words. Struggle in a place like ours is demeaning beyond a certain point, humiliating, beneath us, without merit. As the old joke goes, the definition of a schmuck is somebody who, when you ask how he's doing, tells you.

Now, what if the hurt and suffering I'm talking about is the suffering unto death? What happens to the suffering then if all this is what we have been taught and lived and practiced? What would dying look like then? I think the answer is inescapable. There wouldn't be much of it. And there isn't. We would claim our right and responsibility to be in control of our lives when we are dying, we would use how "in control of things" we felt as a reliable indicator of whether life was still worth living, whether we were continuing to enjoy "quality of life." And we do. We would use our bowel control, the earliest deliberate exercise of dominion over some discreet aspect of our inner selves, as the place where we would plant the flag of our dignity. And we do. We would swear off dying for as long as humanly possible, and a little longer, and employ every drug and medical procedure in the name of "less death for the dying." And we do. This is what would happen to dying people in a place addicted to competence, that dying would be another exercise in not letting them see you sweat. And, mostly, it is. They have a drug for that too.

What does it take for any of this to be different? What does a dying person need so that he or she might make a decision about how they die, about what their dying could mean? How could they make "death" their death? They need collapse or they need courage. Probably they need both. They need a collapse of their hopes of not dying or of dying quickly or of dying and not being there when it happens. They often need the little dust ball of disease symptoms to become a tumbleweed that rolls down every hallway and through every room in their inner house, that shadows every other distraction and feel-good mantra and positive-thinking bromide that friends and caregivers offer with every visit. When these things collapse, dying people can get very lost for a while, and they could throw a real scare into the people who love them. They could be diagnosed as depressed and drugged accordingly, and they often are. Mostly they could be accused of giving up or accuse themselves of giving up. When the symptoms are inadequately persistent or severe enough to justify the collapse of the old way of seeing it all, we figure that the dying person has given up too soon.

When do we let dying people off the meat hook of "trying"? When the symptoms gang up enough on them, become tangible and visible enough to break the positivist will of the most obdurate family member, that's when. Far too often we require a fierce amount of overt suffering, manifest in mounting symptoms, before the idea of "enough already" is ever allowed a place in decision making. Health care professionals will in a similar way rely on mounting symptoms to get the patient "ready" to receive the "bad news." This is the only collapse that seems to have any merit.

It isn't very likely that this collapse will come at a time that still allows for some clear thinking, or clear and heartfelt talk among the people who love each other, but it should. This is what I mean by courage. It takes a towering courage in the face of everything that passes for love and compassion and mental health to *stop trying*. It takes more courage still, or maybe a different, more discerning kind, to stop trying before someone is addled by symptoms and drugs and side effects and cold sweats and twenty-two hours a day in bed and night terrors about what is to become of him or her. Let us say aloud to each other here that being alive is habit-forming. Even when it doesn't go particularly well, still most of us feel the draw of living, and we usually look toward the next new day. It isn't an easy thing to feel otherwise. It is hard as hell, it is counterintuitive, and it is mandatory that *when the time of dying is upon us we have to find a way to stop trying not to die.*

> One early June day I walked the last few steps up from the sidewalk to the front porch of a very fine turn-of-the-century home in a leafy neighborhood of the city I worked in. As always, I waited a moment before ringing the bell, and used the time to get the hurry and the traffic out of me. The referral from the palliative care physician was, as usual, a simple one. The patient in his early fifties, a former captain of industry, was dying vaguely but certainly of cancer. He had metastases to the brain that were complicating his speech and might be affecting his intellectual capacity. (In the middle stages of this disease trajectory it is notoriously difficult—and ultimately pointless—to separate anxiety from depression from anger from brain cancer.) His wife worked as a nurse in the trauma unit of a major hospital. There were no children. The patient was having difficulty adjusting to the changes in his physical condition, and they both seemed to need help understanding that he had rounded the corner from treatment to palliation.

I was led into the living room where the man waited. Three things struck me. The first was that his scalp, very visible under thinning and closely cropped hair, was a series of metastatic eruptions that gave the top of his head a reddened, glistening, lunar look. The second was that he was in perpetual involuntary motion, unable to sit and unable to not sit. It took me a moment to realize that the chair—any chair—was of no use to him. His brain metastases had robbed him of his capacity for equilibrium. He had no sense of being balanced or at rest, and so he was in constant search for that elusive place where his seat, back, legs, and head knew the chair well enough to find some stillness. I was there for about seventy-five minutes, and he never found it. He had no better luck when he slid to the carpet. Laying down, curling in a ball, nothing felt like stillness to him. You could see that he had a perpetual sense of being about to fall off the floor. Whatever success or mastery he had achieved during his life had prepared him not at all for the withering, the terrible resemblance to madness that terminal brain disease had brought. I could tell that he had more practice than he wanted in being able to see himself now as a visitor saw him. He was defiant and humiliated all at once. The third thing that struck me was that his wife assumed a cordial but remote neutrality in the other chair, regarded me as the doctor's unnecessary and unpromising idea, and had almost no response to the man's exhausted teetering. They both looked at me warily, one roiling, the other rigidly alert, and waited.

I struggled with the prospect of asking the man anything. It wasn't clear to me that he would be able to speak, and I didn't want to deepen or complicate his ordeal. After a moment I asked what his understanding was of what was happening to his body and his world. His words came out staccato fashion, in forced, flurried bunches, with great effort. He knew how to make the most of his one-breath sentences. He knew he was seriously ill. He knew that the cancer had gone somewhere in his brain and that he had some serious decisions to make in the coming weeks. He went on to describe the growing challenges to daily life that he was facing and how he and his wife were responding to them. He was having a hard time remembering sequences, the day of the week, what his wife had just asked him. He also knew that he was a burden to her, and that caring for him was slowly becoming an excruciating full-time job. He was sad, he said, that just as they had begun to contemplate early retirement he now had to reconsider what the rest of his life might look like. Eventually his wife spoke in a practiced, reasonable, and supportive way of how she hoped that the new round of radiation that was being offered would reduce the tumors and tremors a little. She was keen that they both enjoy some respite from his escalating symptoms. She also said that she was certain that more treatment should likely give him more time.

Something in the room changed. In a hurry the feeling went from guarded curiosity about me to a practiced compliance with something that didn't have a name. After a moment, the man rotated on the floor with what looked like a spiraling, barely contained, and awful energy, faced his wife for as many constant seconds as he could manage, and, twitching and gesturing, in a strangled, furious voice, said, "Let me go." He said it five times, with a deliberate pause between each. Like Lear.

"Let me go. Let me go. Let me go. Let me go. Let me go."

Each time, the last word was the loudest, a kind of grunt. I have never heard another human make that sound. He was wild with rage, with defeat and humiliation and utter misery. Spent, he turned to me and glared. Or pleaded. It wasn't possible to tell which. I looked at his wife. Silence. She was smiling, very thinly. I could see she wasn't thrown by this at all. I asked her, "What does that mean to you, what your husband just said?"

She said, "Well, he's having a bad day today, as you can see, probably worse than usual. But yesterday he was fine."

After a few minutes it was clear that the meeting shouldn't continue. The husband and wife, each in their own way, were done. There are moments in the death trade, many of them, when there is nothing to be done, but there are very few like that moment, with the utter desolation of what had been done to these people in the name of More Time truer than anything that could be said about it. I was tying my shoes at the front door and, figuring the odds of me being there again remote, risked one more gambit. I asked the wife whether she had ever bought a house. Disarmed for a moment by the non sequitur, she allowed that she had.

"Remember how it went? Looking and looking for months, giving up more than once, your agent pleading with you to just look at this new listing, and you reluctantly driving over. And before you were in the front door you know this was It, the one you'd held out for. And you went from room to room with more excitement, and you were already half moved in, and you called your husband from the new kitchen and announced, 'This is the one.' And you brought him the next day, except this time you saw all the things you didn't see the first time, all the little things that together made you wonder whether it was a good deal after all, and by the time you got home the deal was off, and no one knew what to do anymore, and you were both exhausted." She nodded and remembered something like that.

"If we had given you a mental competency exam that day, you would have failed the part that requires you to have a consistently expressed wish over time. You wouldn't have been allowed to make any significant financial decisions because you failed the test. You wouldn't have been allowed to buy the house anyway, no matter what you decided, because you were not capable of knowing what was best for you. You would have been a candidate for psychotherapy, and maybe for medication." Here her eyes narrowed.

"But nobody held you to that standard, because buying a house can make you nuts. You'd have been given the benefit of the doubt, and everyone would have looked the other way. You would have signed the purchase agreement, or you would have walked away steamed and quitting the whole mess, and everyone would have understood."

I pointed toward the living room where we had just left her exhausted, squirming husband, and said, "So why do we hold him to that standard? How many times does he have to want to die before any of us is persuaded that his wish is real, and earned, and that he's not having a bad day, and that even if he is, given the whole thing, he is entitled to die? That it's his turn?" I asked her just to think about that for a while. I wasn't surprised when I didn't hear from her again. I don't know what became of them, although I did hear that shortly after the visit he took another round of chemotherapy.

I don't say that this man's wife had become heartless any more than I say that he had become depressed. I say only that both of them were barely able to endure having won their wager for More Time. Gaining More Time doesn't mean that dying people get better at dying or that they use their More Time to get ready to die. It is emphatically not inevitable that being obliged to experience more death means people know more about dying, or that they have "better outcomes." Families are now sometimes obliged to provide a level and duration of home care for their dying loved ones that was largely unimagined thirty years ago. The escalating emotional burden of caring for dying people is largely borne by their families, as will the burden of the inevitable trend of early discharge from hospital be borne by them. The promise to care for someone "in sickness and in health" is never undertaken with this kind of dying in mind. Cancer is why people are dying, and palliative medicine is often how they are dying.

The purgatory to which people with "premature" wishes to die are admitted is the holding cell of depression. Antidepressants are almost as common as pain medication in the medical management of dying people. Physicians, counselors, and families are all unhinged when a dying person wants to die before they are able to. The considerable arsenal of medicine, psychology, and family familiarity are stymied and frozen when a dying person asks for help to die "before their time."

Is a dying person who wants to die before they are able to depressed? It isn't a good question. The idea of "depression" isn't challenged to earn its keep as something useful. It is already accepted as a legitimate way of understanding what the wish to die might signal. So we should ask: What are we saying about a person when we say they are depressed? We are saying that they are experiencing, feeling, thinking, and acting in a way that they shouldn't. We are saying that, no matter how devastating the circumstances are, we must leave open the possibility that in time our response can—and ultimately should—be different, less overwhelmed, less confounded. The diagnosis of "depression" is a defense in principle of the obligation to which we hold dying people to *behave*. It trades on the idea that human endurance must be revived. No desire to die, premature or otherwise, could stand up to the accusation implied in the diagnosis: You *should* be able to feel differently. In our culture it is not a given that you should want to die simply because you are or that you should stop trying not to die when you are.

Someone wants to die because they are depressed, not because they are dying: That's how we make sense of it. The problem is, when did this dying start? If they've been dying for a long time are they dying at all? Or have they become "seriously ill," but now for far too long, instead? So, we go about trying to treat the depression "successfully," so that the desire to die is ameliorated by disappearing or by being manageable or livable. How strange it is for me to have lived long enough to see a time in which people are tranquilized for trying to do what they are already doing. "I'm dying." *Don't be negative.* "I want to die." *You're depressed.*

In the earlier story, the wife in a way needed her husband to be depressed. It explained his "mood," his "outbursts," his wish to die, and it gave everyone something to do: antidepressants, psychotherapy, chemotherapy. There was no other way for them to live what was left of their lives knowing what her husband was asking of her, to help him die. But "depression," as a way of understanding our reaction to what befalls us and as a way of helping people who are dying here at the tortured beginning of the twenty-first century, has to earn its keep. It must be informed by what it is like for us to die here and now, and especially by what it is like for us to approach death over and over, as we now do. The sheer cumulative effect of having to keep being who you have become, of carrying the symptoms from month to month, of living your More Time in the shadow of the deferred inevitability of your death, of trying to find a way of ceasing trying when you live in a culture that has no working definition of "enough already": Those things have to be understood before someone well-intentioned obliges the person who wants to die to want otherwise, to keep going.

Most dying people are enormously sad, and they need help in being sad. They don't require a diagnosis. The inability to be sad when it's time to be sad—*not* too much sadness for too long—is something that can depress people. When being sad is hurried through on the royal road to acceptance it is one of the hardest of dying people's tasks. *The antidote for depression is sadness,* and it is sadness that must be taught. To be heartbroken isn't a diagnosis. It's a skill.

People not being *able* to die: That is the nightmare. People wanting to die in the presence of the technological sophistication that obliges people to live: That is the nightmare. All of the debates on euthanasia and suicide, all of the debates on the rights of the disabled, all of the medical ethics reviews and discussions, they all have to contend with this nightmare, with its etiology and its effects and how they are visited on The Dying, and I wish they would. *Dying people as a rule are not traumatized by dying, but, like Lazarus, by having to do it and do it again.*

So this might be the most supreme, most sublime tragedy in the litany of miseries that so often is dying in urban dominant-culture North America: We stop trying to control our dying finally at the point when we have little or no stamina, energy, give-a-shit, and time to give to the honorable and immensely necessary project of dying well, dying lucidly and deliberately, dying purposefully and surely and wisely. I receive emails almost every day from people who are hoping that they die quickly in their sleep and from people who want to die lucid, alert, and aware of what is happening. The chances at the moment aren't too good for either of them to get their wish. Dying in our time and place means having to live all the lunacies and sorrows and slings and arrows described in this book. It asks of all of us grow an immeasurably able, cunning soul to know the hues of madness that color our thousand ways of not dying as we die and to resolutely die anyway. Learning this skill, we could love this part of the human world that is our own, all its human frailties and unwillingness to live when life is hard anyway. We could be sad, a trustworthy achievement. We could bequeath to the young people attending the end of our days—often at too much of a distance—and to the children and babies who will have no memory of us at all a story of a dying life that is faithful to the struggle of being human when the seduction and the pull is so much otherwise, a story so true and indelible that it shines best and brightest in the darkest time, like the stars in a clear, country night sky. This is what is at stake with every terminal diagnosis, every treatment decision, every home death and hospital death, every funeral and memorial service.

You don't learn about all these things in order to not have to do them, or to be able to quit doing them. You learn these things so you can do them well. It means having some sense of grace about getting older and a belief in life going as it must go. That is far beyond the current mantra about acceptance. Acceptance is what you do to the weather when your parade is rained on; love is what you do to your children when they begin living a life that you haven't lived and don't understand. That is loving life, and praising life, and proceeding accordingly. Getting good at dying, for anyone involved in it, doesn't mean that you are fine in spite of it all. It means to be *wrecked on schedule*. It means not wanting to die when you know you are dying. It means saying so. It means wanting more than anything for your loved one not to be dying and telling them this. It means missing people long before they die and telling them so. It means being sad *with* people, instead of "about" them.

It means that people who do what I do won't be asked anymore whether parents should bring their four year old to the funeral, because parents will start bringing them. Every time I have been asked I always respond, "Why wouldn't you?" They usually say something about the child being traumatized, and I ask, "Why would they be traumatized?" They usually say they want their child to remember their grandpa or their brother as they were, and I ask, "Well, how were they?" You know and I know that they mean that they think kids' memories should be free from seeing what time and disease can do to a body, that the only version of someone deserving of being remembered is the most competent, most updated version. They were the most able when they were most themselves: That's our belief, and that's what kids learn from us early on. Children's memories are being selectively anesthetized to banish all the parts that are inconsistent with our idea of happiness and childhood peace of mind. The deeper meaning is that grandpa was only grandpa when he was well and wrestling around on the floor with them. The rest of the story, the ending part, isn't worth remembering, isn't life affirming, isn't true, isn't him.

In fact, it's all life affirming, except the selective anesthesia. Think about all those memorial services you've been to where there's a finely crafted photomontage of the dead person's life, where there are pictures or film clips of that person right up until the ending of their life started to show itself. Then, no more pictures. The kids don't even recognize grandpa in most of the pictures, because that younger, more preferred man didn't exist by the time they were becoming aware of him. This is propaganda. It's the way totalitarian regimes reeducate their populations for the future, by prescribing what they are allowed to remember. Kids deserve a grandpa that died, not one that just stopped being grandpa without saying anything for a month or two and then slipped from view. That's where they'll begin to learn how it is to weaken and die, which will probably be their lot someday. And it's where they'll begin to learn how to be sad in a sad time. That's what we owe children, the chance to learn something besides trauma and aversion, something like a good example that will serve them well when it is their turn and there is no one left from the time that they were kids but themselves.

Dying people don't need our permission to die. That is an expression that should be outlawed. They need our love for them to get out of the way of what they are in some inchoate way trying to do. It is loyalty and a sign of deep love to want your loved one to die when he or she is dying, though it means that something of you will die with them. It is a deep love of being alive that finally helps a dying person want to die. For a long time, dying people are trying to live, and so they do. When the time comes, and the time always comes, the dying person must try to die, in hopes that they might do so. They must be allowed and encouraged and taught if need be to do so. They have to learn what "enough already" looks like, and usually that happens sometime after they get there. Anything that throws them off the scent of their dying must be challenged and made to earn its place alongside the deathbed, just as we all must earn our place alongside it. Greater love hath no man, woman, or child than that one who will love a loved one toward the ending of their days.

A Love Affair in Reverse

With less direct experience of dying we have opinions and feelings instead. These opinions and feelings describe us and our fears and habits much more than they describe dying. How can we know whether our opinions are in any way faithful to what dying is, what it does, how it goes and doesn't go? I would say that, at best, we can't know much about that time of our lives and, at worst, we die badly when we don't have some willingness to learn death well. We should consider shedding some of our opinions the way we shuck our corn, setting the husk of our old opinions aside with some compassion as things that were probably inevitable and seemed so necessary at the time, in favor of sitting quietly and learning things instead. We don't eat the husks, and we would do well to stop trying to nourish our ways of dying and caring for dying people by eating our opinions about it all, and to stop feeding them to others pretending that they are nourishing.

We could begin doing so with a simple question, a question with a quixotic tilt to it: What does dying ask of us? Instead of assuming or insisting on death's malevolence or heartlessness or illusion or supreme disinterest in our well-being, we could just ask of our death what the old stories, the ones that have survived our sophistication, education, and conversion, recommend that we ask of anything that approaches us unbidden from Somewhere Else: What would you have me do? This might seem like divination of a kind, and it is. Teachers of divination don't have their students looking out toward their future or back toward their past, but down at the square foot of holy ground they stand on, and they fix their learning there. Divination doesn't look to tell the way things will be. It pays heavy and faithful attention to the way things are, and from that arduous study has something to say about the likelihoods before us all. Trying to die wisely and well is a kind of divination.

Some of us might be able to recall the epic feel of belonging that we were bathed in in the time before we came into the world. Whether that was in the nine or so months of our being gathered up or in the time before that, still we must have belonged and been at home somehow. That is my best figuring on the subject. How else to understand why it is by force that we are taken from there, driven down, through no wrongdoing of our own, and into the world? How else to understand the look of travail and foreignness most of us bring to those first moments in the blistering light, in the austere air and jangling noise of the world?

So then imagine, as you and I were obliged down the great tunnel, seized by what once held us, the anarchy, the bewildering labor that was forced upon us. We may have had sorrow, something truer than fear, and some kind of knowing about what was becoming of us, a knowing that works the way sorrow works. Not that we knew the outcome, not that we knew that all would be well. Only some greater certainty that this was not the opposite of us, not our undoing. And imagine that as you and I sorrowed that sorrow and worked that work of being born into this world there could have been something like thought. If there was, most of us were not thinking, "Well, this is interesting. Something good could be in the offing here." And most of us were not thinking, "Surely I am surrounded by goodness and mercy, and surely I will be gathered in by able hands waiting just inches away on the other side of this," though for most of us there probably was that goodness and those hands, just inches away.

Somewhere in those moments hovered the end of what we had known and the beginning of our having to learn what we didn't yet know. The world that was to be the ground of our learning and our teacher was the end of what we knew, and the world first came to us not as gravity or livid light or aridity but as our body. This is what was there for us to learn, that there was a body where the world came to us, a body where our home used to be. In the months that followed there would be apprenticeship to hunger, where we would learn the gulf that was even then opening between yearning and the thing yearned for. We would learn the great "not I" of the breast or the bottle, and the unkillable claim that the weight of our body in the world, its gravity, would stake upon us. In all, we would learn the beginnings of a self and how that self was planted in this matted mystery of our body and was growing down into that body.

A little later, after those of us who could do so negotiated the hugeness of our heads well enough to stop keeling over and negotiated the hugeness of our bellies well enough to roll over onto them, and after those of us who could began to make a little sense of being approved of and disapproved of, of the soft voice and the strong one, the open eye and the narrowing eye of those around us, those of us who could slowly learned the great miracle of speech, which would tangle and gild all the rest of our days. The day would come when we would hurt our hand and say "I hurt myself," and this would be a sign that a certain circle of learning had been made whole, where "I" and "my hand" were one.

We live inside that circle of learning for the rest of our lives. At first we learn to have a body, and somewhere along the way we learn to be a body. This has the mark of necessity upon it, which means to me that it is good. Somewhere in this mingled wanting and being wanted we happen upon some willingness and some ability to love this body, this unlikely, wobbly treasure, this one we more and more call "I." Many trials gather along the way. The inevitable amnesia about all of this that comes from getting older, say ten or twelve, will blur or hide altogether this early love. But it is there somewhere in most of us. By then we have become something we call "I," and most of us will use this word as if it had always been, as if it was a solid, enduring fact in the world the way wind and weather are facts, as if it had something of the inevitable about it. We will use it without pause, we will usually sound very sure about who that is, and it will always include the body. In the time to come there will be more swagger and more defeat, more gravity and striving and strife, and they will be known together, the "I" and the one who says the word. The body will have learned the self, and the self the body.

I can hear some objections rising among those who are quite sure that this learning is a kind of mistake that years of meditation and spiritual practice are required to undo. I've read a little about "illusion," but it is something I don't know much about. Karma is popular, but I don't know much about that either. There are teachings that the body is a kind of mistake our consciousness has to recover from, that the world is an illusion, that death is an illusion too. There are books that promise that there is no death, not really.

Now, death is something I know a little about. Just try this out as an idea, just for a moment: What if the body is not a mistake? What if it's not a test for your mind to endure? What if your body is not a con job for your soul or your consciousness to contend with, or to get on the other side of or to sort out? I know it breaks down and won't endure, and I know it isn't the whole story, but the body might be a sign of something more than trouble.

Now ponder this, if you will: Your body is made up of basically everything that makes up the world, chemically, physically, and biodynamically. There are things in the world that are not in the human body, that's true, but there's pretty much nothing in the human body that you won't find in other places in the world. Now, you don't consider the world a con, do you? I hope not. A tree is an illusion? A frog in a frog pond is an illusion? A valley full of reasons to live is an illusion? What if all these things are gifts? What then? Your body is made of the same stuff that makes up all these radical unsought-after gifts that together are called the world. Is your body not worthy of the same regard and awe and gratitude that the world is?

Many cultures have sayings along the lines of "the best way to own someone is to give them a gift." It sounds a little cynical, and I suppose it is, but somewhere in the spirit of those sayings is an effort to contend with the burden that comes with all gifts. Gifts are confounding, mainly because they send up in us an unwelcome tendril of obligation and indebtedness. Yes that's there, but the twin of that obligation is the rumor of your worthiness. Maybe the gift came to you because you were worthy of it, and that had already been decided. It isn't something you have to earn; it's already there. Trying to get out from under that obligation means denying your own worthiness. This is not a good strategy for being human, to deny your indebtedness for your body and for your life in this world, to deny your worthiness for being on the receiving end of all that. Just try knuckling under to both of those "illusions." Just slip on that crazy coat of obligation and worthiness that your body is a sign of. Once you learn how to wear it, you'll look good. And that might encourage other people to look good, dressed up the same way.

Well, this learning I am calling love. It does not mean that the love is constant, any more than most marital love is constant or always in concert. There will be times of almost total amnesia about what the body needs to be well and long days where we will try to escape the body and its limits. But it is more than your companion, this body, and more than shadow. It is your way in the world. In your good days you will notice its impossible persistence and its steady groove, how it answers the call of digestion or locomotion or pleasure before you do, you always playing catch up to the way your breath and pulse have of being themselves. And that attention to your body's ways of being itself will, when you can sustain it long enough, be a kind of love.

With the uncertain benefit of a little fitful hindsight you will come to a steadier notice of your self's body and your body's self just when its moments of asymmetry and struggle begin congealing into the first unbidden suspicion that this steely groove will not last, cannot last. The evidence of time passing, like growth rings in a tree trunk, becomes legible as a story, and then as you. Something cuts across what was the endless highway of your plans and the physical mastery they depended upon. A new weakness in your grip will show itself, a little seizing in your back that doesn't spring to suppleness after a three-hour drive, the inadequacy of light for reading fine print that no one seems to notice but you, these and a few score other bothers become whispers after a while, after they don't pass. They are all saying, "Well, here it is. This is you too, whether you meant it or not, whether you deserve it or not. You ate enough bran or you didn't, you fastened your seatbelt or you didn't, you thought a majority of good thoughts or you didn't, and here it is, regardless. Here is the continuance of your days. Here you are."

This is a time when many begin to look down toward their bodies as if from some greater height or remove, begin to wonder how these changes are happening when there was no prior consultation or assent, begin to have some distaste for that old love. And all of this accelerates when there's an injury that can't be healed, an infirmity that can't be strengthened, an illness that can't be banished. When the news of age comes, it comes to the body first. Strangely enough, we are bound all the more firmly to that old learning, and we are even more our bodies just then, just as our wish that things be otherwise comes on. The news makes us more our bodies.

I remember well a harsh little moment in the grinding inevitability of my mother's hospital death years ago. With her chronic breathing problems we had grown used to yearly admissions, to the point where the news of the next one didn't create much of a stir. We showed up at the hospital in shifts and did what had been done a half dozen times before. The times being what they were, she was in the emergency hallway several days before they found her a room, and this seemed to deepen her keen sense of being disoriented and lost. A day or two later my friend and I visited her in the early afternoon. Keeping a conversation going was hard. She seemed to lose the thread easily, and she was quietly distressed about something she couldn't name or find.

The lunch tray came. No solids. To give the visit some kind of direction or purpose, my friend, bless her, weighed in with the plastic spoon and the mashed apples and started feeding my mother. She took the first spoonful without objection and laid her head on the bed. When the second spoonful came, her mouth was still full with the first. With a little cajoling she made some room for the second, but the third spoonful found the second still there. After one more try, my friend gently encouraging my mother with, "Come, try a little. You need to keep your strength up." My mother opened her mouth with the applesauce in it and glared at my friend and the strange room and the whole, strange world, and growled, "No!" It was the last word I heard her say, even though her death was still weeks away. Her body, at least, was already trying to die, though none of us knew it then.

Probably you have eaten something today. Why? It's an unexpected question I know, but try to answer it. Why did you eat? Probably two answers come to your mind: You were hungry, or the clock or the job or the family said it was time to eat. This is a compensatory understanding of the imperative of eating: You ate some time ago, and so you are eating now to make up for all the time that has gone by since. It's a common answer, but it's not an accurate one. If you have ever fasted for a few days you probably discovered that your appetite seemed to vanish after the initial headaches and wooziness, and the fixation on your eventual next meal eased. The absence of food didn't prompt your hunger, after a while. In a strange way the absence of food often ends hunger, just as the presence of food prompts it. This is a little bit of a grace note written into our biology. We seem to be built in such a way that if there is no food for a while we will not suffer the hunger that will ensue.

So why do we eat, if it is not to make up for the time since our last meal? Eating isn't compensation. It is affirmation. We can have intense memories associated with the smells and the tastes of food. Those may be some of the reasons for eating what and when and where we do, but they are not the *consequences* of eating. When you eat you are voting "yes" to the rest of the day, the rest of your life. You eat to keep on going, not to make up for where you've gone. You eat forward, you could say, not backward. You eat toward what will be so that you can continue. You eat for what will be, the same way you plant seeds indoors in February to have tomatoes in August.

When dying people without announcement or consultation stop eating, their families tend to get very organized around solving this problem, often by changing diet or volume or timing and the like. Anhedonia—the inability to experience pleasure or contentment—and loss of appetite are cardinal points in the compass of depression in the mental health trade, and the mental health trade, like a man with a hammer, misunderstands dying as the easy-to-treat nail of feeling glum. Families too usually take this refusal to eat as a sign that their dying loved one is despondent and giving up the struggle to live. Meal time then becomes an exercise in cajoling and cheerleading, to the chagrin and eventual regret of everyone involved. But eating binds us to life, and each meal nails us to the wheel of the world, and dying people need more than anything else to be able to dissolve a little at a time what binds them to life, especially to the metabolic and physical life. When dying people stop eating they are voting "no" to keeping on. Often it is not even a decision. It is more as though the body's own wisdom, its understanding of how to stop continuing, is announcing itself. It is a wisdom that is absolutely faithful and quietly resolute at the end of a person's life. Dying is groping in a dark room for the door that will let you out, and stopping eating is like turning a knob to see if *that's* the door.

The dying person doesn't need any strength to die. Physical strength makes dying harder, enormously more difficult than it would otherwise be. With dying, as with living, there is such a thing as "enough already." There comes a time when the future has nothing worth wanting or hoping for, and dying people can no longer vote for any future. When they stop eating, they are voting "no."

So dying is a time for untying the knots of strength, competence, and familiarity that have bound us to our bodies. It is a time for excusing our bodies from the heavy labor of getting us around, of being the armature upon which we once draped the cloth of great intent woven in our time of physical mastery. It is a time for watching our bodies being drawn out into the river of life not by typhoon or flood or disaster but by the steady and trustworthy current of how things are and must be. It is a time for learning how to love our bodies not for what they might still do, but for what they have done and will do no longer.

And it is a time for doing all this to the relationships that we have nurtured over the years. Dying people find their way out of life by easing, softening what has bound them to those they know and love. The living often feel abandoned when The Dying stop looking to them and begin to look through them. It is the heavy labor of the dying person to follow the body's wisdom and loosen the ties that bind. It is not the opposite of a love affair, not its annihilation. It is a new way of loving our life, by obeying its way of ending. A love affair, in reverse.

Let's say that you are married now. Perhaps it is your second marriage, perhaps your spouse's second go at it. Both in your late fifties, you've seen enough unhappiness and life now to give you a good appetite for continuing. On your good days you remember that none of this will last, that you've seen more of life by far than you are going to see.

A terminal diagnosis has come elbowing its way into your schemes for contentment. Now is the time for you to know what you've learned about life, whether it feels good or not. This is stand and deliver time. Your deal with each other and with life was going to end one of two ways, either by divorce or by this. If you are the one suddenly, mysteriously dying, you'll almost certainly have the easier road. The disease will do what it does faithfully, and you, faithfully or otherwise, will go along with it.

If you're still reading this, read a little more: Your spouse, unlike you, will probably stumble into his or her dying time unescorted. You won't be there to help. So you'll have to do it now. Here's how. Tell your spouse how it is to be inexplicably dying. If no one on the professional end has had the courage to tell you what is happening, then you be the one who decides what is happening. Then, faithfully report on your ebbing days, the sway of the disease, the unfamiliar absence of energy. Tell your spouse everything he or she doesn't want to know or hear, and don't wait to be asked, and don't aim for acceptance or comfort. Aim at this: I'm going to give you something of your death now, through mine, so you'll have something reliable when you get there, something of me. Let me love you that way.

And if you're the one people will designate as "the survivor," the one who'll write the obituary, you'll have the harder road, friend. Always on the receiving end of news, status changes, test results, you will have to *decide* that you are in the time of dying, whether your spouse gets it or not, whether they agree or not. Here's what you'll have to say, more than once, to plant both of you in the time you're in: "I don't want to be too lonely before I have to be. I'm not going to sit with all this by myself waiting for you to be ready to talk about it. So, here goes. Tell me please what you think about when you look off into the distance, turned entirely inward. Likely I won't have someone to ask me these things when it's my turn. Tell me please, what is it to be dying? What should I learn now, to help me when it's my turn?"

You are not journeying down the road of life together. At this point, you can't. Your dying partner, without meaning to or wanting to, turned off that road when he or she got the news, leaving the rest of us marching along as if we'll be fine. And you'll not be walking the same road again—at least, not until it's your turn. This is how your songs of grief are sung. You see? You don't end up talking about grief after you've begun to learn about it. You don't study it. Instead, grief will be how you talk, how you study, how you see. Instead of being your goal, grief will be your way of going on, not being able to.

It is an uncommon understanding of love, this love that glimpses its end. You might recall perhaps with a little embarrassment when as a child you shamelessly blackmailed a parent or relative into buying you a puppy for Christmas or a birthday. How you squirmed with the thrill of the idea of it. How you angled and jived, and how you defeated every argument and defense against the cost of it, the work of it, with your remarkable and groundless vows to get a job to pay for the dog food, though in truth you wouldn't work for money for another half-dozen years at least, and your vow to do everything the dog needed or wanted done, which to you meant almost exclusively watering and playing. Remember how you finally won, and home the puppy came, and you loved that puppy with a head-locking crazy love that was total, unconditional, and lasted in that form for probably a year or so.

Puppies are love-generating engines, like the small, the guileless and defenseless, the goofily awkward and new of anything, and most of us, even those with allergies, feel the draw of it. Well, you loved the puppiness of the dog, and it lasted as long as the puppy lasted. Maybe it turned into an enduring, labored-over regard for the dog, maybe it became your first great, skilled love project as you and the dog both got older and slipped the newness of being new in the world, together. Maybe not too.

I ask you to consider that this is not love. This is approval. Love of the loveable is like hitting the ground when you fall down: You'll do it, but you can't take much of whatever credit there is, and it isn't a hard thing to do. In fact, you don't really "do it" at all. It is mostly reflex. Loving what isn't easy to love, like an old, half-blind, incontinent, droopy-hipped, white-muzzled dog drooling in the food he can't eat anymore, is love harnessed to the plough of being willing to know life for how it is. This kind of love breaks up the crusted-over field of our comforts and our fears. It is love put to the work of loving the world anyhow.

This isn't approval anymore. What of this can be approved of anyway? This is loving the world anyhow. This is saying some kind of reluctant, hard-earned amen to the way it is, which is what all dying asks of us.

After so much hard talk, maybe another love story is due. There is lots of mystery afoot when sitting with dying people, and there are times of hilarity and softening of the heart toward the hardness of life.

> Louise was like the kind of old lady I remember from my early childhood, and there she was again when I was on the job in my mid-forties. She was well kept, as they say, an English expat who might have come over as a war bride. She maintained her accent, and she kept her feeling for a place for all things and all things in their place, and for decorum. She lived in a classy condo, and each of her rooms looked like a set piece for one of those British family television dramas. She had an extravagant vase full of cut flowers in the living room each time I came, and she was dying.
>
> Louise found a patch of scaly skin on one of her eyelids years before, which turned out not to be eczema but cancer. By the time this was sorted out, she'd lost that eye to the disease. When I met her the remission was over, there were several secondary sites of cancer in her abdomen, and she was wanting someone to talk with about the end of her days. Her husband had died eight years earlier. She was happy to have her children and granddaughters visit without moving in, but no one in the family was keen on the Big Talk. There were a lot of quiet days and nights.
>
> When I first met her, out of concern for my sensitivities I guess, she wore a pair of owlish, massive sunglasses, the kind of fashion-neutral sunglasses you can only

get by prescription. She wore them indoors, for visitors. They were tinted enough that I could see no eye moving behind one of the lenses, but that was all. Louise treated me as her guest, she produced refreshments, she offered lunch, and we talked very subtly at first about her dying.

Probably the third time I came to her home she croaked through the intercom at the front desk, "The door is open. Let yourself in." It was the kind of change in a person's voice I'd heard many times, always a good and faithful sign that the disease was on the rise. When I found her in the living room, she was sitting with her feet up, in real fatigue, and she wore no glasses. It was a moment between us that had a kind of intimacy. This was a kind of sign that we were no longer unknown to each other. She may have been too tired to find them, but I think it more likely that she felt it was better now that I see her. It was an extraordinary thing, that eyeless place in her face. The surgeon had somehow folded the eyelids in with a grace that befit the patient, so that she had a perfect, seamless concavity with a tiny pinprick hole way in the back where her eye once lived, her socket now like a tiny unexpected door in the garden wall, a gate to something. I admit now that I stared. It was not easy to look at, but there was nothing else there in the room with us but her new exhaustion and her eyes uncovered. It was as though one of her eyes was a way in, the other a way out, and by then it seemed as though she could see out of both.

Louise was very proper with me, and only with continued encouragement could I get her to call me by my first name. In this job there are some people you feel more protective of than others, not because they aren't able but because their long lives seem to qualify

313

them for a kind of grace that this world rarely allows. She was a finely wrought kind of person, and I wanted that grace for her. I could see in each visit that she was getting frailer, and that she wasn't likely able to live alone—something she cherished—much longer. Louise knew it too.

Working with dying people asks you for a certain kind of soft focus, a slow gait in your thinking and your speech. As the dying comes on the living moments you have with them get smaller, and they start to resemble the spice instead of the food. You at some point realize that you probably have already had the last deep, sustained talk about the big things. You start to admire certain things just because they are still there, and grief begins to stir when you can count the weeks and then the days that are probably left. One day Louise insisted on walking me to the door, even though it was probably the most taxing thing she was likely to do that day. In a moment like that you could feel guilty that your presence is that demanding on whatever energy and attention she has left. Or you could feel honored that she is spilling a little energy of what she has left on you and that she still wishes to speak with you for a little while the etiquette language of the living. So we stood for a moment at the door, and I thanked her for seeing me and she thanked me for coming.

I had just that week begun to wear reading glasses, and I had found no reliable habit yet to deal with misplacing them. Being unsure of where they were and wanting to let her go to lie down as soon as I could, I with some frantic gestures started patting my pockets in search of them. Louise let this go on for a few seconds, and then in a thinning but very proper English accent said to me, "Oh yes, I know dear. Spectacles, testicles, wallet, and watch." Her timing superb, her face dead-pan, she opened the door and wished me a good day. I said to her, "Louise, I'm not sure I can come back now, you using that kind of language with me. That's some kind of workplace harassment I think." She said, "We'll both be all right." She was in her way untying the last knot of the "counseling relationship" that had until then bound us together and given us a reason to meet, and standing at her threshold we were two people, well met, who were soon to part. And she died a few days after that. Her kids asked me to say something at the funeral, and out in the naked field in a new suburban cemetery in front of a small crowd of fairly proper English people I told that story, and some of them seemed to like it.

As dying people are trying to find their way out of their bodies and out of their lives, the job of the living is to know how hard that is and to get out of their way. Dying is enormously hard. The labor of it—and it is labor, of the same kind as that which brings life into the world—is relentless, demanding. The shock of having to see your days as numbered in the dozens, of seeing your body heading out of town, of seeing yourself as mostly passed, these are in some ways ruinous and costly encounters with the way it is. We've been asking The Dying among us to learn how to die the hard way, on their own, in the middle of the night when the rest of us are sleeping, without much trustworthy guidance and with less first-hand experience than we would provide someone learning how to drive. We should now begin to help The Dying among us to learn how to die by helping them see more of it before it is their turn, by helping them to imagine it out loud without them having to worry about our feelings, especially by helping them grow their love of their lives and of us out past the old promises of staying with us and never leaving.

Those who will do so are those who cultivate the ability to be faithful witnesses, who are willing to learn how things must be even when—especially when—how it must be doesn't include what they wish for. It is this ability that makes being useful to dying people possible. On a good day this is a very demanding thing. It asks a lot of our humanity and our love of life to be willing to serve its end faithfully, to love life in that way too. I've seen people do it, though.

I have a friend who is one of the few people on this continent who still makes some kind of living as a fur trapper. We haven't talked a whole lot about all the moral politics swirling around this thing. We haven't had to. He just brought me out with him on the trap line in the depths of winter a few times after I bothered him enough to do so, and I saw how he was with it and what he believed. It is easy to oppose men like him and what they do. In these days where farms disappear under mall parking lots and jobs where people make things are swallowed by jobs where people service things made by machines, opinions about what you've never seen or done are easy to come up with. This is especially true where dying is concerned. What I saw was that my friend earned his way out onto the trap line, and he earned his opinions about what happens out there. The rest of us could learn something from that.

> One day in late fall, before the snows were on the ground to stay, we were up on the mountain behind my farm checking fisher boxes. Fishers are a bit of a fur-bearing killing machine, and the design of their jaws and head is made to order for what they do best. They are usually trapped in baited boxes with the trap down at the closed end of something that looks like a long wooden shoe box. The traps that are legal now are strong and quick in their business, and the few trappers that I know want the dying to be quick and quiet and unsuspected. It seems like a matter of honor among the best of them. When the traps are well maintained and

well set it usually goes that way. But things can happen out there, even still.

My friend wires a long pole to the trap on the off chance that something happens and the dying isn't quick, so that the animal and the trap can be found close by where it was set. He sent me over a muddy rise to check on one of his traps, and I knew something had happened when it wasn't where he said it would be. It took us a minute or two to find the pole, and the fisher in the trap, but neither of us was ready for finding the fisher still alive, and she was. She was silent in the trap, but the way she was caught up in it you knew meant she was suffering a great deal. When I saw how it was I couldn't understand how the fisher could still be alive. My friend said nothing, and his motions were sure and solid. Using the pole like a long handle he gently turned the fisher on her side. She was snarling as best she could and clawing with her hind feet. With first one muddy boot on the place where her lungs would be, and then the other, he shifted his full weight to that place and stood on the fisher, and stayed there, while she snarled and clawed at his boots. That standing lasted a long time for the fisher, for my friend, and for me. It was a kind of eternity that passed among us that cold, sunny morning. She took a long time to settle, and a long time to stop breathing. She loved her life, just as the other two of us did, and we could see it.

The things we do out of love and respect for life don't always pave the way for things going well. It wasn't a half minute after he took his weight off the fisher that she began against all the odds to stir and claw again. It was stunning to see her cling to it all that fiercely, at least it was to me. If my friend was distressed about it—he was, I know—it didn't cloud his judgment about what

317

his job was. If anything, it guided his judgment. Her suffering gave him his job. He turned her over again, and put his weight back on her lungs, and he stood there a long, long time.

The enormous, sad, faithful willingness of my friend that morning to keep up his end of the bargain was an honest, earned thing. He suffered the dying that morning, felt it come through his boots and the soles of his feet up into the places where he knew things. The great spirit of life to live was there, the great teacher, and he stood where he stood, learning that again. And I saw it all. This is what we need in the presence of life dying, the willingness to feel that dying right in our bones when it isn't our turn to die, to be a faithful witness to how things can go, to the part we play in them and should, to know the old stories that include life dying so that life can live, until it *is* our turn. Maybe then our dying life might feed the life that must go on, after us.

My friend hadn't said a word during all of this, until we were walking back across the muddy rise to the truck parked in the brilliant red morning, back to the rest of our lives, he with the fisher tucked under his arm. He looked up—it was then I could see he was shaken, just a little—and said, "Bad," his assessment, his confession, his debt, his faith all rolled into the word. It is all he has ever said about it since. He said it because something had happened, because he meant well, and still, there it was, because there was honor at stake and a life, because no one wanted it but it came anyway, because he had to do something and because I'd seen him do it. Faithful witness.

This isn't a story I tell you in a covert way to advocate euthanasia or any kind of killing. I include it here because it is good to know how big the world is, how hard life can be, how the sure mystery of it keeps bounding through the bush just ahead of us, making a way for us to follow but not letting us see too much at once. I tell it because it is not an easy thing to be a human being. There are lots of things that seduce us otherwise, and dying is one of those things. *When a hard time is upon us, being hard is not required.* Being supple in your understanding, keeping your willingness close to your memories and your skills, asking your eyes to stay open and wondering what is needed of you in that time is some of what is required. Whatever side of dying we are on, being willing to see things for what they ask of us is something to work at. That is a human skill.

The Words to Say It All

In the lives of dying people and of those who love them, a language that is true to how it is to be dying and to be caring for someone who is dying, a language in which dying people can recognize what is happening to them and what is being asked of them, is something like the Grail: highly prized in principle, and a rumor in everyday life. The words to say it: This is the mother of all our considerable poverties at the end of our lives. We have the technology, we have the medical infrastructure, drugs, and knowhow, and we have no language that does justice to it all, no way of speaking the truth of what has come of us, or why, or what it means. There is real consequence in the poverty of language for our medical care, for the end of our family life, for the stories about us that are told after, for how those who love our dying selves themselves will die. *Without that language, we cannot die well.* It is that fundamental to the great last project of our lives.

I heard an interview years ago with an Inuit elder. The reporter was looking for some drama for his story, and he asked the old lady through a translator what to her mind was the worst thing to befall her people during her long lifetime. The lady took a while in answering, which the reporter seemed to take for elderly confusion. As most white people might do in a similar situation, out of consideration he began to offer her some choices: Perhaps it was the time the caribou failed to appear back in the early 1960s and there were so many deaths from starvation? The old lady kept her faint smile and nodded a little. "Yes," she said, "that was a hard time." Taking this as only partial success, he suggested that maybe it was the time when the government made the people move to government housing, an instant town of prefab houses all close together, off the land, where there was now so much hardship? The old lady smiled a little more, which must have been all the more confusing for the interviewer. "Oh that was a hard time, yes," she said. The same voice, the same nodding agreement. "Well," he asked her, "was there anything worse than that?"

The whole interview so far had gone awkwardly. The reporter wanted a sensitive story, something personal, ethnic, exotic, poignant. The old lady was replying as though he was asking after her health, which he unknowingly was. The reporter seemed to have no thought that the request to speak about something like this was an intrusion without limit, or that the request to speak of the dead might be capricious or dangerous or both. Chances are that the old woman by that time had a good amount of experience dealing with people from the south, and her responses came not from confusion or a rickety memory but from an effort to save them both from harm or humiliation. In this small way she may have been defending her people from this latest incarnation of what might be the worst thing to have befallen them.

So, she gathered all of those concerns for etiquette and ancestor into this answer. She said, "Well, when they brought the TV here. That might be the worst."

"Television?" said the reporter, "Worse than losing your family from starvation or losing your traditional way of life?"

The old lady nodded toward her grandson who was playing on the road outside her government house. "Since TV, we can't speak together. I can't speak TV. He can't speak Inuktituk."

She didn't mean that her grandson watched television instead of talking with her. She meant that he watched television because he couldn't talk with her. She couldn't speak TV—English—and that was the only language he knew. She knew that her culture could survive starvation, as it had done times aplenty in the past. That was *in* her culture. And she knew that there could be enough memory and enough hunger for true things among her people to survive forced relocation, which didn't have to be the end of anything. But she also knew through practice what linguists and anthropologists know through study: The culture lives in the language. When there is a rupture in the teaching and speaking and praying of a language that lasts two generations, when the memory goes the way of the lived experience, it is the real beginning of the end of something. The first generation unable to speak the ancestral tongue, though the language might feel to them like something backward, arcane, or useless and nostalgic, still has the sound of it inside them from their childhood and from the elders that are still alive. The second generation has neither the language nor the experience of hearing it live. That's when a language withers and fades. That's how culture dies.

Another way of saying this with less heartache and more wonder could be this: If you can't say something, you can't see it either. I don't remember where it was or when that this thought came to me. I know that it wasn't there one moment, and in the next it was the only thing there: If you cannot say it, you cannot see it. Remember the scene early in the Genesis story, where Jehovah gives to the muddy human the ability and the power to name all the things of the world. Naming is an exercise in dominion. It is power, and it is an act of conjuring too.

Naming is a way of knowing and retaining and calling forth. Almost all indigenous people on this continent are known to us by outsider names, names they do not use to refer to themselves, names from another language that usually carry an impression or a prejudice of the outsider towards them. Navajo aren't Navajo, not to them. They know themselves as "Dine," the name that remembers their Athapascan origins. "Eskimo" is another example, "Ojibwe" another, and "Huron" another. Many indigenous people have a personal name they are known by on the job, out in the dominant culture or at home, and another name for ceremony and ritual, for partly the same reason. This could be a way of defending themselves against that kind of dominion, a kind of camouflage where they can pass as someone domesticated and safe to be around. Indian agents and missionaries in the nineteenth century insisted all aboriginal people in their charge take on English or French or Spanish first names, mostly taken from the Bible, and then surnames as well, often taken from the agents and missionaries or political notables of the time. This was on the surface to ease the business of running reserves. Look a little deeper though, and you'll see that making native people answer to a foreign name was another way of domesticating and controlling something wilder and unruly. Pretty soon there were no animals or spirit beings in the names people were known by, and pretty soon there were no animals or spirit beings either.

If you can't say it, you can't see it. Our ability to say something with the beauty and elegance of our own language carries our way of knowing that thing. Language is the way the thing is known to us. Language makes a continuity for our knowledge and gives us a way of acting on what we know. This is why the bard or the storyteller is in most every culture the one revered for his or her capacity with words. They are the great rememberers. This is an honorific title in many places in the world. An Anishnaabe elder, a great rememberer, called me that once after hearing me talk, and I was honored by that. I recall sometime after his father died the filmmaker Tim Wilson describing his own grief to me in this way: "When my father died it was like the library burned to the ground." This is a great way of saying it. When his father's voice was stilled, when he could no longer be heard, that was the end of how he knew his father. That's when his father began to pole his boat out into the current of the way of things, away from the Land of the Living and away from Tim's surging desire to have him close. What I think he missed most about his father was not what his father knew, but his way of telling what he knew, the sound of his voice and his way with words.

When our language is used to sell us things, when it is bent toward making deep things obscure or simple and bad ideas the only ideas worth knowing, it is a disaster for us and for our culture. It makes language suspect, untrustworthy, almost sinister. It makes language banal too, annoying and incidental and purely instrumental, which makes for enormous poverty among those who rely upon it every day to know and be known by the people around them. But worse by many times is the mocking or banishment or execution of one's own language by another. Translation, as most bilingual people will tell you, is an exercise in controlled futility. Languages don't translate. They are ways of seeing and knowing, indigenous and faithful to certain places and times and peoples and stories. Because of that, the old way of knowing goes mute in the translation to the new. That's what the Inuit grandma knew. There are no southern words for what she had seen and learned and loved and lost, no way to give those things to her grandson parked in front of the TV, and not much of a way to grandmother him, not the way she was grandmothered.

When I teach people working in palliative care I ask them about the tool, the skill most vital to them on the job. Most people point to their training or the experience on the job, or their motivation or their compassion. Almost no one points to their tongue. Think about how we give so little consideration to the language we use on the job, how we are taught almost nothing about what language to use or why when we are trained for the job: It is the principal delivery mechanism for all the kinds of care unique to working with dying people.

There isn't a drug, a surgical procedure, a medical appliance, a profession, or a conceptual counseling language used to deliver palliative care these days that derives from the physical, social, intellectual, or spiritual realities of dying. All of them are conceived, developed, taught, and perfected elsewhere, in labs and factories and classrooms and boardrooms, and imported to the deathbed. They are carried to peoples' homes and deathbeds and families in the name of caring for them. In the hands of practitioners with some skill they are translated into "end-of-life care." That very phrase is one such translation. "Living with a life-threatening illness" is a translation from generic counseling language into a language used to counsel dying people, predicated on the goals and ideals of coping and healing. By this translation dying people are encouraged to speak in a similar way, and to see their lives in those kinds of terms, and they very often do. The first thing they are forced to do is to choose between living and dying. The language makes them do that, because in normal speech these words are mutually exclusive, and so they can't be doing both at the same time. "Living with a life-threatening illness" is an outsider's language that is used to describe a kind of person that the outsider has never been, a kind of life that the outsider has never lived. "People living with a life-threatening illness" is the same kind of name, carrying the same kind of outsider language and uneasiness and prejudices. So is the phase "The Dying." It means "them." It means "not us." Dying people soon learn that it means "not us." That word—"us"—is a word that dying people cannot use anymore.

Dying people need to hear and speak a language that does justice and bears faithful witness to how dying is. They deserve that kind of language. It is their right. This isn't a language of technical information, prognostic probabilities, and survival rates. It is a language in which dying people can recognize the realities of what they have been living covertly, probably for some considerable time before the tests and the office appointment confirmations of the worst-case scenarios. How else are they able to learn to speak as if what is happening is happening? Remember the grown son of the dying woman in the Maritimes, how he asked her to tell him what he didn't know and what he needed to know? That's what he was doing, trying to find a language. He was saying to his mother, "Tell me how to say it," and she was saying to him, "I don't have any way of saying it." Without such a language there is no way of turning the corner from "if" to "when," from "very sick" to "not going to get better," from "going to die" to "dying." Without such a language there is no way to have a shared understanding between dying people and those they love. There is no way to be sad together.

This is the basic entitlement of all dying people, that they speak and be spoken to faithfully as dying people. They are not people living with a life-threatening illness who, depending on their readiness to hear the bad news and their ability to understand, may or may not be dying. They are not people whose health is failing. What is their health failing to do? Whom is it failing? I don't say that all dying people want such a language, but only that they deserve that language. It is a true thing, an indigenous thing. It isn't pure or unchanging, but it is true to where it comes from. A language for dying would see to it that dying was present whenever it was spoken. If we do not have a language for dying, we cannot see dying when it is present among us. That means that dying people are invisible to themselves and others as dying people, which proves usually to be chief among all the indignities that will be meted out to them during the course of their dying time.

When I told that reporter that I was an Angel of Death, that's what I was doing. I was foraging for a language that was faithful to what was going on. I actually got that line from a woman who was already on her deathbed at home when I first met her. She was struggling like crazy trying to understand what was going on, what all the changes meant, why I, a stranger, was in her home talking with her of intimate things. I told her that usually people are waiting for some kind of sign that tells them without fail that this is what is happening now, that this is the dying time, that this is what it feels like. I told her, "When I come to your house it means that nobody on the medical side is waiting to see how things will go. They know how things will go, usually. When I come to your house, it means that you are dying now. If you've been waiting for a sign, I'm it."

And she looked up from the bed utterly relieved, even a little chipper, and said, "So you're the Angel of Death, then!"

"Yes I am," I said. "Not so bad, is it? Not as bad looking as you thought?"

"Not so bad," she said.

> Years ago I met a woman diagnosed with the same kind of cancer that was coursing through a startling number of women in her family line. She subjected herself to a combination of radical surgery and a round of radiation and chemotherapy that permanently changed the look and feel and workings of her body. I didn't ask her much about it, but I would guess that at the time, given her family history, she probably saw herself first as a victim of the disease and genetics, and then, when she was going through this surgery and treatment, as a fighter. As things turned out, she lived over a decade with no new sign of the disease, and I heard her at that time call herself a survivor. Not too long ago she found some small lumps under her arm, was told by the first doctor she consulted that it was nothing serious, and subsequently discovered that she now had a recurrence of that cancer from years ago. In her first consultation with the oncologist she was told, "You are not a dying woman." The evidence he sighted was not so much her state of health, not the current stage of the tumors, not even that oft-resorted-to statistical probability scale. Instead, he reasoned that she'd had over a decade of disease-free life, and there was no reason that she couldn't have another decade of the same. She walked out of that meeting as if the doctor had seen her future and named her by it.

I am fairly sure that there are no clinical trials or out-come measures he could site that could support that reasoning. I'm just as sure that even within his own practice he couldn't gather enough anecdotal evidence that people with a decade of remission routinely enjoy another decade of remission. Clinical experience with cancer treatment protocols didn't lead him to make that declaration. What led him there was a contorted kind of compassion and a dearth of any language that was true to the fact that *things had changed*. The language hadn't.

On the basis of reasoning and probability alone, her having had a decade of remission could just as likely—more likely, in fact—oblige them both to conclude that she had received her share of what everyone in that po-sition hopes and prays for, More Time, and that the recurrence was the sign that this more time was now at its fullness. It took months of more chemotherapy, more symptoms, more drugs and side effects, and hope and side effects of being hopeful for the oncologist to change his language. When he did, as the procedures had less and less of the desired effect on the tumors, ap-ropos of nothing in one of their five-minute meetings to review her situation, he simply said, "Well, what do you want to do?"

The signal to her and her husband was jarring, ob-scure, coded, aloof. He had never asked her this ques-tion before. He had always told her what would be wise to consider. Without knowing quite why or how, she gathered from his question that she was now on her own. A few months prior, all the language was about what *we're* going to do, how *we're* going to fight this. Add a little more disease, a little less promising response to the treatment, and it became, What do *you* want to

do? By then no one was talking about her having another good ten years. A few weeks later, during one of
several hospital admissions to try to get a better handle on the management of her pain, a hospital social
worker, a well-intended person who didn't know this
woman at all except as a referral, came to her bedside
and offered this well-intended reorientation: "You are
not dying with cancer. You are living with cancer." That
is what the social worker called her, a not-dying hospi-
talized cancer patient receiving pain management and
symptom control. Another christening, another job description, another thing to do about what no one can
do anything about.

What the oncologist needed, more than his medical training and years
of experience and secure position at the hospital, and what the social
worker needed, more than a welcome and timely referral from a physician
often reluctant to refer a palliative patient for counsel, was a way of saying
what was probably true, increasingly true, sadly and madly and deeply
true. It was certainly what the woman with the cancer needed. Each of
them needed a language that did not come from the cheerleading mantras
of positive thinking or from the half-speak orthodoxy of self-help or from
the guideless generic counsel talk of patient-centered care. They needed a
language that testified to what was there to be known. They needed a language that didn't come from cancer care, but from now, finally, beginning
to die while in cancer care. They didn't need another round of patient-centered care. They needed the recognizable beginning and the true language
of dying-centered care.

The language of "breaking bad news" is what makes it bad news. It is
a language its users count on to be kind, gradual, hopeful but realistic,
problem solving, comforting, looking with some pliable solace toward the
future. But you will never get such a language from the "breaking bad
news" training ground. The bad news language is a language that comes
from exhaustion. It is used when the worst outcome is suspected, when

hope looks ludicrous or feels like it begins to border on malpractice. It is used when the med-tech arsenal is reduced to balms, when the high-powered express train of treatment has been downsized and triaged to a small commuter bus of pain and symptom management. The bad news language is used when the patient has turned down the one-way street of palliation, away from the homes and jobs and lives of the healthy, the living. Worst of all, it is not a language that knows anything more about dying than the language of treatment and surviving and coping does. It is a language that teaches only what it lacks.

I know there is tremendous resistance all over the place to using a language for dying where the truth of the dying is in the language. We traffic in euphemism instead, as if the dying can survive the euphemizing. I don't think it ever does. I don't think it can. We usually use the words we use to banish dying from the dying room. When we keep doing that, everyone involved tends to lose track of what is going on, and of what their job is. They say that war's first casualty is the truth. It certainly seems to be the first casualty of the war on cancer.

A few years ago the National Film Board of Canada produced a documentary film called *Griefwalker* about some of my work and ideas. The more times I have seen it, the more I have realized how strong and agile an introduction it is to how we die and how we struggle not to die in our time and place, and I am glad that it is in the world. I was asked once to be present at a private, invitation-only screening of *Griefwalker*. When the evening came my wife and I drove down a beautiful cul-de-sac on the sea shore. The house was of a kind I was not born to, and we had trouble figuring out which of the several entrances we should present ourselves to. We took a chance on the more formal-looking doorway and rang the bell. We introduced ourselves to the man who opened the door, who didn't seem too impressed either with my appearance on the scene or with the event itself. When all was in readiness I introduced the film to a group of mostly therapists and counselors, and then offered to stay afterward for questions and discussion. When the house lights came up seventy minutes later, the crowd was silent for quite a while. Finally a tall fellow asked me something. He said, "Well I have a question. What gives you the right to be so direct with people who are dying?" He asked this in a fairly aggressive way, the crowd took a collective breath, and things got a little tense right away. Gads, I thought, if this is where the talk is starting, where's it going to go from here?

His question came of course from a therapist's concern for someone in heartache and travail. That's partly where it came from. It also came from the standard death-phobic gospel that there is little merit in knowing that you are dying, little merit in telling someone that they are dying, little merit in talking as if that were so. The way the therapist was coming at it, I had to defend my practice of doing things differently. So I said to him, "Well, okay. That's a pretty challenging question to get us going, but why not? So I'll strike a deal with you. I'll go to great lengths to answer the question you have asked me, right after you answer a question of mine: What gives you the right to be so indirect with people who are dying?"

And that is a crucial question for us all to ask ourselves. The instinct to understate things is not tolerated when we're talking about domestic violence, about residential schools, about the safety of our food supply. It's not respectful or kind then. When it comes to talking with people who are dying, or about them, obfuscation, obscuritanism, and euphemizing all take up enormous room in how we theorize and teach and practice palliative care, and yet these practices are rarely asked to pay their way. The practice of "directness," which to me is a practice of fidelity and authentic witness to the contending truths of dying in a death-phobic time and place, is regularly challenged and sometimes vilified, and the practice of weaving and reweaving the pall stands for compassion and passes without comment. I have been told by palliative care doctors many times that they have to "undersell the palliative stuff" just to be able to get in the door of a dying person's house. They have told me that they have to establish a relationship of trust with the patient, and this trust often is forged by not being candid about the inevitable outcome of the disease or about the purpose of the doctor's appearance on the scene, at least not until the patient signals that they are willing to be spoken to as if that is what's happening. It's understandable, but it's bizarre: a relationship of trust based on being compassionately obscure. "When do you get to be honest?" I ask them, and they say, "When the patient's ready." Well, how do they get ready?

Dying is not getting the news that you are dying. It isn't "getting the information." Tolstoy's Ivan Ilyich, like most people, "in the depth of his heart knew that he was dying but not only was he unaccustomed to such an idea, he simply could not grasp it, could not grasp it at all. And it simply was not possible that he should have to die. That would be too terrible. And so his feelings went" (Tolstoy, pg. 93). This is a very honest way of saying it: *He knows that he is dying, and he doesn't understand it.* This is why I keep challenging the idea that everyone knows they are going to die. It is possible—and in a death-phobic culture it is almost inevitable—to know this in some fashion and not allow the knowledge any consequence or meaning in how a life gets lived.

Tolstoy wrote that Ivan Ilyich suffered most from "the Lie," and his book shows so well that one of the places that you die—that you know that you are dying—is in the eyes of another person who is willing to know that with you and not blink, who is willing to struggle with you in understanding this unprecedented thing by talking toward it. Remember the dream you have probably had where you are the only one who seems to see the impending mayhem, and try as you might you cannot get the others in your dream to turn around and see the thing? Remember the raw panic of being the only one who knows something is coming, while everyone else carries on as usual? Now imagine lying in what you have grown sure is your deathbed, with everyone around you speaking and acting as if you are ill, or as if not much has changed when it has. Imagine the power of that to rattle you beyond measure and to make you wonder if you know what you know, and to make you question your sanity. Imagine the power of it to make you disappear. Solemn lying, whatever its motivation, has to answer for itself.

Whether it is compassionate or not isn't my issue. I am asking over and over only how we know that it results in what we think it results in: an ordered, naturally unfolding, graduated awareness that gives the dying person and their kin the chance to come to hard things according to their willingness and capacity. This then brings us to the question of how do you get ready to do something you desperately do not want to do? What are we asking of a dying person when we ask them to be ready before we begin speaking and behaving with them as if they are dying?

We could start with a little Word Voodoo of our own. We could start making a language in which dying actually shows up and using it at every opportunity. This "live like you were dying" stuff is shite, forgive me for saying so. This how people who will die but are not dying talk. This is what they imagine is possible, and it is what they want for others. It comes directly from that adolescent caper that most have been in on: If you found out that you had a week or a month to live, what would you do? Giddy excess is the almost universal reply. Dying people aren't usually physically capable of extravagant excess, and they aren't "living *like* they're dying." Mostly they *are* dying, and they don't know how. They don't have the words to say it. So we could work toward a day when you ask a dying person, "So, how are you doing?" and the dying person says, "I'm dying. How are you?" Just as a start.

10

KIDS

If you've a good recollection of your early years, you'll remember the sadness of others more deeply than sadness that was your own—if there is any such thing as your own sadness in those years. Maybe there is only the sadness that comes first from knowing the sadness of others and theirs from knowing you. Maybe that is how you come to it, knowing what sadness is by knowing others a little and being known by them as much. It could be that all the human yearning—for closeness, for understanding and recognition—comes from that.

So I remember being three years old very well. I remember the growing remoteness that would within the year part my parents. I remember my sister's appearance in life, how my parents looked to her to make their life together worth the effort. I remember the short hill I had to climb to see the neighbor, and how a long way's off that neighbor's house looked to be. And I remember suddenly beginning to go out of life and my mother's sadness because of it.

> In 1958 some places on this continent were booming,
> and I was in one of those places. There was a refriger-

ator for everyone, probably a car. There were houses spilling into fields. The code was being written on the hide of the world: There is no visible bottom to what can be. And in the midst of all that there wasn't much that could be done for kids with meningitis. One day in the land of plenty, I was picking up bees I thought had fallen into flowers, to find that they were still very alive. And then I was in a hospital, going out of life. No one knew what was wrong with me at first. I remember being wheeled into a small room that had a doctor off in the corner, a large nurse standing in front of a wooden stool on which I was perched, and a green towel on which lay the biggest needle ever made. The nurse took the back of my head and pressed my chest to my knees, and laid her considerable self on top of me so I couldn't move. When the needle was deep in the small of my back she scolded me for yelling, specifically for waking up all kinds of people in the hospital. They wheeled me back to my room after the lumbar puncture, and I was going out of life.

People regard dying children as they do no one else. A fierceness can come into some of them, and they take their position on the ramparts, for war. When I was three years old, there were nurses there that put their bodies in the way of my dying. I remember how they touched me. They were laying claim to me. Even the big nurse who shushed me and forced the wind out of me with her weight: She had to feel that fear and that pain running in me during that lumbar puncture through her whole body, and she did. They were all declaring for me citizenship in the land of the living and would take on anyone or anything that would have it otherwise. All of this was in their touch. That is how it came to me, through how they touched me. People should hold you in times like that, and those nurses held me. You will remember if they do, and I remember it well. My countryman the poet Alden Nowlan, who nearly died several times of heart troubles and operations before he finally died, had his way of remembering the change in touch that often accompanies the time of dying, rendered in an adult way. He grew sure toward the end of his life that everyone, in the end, wants, more than fame or infamy or self esteem or even love, to be held.

Well, in 1958 I was held that way, and bathed and dressed and needled, but there wasn't much they could do to stop the meningitis doing what it was doing to me. And I remember that sometime after the first day at the hospital, at the end of their testing, things changed. They touched me like I wasn't going to be staying around. They didn't pull me to themselves in the same way, as I began going out of life. I know now that they were trying to get ready for what everyone knew was coming. I know that they had to find ways of being able to come to work the next day, after a child they had laid claim to died on their watch. I don't say that they touched me any less, or that they were aloof or indelicate, or that they'd stopped caring for me. I only say that I remember well how they were making a way for themselves, and for me, for this to be over soon. They were loosening their hold on me.

I remember the nurses' touch more than my mother's because that is how it was in those days. There were rules and visiting hours, and the nurses had to enforce those too. So my mother couldn't be with me as much and couldn't touch me as much as they could. I imagine now how it must have been in those days, in the middle of all that prosperity, mothers and fathers watching their children going out from among them, the rules of hygiene and profession obeyed over and over, so much loneliness. I remember her face framed in the small safety-glassed window of the big door, after the intercom voice had announced the end of visiting hours, after they had finally helped her out the door, how she had turned around and looked at me through the glass, and I was looked at as someone who may not be seen again. It is a powerful thing, to be looked at that way. It stays with you.

I didn't die, but I very nearly did. That's what they told my mother, that I had somehow survived, that their drugs didn't have much to do with it. The doctor in charge took no credit. He told her that there was something else at work. One day I was dying, the next I wasn't, my life suddenly spectacular for what did not happen. The days come and go. Your childhood goes on, you come into your adolescence, and you can get used to having nearly died. By then it is a war story from the old days, or your mother's embarrassing exaggeration. Your memory of it quiets down. The fact of the thing you can remember, but the truth of it you forget. I wish it wasn't so easy to do—it is such an enormous thing, and it *should* change you utterly—but it is. You can easily mistake having nearly died for the way things just go, or at least for the way things went for you. You fold it into your memory drawer and your life gets piled on top of it. Maybe there were no witnesses or, eventually, they're all gone. You can forget that it came from somewhere unbidden, as a gift can do, whirling out of the peripheral mists to give you back your days, and you stop making a place for having nearly died. You stop thinking of yourself that way, as a kid who nearly died. You might even take a little credit for it. All these are ways of forgetting, shredding the great mystery, letting it scatter. Having nearly died once, damn it, can't do much to keep you alive in the time to come, not necessarily.

Years and years after wrestling with the meningitis angel, I ended up with breathing troubles from secondhand smoke that have stayed with me since. A traditional Chinese medicine woman I know says, "Too much sadness, here," and she touches my sternum gently. Probably true too. So it happened that I got a case of what I call Leather Lung. I couldn't get good breath, it went on for weeks, and I dissipated to a played-out, dehydrated, crusty state of premature oldness. That happened when I was somewhere around twenty years old, and I ended up in the hospital again, self-admitted this time. It makes you feel sorrowfully grown-up, admitting yourself to the hospital for the first time, like you've reached a degree of taking care of yourself that you never wanted. I had the paper blue gown with the fine ventilation in the back to go with the paper blanket on the rubber bed. I had the semi-private room with someone in a lot worse shape than me. In my arm I had the saline IV hanging from a rolling four-wheeled stainless steel tree. When the mood struck, I could float the hall, well togged out in shades of pale blue right down to my paper slippers with the seam running down the length of my sole, looking very white and wretched, a little ghostly, as if I came from nowhere.

I was just sick enough not to be able to read. When I reached my limit of ceiling tile observation one day I lurched to a half sit, heaved my legs over the side, got a good hold on the IV pole and, papered up, clattered the hall. From the eastern window at one end down to the western window at the other I passed doorways that flashed instant stories of gloom, boredom, panic, time-killing, and ordinary sickness. They were the rooms you couldn't look into and you couldn't not look into. Who knows what the etiquette is, all of us unexpectedly blown together like cross-country passengers in a snow-stormed bus station, a coed dorm of mostly strangers too old for this, people who had other plans, waiting it out. Who knows how fast you should go down the hall, how slow— if you're walking, are you bragging? I was, from what I could, see the youngest person there.

I'd been in the hospital a week or so, long enough to feel the ennui of having my life rerouted to this. Instead of walking my typical wheezy beat, I sat on the window sill on the tenth floor at midday, pale and thin, facing west.

Sweat lodge leaders tend to be very careful about the seating arrangement for the ceremony. In my part of the world the lodge's door is to the east, Waabnong, the dawning place where the old grandfather stones that will cook you come into the lodge. The people seated in the cardinal directions have ceremonial jobs to do. The one sitting opposite the door, in the west, Ebnigishmaag, is often the leader or the elder, and that one is in the line of ceremonial fire. For one thing, that is the place of being particularly well cooked, since the wet heat tends to go there first. But the western door is also the place where everything heads to, at day's end, at life's end. That is where the dead make their way along the Bridge of Sighs to join their kin, if they are well remembered and loved by the living enough to have endurance for the journey. So sitting in the west is sitting in the slipstream of the dead.

I didn't know any of this that day. I knew hospitals well, though, and I knew how it was to catch the scent of dying a little. I sat there in the thin light of winter and remembered all the other hospital admissions when I was younger, the panicked midnight runs to the emergency room, the adrenaline shots. I was sad for myself, sad for how little of what I'd seen of the place I'd been born to and felt like home after twenty years, sad for finding no place so far where people loved life together, sad for the turning wheel of the world.

Ten floors below me, it turned out, was the service entrance to the hospital. I looked down and saw a garbage truck make its lumbering backward climb, butt-end toward the doors. The driver jerked the truck to a halt and geared the thing for packing and grinding. Someone tucked inside the hospital's heated service entrance fired bagged trash into the truck's maw for a minute or two. I could only see the green bags, maybe thirty of them, arc out of the door ten floors below and, without a sound, fill the truck. The driver climbed back in, smudged the whole place with blue exhaust, and was done and gone. An ordinary thing, no wonder in it. I sat the distracted sitting of a winded, homeless patient, waiting to get better and get out.

Maybe it was twenty minutes later, maybe an hour. Up that same paved road slid a silent, sparkling, blue-black hearse. It had the shined metal, high-buff shine of pure efficiency, and it came in business-end first. The hearse backed to the same entrance. The driver, decked in the black and white rayon of the dismal trade, came round to open the hatch of the hearse. There was only enough room between the hatch and the building for me to see first one and then the other, two silver fish slide without any ruckus or sound into the hearse's belly.

Two high-buff metal caskets rolled down the castered gangway into the dark. Down the hatch came, down the lane the hearse slid, back into traffic, back to the world, out of sight, gone.

These two things swam toward each other in my heart. It took a few moments, but like the newly married, they perched awkwardly hand in hand on the twin thrones of my sadness and my aching for home. I still sat on the window ledge, but inside I staggered. Hearses and garbage trucks. Garbage and coffins. Me here and two people gone, the living and the dead together. It came rising up through the storm in me: While I lay and panted and sorrowed and slept, first one person and then another had died here, in the same building, breathing the same air and then not, hearing the same whirrs and hums and then not. Maybe they prayed and quit just above or below where I laid and pined. They had died alongside me. A few hours, maybe a day later, they were gathered up, taken to Shipping and Receiving alongside the garbage, and sent out into the tidal sway of the way things are, no more, gone.

Pinned to my own whirring heart I went back to lie down. The mystery of ordinary things was spilling in all directions. I knew myself to be alive, and I took it for a blessing. I wanted to thank someone, I wanted to tell someone. I had to go somewhere, I had nowhere to go. Minutes crowded together. Whatever I'd imagined to be true about life was in a small bag by the door. Something immense had come to claim me.

Somewhere in this staggering revelry a nurse came into the room. I'd never seen her before. She was in the full starched uniform with that crazy headpiece that nurses used to wear, a little watch pinned to her chest. She was only a few years older than me. She introduced herself as Miss Needles—it said so on her name tag too—and asked me how I was feeling. I reached toward what had just happened, what was still happening, and tried to coax a few words from it. I told her about the garbage truck and the hearse, about the light in the window, about unexpectedly being alive and unexpectedly being heartbroken about it. I couldn't corral the thing. After a minute I stopped. She looked at me for a bit, then started to tell me about a patient she had spent months caring for, about how she had gotten to know him so well and how he had talked to her about wanting to get better, about how she had gotten close to his family too, even though her colleagues warned her, and how he'd taken a turn yesterday and without anyone being there in the room with him he had died, just last night, one floor up, when she was off shift, and because she was so distraught they moved her to this floor for the day, and so to this room, and to me. She wept then, without hiding it. Both of us there bewildered and barely twenty, both sorrowed, both alive and brokenhearted by it.

The spiral mystery of being alive and being close to death whirled and I did too. After Miss Needles left, many years went by as I lay there. I began to write something, and it turned into a thank-you letter to my mother for giving me birth and life against the odds. That's what seeing death can do, make you fall in love with being alive. It didn't look like a love letter, but it was. She kept that thank-you in her purse for years, until it was just faded fibers in Scotch Tape. Anyone who might have found it by accident wouldn't have known what it was or how much was written on the page. I have tried to keep my version of that note in my pocket ever since too. This book is a few lines taken from the note, as best as I can remember them.

How does it happen again, the making of human beings by human beings? It has nothing to do with parenting. Parents are nowhere to be found during the initiation of their children, because their hopes for their kids will inevitably mess with their discernment about what initiation will ask of their kids. Their parenthood disqualifies them. Puberty rites are performed by people only distantly related to the children, and they take dead aim at childhood and by various means calculate and engineer its annihilation. No child in their right mind relinquishes their childhood willingly, and intact cultures know this.

Good ceremonialists have good memories. They recall their own childhood, not just their own initiation, and they know this tenacity and persistence for the natural things they are. A child must have their childhood killed out from under them. Anthropologists say that this is done by ceremonial segregation, ritual scarification, or dietary deprivation, but this is the language of someone who has not been through it. Childhood is killed off in the same fire in which personhood is forged: through a deliberate, orchestrated exposure to the smell, texture, and certainty of death, and in particular to the initiate's own personal death.

Initiation makes personal death the initiate's lifelong, faithful, and just companion. And why is this typically undertaken at puberty? Because puberty detonates the full-bodied, unchildish capacity for being drawn by the looming, urgent tidal sway of another body, another person. Indigenous wisdom knows that learning how to love someone well means learning the inevitability of one of you leaving the other by dying. Love and death co-conspire. They fertilize each other, and become true only in each other's presence. *Eros* and *Thanatos* are kin, twins of a sort. This is true. There is wisdom in it. Western psychology knows this too.

Loving someone isn't inevitable; loving someone who will die is. Loving *as* someone who will die is human work. The realization of this, if it is randomly experienced without the guidance of elders and a culturally endorsed ceremonial life to hold things, is too crushing for anyone, never mind their age. Without that guidance and ceremony there is no wisdom that accrues to experience, and limit-defying adolescents remain adolescent well into their middle age, becoming fragile and remote, looking for someone who through love or sex or through the habit of coming home from work every night can perform the holy labor of saving them from loss, frailty, and death. Instead, people tutored in these things make a place for children to learn the beginnings of living and dying by ending their childhood, by making for those children a well-known friend of their death, and by giving them a chance later in life to love a human who will not, no matter how good that love is, defend them from dying at the ending of their days.

I, on the other hand, was born and educated in a culture that believes that human beings are born whole, pre-wired and ready to be human. So it goes that my culture provides its children with free passes into adulthood. There are no rituals or ceremonies whose purpose is to make human beings out of children, none at all. Being afraid you'll forget a line in a recitation you hardly understand and will probably never use again, being embarrassed by dressing in new, uncool clothes in front of your friends, throwing up from drinking too much on your age-of-consent birthday or before, none of these constitute failure or danger, and none are rituals. The only qualification for adulthood in this culture seems to be living long enough to get there. The things we think of as "rites of passage" are mostly empty, sentimental, and nostalgic gestures, because no one believes that they *make* anything of the young person. They are rubber stamps, not alchemy. The teenagers don't ask for the rites of passage and don't seem to need them any more than the culture seems to need the teenagers. The events of excess are a reward for getting there, nothing more.

Uninitiated young people look the part of human beings, to some degree, but they are capable of treachery, self-harm, and intoxicating self-absorption in the name of a self-appointed and unguided search for "personal identity." Without the endorsement and support of the culture, which could come to them through elder-directed ceremony, the unformed yearning for love turns into a cruder, more inarticulate, and camouflaged stumble in the direction of intensity of all kinds. When the body begins to know the yearning for another, the gravitational pull that stirs brings that yearning's twin, death, with it. It whispers, "By this you can melt whatever separates you from the Big Story," which is code for dying. But this gives parents and teachers cold sweats, and most of them do their best to throw the kids they are responsible for off the scent of death. Managing adolescents in our part of the world is mostly a conspiracy to keep dying at a distance, in deference to being "in the prime of life" or in the name of "having your whole life ahead of you," by making what they call now "good decisions for yourself." No one says, "You have your whole death ahead of you." Almost no one can make any sense of it that helps. The kids are on their own, ducking parents' fears about what they are exposed to every day and text messaging each other about another friend who went all the way. This culture can't decide when a person becomes a living thing—that is what the abortion debates show, where the preference is for the term "viable fetus"—but it has no hesitation announcing that everyone is human once they make it here, and adult once they can pay their own bills.

> I was driving along the north shore of Lake Superior on my way to a meeting with the high school kids at a small town on the rocky, windblown shore to talk with them about dying. Long highway trips might be a little out of fashion now considering how much gas they burn, but the rhythm of things going by and the vast, humanless distances can conjure unbidden Big Thoughts. As always, I was asking for help, for some nudge that would guide me to do something useful in our time together. Teetering little piles of stones flashed by.
>
> I knew the sign each time that I was getting close to a town or village, and it was the same as I was leaving one: the rock cut faces were sprayed with initials and pairs of initials, most down along the highway, some away up in hard to reach places, dangerous places to get to. I had my nudge, as much as I was going to get that day.

The kids were probably not used to a lot of strangers in the school. They sat quietly in long rows in the gym, waiting to see what I was about. A few early questions got no response, and so I told a few stories. Things got a little easier, and then I asked them: "Why is it do you think that people paint their initials and names on the rock faces by the highway?" No response. "I'm pretty sure you guys know about this. Why, do you suppose?" A teacher pointed out that this was illegal. I said, "I'm not asking for confessions. I'm asking for ideas."

After a little more silence one of the boys said, "It looks cool, if it's done good," and everybody laughed.

"Okay," I said, "how about this: Why do people paint where they do? Why don't they go into the bush, find a nice smooth rock, and paint it there?" A different kind of quiet was in the room now. "Why don't you go down to the beach and write your initials in the sand instead? Why is it always paint on stone?"

Someone said, "Because the wind would blow it away." Someone else said, "Because it wouldn't last." And someone else: "I want it to be there for a long time."

"All right," I said, "so why do it by the highway, where you can get busted for it?"

Someone answered, "Because we want people to see it."

Most adolescents you know have some kind of at least passing fascination with death and suicide. Teachers are on the lookout for it in essays and short stories written for class. Counselors and parents are pretty sure it is a sign of depression. I'm pretty sure it is a sign of a yearning for some kind of initiatory event, some kind of purposeful intensity, some visitation from the Other World. You can see that most kids are drawn to the enormity and the mystery of death as a way of making sense of being alive. Thinking about suicide is a way of conjuring death without waiting for disease to get you there. This comes up for most kids when they start wondering about other hearts and other bodies. The idea of union, of melting into another, is a balm for social awkwardness at a vulnerable age, but more than that happens. When someone says "yes" to you at that age, it has never been like that before. It is mutual, it is powerful, and it instantly brings you to a nascent understanding you never bargained for, that it all could end, that something of you will not survive it. Kids write "Forever!" in each other's yearbooks because they have glimpsed for the first time what "No More" could be like. This kind of attraction has the end of attraction in it, and this way of living has the end of living in it. They are twins.

And so the initials are sprayed so often in pairs, in places that can be witnessed by others, in some kind of medium that will last longer than high school will last, longer than they will last. By that time kids have tasted the finitude and finality that mingles with their hormones. They're telling everyone, in hopes that somebody in the know will corroborate their fugitive hope that it is all worth it, that it can be done, that life can be lived, that things not lasting forever isn't the same thing as everything being meaningless. When kids write their names across the landscape, when they think about death, when they flirt with all manner of self-harm to see what "all the way" might be like, they're telling us that we have left them adrift, that they could use a little help here. They're asking, "What's the point?" and it isn't a rhetorical question. I'm not saying that they are asking to be saved from feeling the edges of life, nor that they are asking to be prevented from groping with each other in the dark. No kid, intact culture or not, wants their childhood to end, not really. It has to be taken from them. Real tutelage is, without them ever saying so, what their lives are asking for. Being fascinated with death is how they ask for it.

Our culture has psychology in its eyes. Wherever it looks, psychology is what it sees. For us, psychology is fate. Whichever parents you were born to, however they parented you through the first four or five years of your life, you will spend the rest of your life responding in one way or another to that parenting. The contentious, spikey reactivity that often floats between parents and their children's schools comes from the uncertain frontier where the parents' right and obligation to form their children's identity gives way in some fashion to the school's right and obligation to "socialize" that identity for the greater good. Is all of this true the world over? Not at all. Why is this not a global constant? Simply, there are cultures in the world, and certainly there are in what survives of the indigenous world, that proceed with the certainty that when children are born there is already someone there. We proceed from each birth as if that child was born essentially blank, a protein unit awaiting an identity. Indigenous parenting, to make a debatable generalization, has the responsibility of elegantly, deeply, and with love getting out of the way of the child's turning into himself or herself, and it is the community's job to make that happen. Our parenting has the responsibility of writing some identity on the child before anyone else gets a chance to. That's why there's so much focus on the first five years of life in our world: You still have a chance to compensate for what the crazy world will do to them, proactively.

Oh no, some may object, I know my child was born with their own character; nothing to do with me. That might be true for you, but consider two things. First, watch how keen parents are to find themselves—their influence and their personality—in the emerging, peculiar zaniness of their child. Second, the Greek cognate of our word "character" refers to the marks or lines scored into a surface by a pointed writing implement or stylus. The character lines in your face are etched there by life, and your personal character was etched upon you primarily by the parenting you were subject to. This belief is written into the language we use, and so into us.

Now if you would, take all of this understanding and use it to sort out what happens when a child is dying here in our part of the world. That child's grief-riven parents go through torment without end deciding how, or if, their child should be told that they are dying. I've heard four reasons parents give for wanting their children to die uninformed. They believe that knowing by itself will cause avoidable and unnecessary pain and suffering; that children cannot remain children if they are told that they are dying, because the knowledge of dying destroys childhood unnecessarily and too soon. Going along with the psychologists' theories that they've read on the internet, they believe that children have no capacity to grasp the concepts of permanence and end. They believe that they know their child best and that they know what is best for them. Taken together these are arguments for allowing the parents to be the ones who, having done nothing like this before in their lives, guide what dying will be like for a child who does not know, or doesn't seem to know, or who won't let on that they know they are dying.

Typically dying children know three things, from what I've seen. They know somehow that they are dying, that they are not allowed to know that they are dying, and that their parents likely cannot endure knowing that they are dying. Children have the keen eye for detail that all living things have who depend for their survival on those around them, and they take many cues from their parents. If as I've been saying dying changes everything if it is allowed to, then it surely changes the person dying into a dying person. The dying child is not the same child that the parents knew when he or she was well, and the parents' claims of familiarity are often more hopeful than accurate.

When all of these hopes and assumptions and opinions are allowed to stand, you often get something like this. A child is in hospital for a third round of chemotherapy. They have begun to figure out that they aren't feeling any better, even after the side effects wear off. They can tell by the kind of questions they are asked, the tones of voice they hear around them, the kind of touch they feel from hospital staff, that people are worried or afraid, a big step beyond "concerned." They have seen that answering the question, "How are you feeling?" is a trauma for everyone. They can feel the presence of the thing that isn't being said. They're not sure about the content—the when and the how of their dying—but they are fairly sure about the shape: fear, torment, heartache. What can you possibly keep from dying children that isn't already in the room with them? What do they deserve from you and me when that time comes?

Let us with some humility be tutored by cultures that have been trying to do the work of person making longer than our culture has, in particular regarding this idea of initiation. Where could we start? The idea of uninitiated people doing some kind of weekend initiation with teenagers is not a trustworthy proposition. The teaching that is *in* initiation though, that can help. It shows us that the end of childhood is the beginning of personhood, and that childhood ends with a deliberate, purposeful, choreographed, culturally endorsed exposure to death. That is the meaning that initiation gives to death: *It is the beginning of the life you seek,* and it kicks in just when you want to begin taking up a place in the world and when you want to lose yourself in someone else. What is true is that you will die. It has always been true, but initiation turns dying from a feared thing into a known thing. This is the sanest reversal imaginable of our insistence that knowing you will die is the thing that will traumatize you and cause you suffering. This understanding stubbornly insists on knowing the real limits to one's life. It gives initiated people some skill at suffering by making the stories of their lives and deaths purposeful stories, and it starts early in life. The news of your death brings the rest of your life toward you, it forges kinship to go along with identity, and it is news that young people deserve as a part of their adolescence.

We deserve that kind of understanding of life early in our lives, but we do not often get it then. We almost never get it by careful orchestration. Mayhem is more often our teacher of the bigger things. We certainly deserve to have that kind of understanding sometime before getting a terminal diagnosis. Well, imagine how it all could be among us if we began to understand all the talk about dying and the news about dying and the visits to the hospital and the deathbed and the grave side and the memorial service, and all the sorrows and grief of life, as our initiation into personhood. We could change it from trauma and loss and therapy and depression into tempering and emotional intelligence and spiritual maturity and wisdom. *We could make our way of dying into our way of person making.* Every death that precedes our own could be our school, our initiation hut, every dying person and every witness our fierce teacher. Our own death could be that for everyone who attends it and hears about it, if it is messy enough to give everybody lots to do.

For that to happen we have to begin understanding our dying as an obligation we have to the people around us. If that happens we will change
what dying means and what dying does to us. When that happens, dying
isn't an intrusion into the natural order of true things. It *is* the natural
order of things. It is life's way of gathering you to itself, making sure you
aren't left on your own. Dying isn't the end of true things—which is what
most people mean when they grudgingly admit that dying is part of life—
or the euchre of true things. It is one of the true things, that is all. One of
the eternal verities, an obligation we have to the life that has been given to
us. When dying is understood as justice, mercy, a sign of the compassion
that is stitched into the fabric of life itself, that understanding is a midwife
that can bring us into a world-loving, community-serving love of life.
That is its power. The news of our dying is the initiation into life that we
are seeking.

Here is what that might look like.

> Martín Prechtel told this story a good number of years
> ago, and I was lucky enough to be there when he did.
> I'll probably add a little without knowing it and leave
> out something important, but I think the bones of
> the story are here. He was sitting one day with the old
> man who was his teacher. Maybe they were making
> things, or passing time together. All at once outside the
> house there was a great hue and cry going on. People
> were calling the old man's name and generally in an
> uproar. The old man asked them in, and got them to
> calm themselves enough to say what their worry was.
> It seemed that the Protestant missionary that had set
> up shop in town months before was having a revival of
> some description in the town square. Most of the folk
> had shown up. He'd whipped them up to a considerable
> torment with his stories of hell and sin and the rest,
> and these people took it to heart. So the old man had
> to come quick.

Now this old man was the head shaman to many thousands of people in that part of the country. He'd lived long enough to see just about everything, at least once, and his elaborate way of living with the unseen was duly noted far and wide. So of course he knew what was happening in the town square and what was at stake. This missionary was one part of the latest wave of a thorough legislative, religious, and military assault on indigenous people in that area and their way of life that had been ebbing and flowing for several hundred years. Off the old man went in the direction of the clamor.

He found the missionary in full fervor, dealing in sin and redemption in a slurry of badly managed Mayan. He found many of the people in real disarray and torment, particularly regarding this idea of hell. Most of us would probably guess that they feared ending up there. But the hardest part of his message for them was the possibility that their relatives and friends who had died without being saved were doomed and writhing at that very moment. They took their relationship with their dead, and their obligations to them, very seriously.

The missionary knew the old man to be a staunch traditionalist and kingpin of the village hierarchy. The old man hadn't yet appeared at the missionary's performances, and many a thing looked to hang in the balance. If he could get the old man to sway, the whole place might come over to his particular Jesus. All eyes were trained on his unlikely and sudden appearance. The old man sat himself not at the periphery or somewhere in the crowd, withholding his attention, arms folded in sullen resentment, but right under the missionary's nose, and he gave the acrobatic stranger his full face. The missionary turned his full zealous swagger on the crown of the old man's head.

After a few minutes the old man began to nod in agreement with some of what he was hearing. He could be heard in a kind of stage whisper admiring the snake and garden story, the tower and the babble story. A few minutes more and he began to show signs of real distress, holding his head and moaning a little. All eyes were upon him, and all—missionary, traditionalists, Protestant converts, Catholic stalwarts—were astonished at how quickly he was being made to see the light. Sensing that it was probably time to sink the hook, the missionary launched himself into a full articulation of the wages of sin, and then stopped.

"It needn't be that way, brothers and sisters," he said. "None of this need come to pass. If you take Jesus now as your own personal savior, you will gain the gift. Take Jesus, now, and the life everlasting will be yours. You don't have to die."

The old man was in full lament, but suddenly stopped. He lifted up his face, now wearing something like wonder with a hint of having known all along. "What? What was that you said, son? I won't die?"

"No, grandfather. That's what I said. This is the news we all want, and it is there for you. You won't die." The missionary was fairly sure he could smell fear, self-interest, and conversion (the usual brew in times like these) in the air.

The old man stood up slowly and gave the missionary a kind face. "Oh son you know, you almost had me. You almost had me there, you did."

The missionary asked him, "'I almost had you'? What do you mean, grandfather?"

"Well, you know that we've been here for a long time, us Indians, and we've thought of a few good things. But that story of the garden and the snake, that was a good one. We don't have anything like that. And your God sounds like a good one, giving us His son because He loves us. The water and the wine. Good ones, those. I liked everything I heard, until that part about not dying. Oh, no. You lost me there, son, and you won't get me back."

The Gothic cathedral of the missionary's vision began to shift and moan and crack under the weight of this withered old man's refusal of the gift of being saved from death. "But that's the best part, grandfather. That's the answer to all the fear and the suffering, and the sins."

"I know you think so, son. It probably *is* the best part, where you come from. But listen to me. I've learned some things in my time. You see all these people who have been listening to you? They come to me quite a bit for help and advice, and I try to teach them what I know. The truth is, no matter how long I talk with them from here on, even in big groups like you do, I'd never be able to tell them all the things I've gathered up through the years that could help them in their lives. They'll have to wait for me to die to hear the rest.

"Listen. We have a crazy old custom here. When I die they'll make a big feast for me, and I'll be there! They'll dress me up good. They'll start telling stories about me, true ones and some they'll make up, and they'll start remembering all their people who have died too and telling their stories, and they'll soon see their own death coming along some day and the ceremony that'll be done for them, and how life is, and that's how the rest of what I wish I could tell them will get told. They'll tell the rest to each other. That's how it will get spilled out for them. But if I take your Jesus, you say I won't die. And if I don't die there'll be no feast. And without the feast, all these people won't eat what I have learned.

And they'll starve a little. So I've thought about it, and I'm not going to starve them. Life here is hard enough, without having not to die." The old man turned to the villagers and said, "Me, I'm going to get ready to die. You people can do what you want with what our friend here is telling you." The old man dusted himself off, gave a good nod to everyone, and headed back to his house for supper.

I don't tell you this story to ridicule missionaries, much as I feel the destruction that is done by them, unwittingly or not. I don't tell it to lampoon theological sophistication or anyone's one God religion, nor to whisper that every indigenous person has got it figured out and we don't. But imagine being a kid in that crowd, hearing all that. The old man's act of hard-earned faith in the way things are, his willingness for his life to be gathered up into Life, all during his life and at the hour of his death, his willingness to really die so his people could live, just as the corn in his field does, is the best teaching there can be on what it looks like for someone to be at home, living something that to him looks a lot like Heaven, making his dying mean something to the faithful witnesses around him, without rancor or argument, without having just visited the world. If heroism it is, then his heroism is the kind that has no enemy and no fight. Instead, his way of loving his culture was to hold himself out to it in service by loving his life and by insisting that his way of dying serves life too. He wasn't fighting with the missionary or with monotheism or with Jesus, I don't think. He was wrestling the angel of what all of our lives are made of, endings of all kinds, and insisting on making there justice and mercy and meaning, without demonizing anything of what brings us there.

This is not faith or hope, nor is it fueled by a sense of entitlement to life or a feeling that the life one lives is a personal possession to do with as one will. It is a faithful witness to the way it is. Imagine living in a place and knowing that the people around you will be sustained by your way of going out from among them. Imagine how your feelings about what your own death means would change then. Imagine an old man or old woman like that charged with initiating you into life, and imagine this insistence on you dying was his or her way of serving you. Imagine that something of this is possible for our children and our grandchildren. It is. Amen..

11

AH, MY FRIEND THE ENEMY

On the bridge over the canal
You smiled as if . . .
Mortality
Was a divinity
Glimmering under a lintel.

Paul Durcan, "Birthday Present,"
in *Daddy, Daddy,* page 128

Once I Had a Brother

I've heard that if you work very hard at your dying, if you learn what needs learning and find a way to gracefully untie all the web of habit and devotion and love that bound you to your body, your friends, and your life, then your fontanel might open again just as your final hours of living come on. I've heard this little gate, the place that was for your parents such a dangerous vulnerability, opens enough to give you a way out of here. I don't know much about that, but I wouldn't be surprised. It is such a wild idea that, if it's not true, maybe it should be. Something like that should be part of the story of your dying and mine. What I do know is that if you tell this certain story very well, if you learn the vast detail and the enduring architecture of the thing and tell it in a language that suits it just as it should be, then the people listening cannot tell if it is the story of being born or the story of dying. They are for the most part the same story—from the outside and from the inside too, if we are willing.

Good teachers are hard to find. Teachers who are faithful to you are rare, and hen's teeth are those teachers who are faithful to what you seek when you are not so faithful, who mysteriously don't turn away from you when you turn away from the things worth seeking. They lean against the portal, nursing a little grief for you, not drawing too much attention to themselves, patient with your many strivings and your penchant for self-harm and for sabotaging your best intent. Wherever they are, no matter what you say, that is where you are trying to go. Would that all of us could know such a person at least once in our lives and that we might be that person for others someday. My great good fortune so far in life is to have had several of the first kind, a few of the second kind, and probably two of the third. Rich indeed am I, and too lucky to imagine. This story is something I learned from one of those two.

Brother Blue could tell stories that would open your fontanel again, which is a powerful thing. We met in Cambridge, Massachusetts, when I was in my early twenties, and by some mystery I became, for a time, his band. He was the bard, the bad man, enormously funny, a rhythm king and a wordsmith and rapping minstrel without equal. He was the North American equivalent of an Indian holy man, utterly faithful to what had claimed him, a servant of life, and if you didn't hear him at least once you missed something that won't come again in our lifetime, maybe longer. Over seven years or so he and I and his steady wife Ruth toured over the eastern U.S. and Canada. During that time we performed in scores of unlikely places, some dangerous ones, and slowly I began to learn what a human being is capable of. He was a master of tragedy, the father of my soul, a true village man and a gift to this world. He was a relentless praise master, and his ability to love life was an ancient tower around which many of us who knew him spiraled.

He knew—just to give you a feel for how it was with him—the entire Shakespearean canon by heart, all the parts, in Elizabethan diction, and could deliver it with a flourish worthy of Stratford on Avon. He could also do the same plays, all the parts, in rhythmed and rhymed staccato black urban hip-hop rap before there was such a thing on the radio, such was his soul. He knew soul-rending folk stories from all the continents, and he could improvise lyrically and musically from pocket lint or muddy shoes or a child's shyness or a bird's song. He was a jazz tycoon, a master of the language, a towering exemplar of erudition and hortatory power, and he knew about loving this world. On your best days he made you want to be better.

His best stories, for me, were those that grew like steady oaks out of his own early years. He had one called "Once I Had a Brother." He grew up with a younger brother who had severe learning problems, in a time where there was no such thing as special education, in a place where he described himself as "one black button in a field of snow." A kid's limitations and differences are lightning rods for childhood cruelty, and Blue's story tells impossible-to-bear scenes of playground taunting and humiliation. So Blue was his brother's keeper in those days. It happened when he got a bit older that Blue won an academic scholarship that was his ticket out, but he refused it knowing that with both parents working just to keep the family afloat there would be no one to care for Tommy. His mother overrode his decision by holding him to the responsibility of bringing honor to the family with the keenness of his mind and by promising him that she would quit her home-cleaning work and stay home with his brother.

As Blue told it, he got a call a few weeks after going away to Harvard telling him to come home for a few days and bring his good suit with him. It turned out that, knowing how fiercely her son defended his brother's soul against the cruelty of the world, she made a promise to him that because of the poverty of the time she couldn't keep. She had taken Tommy to a home to be cared for while his parents were working. For no medical cause that could be found he had died there after a few weeks, the world too hard a place for his soul. As he got to the end of the story Blue would look around the audience for his brother, literally. He would say, "Is it you? Is it you that is too fine a soul for this world? Is it you who's thinking of getting out?" When Blue told this story—I performed it with him maybe fifty, maybe a hundred times over the years—some people just couldn't bear the heartache of the thing. People would be sobbing. Most would be silent. It was an epic of human sorrow, and I tell you just the bones of the thing here to give you a way of hearing the story I want to tell you now.

One day, in the midst of one of our tours, Blue and I did something that was one of the few "normal" things, given the demands of touring and the typical extremes of the heart that his performances brought us all to, we ever did together. We went to a matinee movie. As it happened, *The Elephant Man* was playing. It is a black-and-white story set in Victorian England, based on the life of John Merrick, a man so disfigured by a congenital affliction that he ended up a circus freak. Well-intended scientists rescue him from this life, only to subject him to a subtler kind of investigation and segregation. Toward the end there is a scene that is an extended soliloquy of Merrick primping his deformed self in front of a mirror, the mirror being where the camera is, and so he is looking at you, fixing the few hairs on his head, rearranging the ruffles at his wrist and retelling the story of his life that you have just watched. But instead of the panorama of human cruelty and heartache, he tells it as an unlikely, mythic journey of challenge and wonder that has all been gathered into the extraordinary happening that he now finds himself with people who care for him. He has friends. When he says it—"I have friends"—it sounds like he is describing a miraculous gift that has come to him without reason or warning, the same thing that most of us probably take as a given. I was pretty weepy watching that scene.

Because of his deformity the Elephant Man couldn't lay down, and he'd spent all his sleeping hours in a half-sitting position. After this soliloquy he moves off camera. After a moment you hear his bedsprings creak. And then you hear his labored breathing, and it takes another moment yet for you to realize what he has done. Everything inside you rises up and says, "Oh no. Not now. Any time before now, I'd understand it, but not now. You just said you had friends. You just turned your life into something worth living, or more. You just made an impossible case for keeping on going. You can't end it now. Get up!" And that's how it ends as I recall, you knowing that his life was suddenly full enough and good enough, that it didn't have to last forever to be worth living.

The lights came up in the theater. There were only about seven people there. We sat a long time without moving. When the cleaner started sweeping the popcorn from the back rows, we got up and slowly made our way up the aisle. I was talking away about the movie, about what it did to me and so on. Blue didn't say a word during my long response. We walked through the foyer and out into the busy afternoon street. We stood there a long while, in silence. Then he turned and looked at me the way he could look, some kind of epic understanding sweeping through his eyes, and this is what he said: "My heart is broken. I never want it to mend."

I carried those two sentences around for years without understanding a word. It came to me slowly that this was more than him talking about the movie or about how he felt. This was a prayer. Blue was praying for a broken heart. I have never heard anyone do that, not before and not since. Most everyone prays for their heart to mend, to get on with their lives, to have no broken heart at all, a grief-free or grief-contained life. He was praying for what almost no one else wants. He knew so many vast things about human life, about how we are in the face of mayhem and sorrow. He taught me well, and I've seen it hundreds of times in my work in the death trade, how so many of us believe in amnesia, how getting over hard things is so much like forgetting them. He knew—probably he knew this from a young age—that remembering means gathering back together again something that was once whole and has been scattered, and that the human heart was built to break, and that feeling that heartbreak each time is remembering again the deep things of life that need remembering. He knew that heartbreak is something like the orphaned or disowned sibling of love. So he was willing to know sorrow, that older brother of love, and he prayed for it, so that no passage of time would heal over his memory and his ability to love how life is. He was my first teacher and still the most able in the skill of broken heartedness.

There is a belief that clunks along during the course of someone's last days that is almost as common in the death trade as it is in the general population. It is the strong belief that crises, and dying in particular, bring out the best in people. People seem to expect this of each other, and they especially expect it of themselves. Most of us count on a kind of saintly capacity descending with a terminal diagnosis that gives sure and remarkable discernment and allows people bound by love and life experience to choose correct behavior, to know what is best at a time like that, to know what is needed most, and to put aside any character wrinkle or family mayhem that would interfere with delivering from the best part of themselves. If there is ever a time in life when the power of the moment itself could give people a way of setting themselves aside for the sake of the greater good, or for the sake of the person they love, the time of dying must be it. Surely then the best part of most of us comes forward, when there is nothing more to lose, when there is no longer any good reason for it not to.

Turns out that there are often lots of good reasons for it not to. In the film *Griefwalker* I said that it often happens that dying people discover that they were wrong about what they were afraid of. Most of us will be pain-managed and in the midnight grip of a low-grade terror that doesn't know how to break the surface of coping. My experience tells me that most people fear disappearing, fear what their families and friends and rest of us are going to do with them after they die, fear our well-known ability to get on with our lives. They are afraid of the surface of life closing over their heads, slipping beneath the waves and disappearing from view and from mind and from life itself. That is the death they fear, in my experience. It isn't something that healthy people think about much, except as a philosophical proposition to noodle over. But for dying people it often is the only show in town. They'll tell you that they want you to get married again, or to get out there and be happy, and they aren't lying. But they won't tell you that they're afraid you'll be able to do just that, to start living someday as if they'd never been.

When people get a terminal diagnosis they eventually start thinking about how it will be for their spouses and their kids and the rest of the family after they die. Often they are worried about whether their families will survive at all. They start thinking about all the milestones they'll miss, the graduations and the weddings and the grandchild births. Often they'll start making home movies. Most of the ones I've heard about dispense good wishes and advice about married life, about growing up, about being a parent. The idea is that these movies will be played at the events that they won't live long enough to see. When they are played it is often a very emotional thing. It sounds like in this case having the technology is entirely a feel-good thing. It sounds very life affirming.

I've never seen it that way. Why are these movies being made? They are being made to give the dying person a chance to say something important to someone they care about from beyond the grave, that's true. That's the motivation. Why is it *necessary* though?

This is the dying person's way of seeing to it that he or she will have some presence at these events. Why do they have to make these movies to guarantee that presence? They are not sure that they will be present if they leave it up to the rest of us. Why would they doubt it? Is it because they don't think we will love them or miss them enough? Not usually. It is more because, as they have begun to die and to ponder what that means, they've begun to think a lot about whether when the time was upon them they made sure that those who had died before them had a presence at the weddings and confirmations and in everyday life. And they've begun to realize that they didn't do it, though it never seemed like much of an issue, never mind a dereliction of duty, until now. Now they've begun to see how easy it is in our way of life to let the dead slip from view and from memory, how easy it is to disappear. They've seen that the only presence you can have after death is that which the living grant to you. So somewhere deep inside them, dying people making home movies have realized that asking the rest of us to remember them well, and to see to it that a place at the table in the banquet hall of life is made for them when the times come, might be asking too much. So they ask us to press "Play" instead.

These movies are an indictment of our way of pathologizing and counseling grief. They are an indictment of our comfort seeking and our addiction to competence and mastery. They are a resolute lament over our continuing reluctance and inability to carry our dead with us through our days, to even imagine that such a thing is possible, or necessary. They are a way of engineering our legacy when the chances of us having much of one at all are sketchy. The truth is that we cannot, nor should we be able to, choreograph the way in which we will be remembered, if we will be remembered at all. We can try, and we do, but we cannot die getting remembered. The consequence of doing so is to bequeath to those after us a legacy of fear, faceless anonymity, and terminal futility that will hatch out into another generation of dying miserably when the time comes for them. Where do you think we got our fear of disappearing from? We got it from those who feared disappearing as they died. Mostly, their fears have proven warranted. Mostly, if we don't begin doing all of this much differently, our fears will prove out in the same way.

Instead we have to go along as if it is true that The Dying do need the living to carry them. It is the only way that dying people will continue to have presence among their kin. It is one of the responsibilities of village-minded people and human beings everywhere to carry their dead with them as they walk through their days. Even if dying people have left off doing so until the time of their own dying—*especially* if they have— when the realization has set in of their reluctance or their failure or their never having suspected that this is what was needed and not done, still it is not too late for them to live the rest of their lives as if there were people who died on their watch who needed and wanted to be remembered, and to remember them aloud now to those who are about to get on with their lives. Among the bundle of tasks that come with dying in a sane time and place this might be chief. *Dying people must stop dying trying to be remembered and begin to die remembering.*

Heart Like a Seed

People die the way they live, mostly. That could be grim, or it could be, in a quiet and unexpected way, great news. It means that you can begin to learn how to die well long before your turn comes. It means that you can practice it in all the mundane corners of daily life. It means there's nothing to wait for. There's no one to give you the news. Getting up again the next morning, until you can't: That's pretty much all the news you're going to get to keep you in the know. Being able to eat again, until you can't: That's the news. Everyone else's dying and death before yours is the news washing up on your shore. That's your chance to get it figured, to get it in view. Nothing morbid about it, nothing at all. How you die has enormous consequence that ripples out from your dying time, that doesn't end when your life ends. How you die is the next generation's teacher. It means that you can sign up with the Dalai Lama, who describes his life work as being a simple monk who is preparing for his death. Not a bad example to carry around of how it all could be.

Grief. Just saying the word makes something happen. In the death trade it might be the word most spoken, but it is the word least spoken about. When I worked there I heard it used almost always as a synonym. It was code for misery, depression, loss, bereavement, sorrow. Most people speak of grief as if it comes out of nowhere, *with cause but without purpose,* like hail. It is something that careens into the natural order of things, an intrusion or a rupture, depending on who he or she was to you. It is an affliction that has to be borne. It has a shelf life, a best-before date, after which it turns into something virulent. Grieving for a seemly period is proper and called for. The psychology trade has words describing a grief that goes on too long: complicated grief, or morbid grief, or pathological grief. Too much of the same thing for too long, and then comes the time for therapy. Grief is supposed to be fitted into your life, for a fairly short while. It is supposed to shift your priorities where appropriate, help you think big thoughts eventually, and eventually leave you altogether to get on with your life, grief-free, shaken but not stirred. Nobody wants to be the old Italian lady who lives down the block, all in black for the last thirty-five years of her life, especially not young Italian ladies. And grief is just about always talked about as something that happens to you, something that is inevitable. Without thinking about it much, most of us think of grief as something that will befall us, inevitably, when the time comes: When the grief-detonating thing rolls in, we will grieve. And then, all going according to Hoyle and health being what it should be, we won't.

Such is the illiteracy that abounds among us about grief. We have all this inherited content about what grief is, but very little wisdom about what grief is for. This is mainly because we routinely figure on what grief does to us instead of what grief asks of us. Ask one question, though, and things change in a hurry. You'll probably remember this one from earlier in the book: Is grief something that happens to you, or is grief something you do? Please find some way of imagining that it is nothing *but* what you do. My years in the death trade and my life outside of it have shown me over and over that grief is not an inner feeling, not a complex little knot of inner feelings, not a coaxial cable of feelings. Grief is not a felt thing at all, though we seem to have many feelings about it. This is what sorrow, depression, loss, and the rest are—descriptions of the inner experience and what they mean for us—and that's why we have distinct words for them. Grief is not a synonym for those things, nor is it what happens to you when you feel all those things for too long. It is an important distinction. When your focus is on how you feel about things in the world, then the things of the world slip from view, your little boat of learning things for what they are swamped by the swells of how you feel about them. With hard work and with learning, the things of the world are still somehow out there, waiting for you to know about them, no matter how you feel. They survive how you feel about them, and they are there before and after the storms of your feelings roar through and abate. Feelings aren't much of a compass to go by.

Grief doesn't come from nowhere, an intrusion into the natural order of things. It *is* the natural order of things. Grief is a recognition of how it is and how it must be, how it can be if we stay our hand long enough to let it be so. Grief: A sign of life stirring toward itself. To go back to *Griefwalker* again: The filmmaker asks me toward the end of the movie about grief. He asks me if it's what happens to you when you finally realize, perhaps belatedly, that you've been … Then his questions hesitates, maybe because he isn't sure how grief could be a realization instead of an affliction. So I finished the sentence for him: "On the take," I said.

Though it isn't inevitable, it happens sometime around the halfway point in our lives, maybe a little after, that many of us begin to see that our way of life has mostly been spent on the receiving end, trying to get our needs met, trying to get happy, looking for love in all kinds of places. Maybe because of a massive calamity, maybe because of the umpteenth time that things didn't go the way we wanted, we are more or less dragged to the reluctant understanding that things not "working out" doesn't come from how life is, but from what we keep asking from life and from our little corner of it. It comes from realizing that relationships aren't need-gratification machines, plugged into the power grid, humming along, waiting for us to slip our money into the slot and pull the lever. They are living things that need care and feeding, that need us.

It's the same with the world. Maybe you awaken to the fact that the world isn't there for your extractive pleasure, or mine. Maybe we've taken too much. Maybe the whole matrix is suffering and coming loose at the seams because we've been taking too much, going along for years as if we're needy, giving job security to therapists and the wholesalers, instead of risking being accused of arrogance or inflation and *going along as if we're needed*. When you see that, then something can happen.

When you glimpse this, hopefully, you grieve. Feeling bad won't be much use. Feeling an avalanche of paralyzing guilt about the rainforest or the plight of aboriginal people or the biosphere or your buying habits is understandable, but it's just more of the same. Self-hatred is of the same order of disturbance as self-absorption. Grieving is being willing to see now what has become of us, what we have been and done. Grieving is understanding. It is knowledge. It isn't how you feel about what you know. It is being a faithful witness to the story of how it has been with us and crafting a language that does it justice, and testifying occasionally.

And then, if you work hard, if you are willing to understand that you are dying when you are, say, when finally you're willing to die, then your grief hatches out as a capacity, a skill. It doesn't arise only from seeing how you have or haven't lived. It comes from seeing how life is, no matter what you've done. The filmmaker objected a little to what I was saying about many of us being on the take, and properly so. He asked me, "What about people who are just happy to see a new sunrise, who are happy to see a flower?"

I said, "What season are we in right now? The dying away of the very flower we're talking about."

Most of us will vote "yes" to flowers, assuming without asking that we are talking about flowers in bloom. But flowers in bloom are working their way toward their death, maybe like the Dalai Lama. That's what their openness means, that the petals will peel off and fall soon, that the heart of the flower will be all that's left for a while, skewered on the end of a brittle shaft in the thinning sun. It is in the flower's nature to give itself away unto its death in the act of being itself. Until we learn how to see the flower's end, until we are willing to see it, how much of the flower do we see? Only the part that makes us feel the feeling we're looking for.

Grief is that learning and that ability of seeing the story of the thing, the whole story.

Grief has to be learned, which means it has to be taught. Which means it is possible not to learn it. When we keep insisting on grief being a feeling, or a process that needs management and closure, we are talking about grief as an affliction, the same way we talk about dying. But something changes when we start seeing grief as a skill that needs learning, which is what it is. As a culture we are grief-impaired not because we don't have what we need to feel bad, but because *we are grief-illiterate.* We aren't taught to grieve; we are taught to handle grief, to resolve grief, to get on the other side of it. We need grief teachers and practitioners, not grief counselors, until the day dawns when they've become the same thing.

You can read about cultures that have professional grievers whose job it is to show up at the appointed ceremonial hour and get the river of grief rolling for everybody else. We might find that contrived or inauthentic, but every culture with such a profession knows that *grieving in a moment made for grief, pleading for grief, is not inevitable.* There is much inside us that moves away from grieving when the time comes, that doesn't want to do it. Professional grievers are those who seem to have been born naturally and inevitably sensitive to the tones and the events around them, obedient to the nap of life. When the time for grief is upon them, they grieve, because they know how. They are prone to the world, and their very valuable service to the rest of us is to detonate the sorrow that is set aside or buried under the burden of trying to make it through our days. We have those people in our midst today, but they are not usually employed in such an honoring way. Often they are medicated, or in special education, or living in a cardboard shelter under a bridge.

I've often called myself a grief monger, a very accurate portrayal of my life's work, and so far I haven't had many takers. In a land of competence and comfort and grief-illiteracy it is a hard sell, I tell you. Real learning is an intense and costly event. It plays havoc with what we are used to and with what has comforted us in the past. The tuition for this learning is drawn from the account of what we once believed was trustworthy and true, and usually it isn't paid willingly or in generous amounts. As you begin to lose some faith in the old ways of thinking and doing, it feels less like tuition and more like casualty.

When I teach these things I try to arrange at least a full day for people having this kind of experience to be together because learning takes time, and because there isn't much that is self-evident about what I am teaching, and because learning is good and has a chance of surviving a normal working day when it is done with others. It is simple but not self-evident. Somewhere around the midafternoon break someone in the group will blow a gasket, as my mother used to call it, and say something like this: "Okay. It's close to three o'clock. We've been devastated since about 9:30 this morning. What do we do now? You can't just leave us like this. How can things ever be any different?' I understand that response. I have had it many times myself, especially in the early days when I began to get the haunting sense that not much was as it seemed, that dying people's sedation wasn't necessarily the equivalent of dying well, that "resting comfortably" wasn't necessarily what we bargained it was, that the emptiness that followed the death of loved ones didn't come from their deaths nearly as much as it came from how they died, and how they refused to die, and especially how many of us in the death trade were complicit in serving that refusal.

So around three o'clock I'll do this.

> I find a potted plant somewhere in the place. I hold it up and say, "Okay. This is the easy part. Tell me what you see." Almost everybody gets ethereal right away. They see the Life Force, they see nature, or the eternal purpose or green energy or Gaia. You see how the plant instantly disappears, as soon as you ask people to see it? It's amazing. Many people seem to have an unkillable instinct for making metaphors of ordinary things so the ordinariness doesn't show through. I slow them down a bit. "Try to get simple with this. What can you see?"
>
> Someone will ask, "Do you mean, like, see with my eyes?"

"Yes. Get fleshy. Incarnate the thing."

Then, finally, they see flowers, they see green leaves and stems and stalks. And the pot. That's it. I have to cajole them some more. Finally somebody throws out, as an afterthought or a question, "Dirt?"

Dirt, yes. The one that seems always to go without saying. Dirt seems to be just beyond the edge of the known world for us, terra incognita itself. "What is it?" I ask. People say instantly that it is life. "You're losing your way again. Get simple."

They might start guessing as if this is a riddle: Soil? Earth? Land? Some know the chemical makeup of the stuff. Somebody will eventually say "Decayed vegetable matter." It's almost always the vegetables they mention, the only things that seem to go into the ground in the supermarket take on things.

"What else?" I ask. Most go blank. "Okay then. What has to happen to end up with it? How do you get it?" This goes on for many minutes usually.

Then, another afterthought: "Plants have to die."

Well friends, not just plants. Yes, insects and animals, but not just them. Us too. That's how long it usually takes to get to the point where I can hold up a potted plant and a room full of people who work in the death trade see death in my hand. We can see plants and insects in the potting soil, but we can't see Uncle Frank. And we can't see ourselves, not until we are pretty much dragged there. And then, for almost everyone, it's a euphemism. We just don't see ourselves or those we love or those we come from in the ashes and the dust. What the potted plant is willing to teach us is that every living thing needs something to die in order to live. In the case of humans, and hugely in the case of urban North Americans, we need scores of things to die every minute in order for us and our way of life to keep on going. It's the same for vegans and vegetarians, pretty much. Life doesn't feed on life. Life doesn't nourish life. Death feeds life.

Every rooted thing knows that and proceeds accordingly. Death is the life-giving thing. That is the proposition that life offers, that grief endorses. Everything dear to you will perish so that life might continue. Our deaths can, in every sense the word can be meant, feed life—unless we refuse to die, or fight dying, or curse dying, or spend all our dying time not dying. When we do that we exempt ourselves from the biodynamic imperative and the great caravan of how it is. When we exercise our right to not die until we are ready, when we employ enormously expensive drugs and technology, expensive both spiritually and materially, to stand in the way of life being itself and us joining the parade, something begins to starve. Every person exposed to that refusal begins to feel the pangs of not being nourished, which turn into fear or entitlement. Every person who hears another story of deathbed misery and torment begins to starve a little. Every child who is kept from the graveside is starving for a story of how life is, and why, and whether that is just. Instead they get the saccharine drip of blanket reassurance or the empty calories of platitude and metaphor.

> I was with a small group of people on a small island on the West Coast. As usual they were mostly in their forties or older. Any younger people coming to a teaching event about dying, when they come at all, usually sit at the back or close to the door. We watched *Griefwalker* together and a spirited discussion followed. Toward the end, the youngest man there told us about his grandmother. As in so many other families his had spread out across the continent, while his grandmother had stayed alone in a small apartment in the town they were from. It happened that several months before our meeting someone in the family had found her there. She'd been dead for a couple of days. She had left a note. She had known that she was dying for a while, she'd gotten her affairs in order, she'd left nothing for anyone to do. She'd been a burden to no one, as had been her wish. It was an orderly, invisible event. He told this story in the

emptiest voice imaginable. At the end he looked up and said, "I used to think that was a good death, the kind I wanted for myself. Until tonight. Now, I'm not so sure."

Well, praise all the Gods for that uncertainty. She had exercised her right still vigorously defended in our culture to a private disappearance. What the young man lost by that exercise—and he knew it now—was the chance to be a grandson to a dying old woman, which is a different kind of relationship, one that is forged in the shared knowledge that one of them is dying. When you don't let dying change how you live together, whatever the motivation, the consequence is missed last chances for authentic talk between you, shared sorrow, teaching, learning how to live as if what is happening is happening. That loss endures and compounds. Everyone is the poorer for it, and it doesn't end with the funeral or the distribution of the estate among the beneficiaries.

There are big things to know, and many of them hurt. At least they hurt the first few times you learn them. After that, after learning how to be devastated by how it is through this way of initiation, you might learn how to live as if how it is has justice and mercy and necessity to it. You can learn how to be a faithful witness, to be wrecked on schedule, to put your grief in your carry-on bag together with your other treasured things. My friend has twin daughters who are about eleven years old now. He split with their mom years ago, and sometimes you can see a little of the sadness stitched into the lining of their play clothes. One spring, when they learned that my wife and I would be on the road teaching and wouldn't be able to plant seeds on our farm, the girls got some seedlings up and running for us, their first. In May they invited us to their house and presented us with some squash and tomato plants, a little spindly from want of sun and air but ready to carry on. In the fall, when they came to the farm for a visit, we had the squash for dinner. This is what I told them:

Most of the seeds that I've planted over the years, even the tiny ones, have a seam running down the middle of them. It's the place where the two halves meet, or it's the thing that keeps them from quite meeting, or it's all of that. It's a fissure or it's a weld, or it's both. Did you ever notice how almost every seed looks like a heart in some way? A little eccentric or lopsided, a little lumpy, the way most hearts are, maybe having more than two sides to them, but always that seam. That's the place where they break. It's not a metaphor. You can see it.

When we put seeds into the ground we have a feeling of hope for the future, maybe a feeling of promise for some kind of bounty on the other end of it all. It would do us all good to plant more seeds, probably. It would be a good thing if we thought a little about what we're asking when we plant seeds, what we're asking of the seed, what we're doing to it. The seed catalogues won't tell you this part, but it is true. First, it's a little hard to tell if the seed is the youngest part of the plant or the oldest, or mysteriously both at once. Whatever it is, we make a hole in the dark earth and we bury it. We make as if it is dead, and we bury it. Or we are asking it to die by burying it. Or both. We are losing sight of it, that little heart-shaped thing, and we won't see again. When you call it "planting" you don't quite get the feel of what you are doing to the seed. When you say you are asking the seed, the grandfather or the grandchild of the plant you want to see, to die, you're getting close. You're getting a little of the feel of things, a little of the consequence of what you're asking.

In the cool, dark ground, if all goes well, the seed breaks. We don't break it by burying it exactly, but we keep up our end of things and it breaks. If it doesn't break, that's it. It is gone. If it does break, it is gone. Either way, that's the end of the seed. It seems to know how to break, right along that weld. If it breaks, something starts to happen. Some green thread begins to unspool like the spring of a broken clock, and it wends its obedient way first down into the dark and then up toward the surface, past we who buried it, and toward the light. We don't get to see it break. That's just what happens when we ask it to live and to feed us.

Anything that shape seems to know how to break. I don't know if that means it is willing to break, but breaking seems inherent in it being shaped that way. And it seems that it can't break on its own, sitting in a jar on a shelf somewhere. Some subtle combination of things has to congeal, and then it can break. There seem to be thousands of ways those things can combine—lots of water or not much, cold or cool or warm temperatures, who knows what kind of soil nutrient combinations—but for all that it still seems a delicate, unguaranteed thing that against the odds happens anyway. It breaks, and then life comes. It has to be brought to the ground to break. It isn't a metaphor any more than your heart is a metaphor, or your grief, or your death. It is this way with our life and with our inner life. Everything we treasure deeply, and even our way of treasuring deeply, has that shape, has that weld, that way of knowing how to break. Our job is not to break it. That is the job of the world, which knows very well how to break it. Our job is to be willing to have it broken and to learn to live that way. Our job is to make a little hole in the field of our days with an old digging stick, to ask the heart-shaped desires we have for our lives to die, to lose sight of them, and to learn to recognize the new life tendril that has cleared the surface sometime after we forget where that heart-shaped thing went into the ground. Simple.

The unlikely, ordinary miracle of this rises up out of the earth of our life dangling the seed sheath that once was who we thought we were and what we thought most deserved to last, almost split in two but joined close to the new shoot. The sheath that was the heart-shaped thing is brown and withered. It's one half is our sorrowing realization that life asks, nudges, sometimes forces the heart of each living thing to break, so that life can live. It is the grief that grows from giving in to the greater understanding that life is bigger in every way than the human life span, and must be. The other half is the awe and the love of life that begin to stir in us, born from seeing that this has all been going on without us knowing it, feeding us the whole time, waiting for us to come to this understanding and to take our place in the story and to keep up our end. Keeping up our end means awakening to the obligation we have to all that has given us life, to all that has lived and died before us. With it all comes an unbidden understanding that each of us is incalculably, inextinguishably obligated to life for our life, and that this is a debt that we cannot and should not be able to repay. It will always be so. With the soil temperature and the chemistry and the moisture—that is, with the heat of the heavy labor of learning all this, with the elixir of willingness and capacity of the heart that this learning makes in you, with the tears of knowing that there are tears in all things—just so, your broken heartedness becomes your life, where all this understanding is lived.

Just keep up your end and let your heart be planted. Then, without you meaning for this to be so, your time of dying can turn into an old field with all the plough ruts mostly filled in by the wind, where others who are out for a walk unexpectedly, finally, and without seeking it get a chance to learn big things. They don't know they are walking through the windblown field of your ending days. They just hear a bit of the story, they might turn to face the wind, and it begins. Even your loved ones will lose sight of you for a time, by asking you to die finally and by getting out of the way and by helping you do it, more and more heartbroken all the while. If your dying time is messy enough and gives a whole village of people lots to do, your heart is planted in the soil of their lives. By finding in the little tendril that comes from your broken heart and theirs, the green straining toward life, you live. By learning what you meant to them while you remember all those who until now have been unremembered as you went your way, you grow kinship. By asking the Old Ones to remember you now, and to make a place for you among them: That is how grief waters life. That is how grief gets learned. That is how a village is made, by your life being spilled on the groaning board in the banquet hall of life, where all the big stories are told again. That is what human redemption looks like.

With all of this, of course there are regrets. Of course. Down along the fence line in the back forty of your life there is a pile of stones—your regrets. If you don't go down there to visit them often, you'll end up thinking either that they're not there at all or that they make a pile a mile high. Here it is: They're almost always there, and the pile is rarely as high as you think. When the ending of days comes into view, that's a good time to visit that little altar. Here's my advice. Don't add another stone to the pile by the way you are with the ending of days. Just remember. Then, climb that little hill, picking up one stone at a time and putting it back in place, remembering. It's not all bad. When you get to the top, look around. That's the great pasture and field of your life, with everything it was now visible. You can only really see it from up there. That's the big story.

Fail to Live Forever

Because it must be learned instead of inherited and because it has a costly tuition, grief is a crafted, agile savvy. It is not a skill of coping and hoping and, when they fail, doping. Grief is not hanging on to what you've got for dear life no matter what, and it is not scraping through or getting by until the hard parts of life are done with us. Grief is an ability to know certain things about life well and an ability to proceed in your life as if they are true. Grief is what you do with what comes to you. Very few people seek it out or want to get good at it, but grief is an ability as vital to our emotional and spiritual and community life as the skill of love. We may be born with the need of them, maybe even with the longing for them, but we are not born knowing how to do either. They have to be learned, and by some ordinary miracle they are both learned in the same way.

You see, grief is a maker of human being. More than a staging area for human strength or endurance, grieving conjures humanity. Grieving gives us a chance to practice unlikely gratitude for that which doesn't seem to benefit us. There are people who are very good with animals, particularly sorrowing or traumatized animals, and these days they are called "whisperers." Grief is a kind of human whisperer.

A young person learns how to love by first being on the receiving end of someone else's love. Some kind of gaze, some kind of sound in the voice, some kind of swaddling regard, some way the nurse or a mother or father has of touching you that lays a claim upon you and gathers you into the land of the living—they all conspire to give the young one a feeling of being the cause of those things that add up to love, and from that stirs a rumor of worthiness. Being on the receiving end of that love teaches first that such a thing is possible. If that worthiness is nurtured over the young one's childhood it can swell into *a capacity to feel worthy,* especially in those times when the slings and arrows cause other suspicions. That feeling of worthiness that comes from being well loved is a skill that carries under its arm the possibility of loving. You have to feel worthy of love—you have to be able to be loved, a separate skill—to be able to love. That's what you can learn by being loved. That's why loving each other and loving the world count for so much.

So it is with love's older and probably wiser sibling. Grief, the epic humanness of being willing to know life well, you learn first by being fretted over and missed and mourned over by others, by being on the receiving end. It grows in you the same kind of worthiness. Maybe you are moving away from a job or a community of people that grew to know you and count on you, and in their melancholy farewells in the office hallway or over the back fence you recognize something of how on your better days you tried to live. The feel of people longing after you and missing you begins your ability to grieve. To feel the consequence of *your* absence is what awakens in you the ability to feel absence. Seeing the end of something precious to you gives you the chance of loving it well. Loving and grieving are joined at the hip, for all the beauty, soul, and travail that brings. *Grief is a way of loving what has slipped from view. Love is a way of grieving that which has not yet done so.* We would do well to say this aloud for many days, to help get it learned: Grief is a way of loving, love is a way of grieving. They need each other in order to be themselves.

> I was interviewed at a small underground radio station in the village close to where I live. The sound insulation was egg cartons stapled to the ceiling. The host asked me to bring along a half-dozen tunes to go along with our theme: What is it about dying that is so hard in our time? I changed the theme a little during the interview: What is it about our time that makes dying so hard? He was concerned that we might run out of things to talk about, I suppose. He brought a half-dozen songs too, thinking there'd be plenty of opportunity over the two hours to get all that music in. I was pretty sure that wasn't going to happen.
>
> We had about fifteen minutes left and he'd played one song so far. He asked me to choose one from the

six I'd brought, and I had him play a Tuvan song that was about the longing for a long gone friend. After the haunting, soulful tune's last notes hung in the air for a few long seconds, the host asked me, "Why did you want us to play that one?"

I told him, "Imagine that you had lived in such a way that, sometime after your death, your friends' longing for you could stir them so deeply that they could make that kind of music. Imagine that someone who never knew you would hear something that could only come from your dying, and it made them fall in love with being alive. I wanted the people listening to hear what their life could sound like after they die, what their dying could be. That is how it all could be."

In one of our fields we have a Mongolian ger, which looks to be a grandparent to the tepee. All the woodwork is hand-painted spirals and road maps and star maps on a field of blood red, and we have many meetings there. I teach my school in the ger, and people seem to enjoy it. Most people who have heard of the ger have not seen one, and they marvel when they do. It is, as with all the material culture of nomadic peoples, a mingled genius of light and faithful living that indisputably works, with no diminishing of the life around it. Here is one gorgeous detail: When you are putting it up it is a rickety, swaying affair that seems to lean together according to a blurry blueprint of naïve hope that the thing will endure. There is no metal in it, nothing that nails or screws together, nothing that binds in ninety-degree obedience. It just teeters. But the ger miraculously becomes stable, without losing its flex or becoming rigid, when the load of felt is piled on top. It firms into place, it becomes something like a body, all the parts finding the web of connectedness, one to the other, by being asked to hold. The ger is a teacher, and it shows something of the skill of being alive. It finds itself when it is asked to carry burden, when it is employed in sheltering a life living within it. Its burden makes it a home.

And so it could be with us. Our grief and our love of life, both faithful and both hard earned, both burdensome things that will not leave us alone once we find them. They are our kinship with all people, with those who are gone from among us and with those not yet here who we will not live long enough to see. They are our kinship with the world that has sheltered and weathered and fed us all along. They are our truest companions, as faithful as the earth that will one day cradle us again. They are the unlikely grace of being alive for a time, and the fealty we owe for that gift. The overflowing burden of knowing something of the ending of days, that is what gives you your days and your love for them, and makes of you a treasure for the rest of us, and makes of your life a story worth knowing. You become example enough and reason enough for those wrecked on schedule and those refusing to be so to continue for a while. It makes of you the rumored, honorable ancestor. You won't be there to see it, but your willingness to live your death, to die wise, ennobles those who come after.

AFTERWARDS: DAWN

It isn't dawn, not yet, but the signs are there. The dazzle of stars has already begun to quiet. First light is elusive, like the morning's first wave on the beach, or the first thought upon awakening. The Bridge of Sighs and its swell of time and light has already faded without notice, and so the lost nation road is about to be lost again. Perhaps. We'll see.

The night of our contemplation was long. Like every ordeal that threatens eternity, the end of this wondering has come suddenly, a little too soon, finding us not entirely ready. We grew certain again that this was too much, too long, that this death wonder and its orphan wisdom had overstayed and shed whatever use it once promised. This is a sign that dawn is near. It comes just before we're ready for it, or just after. The night sky and the river of your days you can't tell apart, both starry, both indigo. The dawn sky and the river of your days: both stirring toward a light not yet here, both holding memory of the starlight of what went before.

If, much against the odds of our time, you began this wondering with companions, you'll see with the coming light that some of them have parted company with you and gone to a needed sleep. Some have chosen companions more affable and contemplations more comforting, more in the manner of hope. Some have chosen gentler commandments, clearer lineages, more familiar despairs. But a few of them have stayed by your side, and you by theirs, quiet witnesses to a willingness to go the distance and to learn. Perhaps your endurance of this night of dying wisdom has drawn an unlikely companion or two as it went on. However it has gone, you've come to the end of this wonder differently than you began it, with different companions and concerns, to different purpose. The clarity of night wisdom is about to fade, and the murmuring of dawn will add many voices and convictions to your own.

It is at just this moment, when you look up from the last page or turn from the last thought, the last disturbance or the last heartache, that you find the seed of a better day tucked into the folds of your palm. First light is the end of the clarity of stars, but it is the beginning of planting that hard-won seed in the field of your days. This is the great act of faith our time requires of us, that we live as if we have been entrusted with something precious and mandatory, as people needed by an imperiled time. That is what farmers, those of us left, have become now: We preserve heritage seeds mostly by planting them.

You and I will die. This is a given, entirely proper. It is a whorl in the thumbprint of the Maker of Life. But the manner of our dying is not a given. That, with deep labor, is up to us. This is one of the life gifts entrusted to us at birth, dazzling as the night sky and burdensome as any vision is of how it all could be.

People die in the manner of their living. Lately that hasn't been good, and we've wished otherwise for ourselves and for them. This is the DNA of dying though, that it faithfully bears the imprint of how we've carried our days and been carried by them. So there's nothing more to wait for, no more portentous morning, auspicious afternoon, or providential night. This is what we're granted, and we've been spared to see it.

The dark is faded now, the horizon of our days coming into view, the clamor of those undisturbed by the wisdom of dying stirring again in the marketplace of our mutual life. There may be some dusty old people there, unclaimed by the madding crowd and the striving, all atangle with their dead. If there are, lean in respectful and close, and listen.

If not, mourn for a good while. Then surrender to this dying wisdom. Be plaited by your years, an elder in training, anointed. Uninvited and unsought, take the empty seat in the raucous marketplace, you all atangle with your dead. Someone alongside you could lean in, respectful and close, listening. Be ready for them.

BIBLIOGRAPHY

Durcan, Paul. *Daddy, Daddy.* Saskatoon, SK: Thistledown Press, 1990.

Herodotus. *The Histories.* Translated by A. de Selincourt. London: Penguin Books, 1954.

Rumi. *The Essential Rumi.* Translated by Coleman Barks. New York: Harper Collins, 1995.

Smith, Thomas. *Keeping the Star.* St. Paul, MN: Two Rivers Press, 1988.

Tolstoy, Leo. *The Death of Ivan Ilyich.* Translated by Lynn Solotaroff. New York: Bantam Books, 1981.

INDEX

Unexpected death, 27, 37, 44, 229–230
Uninitiated people
    dying and, 196
    teenagers and, 349
Untreated death, 27

W

Whole-person care, 31
Whose Life Is It Anyway? (film), 147
Wilder, Amos, 189
Wilder, Thornton, 189

Wilson, Tim, 198
Wishes, for life and death, 58–59
Wizard of Oz, 140
Wonder
    ability of, 117–118
    mystery and, 217
Word Voodoo, 40, 68, 134, 332
World
    exploitation of, 21
    responding to needs, 21
Wrestling death, 113, 114, 116

THE WRITER

Conceived while the ash of the Second World War settled. A sustained and sustaining influence thereafter.

I am read to beginning then, and for years afterward. Some ability to story-hear and story-see comes to me, and persists.

Very young and, mysteriously, dying. Physicians can't explain when, a week later, I don't die after all. Eventually, everyone in the house gets used to this, and it is forgotten. Shipwrecked in the Mediterranean. A stone mason in Gibraltar. An angel visits me in Notre Dame Cathedral. Other misadventures deepen my days.

Harvard University (Master of Theology): Fall in love with learning, receive an unearned scholarship and become a legal alien. In the normal confusion of such a thing I enlist in training for the priesthood, having never been to church. I am counseled otherwise, which was a good idea for everyone involved. The strange dream of a devotional life is traded for learning something of the history of the world.

Gathered up into an undeclared apprenticeship to a magisterial black storyteller in America, a man aflame, and from him learn the majesty of the spoken word. Here I see incarnate human courage conjured by an endangered, endangering time, and everything changes.

University of Toronto (Master of Social Work): Here I obtain a working visa that grants me entry to the helping professions. Years are spent learning the elaborations of human sorrow. Marriage and children. The limits of all things psychological become clear. The mythic and poetic poverty of my time becomes clearer. This is the principal affliction.

I begin a decade in the desert unawares. Learn some skills of the hand: stone carving, canoe making. Build a house and swear I'll never do it again.

I write a book about money and what I imagine are the soul's desires. The publisher goes bankrupt. The book is discontinued before it is continued. I buy cases of it from a bargain book outlet in a mall, and swear I'll never do it again. Somewhere in there I enter the second half of my life.

Though clearly not organizational material I am courted into the health care system. Unwisely I accept. First encounters with the mysteries of palliative care. I am now in the death trade unawares, where no one wants to die. The unadorned madness of a death phobic culture invites me to dance, and I dance. I appoint myself its adversary. The beneficiary of administrative benign neglect, I inadvertently begin the revolution of death-centered care. For a while it works: creator of a center for children's grief, assistant professor in a medical school. The revolt is time sensitive: I am counseled otherwise again. Marriage again. The National Film Board of Canada produces a documentary on my work from this time: *Griefwalker*. I build another house and swear…

People bereft of ceremonial tuition ask me to do their weddings, their baby blessings and house blessings and funerals, and I do them. The great longing for ancestry and for elders is under it all. An Anishnaabe elder calls me "a great rememberer," another worthy assignment. I begin farming. Desirous of big learning I conjure a school for orphan wisdom that might teach the unauthorized history of North America and other things, certain that no one will come. I'm wrong again: they do. Teaching across the continent and in Europe ensues. Life resembles an extended rock-and-roll tour, minus everything you can think of. Grandchildren.

Somewhere in there I decide to testify to what came to me during my time in the death trade. My breathing is troubled, continuing to live becomes iffy, we go to Mexico in the event that this is it. I write the dying book in the shadow of an overlooked Aztec pyramid. I call it *Die Wise: A Manifesto for Sanity and Soul*. The "manifesto" part troubles some people, but I decide to be honest about it.

I don't die after all, again. I go on.

Stephen Jenkinson, MTS, MSW
www.orphanwisdom.com

About North Atlantic Books

North Atlantic Books (NAB) is an independent, nonprofit publisher committed to a bold exploration of the relationships between mind, body, spirit, and nature. Founded in 1974, NAB aims to nurture a holistic view of the arts, sciences, humanities, and healing. To make a donation or to learn more about our books, authors, events, and newsletter, please visit www.northatlanticbooks.com.

North Atlantic Books is the publishing arm of the Society for the Study of Native Arts and Sciences, a 501(c)(3) nonprofit educational organization that promotes cross-cultural perspectives linking scientific, social, and artistic fields. To learn how you can support us, please visit our website.